Film Review
2004-2005

Film Review

2004-2005

JAMES CAMERON-WILSON
ADAM KEEN

JULY 2003 - JUNE 2004

Reynolds & Hearn Ltd
London

Acknowledgements

The authors would like to acknowledge their uncontained debt to the following, without whom this book would have been rather different: Dave Aldridge, Charles Bacon, Cate Blanchett, Ian Crane, Joel Finler, Marcus Hearn, Tony Hillman, Peter Jaques, Mike Leigh, Lorna Mann, Nigel Mulock, Scot Woodward Myers, Daniel O'Brien, Alan Parker, David Quinlan, Carolynn Reynolds, Richard Reynolds and our respective wives. And a very, very special display of appreciation must go to our colleague and virtual co-editor Mansel Stimpson. Thank you all.

Picture Credits
Rex Features: Pages 7, 147-154, 158, 160, 169
The Joel Finler Collection: Pages 178-187
The Tony Hillman Collection: Pages 178-187

First published in 2004 by
Reynolds & Hearn Ltd
61a Priory Road
Kew Gardens
Richmond
Surrey TW9 3DH

© James Cameron-Wilson 2004

A CIP catalogue record for this book is available from the British Library.

ISBN 1 903111 87 0

Designed by James King

Printed and bound in Great Britain by Biddles Ltd, Guildford, Surrey.

Contents

Introduction

Sixty glorious years. Great name for a movie and the length of time that this book has been going. When F. Maurice Speed kick-started the world's longest-running film publication (back in 1944), he cannot have foreseen the changes that would manipulate the medium of cinema. Long before the advent of video, DVD, computer animation and Quentin Tarantino, Maurice was besotted with the magic of Carmen Miranda, Sonja Henie and Lassie. Back then, Maurice – a ten-year veteran of film reviewing – was obliged to 'cable' the Hollywood companies for colour transparencies, which were a relatively new phenomenon. Now we just download them off the internet.

It was the year that Bing Crosby won the Oscar for *Going My Way*, the year that the ballpoint pen was patented (by the Hungarian hypnotist Lasalo Biro) and the year that over 4,000 ships chugged across the English Channel to wrest France from the Nazis. It was also the year that introduced pink, sticky versions of George Lucas, Michael Douglas, Chevy Chase and Danny DeVito to the world.

Even so, in his very first introduction, Maurice lamented that 1944 was not a very remarkable year. Of course, he was talking cinematically. 'There have been no great technical advances, no astonishingly successful – or even astonishing – experiments,' he wrote. He also confided that, 'it is greatly to be regretted that no full-length Disney film has found its way to the screen.' Not so

in the period covered by this book. With the double assault of *Finding Nemo* and *Pirates of the Caribbean*, the Mouse House had the summer of 2003 wrapped up.

However, the summer of 2004 was of a very different hue (not green, that's for sure). First off, CEO Michael Eisner ditched Michael Moore's *Fahrenheit 9/11* – for fears that its anti-Bush agenda would jeopardise the tax breaks granted

Uma Thurman provides new edge to the cinematic platter

Michael Moore accepts his
Palme d'Or and, for once,
is speechless

The Village is not the success
that Disney had hoped

to his theme park and hotels in Florida (for Florida, read Jeb Bush). Instead, Lions Gate distributed the film which, financed by Disney's Miramax to the tune of $6 million, was a pretty cheap acquisition. So imagine the company's stupefaction when the little documentary grossed $24 million in its opening *weekend*. I mean, documentaries find it hard to penetrate the top ten, but to beat all comers? In the end, *Fahrenheit 9/11* grossed over $118m in the US, making it the most successful documentary in history. Had it made half that, it would still have been the most successful documentary in history. And to think that Disney could have been manoeuvring its purse strings.

Instead, the company had the $110m *Around the World in 80 Days* to call its own, a flop that limped to the finishing line with $23m in its pocket. Disney also produced Jerry Bruckheimer's $90m Arthurian romp *King Arthur*, another flop, and M. Night Shyamalan's *The Village*, which insiders had predicted would be the surprise hit of the summer. It wasn't. In fact, the only Disney release besides *The Village* to reach number one in the May-September window was a Chinese film, Zhang Yimou's *Hero*.

If the first nine months of

2004 proved hard for Disney, it was no less a rosy picture for the British cinema. There were no British wins at Cannes (indeed, no truly British film was even selected for the competition) and, for once, we had nothing to bleat about at the Oscars. To stretch a point, the only Oscar that the British won was a third of the Best Song category, which was scooped up by 'Into the West' from *The Lord of the Rings: Return of the King*, co-written by New Zealand's Fran Walsh, Canada's Howard Shore and Scotland's Annie Lennox. Big deal.

To be fair, the British had every reason to register *nil point* – it was producing garbage. Indeed, *Sex Lives of the Potato Men* drove critics to scramble for new superlatives. According to Mark Lawson in *The Guardian*, 'saying that *Sex Lives of the Potato Men* has had bad reviews is like suggesting that some people found Stalin a bit nasty.' There was a rumour going round that Chancellor of the Exchequer Gordon Brown had caught an early screening of the film (which was part-funded by the UK Film Council) and afterwards closed the tax loophole in British film finance. This measure sent shockwaves through the industry and stalled the production of around 50 British movies, notably killing off John

Madden's $45m *Tulip Fever* which was to have starred Jude Law, Keira Knightley and Jim Broadbent. The film's producer, Alison Owen, who was expecting a third of her budget to come from government-sanctioned tax breaks, gave the actors and crew one week's notice.

That was then. On Saturday, 17 September, Mike Leigh's *Vera Drake* won the coveted Golden Lion at the Venice Film Festival and its star, Imelda Staunton, was named best actress. Leigh, picking up the award, took the opportunity to berate Cannes for not even allowing his film into the competition. There were also a slew of fine British films coming up: Sir Richard Eyre's *Stage Beauty*, Ken Loach's *Ae Fond Kiss*, Michael Winterbottom's *Code 46*, Roger Michell's *Enduring Love*, Danny Boyle's *Millions* and, marking an extraordinary debut from the stills photographer Shona Auerbach, *Dear Frankie*, a superbly crafted, profoundly moving tale of a single mother (Emily Mortimer) who invents an imaginary father for her nine-year-old son.

With this lot lining up for next year's annual, F. Maurice Speed could not complain of an unremarkable year.

James Cameron-Wilson
September 2004

Capitol Hill suit John Tanner is harangued by Michael Moore about Iraq

Top 20 UK Box-Office Hits
July 2004 – June 2005

1. The Lord of the Rings: The Return of the King
2. Harry Potter and the Prisoner of Azkaban
3. Love Actually
4. Finding Nemo
5. Pirates of the Caribbean: The Curse of the Black Pearl
6. The Day After Tomorrow
7. Bruce Almighty
8. Calendar Girls
9. Troy
10. The Matrix Revolutions
11. Elf
12. Scooby Doo 2: Monsters Unleashed
13. Terminator 3: Rise of the Machines
14. Shrek 2
15. American Wedding
16. Van Helsing
17. Starsky and Hutch
18. The Last Samurai
19. Kill Bill Vol. 1
20. School of Rock

Top 10 Box-Office Stars

Star of the Year: Jim Carrey

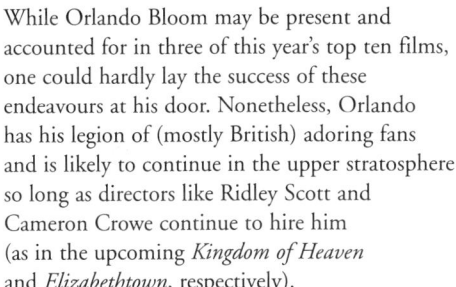

2. Hugh Grant

3. Johnny Depp

4. Brad Pitt

5. Orlando Bloom

6. Mike Myers

7. Ben Stiller

8. Keanu Reeves

9. Will Ferrell

10. Tom Cruise

While Orlando Bloom may be present and accounted for in three of this year's top ten films, one could hardly lay the success of these endeavours at his door. Nonetheless, Orlando has his legion of (mostly British) adoring fans and is likely to continue in the upper stratosphere so long as directors like Ridley Scott and Cameron Crowe continue to hire him (as in the upcoming *Kingdom of Heaven* and *Elizabethtown*, respectively).

A more obvious draw at the British box-office is Hugh Grant, who repeatedly appears on this list, snatching the top position in 2001-2002 and 2000-2001. With the remarkable success of Richard Curtis's *Love Actually*, he has bounded back, although considering the film is an ensemble piece he will have to concede the No. 1 slot to Jim Carrey. Carrey is a regular feature of the UK box-office and the outstanding success of *Bruce Almighty* is primarily his fault. Likewise, Brad Pitt's presence added considerably to the handsome coffers of *Troy*, while Johnny Depp crossed into the mainstream with his wicked portrayal of a pirate modelled on Keith Richards. As for Ben Stiller, well, he was just everywhere, whether chasing Polly or Hutch or just playing *Dodgeball*. Runners up include: Arnold Schwarzenegger, Eddie Murphy, Jennifer Aniston, Adam Sandler and Will Smith. JC-W

Releases of the Year

This section contains details of all the films released in Great Britain from 1 July 2003 to the end of June 2004 – the period covered by all the reference features in this book.

Leading actors are normally credited with the roles they played, followed by a summary of supporting players. Where an actor further down a cast list is of special interest then his/her role is generally credited as well.

For technical credits the normal abbreviations operate, and are as follows: Dir – for Director; Pro – for Producer; Ex Pro – for Executive Producer; Co Pro – for Co-Producer; Ass Pro – for Associate Producer; Line Pro – for Line Producer; Scr – for Screenwriter; Ph – for Cinematographer; Ed – for Editor; Pro Des – for Production Designer; and M – for composer.

Abbreviations for the names of film companies are also obvious when used, such as Fox for Twentieth Century Fox, and UIP for Universal International Pictures. The production company (or companies) is given first, the distribution company last.

Information at the foot of each entry is presented in the following order: running time/country of origin/year of copyright/date of British release/British certification.

Reviewers: Charles Bacon, James Cameron-Wilson, Marcus Hearn, Adam Keen, Scot Woodward Myers, Daniel O'Brien and Mansel Stimpson.

Star ratings
★★★★★ **Wonderful**
★★★★ **Very good**
★★★ **Good**
★★ **Mediocre**
★ **Insulting**

L'Afrance ★★★¹/₂

This is a deeply committed first feature but one overshadowed by *Waiting for Happiness* [qv]. In the latter it's Mauritania which lies at the heart of the work whereas here it's Senegal, but in each film the concern is with youngsters who can only truly learn and develop elsewhere (*L'Afrance* is set in Paris). That such a situation is a threat to the survival of the home country as the source of a rich and individual culture is common to both. However, *L'Afrance* is less poetic and less memorable visually. Also it's none too well structured with, arguably, too much emphasis on the hero's relationship with an attractive Parisienne and too many ill-defined subsidiary characters. Nevertheless, this is a film which has something to say and says it loud and clear. MS

• *El Hadj Diop* Djolof Mbengue, *Myriam Bechet* Delphine Zingg, *Khalid* Samir Guesmi, *Demba* Théophile Sowié, *Chérif* Bass Dhem, *Oumar* Albert Mendy, *le père* Thierno Ndiaye, *Papis* Oumar N'Diaye, *teacher* Louis Beyler, *Awa* Joséphine Mboub, *Jean* Seybani Sougou.
• *Dir* Alain Gomis, *Pro* Anne-Cécile Berthomeau and Edouard Mauriat, *Ex Pro* Eric Idriss Kanango, *Screenplay* Gomis, Xavier Christiaens, Alain Pierre Schöller, Nathalie Stragier and Marc Wels, *Ph* Pascal Stoeber, *Pro Des* Philippe Barthelemy, *Ed* Fabrice Rouaud, *M* Patrice Gomis, *Costumes* Claire Chanat.

Centre National de la Cinématographie/Mille et Une Productions-Gala.
90 mins. France/Senegal. 2003. Rel 14 November 2003. Cert U.

After Life
See *Trilogie, La*

Against the Ropes ★¹/₂

The daughter of a local boxing hero, Jackie Kallen dreams of becoming a promoter. But in a chauvinistic sport, she just can't get a break. That is, until the local kingpin drops the contract of a promising but undisciplined fighter onto her lap for the joke sum of $1. Can she turn her young charge around and make it big in the testosterone playground of professional boxing? The film is based on the real Jackie Kallen, who (if Meg Ryan's wardrobe is to be believed) is still the only professional boxing promoter in a mini-skirt and high heels. But the story of her success is so heavily fictionalised that, unless we are to believe that life really does imitate schlock, there are no inspirational emancipatory insights to be had from her rise and rise. Ryan's acting is forced and uninspired amidst a cast that cannot help but look foolish in the glare of this over-processed biopic. Only Omar Epps as the young boxer Luther Shaw delivers on the dramatic front, and shows off some tidy looking skills in the ring. AK

• *Jackie Kallen* Meg Ryan, *Luther Shaw* Omar Epps, *Sam LaRocca* Tony Shalhoub, *Gavin Reese* Tim Daly, *Renee* Kerry Washington, *Felix Reynolds* Charles S. Dutton, *Irving Abel* Joe Cortese, *with* Sean Bell, Dean McDermott, Beau Starr, Jackie Kallen.
• *Dir* Charles S. Dutton, *Pro* Robert W. Cort and David Madden, *Ex Pro* Steven Roffer, Jonathan Pillot and Scarlett Lacey, *Screenplay* Cheryl Edwards,

Ph Jack N. Green, *Pro Des* Sandra Kybartas, *Ed* Eric L. Beason, *M* Michael Kamen; songs performed by Jackie Wilson, DMX, Hugh Masekela, Lucinda Williams, Al Jarreau, Mana, etc, *Costumes* Ruth Carter, *Stunt coordinator/boxing choreographer* Roy T. Anderson.

Paramount/Cort/Madden-UIP.
110 mins. USA/Germany. 2003. Rel: 14th May 2004. Cert 12A.

Agent Cody Banks ★¹/₂

Harriet the Spy meets *Spy Kids* in this teenage spoof of, yep, you guessed it, James Bond. No sooner has Johnny English wrested the future of Great Britain out of the clammy hands of John Malkovich, than along comes the pint-sized Frankie Muniz to step into his place. The twist is that Cody is 15-years-old and while he is smart and athletic, he is hardly a smooth-talker where the women are concerned. Yet it is the last-named attribute that he needs to call on to fulfil his obligation to the CIA. They need him to romance teenage dreamboat Natalie Connors in order to get closer to her father, who is in cahoots with a criminal warlord. The fun part is watching Cody hoodwink his docile parents and cock-up his romantic overtures to Natalie (he thinks T.S. Eliot, her favourite author, is a woman). But as soon as the film kicks into action mode it becomes a pale imitation of the real thing. Indeed, the stunt sequences leave a lot to be desired, culminating in a shambolic climax virtually devoid of ingenuity, humour or suspense. JC-W

• *Cody Banks* Frankie Muniz, *Natalie Connors* Hilary Duff, *Ronica Miles* Angie Harmon, *CIA Director* Keith David, *Brinkman* Ian McShane, *with* Arnold Vosloo, Martin Donovan, Cynthia Stevenson, Daniel Roebuck.
• *Dir* Harald Zwart, *Pro* David C. Glasser, Andreas Klein, Guy Oseary, Dylan Sellers and David Nicksay, *Ex Pro* Mark Morgan, Jason Alexander, Jennifer Birchfield-Eick, Kerry David, Danny Gold, Michael Jackman, Madonna and Bob Yari, *Screenplay* Ashley Edward Miller, Zack Stentz, Scott Alexander and Larry Karaszewski, *Story* Jeffrey Jurgensen, *Ph* Denis Crossan, *Pro Des* Rusty Smith, *Art Dir* Kelvin Humenny, *Sets* Lesley Beale, *Ed* Jim Miller, *M* John Powell, *Stunt Coordinator* Scott Ateah, *Visual Effects Supervisor* Raymond McIntyre Jr., *Costumes* Suzanne McCabe.

Dylan Sellers Productions/Maverick Entertainment Inc./MGM/Splendid Pictures-Fox.
102 mins. US/Canada. 2003. Rel 25 July 2003. Cert 12.

Agent Cody Banks 2: Destination London ★

Frankie Munz returns as Cody Banks, teenage secret agent. Second time out, the CIA dispatch Banks to the UK, where mysterious megalomaniac villains threaten the royal family. Even the Blair-lookalike Prime Minister falls under their spell (what else is new?). Filled with lazy stereotypes and tourist views of London, this thin sequel is a poor excuse for a kids' movie. Once again, *Malcolm in the Middle* star Munz fails to extend his television appeal to the big screen. Stuck with second rate material, director Kevin Allen delivers precious few laughs. That said, Allen's *Twin Town* and *The Big Tease* weren't much better. The *Cody Banks* franchise remains a poor man's *Spy Kids*. DO

• *Cody Banks* Frankie Muniz, *Derek* Anthony Anderson, *Mrs Banks* Cynthia Stevenson, *Mr Banks* Daniel Roebuck, *Emily* Hannah Spearritt, *CIA Director* Keith David, *Jo Kenworth* Anna Chancellor, *Diaz* Keith Allen, *Kenworth* James Faulkner, *with* David Kelly, Santiago Segura, Paul Kaye, Harry Burton, Julian Firth, Damien Hirst, Mark Williams, James Dreyfus, Patti Love, *US president* Sam Douglas.
• *Dir* Kevin Allen, *Pro* Dylan Sellers, Guy Oseary, David C. Glasser, Bob Yari and David Nicksay, *Ex Pro* Madonna, Jason Alexander, Jennifer Birchfield-Eick, Kerry David, Danny Gold, Michael Jackman, Andreas Klein and Mark Morgan , *Screenplay* Don Rhymer, from a story by Rhymer, Harald Zwart and Dylan Sellers, based on characters created by Jeffrey Jurgensen, *Ph* Denis Crossan, *Pro Des* Richard Holland, *Ed* Andrew MacRitchie, *M* Mark Thomas, *Costumes* Steven Noble.

MGM /Maverick Films-Fox.
100 mins. USA. 2004. Rel: 26 March 2004. Cert PG.

Aileen: Life and Death of a Serial Killer ★★★★

As powerful as any drama, this is the second feature length documentary made by Nick Broomfield about the late Aileen Wuornos. The earlier film dealt with the media exploitation of the woman condemned as America's first female serial killer. After a decade on death row, her final appeal came up and Broomfield was subpoenaed as a witness. The present film shows the failure of that appeal leading to her execution, but it also finds the filmmaker investigating her past as he attempts to decide whether the truth lay in her original defence of provocation or in her later withdrawal of that plea. This is gripping in its own right, but the film also challenges the validity of capital punishment on grounds I don't recall being broached in any other movie. MS

• *With* Aileen Wuornos, Nick Broomfield, Joe Hobson, Steve Glazer aka 'Dr Legal', Governor Jeb Bush, Jesse 'The Human Bomb' Aviles, Diane

Wuornos, Joan Churchill, etc.
• *Dir* Nick Broomfield and Joan Churchill, *Pro* Jo Human, *Ph* Joan Churchill, *Ed* Claire Ferguson, *M* Rob Lane.

Lafayette Films/Channel Four-Optimum.
92 minutes. UK. 2003. Rel 21 November 2003. Cert 15.

All the Real Girls ★★★★

A major advance on the overrated *George Washington*, this is a remarkably insightful and perceptive study of adolescent emotions from David Gordon Green. The approach is novel since the relationship of the central couple is threatened by the hostility of the girl's brother. The boy now drawn to his sister may be his best friend, but he knows him for a philanderer and fails to realise that, genuinely in love for the first time, his friend has reformed. Paul Schneider and Zooey Deschanel in the lead roles are first class and we really feel for their characters, but there are drawbacks. While the setting of North Carolina is atmospheric, the accents pose problems of audibility at times and the later stages of the film are less clearly detailed plot-wise. But despite these imperfections this is a memorable movie, so truthful that at its best it touches greatness. MS

• *Paul* Paul Schneider, *Noel* Zooey Deschanel, *Elvira Fine* Patricia Clarkson, *Leland* Benjamin Mouton, *Bo* Maurice Compte, *Bust-Ass* Danny McBride, *Tip* Shea Wingham.
• *Dir* and *Screenplay* David Gordon Green, from a story by Green and Paul Schneider, *Pro* Jean Doumanian and Lisa Muskat, *Assoc Pro* Kim Jose, *Ph* Tim Orr, *Pro Des* Richard Wright, *Ed* Zene Bakel and Steven Gonzales, *M* David Wingo and Michael Linnen, *Costumes* Erin Aldridge Orr, *Sound* Mark Gingras.

Sony Pictures Classics-Columbia TriStar.
108 mins. USA. 2003. Rel: 1 August 2003. Cert. 15.

All Tomorrow's Parties ★★★

(*Mingri tianya*)
The futuristic setting of this Chinese film does not prevent the piece from playing as a timeless portrayal of a dictatorial regime: we think of the Taliban and of Orwell's *1984*. The lack of any detailed background increases the general validity, but the story of two brothers sent to a re-education centre and of a single mother with a young child develops confusingly. Stylised imagery sometimes adds to the sense of novelty prompted by the location, but exactly what message the film is trying to convey is ultimately obscure, with the second half of the picture far less satisfactory than the first. MS

• *Xuelan* Yong Won-cho, *Xiao Zhuai* Diao Yi-nan,

Xiao Mian Wei Wei Zhao.
• *Dir* and *Screenplay* Nelson Yu Lik-wai, *Ph* Yiu-Fai Lai, *Ed* Keung Chow, *M* Yoshihiro Hanno.

Lumen Films-ICA Projects.
96 mins. France/Hong Kong/South Korea/Netherlands/Switzerland. 2003. Rel: 2 April 2004.

Almost Peaceful ★★★½

(*Un Monde Presque Paisible*)
Whereas such recent French productions as *Bon Voyage* and *Strange Gardens* have looked back to the war years, this superior movie is set in Paris in 1946. By studying the lives of a group of characters working for a Jewish tailor, it shows people adjusting to post-war life as well as coming to terms with the loss of those who have not survived. Indeed, what starts like an exercise in nostalgia becomes a film not afraid to take on board the darker elements. This is however a very traditional piece of filmmaking despite the fact that it was directed by Michel Deville best known here for *La Lectrice* and, as such, it works well, albeit without ever approaching the harsh edge of reality found in a masterpiece like *Au Revoir Les Enfants*. There's also the fact that it fails to handle its last scenes to best effect, but it's a pleasing work for all that. MS

• *M. Albert* Simon Abkarian, *Jacqueline* Lubna Azabal, *Léa* Zabou Breitman, *Simone* Clotilde Courau, *Léon* Vincent Elbaz, *Mme Andrée* Julie Gayet, *Maurice* Stanislas Merhar, *Charles* Denis Podalydès, *Joseph* Malik Zidi, *Mme Himmelfarb* Judith D'Aléazzo.
• *Dir* Michel Deville, *Pro* Rosalinde Deville, *Screenplay* Michel Deville, Rosalinde Deville and Robert Bober, based on the novel *Quoi de neuf sur la guerre'*, *Ph* André Diot, *Pro Des* Arnaud de Moleron, *Ed* Andrea Sedláčková, *M* Giovanni Bottesini, *Costumes* Madeline Fontaine.

Canal Plus/Centre National de la Cinématographie (CNC)/Eléfilm/France 3 Cinéma/France Télévision Images 2/Gimages 6-Miracle.
94 mins. France. 2002. Rel: 18 June 2004. Cert 15.

Along Came Polly ★★★

Ben Stiller is a very funny man – but only when he's not trying to be. As he exhibited in *There's Something About Mary* and *Meet the Parents*, he's a great straight guy. Having foundered in such movies as *Mystery Men* and *Zoolander*, Stiller returns as the lost nebbish in a world of demented individuals. He is Reuben Feffer, an insurance risk assessor and by definition a professional worrier. By nature he is also a compulsive obsessive, given to designing programmes on his laptop that calculate the risk of any given situation, be they financial or romantic. He did feel pretty secure in his new bride, but when she sleeps with a scuba diver on the first day of their honeymoon his life falls apart. Then along comes Polly, a spontaneous, absent-minded waitress with a passion for spicy food and with less than discriminating ideas on hygiene… As Feffer battles the monsters of his day-to-day existence (that is, everybody he comes in contact with), so the chuckles arrive thick and fast, as do the toilet gags. Cheerfully offensive, the film is strong on smiles, although its attempts at human comedy are way off the mark. Previously known as *Captured.* JC-W

• *Reuben Feffer* Ben Stiller, *Polly Prince* Jennifer Aniston, *Sandy Lyle* Philip Seymour Hoffman, *Lisa Kramer* Debra Messing, *Claude* Hank Azaria, *Leland Van Lew* Bryan Brown, *Stan Indursky* Alec Baldwin, *Javier* Jsu Garcia, *Vivian Feffer* Michele Lee, *Irving Feffer* Bob Dishy, *with* Missi Pyle, Judah Friedlander, Caroline Aaron.
• *Dir* and *Screenplay* John Hamburg, *Pro* Danny DeVito, Michael Shamberg and Stacey Sher, *Ex Pro* Jane Bartelme and Dan Levine, *Assoc Pro* Anders Bard, *Ph* Seamus McGarvey, *Pro Des* Andrew Laws, *Ed* William Kerr and Nick Moore, *M* Theodore Shapiro, *Costumes* Cindy Evans, *Choreography* JoAnn Fregalette Jansen and Anne Fletcher.

Universal/Jersey Films-UIP.
90 mins. USA. 2004. 27 February 2004. Cert 12A.

Amandla! ★★★

Subtitled *A Revolution in Four-Part Harmony*, this feature-length documentary looks at the history of apartheid but principally emphasises the role played by music in the struggle by those oppressed. Filmmaker Lee Hirsch is deeply committed, and his film has some powerful and moving moments. However, these stem mainly from the footage of historical events (the Sharpeville Massacre, violence in Soweto, Nelson Mandela seen before and after his imprisonment). With exceptions, the music is not strong enough to justify being the centre of focus in a film lasting 102 minutes. But for anyone with a specialised interest in the changing style and function of these songs the film is well worth seeing. The most memorable comment included may be missed by many because it comes at the end of the final credits. MS

• *With* African Devoted Artists, Hugh Masekela, Abdullah Ibrahim, Miriam Makeba, Vusi Mahlasela, Sibongile Khumalo, Sophie Mgcina, Dolly Rathebe, Sifiso Ntuli, Duma Ka Ndlovu, Sibusiso Nxumalo, Thandi Modise, Lindiwe Zulu.
• *Dir* Lee Hirsch, *Pro* Hirsch and Sherry Simpson Dean, *Ex Pro* Simpson Dean, *Co-Pro* Desireé Markgraaff, *Ph* Clive Sacke, Ivan Leathers and Brand Jordaan, *Ed* Johanna Demetrakas.

Kwela Prods/Bomb Films/HBO/Cinemax Documentary Films-Metrodome.
103 mins. USA/ South Africa. 2002.
Rel: 19 December 2003. Cert 12A.

An Amazing Couple
See *La Trilogie*

American Cousins ★★¹/₂

What's a New Jersey wiseguy to do when he falls foul of the Ukranian mafia? Dan Hedaya's aging mobster hotfoots it from Kiev to Glasgow, hiding out with his Italian-Scottish relatives. Unlike their American cousin, these are law-abiding people, with a fish and chip shop and ice cream business. Inevitably, Hedaya and young sidekick Danny Nucci are seduced by this gentler way of life. They also help fight off the thugs threatening their relatives' livelihood. Directed by Donald Coutts, *American Cousins* is an amiable, if sentimental comedy. The Clydeside setting invites comparisons with Bill Forsyth's *Comfort and Joy*, which played Glasgow's vicious 'ice cream wars' for uncertain laughs. While *American Cousins* doesn't compare with the best of Forsyth, it has more than its share of good moments. Highpoint: Dan Hedaya dancing the Dashing White Sergeant. DO

• *Gino* Danny Nucci, *Alice* Shirley Henderson, *Roberto* Gerald Lepkowski, *Tony* Vincent Pastore, *Settimo* Dan Hedaya, *Nonno* Russell Hunter, *Jojo* Stevan Rimkus, *young sundae girl* Eva Coutts, *with* Stephen Graham, Jake Abraham, Alan McQueen, John Henshaw.
• *Dir* Don Coutts, *Pro* Margaret Matheson, *Ex Pro* Robert Bevan, Keith Hayley, Amanda Coombes, Amit Barooah and Charlie Savill, *Line Pro* Peter Gallagher, *Screenplay* Sergio Casci, *Ph* Jerry Kelly, *Pro Des* Andy Harris, *Ed* Lindy Cameron, *M* Donald Shaw, *Costumes* Lynn Aitken.

Little Wing Films/Bard Entertainments/Scottish Screen/National Lottery/Glasgow Film Office Script Factory-Bard Entertainments.
93 mins. UK. 2002. Rel: 28 November 2003. Cert 15.

American Pie: The Wedding ★★¹/₂
(US title: *American Wedding*)
Like a high-school reunion planned too early (just after college graduation, in fact), the third (and blissfully final) gross-out film party is an awkward farce that rarely echoes of the subversive wit made the first film great. The story opens with Jim and Michelle (Alyson Hannigan, again outclassing everyone else on screen bar Eugene Levy) setting up a wrenchingly hilarious scene that has Jim proposing

marriage with his cock out. We move swiftly to the engagement party, which an uninvited Stiffler crashes, causing another momentously embarrassing tableau involving him, a half-naked Jim, and two shameless (and horny) dogs. The other set-pieces are forced and reek of creative desperation: stuffy in-laws stumbling into an X-rated stag party; a fight over a 'dog poo' chocolate truffle, an 'I'm Too Sexy' dance-off in a Chicago gay bar are garish examples of twisted imagination begging you to laugh. This really is third-tier sitcom trash. AK

• *Jim Levenstein* Jason Biggs, *Michelle Annabeth Flaherty* Alyson Hannigan, *Cadence Flaherty* January Jones, *Kevin Myers* Thomas Ian Nicholas, *Steve Stifler* Seann William Scott, *Paul Finch* Eddie Kaye Thomas, *Harold Flaherty* Fred Willard, *Mary Flaherty* Deborah Rush, *Jim's dad* Eugene Levy, *with* Jennifer Coolidge.
• *Dir* Jesse Dylan, *Pro* Warren Zide, Craig Perry, Chris Moore, Adam Herz and Chris Bender, *Screenplay* Adam Herz, *Ph* Lloyd Ahern, *Pro Des* Clayton Hartley, *Ed* Stuart Pappé, *M* Christophe Beck.

Universal Pictures/Zide-Perry Productions/LivePlanet-UIP.
96 mins. USA. 2002. Rel 15 August 2003. Cert 15.

American Splendor ★★★★¹/₂

Cleveland, 1990-ish. Born loser Harvey Pekar turns his drab and angry existence into the inspiration for a series of indie comic books that have won him an enormous underground audience, thanks in part to his friendship with renowned comic artists like Robert Crumb, who draws some of the original American Splendour titles. Pekar's gift is his ability to distil the frustrations of his profoundly unglamorous life into a black humour full of home truths. Shari Springer Berman and Robert Pulcini mirror the translation from life to art by producing a dramatised documentary starring Paul Giamatti as Pekar that also has Pekar narrating and appearing as himself in stylised 'backstage' scenes, commenting on the making of the 'fake' documentary of his life. It's the most entertaining deconstructionist ploy I have ever seen. AK

• *Harvey Pekar* Paul Giamatti, *Joyce Brabner* Hope Davis, *himself* Harvey Pekar, *interviewer* Shari Springer Berman, *Mr Boats* Earl Billings, *Robert Crumb* James Urbaniak, *Toby Radloff* Judah Friedlander, *Bob, the director* Robert Pulcini, *real Toby* Toby Radloff, *real Joyce* Joyce Brabner, *stage actor Harvey* Donal Logue, *stage actor Joyce* Molly Shannon, *Fred* James McCaffrey, *Danielle* Madylin Sweeten, *real Danielle* Danielle Batone.
• *Dir* and *Screenplay* Shari Springer Berman and Robert Pulcini, based on the *American Splendor* comics by Harvey Pekar and *Our Cancer Year* by

Pekar and Joyce Brabner, *Pro* Ted Hope, *Assoc Pro* Julia King, *Ph* Terry Stacey, *Pro Des* Thérèse DePrez, *Set decorator* Robert Desue, *Ed* Mr Pulcini, *M* Mark Suozzo, *Music supervisor* Linda Cohen, *Costumes* Michael Wilkinson, *Animation and visual effects* Twinkle.

Good Machine/HBO-Optimum Releasing
100 mins. USA. 2003. Rel: 2 January 2004. Cert 15.

Anazapta ★★¹/₂

Set in England in 1348, this revenge drama is most likely to appeal to those looking for a medieval variant on ripe Gothic. Soldiers return from France to an English village where a rich old brew develops: mysterious deaths, a venal bishop who imposes sexual forfeits for postponing payment of a debt, ploys involving a valuable hostage and a hidden family secret. Despite some striking images, it's all hog-wash and wastes some good players, not least Lena Headey. At least it keeps moving but, with sex and violence as garnish for contemporary tastes, this is one for the video stores where it can be sought out by those who favour over-the-top material played straight. MS

• *Lady Matilda Mellerby* Lena Headey, *Jacques de Saint Amant* David La Haye, *Nicholas* Jason Flemyng, *Steward* Christopher Fairbank, *Sir Walter de Mellerby* Jon Finch, *bishop* Ian McNeice, *priest* Jeff Nuttall, *Randall* Anthony O'Donnell, *Physician* Ralph Riach, *with* Stevan Rimkus, Hayley Carmichael, Craig Russell, Nick Holder, Tony Aitkin.
• *Dir* Alberto Sciamma, *Pro* David Ball, Adam Betteridge, Alex Marshall and David Rogers, *Ex Pro* Jason Piette and Clive Waldron, *Assoc Pro* Michael Cowan, *Screenplay* Harriet Sand and Alberto Sciamma, *Ph* Alastair Meux, *Pro Des* Keith Maxwell, *Ed* George Akers, *M* Dan Jones, *Costumes* Ffion Elinor.

Beyond International/ Spice Factory/
Great British Films-Guerilla Films.
115 mins. UK/Australia. 2001. Rel: 7 May 2004. Cert 15.

Angela ★★★¹/₂

Decidedly interesting even if not ultimately satisfactory, this drama set in Palermo introduces two striking new talents. The story, freely adapting real events, is about a married couple, the eponymous Angela and Saro (Pupella), who deal in drugs under cover of running a shoe shop. Director Roberta Torre uses fashionable hand-held cameras but is marked out as a director of distinct originality by the rhythms of the film and by its swift presentation of the set-up as though both businesses were everyday enterprises. The other stand-out is the splendid Donatella Finocchiaro whose debut as Angela prompts comparisons with Anna Magnani in her prime. But the second half finds Angela, despite her love for Saro, taking up with a younger man who is both criminal and killer (di Stefano). The film's attempt to pass off these two as tragic lovers when both behave reprehensibly simply won't do. MS

• *Angela* Donatella Finocchiaro, *Masino* Andrea di Stefano, *Saro* Mario Pupella.
• *Dir* Roberta Torre, Lierka and Rita Rusic, *Screenplay* Roberta Torre and Massimo D'Anolfi, *Ph* Daniele Cipri, *Ed* Roberto Missiroli, *Art Dir* Enrico Serafini, *M* Andrea Guerra.

Movieweb/Rita Rusic Co/Sister Film-Optimum Releasing. 91 mins. Italy. 2003. Rel: 15 August 2003. Cert 15.

Animal Factory ★★★★
Based on the biographical confessions of writer Edward Bunker, *Animal Factory* is an unassuming yet hugely impressive actor's showpiece. The film follows a young hood's initiation into the hard world of prison life. Ron Decker starts out as a petulant and cocky middle-class brat and ends up much wizened for his scars. Along the way he is 'adopted' by the veteran jailbird, yard-king and fixer Earl Copen, played with awesome subtlety by Willem Defoe. The unforced air that pervades a film so dense with incident, atmosphere and character is a marvel. The paradox carries all the way to the finale, which is as uplifting as it is sad. AK

• *Earl Copen* Willem Dafoe, *Ron Decker* Edward Furlong, *Jan the Actress* Mickey Rourke, *Buck Rowan* Tom Arnold, *A. R. Hosspack* Steve Buscemi, *James Decker* John Heard, *Buzzard* Edward Bunker, *with* Seymour Cassel.
• *Dir* Steve Buscemi, *Screenplay* Edward Bunker and John Steppling, based on the novel by Bunker, *Pro* Julie Yorn, Elie Samaha, Andrew Stevens and Steve Buscemi, *Ph* Phil Parmet, *Pro Des* Steven Rosenzweig, *Ed* Kate Williams, *M* John Lurie.

Animal Productions/Arts Production Corporation/Franchise Pictures/Industry Entertainment/Phoenician Entertainment-Optimum Releasing 94 mins. USA. 2003. Rel 4 July 2003. Cert 15.

Après la vie
See *Trilogie, La*

Ash Wednesday ★½
Producer-director-writer-actor Edwards Burns has carved a niche with New York dramas centring on blue collar Irish-Americans. While his no-budget debut *The Brothers McMullen* proved a modest 'sleeper' hit, the higher profile *She's the One* suggested that Burns was a filmmaker of limited range. Shelved for several years, *Ash Wednesday* does little to alter

this impression. Set in the early 1980s, the film stars Burns as Francis Sullivan, a retired mob enforcer who now runs a bar in Manhattan's Hell's Kitchen. When Francis' younger brother Sean kills three Mafia thugs, he has to be whisked out of town and declared dead to avoid reprisals. This deception is eventually discovered, Frances drawn back into the criminal underworld he'd hoped to escape. As the title suggests, *Ash Wednesday* is heavy on religious significance, with plenty of Catholic guilt and redemption. The atmospheric visuals and profanity-laden dialogue fail to disguise a creaking plot burdened by cumbersome story exposition. Burns' direction is unexceptional and the performances seem tentative. DO

• *Francis Sullivan* Edward Burns, *Sean Sullivan* Elijah Wood, *Grace Quinonez* Rosario Dawson, *Moran* Oliver Platt, *Father Mahoney* James Handy, *with* Brain Burns, James Cummings, Pat McNamara, Malachy McCourt.
• *Dir* and *Screenplay* Edward Burns, *Pro* Burns and Margot Bridger, *Ex Pro* Jonathan Sehring, Caroline Kaplan and Glen Basner, *Ph* Russell Lee Fine, *Pro Des* Susan Block, *Ed* David Greenwald, *M* David Shire, *Costumes* Catherine Marie Thomas.

IFC Productions/Marlboro Road Gang-Redbus. 98 mins. USA. 2002. Rel: 19 March 2004. Cert 18.

At 5 in the Afternoon ★★★½
Stunningly photographed by Ebrahim Ghafoori, this view of life in Afghanistan following the defeat of the Taliban is handled by Samira Makhmalbaf with both commitment and artistry. The story-line centres on one family with a traditionalist at its head and the leading character is his daughter (Agheleh Rezaee) who secretly takes advantage of new opportunities for women to study. Meanwhile her sister-in-law, whose husband has gone missing in the fighting, struggles to keep her baby alive despite suffering both poverty and cold. It's a bleak picture, easier to admire than to enjoy, and, bearing in mind the involving impact of *Osama* that other recent film about Afghanistan, one regrets that Samara Makhmalbaf appears so wary of expressing warmth for her characters for fear of sentimentality. MS

• *Noqreh* Agheleh Rezaee, *father* Abdolghani Yusef-zay, *poet* Razi Mohebi, *Leylomah* Marzieh Amiri.
• *Dir* Samira Makhmalbaf, *Pro* Mohsen Makhmalbaf, *Ex Pro* Syamak Alagheband, *Screenplay* Samira and Mohsen Makhmalbaf, *Ph* Ebrahim Ghafori, *Ed* Mohsen Makhmalbaf, *M* Mohammad-Reza Darvishi.

Makhmalbaf Film House/Wild Bunch/ BAC Films-Artificial Eye. 106 mins. Iran/France. 2003. Rel: 16 April 2004. Cert. U.

Bad Boys II ★★

Miami, the present. This shamelessly flabby sequel to the buddy-cop actioner that put Will Smith and Martin Lawrence on the A-list is set eight years after Detectives Marcus Burnett (Lawrence) and Mike Lowrey (Smith) last explosive drug bust. We pick them up on the verge of their next big drug bust, featuring ecstasy smuggled in the cavities of dead bodies and culminating in an hysterical 'unofficial' invasion of Cuba. The testosterone remains laid heavily throughout and the relentless odd-couple bickering is as stale as last week's cold pizza. In fact, this is the same old movie: louder, longer and thoroughly blinged-up but otherwise a clone. Director Michael Bay and producer Jerry Bruckheimer understand well that restraint and change are not what fans of the original movie want. They want more car chases, more gun battles, more psycho baddies and more gorgeous women. And, boy, do they get them. The pummelling amusement park experience that is *Bad Boys 2* showers the audience with these generic treats until only the most hardcore fans can stomach the excesses without wincing. AK

• *Det. Marcus Burnett* Martin Lawrence, *Det. Mike Lowrey* Will Smith, *Johnny Tapia* Jordi Molla, *Syd Burnett* Gabrielle Union, *Alexei* Peter Stormare, *Theresa Burnett* Theresa Randle, *Capt. Howard* Joe Pantoliano, *Floyd Poteet* Michael Shannon, *Roberto* Jon Seda, *Detective Mateo Reyes* Yul Vazquez, *Det. Marco Vargas* Jason Manuel Olazábal, *Carlos* Otto Sanchez, *TNT leader* Henry Rollins, *with* Antoni Corone, Oleg Taktarov, Treva Etienne, *crappy cab driver* Michael Bay, Dan Marino.

• *Dir* Michael Bay, *Pro* Jerry Bruckheimer, *Ex Pro* Mike Stenson, Chad Oman and Barry Waldman, *Screenplay* Ron Shelton and Jerry Stahl, *Ph* Amir Mokri, *Pro Des* Dominic Watkins, *Ed* Mark Goldblatt, Thomas A. Muldoon and Roger Barton, *M* Trevor Rabin; additional *M* Dr. Dre, *Costumes* Deborah L. Scott and Carol Ramsey.

Columbia Pictures/Don Simpson/Jerry Bruckheimer-Columbia TriStar.
146 mins. USA. 2003. Rel: 3 October 2003. Cert 15.

Bad Education ★★★
(*La mala educación*)

Anyone hoping that this latest from Almodóvar will maintain the depth of his two most mature works, *All About my Mother* and *Talk To Her*, will be disappointed, but those who prefer his more outrageous pieces may relish this return to the tone of 1986's *Law Of Desire*. A complex tale that plays with fictional versions of the story we are asked to believe in, *Bad Education* concerns a filmmaker and the would-be actor and writer who claims to be his childhood friend who suffered sexual abuse from the head of a Catholic school. Despite the seriousness of this, the film is often playful but, as a melodrama that unfolds like a series of Chinese boxes, it lacks a consistent tone and is emotionally uninvolving. Melodrama can be a style housing serious comment or something to be relished for its camp appeal. Here Almodóvar unwisely opts for a bit of each, but the fact that it's his gayest film for some time and stars a persuasive Gael García Bernal will ensure its appeal for some. MS

Left: About face: Gabriel García Bernal (left) in Pedro Almodóvar's complex, melodramatic *Bad Education* (from Pathé)

• *Angel/Zahara/Juan* Gael García Bernal, *Enrique Goded* Fele Martínez, *Father Manolo* Daniel Gimenez Cacho, *Sr Berenguer* Lluis Homar, *Paca* Javier Camara, *Mother* Petra Martinez, *Young Ignacio* Nacho Perez, *young Enrique* Raul Garcia Forneiro, *Monica* Leonar Watling.
• *Dir* and *Screenplay* Pedro Almodóvar, *Pro* Agustín Almodovar, *Ex Pro* Esther Garcia, *Ph* Jose Luis Alcaine, *Pro Des* Antxon Gomez, *Ed* Jose Salcedo, *M* Alberto Iglesias, *Costumes* Paco Delgado and Jean-Paul Gaultier.

El Deseo, DA/ICAA/Canal Plus-Pathé.
105 mins. Spain. 2004. Rel: 21 May 2004. Cert 15.

Bad Guy ★★
(*Nabbeun Namja*)
Pimp and gang-leader Han-Gi is smitten by Sun-Hwa and hijacks her life in a sting which, due to the peculiarities of the Korean loan-sharking system, finds her working in one of his brothels. As her spirit is broken by the degradations heaped upon her, Han-Gi watches her through a mirror, waiting for the right moment to reveal how he feels about her … Writer-director Kim Ki-duk holds together this seedy nightmare (thematically kin to *The Taming of The Shrew*) for a surprising while with interesting lens work and a charismatic lead actor. But when the soundtrack changes from trippy samples to drippy pop ballads, the edge is lost, along with most of the psychological tension built up by Han-Gi's obsession. AK

• *Han-Gi* Jo Je-hyeon, *Sun-Hwa* Seo Won, *Hyun-su*

Nam Gung-min, *with* Kim Yun-tae, Choi Duek-mun, Kim Yoon-young.
• *Dir* and *Screenplay* Kim Ki-duk, *Pro* Seung-jae Lee, *Ex Pro* Seung-beom Kim, *Ph* Cheol-hyeon Hwang, *Ed* Seong-won Hang, *M* Ho-jun Park.

LJ Films-Metro Tartan.
102 minutes. 2003. South Korea. Rel: 11 July 2003. Cert 18.

The Barbarian Invasions ★★★★
(*Les Invasions Barbares*)
This belated sequel to *The Decline of the American Empire* stands on its own and won for its writer/director Denys Arcand the 2004 Oscar for Best Foreign-Language Film. Combining satire and sadness, the grandiose title hides an almost Chekhovian study of a group of cultured friends whose attitudes were shaped by the trends and hopes of the sixties. They are reunited by the fact that Rémy (Rémy Girard), a key figure in the group, is dying. There is also a beautifully handled sub-plot in which Rémy makes peace with the son who represents a material generation holding a quite different outlook. There may be autobiographical elements here and the last scenes are over-generous in forgiving Rémy his faults, but this is top quality filmmaking. Recognition that what really matters in life is friendship and affection becomes the film's central theme, and Rémy Girard's performance is outstanding. MS

• *Rémy* Rémy Girard, *Sébastien* Stéphane Rousseau, *Nathalie* Marie-Josée Croze, *Gaëlle* Marina Hands,

Right: Flight of the Intruder: Stéphane Rousseau and Marina Hands in Denys Arcand's Oscar-winning *The Barbarian Invasions* (from Artificial Eye)

Louise Dorothée Berryman, *Sister Constance* Johanne Marie Tremblay, *Pierre* Pierre Curzi, *Claude* Yves Jacques, *Diane* Louise Portal, *Dominique* Dominique Michel, *nurse Carol* Micheline Lanctôt
• *Dir* and *Screenplay* Denys Arcand, *Pro* Denise Robert and Daniel Louis, *Ph* Guy Dufaux, *Pro Des* François Séguin, *Ed* Isabelle Dedieu, *M* Pierre Aviat, *Costumes* Denis Sperdouklis.

Cinemaginaire/Pyramide/Télefilm Canada, etc-Artificial Eye.
99 mins. Canada/France. 2003. Rel: 20 February 2004. Cert 18.

Barbershop 2: Back in Business ★★★¹/₂

The sleeper success of *Barbershop*, a modestly budgeted hairdressers-in-the-hood comedy, made a sequel more or less inevitable. On Chicago's South Side, Calvin is still packing them in at his barbershop, a focal point for the local community. *Barbershop 2* gives centre stage to veteran barber Eddie, whose debunking of black icons in *Barbershop* drew the wrath of Jesse Jackson and Al Sharpton. There are flashbacks to the 1960s, where the young Eddie learns some harsh life lessons in the pre-Civil Rights era. The film also explores the theme of Black Americans selling out their culture and heritage. Calvin stands to make money – but lose his shop – when rival hairdresser Nappy Cutz appears on the scene and the area is redeveloped for wealthy white residents. Both funny and intelligent for much of its running time, *Barbershop 2* lacks the freshness of the first film. The non-PC element has also been toned down. DO

• *Calvin* Ice Cube, *Eddie* Cedric the Entertainer, *Jimmy* Sean Patrick Thomas, *Terri* Eve, *Isaac* Troy Garity, *Ricky* Michael Ealy, *Dinka Leonard* Earl Howze, *Quentin Leroux* Harry Lennix, *Alderman Brown* Robert Wisdom, *Kenard* Kenan Thompson, *Gina* Queen Latifah, *Loretta* Garcelle Beauvais-Nilon, *Miss Emma* Jackie Taylor.
• *Dir* Kevin Rodney Sullivan, *Pro* Robert Teitel, George Tillman Jr. and Alex Gartner, *Ex Pro* Ice Cube, Matt Alvarez and Mark Brown, *Screenplay* Don D. Scott, *Ph* Tom Priestley, *Pro Des* Robb Wilson King, *Ed* Paul Seydor, *M* Richard Gibbs, *Costumes* Jennifer Bryan.

MGM/State Street Pictures/Cube Vision-Fox.
105 mins. USA. 2004. Rel: 16 April 2004. Cert 12A.

Bartleby ★★★¹/₂

That Herman Melville's story about the scrivener who stands up against the spirit-sapping agenda of the modern workplace retains such resonance a century later, in an age rife with management

theories, employee wellness programmes and worker's rights is amusing enough in horrifying fashion. In Jonathan Parker's excellent tragic-comic absurdist modernisation, Crispin Glover plays Bartleby as a municipal records clerk whose staged descent into wage-slave *hara-kiri* confronts the futility and idiocy of the modern workplace in line with the work of cartoon-strip heroes like Dilbert and the highly successful BBC TV series *The Office*, but with deadlier intent. Glover is the perfect image of bureaucratic greyness, whose signature phrase 'I would prefer not to' becomes the battle-cry for a quiet revolution against a culturally sanctioned regime that common-sense *still* declares as unworthy of anything by contempt. So, this is what a salaryman's horror movie looks like … AK

• *The Boss* David Paymer, *Bartleby* Crispin Glover, *Vivian* Glenne Headly, *Rocky* Joe Piscopo, *Ernie* Maury Chaykin, *Frank Waxman* Seymour Cassel, *book publisher* Carrie Snodgress, *the mayor* Dick Martin, *with* Josh Kornbluth, Olivier Parker.
• *Dir* and *Pro* Jonathan Parker, *Co-Pro* Catherine Di Napoli, *Assoc Pro* Denise L. Hardy, *Screenplay* Parker and Catherine Di Napoli, based on the story *Bartleby the Scrivener* by Herman Melville, *Ph* Wah Ho Chan, *Pro Des* Rasario Provenza, *Ed* Rick LeCompte, *M* Mozart, Debussy, *Costumes* Morganne Newson.

Parker Film Co-Mandrake Media.
83 mins. USA. 2001. Rel: 2 January 2004. Cert PG.

The Basque Ball: Skin Against Stone ★★★★

(*La Pelota vasca. La piel contra la piedra*)
Much to his credit this documentary feature finds Julio Medem turning away from fiction to tackle head on the need in real life for talk where there is conflict. He applies this to the issue of the claims of the Basque Separatist Movement, but the world situation is such that it's an attitude that resonates beyond this particular example. Having wanted to give a platform to all opinions, Medem regrets that no members of ETA or of Spain's centre right party then in power agreed to appear, but the film brings together artists, priests, politicians and academics to express a range of views. Despite the movie's visual quality and the adroit use of music, it can be faulted in several ways (it's too long and taking in the identity of speakers indicated alongside their words is often difficult). However, nothing could be more honourable than for Medem to have spent his own money on a film that he rightly describes as an invitation to discussion. MS

• *With*: Xabier Arzalluz, Bernardo Atxaga, Txetxo Bengoetxea, Iñaki Gabilondo, Felipe González, Juan

José Ibarretxe, Fermín Muguruza, Arnaldo Otegi, Ana Torrent, Yoyes (archive footage), José María Aznar.
• *Dir* and *Screenplay* Julio Medem, *Ex Pro* Medem and Koldo Zuazua, *Ph* Javier Aguirre, Jon Elizegi and Ricardo de Gracia, *Ed* Julio Medem, *M* Mikel Laboa, Pascal Gaigne, Josetxo Silguero and Iker Goenaga.

Alicia Produce/Canal Plus España-Tartan Films. 110 mins. Spain. 2003. Rel: 7th May 2004. Cert 15.

Belleville Rendezvous ★★★★

(*Les Triplettes de Belleville*)
Breathtakingly drawn, this surreal animated adventure is about a boy called Champion who matures into a single-minded professional cyclist (albeit not a very successful one – his club-footed grandma appears to be his trainer and fan-club all rolled into one potato-shaped package), who is kidnapped by the French mafia (ha!) and taken to the New York-ish city of Belleville to race on a ludicrous contraption as part of a gladiatorial gambling spectacle. Only his gran can save him, with the help of a trio of decrepit frog-guzzling, jazz-singing, skiffle-playing sisters ... If Disney Studios worshipped the Tour de France, then *Belleville Rendezvous* is the hallucination they might have had from a death-defying dose of LSD. The man behind the delicious madness is comic artist Sylvain Chomet. His world is peopled by wonderful physical exaggerations of personal characteristics. As a smorgasbord of fabulously twisted imagination unapologetic of its elaborate childishness, there is nothing to compare.
AK

• *Voices*: Jean-Claude Donda, Michel Robin, Monica Viegas (characters) M, Béatrice Bonifassi, Charles Prevost Linton (songs).
• *Dir* and *Screenplay* Sylvain Chomet, *Pro* Didier Brunner and Paul Cadieux, *3-D Animation Direction* and *Special Effects Compositing Design* Pieter Van Houte, *Animation Supervisor* Jean-Christophe Lie, *Ed* Chantal Colibert Brunner, *Pro Des* Evgeni Tomov, *M* Benoît Cherest.

BBC (Bristol)/BBC Worldwide/Canadian Cable Industry/Canadian Television Fund/Canal Plus/Centre National de la Cinématographie (CNC)/Cofimage 12/Fonds Film in Vlaanderen/France 3 Cinéma/Gimages 3/Les Armateurs/UK National Lottery/Procirep/Production Champion / RGP France/Société de Développement des Entreprises Culturelles (SODEC)/Téléfilm Canada/Vivi Film-Metro Tartan. 80 mins. France/Belgium/Canada/UK. 2003. Rel 29 August 2003. Cert 12A.

Benzina ★★★

(*Gasoline*)
It's the storyline which lets down this feature debut from Italy's Monica Lisa Stambrini. Her use of the wide screen displays instinctive feeling for moving images and she creates genuinely sympathetic heroines in a lesbian couple who run a small petrol station and bar. One of them has a homophobic mother whose death, accidentally caused, has the lovers seeking to drive away with her body and hide it. Alas, a trio of nasty youngsters keep turning up to spoil their scheme but this seems more like a plot contrivance than anything we can believe in, just as the overextended ending smacks only of a desire to emulate *Thelma and Louise*. But, despite all the misjudgments, there are appealing elements here and some pleasingly idiosyncratic characterisations. MS

• *Stella* Maya Sansa, *Lenni* Regina Orioli, *Madre di Eleonora* Mariella Valentini, *Padre Gabriele* Luigi Maria Burruano, *Pippi* Chiara Conti, *Sandro* Marco Quaglia, *Filippo* Pietro Ragusa.
• *Dir* Monica Stambrini, *Pro* Galliano Juso, *Screenplay* Monica Stambrini, Elena Stancanelli and AnneRitte Ciccone, based on the novel by Stancanelli, *Ph* Fabio Cianchetti, *Art Dir* Alessandro Rosa, *Ed* Paola Freddi, *M* Massimo Zamboni, Luca Rossi and Simone Filippi, *Costumes* Antonella Cannarozzi.

Galliano Juso-Millivres Multimedia. 88 mins. Italy. 2001. Rel: 14 November 2003. Cert 15.

Big Fish ★★★

Tim Burton's latest is characteristically adventurous but surprisingly sentimental. It shows a son (Billy Crudup, excellent) attending on his dying father (Albert Finney) who had always hidden behind his gift for telling tall stories. These purportedly autobiographical tales, a series of fantasies lacking consistency of style, are incorporated into the film and Ewan McGregor portrays the father in his youth. At times this is engaging, but the diversity does not help the film to achieve a sense of unity and at around two hours it outstays its welcome. Ultimately, the whimsical treatment of the father's death simply marks a retreat from the son's valid criticism of a man afraid to let himself be truly known. Marian Cotillard playing the daughter-in-law is a most promising newcomer. MS

• *Ed Bloom (young)* Ewan McGregor, *Ed Bloom (senior)* Albert Finney, *Will Bloom* Billy Crudup, *Sandra Bloom (senior)* Jessica Lange, *Jenny (young & senior)/the witch* Helena Bonham Carter, *Sandra Bloom (young)* Alison Lohman, *Norther Winslow* Steve Buscemi, *Amos Calloway* Danny DeVito, *Dr Bennett (senior)* Robert Guillaume, *Josephine* Marion

Cotillard, *Karl the giant* Matthew McGrory, *Don Price (aged 18-22)* David Denman, *Mildred* Missi Pyle, *Beamen* Loudon Wainwright, *Ping* Ada Tai, *Jing* Arlene Tai, *with* Deep Roy, R. Keith Harris, Daniel Wallace.
• *Dir* Tim Burton, *Pro* Richard D. Zanuck, Bruce Cohen and Dan Jinks, *Ex Pro* Arne L. Schmidt, *Assoc Pro* Katterli Frauenfelder, *Screenplay* John August, based on the novel *Big Fish, A Story of Mythic Proportions* by Daniel Wallace, *Ph* Philippe Rousselot, *Pro Des* Dennis Gassner, *Ed* Chris Lebenzon, *M* Danny Elfman, *Costumes* Colleen Atwood, *Choreography* Cynthia Onrubia, *Visual effects supervisor* Kevin Mack, *Animatronic and makeup effects* Stan Winston Studio.

Columbia Pictures/Jinks/Cohen Co./Zanuck Co-Columbia Tristar.
125 mins. USA. 2003. Rel: 16 January 2004. Cert PG.

Black and White ★★¹/₂

This Australian movie concerns an Aborigine accused of raping and killing a ten-year-old white girl. Encompassing such issues as racial prejudice, injustice and police corruption, it expresses all the right sentiments. However, taking a story from real life is no guarantee of creating convincing drama and Louis Nowra's screenplay offers a great deal that is implausible. This extends to the stereotypical portrayal of the Establishment characters including the Crown Solicitor who when prosecuting sneers as only Charles Dance can (and rather too often does). Supporting players fare better, as witness Colin Friels and Ben Mendelsohn as the young Rupert Murdoch who threw the weight of his newspaper behind a campaign demanding justice for the accused. Kerry Fox however is sadly wasted. It's a case of fascinating material ineptly handled. MS

• *David O'Sullivan* Robert Carlyle, *Roderic Chamberlain* Charles Dance, *Helen Devaney* Kerry Fox, *Father Tom Dixon* Colin Friels, *Rupert Murdoch* Ben Mendelsohn, *Max Stuart* David Ngoombujarra, *Det-Sgt Turner* Roy Billing, *Thomas Playford* Bille Brown, *Rohan Rivett* John Gregg, *Roma Chamberlain* Heather Mitchell, *Const. Jones* Garry Waddell, *Justice Reed* Frank Gallacher, *Justice Abbott* Rhys McConnochie, *Chief Justice Napier* Vincent Ball, *Karskens* Chris Haywood, *Justice Windeyer* Peter Whitford, *Viscount Simonds* Peter Carroll, *Mrs Aston* Penne Hackforth-Jones, *Dr Strehlow* Petru Gheorghiu, *Dr Thompson* Susan Lyons, *Ed Montale* Scott Harrison, *Bishop* Paul Sonkkila, *Dawson* Edmund Pegge, *Barmaid* Josephine Byrnes, *Mr King* Tim Robertson, *Govt. Prosecutor* Edwin Hodgeman, *Det-Sgt Karskens* Chris Haywood.
• *Dir* Craig Lahiff, *Pro* Helen Leake and Nik Powell, *Screenplay* Louis Nowra, *Ph* Geoffrey Simpson, *Pro*

Des Murray Pickett, *Ed* Lee Smith, *M* Cezary Skubiszewski; Mozart, *Costumes* Annie Marshall.

Svensk Filmindustri/Duo Art/Scala/Australian Film Finance Corporation-Tartan Films.
99 mins. Australia/UK/Sweden. 2002.
Rel: 9 January 2004. Cert 15.

Blackball ★★

The gentlemanly game of lawn bowls is a quintessentially English pastime. In bowls, according to Torquay's reigning champion Ray Speight, the key to success is 'composure.' Local bad boy and self-proclaimed 'sexual theme park' Cliff Starkey would beg to differ. With all the arrogance of John McEnroe and Liam Gallagher combined, Starkey is a natural on the green and is determined to dismantle the smug pretentiousness of the game. To Speight's horror, Starkey beats him hands down and is crowned champion of the Southern league. But when Starkey defaces the property of the club, he is banned from the game for 15 years. Which is a shame, as the club is offered £2,400,000 in sponsorship money if Starkey is allowed to play in the next championship... Marking the feature film debut of TV comic Paul Kaye (*Anyone for Pennis?*), *Blackball* is a slick, formulaic comedy that is high on novelty value if low on laughs. Cliff Starkey is also too obnoxious and one-dimensional to take to heart, which is a shame as Kaye is obviously a talent to watch. JC-W

• *Cliff Starkey* Paul Kaye, *Ray Speight* James Cromwell, *Kerry Speight* Alice Evans, *Mutley* Bernard Cribbins, *Trevor* Johnny Vegas, *Bridget* Imelda Staunton, *Rick Schwartz* Vince Vaughn, *Alan the Pipe* James Fleet, *Giles Wilton* David Ryall, *Hugh the Sideburns* Ian McNeice, *with* Kenneth Cranham, Terry Alderton, Christopher Godwin, Mark Little, Jeff Rawle, Tony Slattery, Jon Snow.
• *Dir* Mel Smith, *Pro* James Gay-Rees, *Ex Pro* Smith, Steve Christian, Bruce Davey and Duncan Reid, *Scr* Tim Firth, *Ph* Vernon Layton, *Pro Des* Grenville Horner, *Ed* Christopher Blunden, *M* Stephen Warbeck; Elgar, Mozart; songs performed by The Libertines, Madness, Queen, Delays, The Who, Elastica, Eddie & The Hot Rods, M.A.S.S., Doves, U2, Caesars, Hoggboy, and Steve Harley and Cockney Rebel, *Costumes* Nigel Egerton and Anja Mai.

Icon/Isle of Man Film Commission/Inside Track/Midfield Films/Working Title-Icon.
96 mins. 2003. UK. Rel: 5 September 2003. Cert. 15.

Blind Flight ★★★

Eschewing any wider political comment, this is a

portrayal of real-life suffering. It's the story of how two contrasted men, Brian Keenan and John McCarthy, came to share a cell-like room in the Lebanon after Keenan, a teacher, had been seized as a hostage in Beirut and put initially in solitary confinement. Their years of imprisonment led to a friendship which has extended beyond their release. There's nothing exploitative about this film, and the acting – Ian Hart as Keenan and Linus Roache as McCarthy – is first class. It's also a triumph of reconstruction since it was not possible to film in the Lebanon. Nevertheless, the rating has to reflect the fact that the film proves to be an endurance test for the audience – that's because the experiences depicted, however heroic and tragic, do not really lend themselves to effective dramatisation. MS

• *Brian Keenan* Ian Hart, *John McCarthy* Linus Roache, *with* Bassem Breish, Mohamad Chamas, Ziad Lahoud, Lynne Farleigh, Brian Devlin.
• *Dir* and *Screenplay* John Furse, *Pro* Sally Hibbin, *Line Pro* Veronica Castillo, *Co-Pro* David Collins and Eddie Dick, *Ex Pro* John Furse and Luke Randolph, *Ph* Ian Wilson, *Pro Des* Andrew Sanders, *Ed* Kristina Hetherington, *M* Stephen McKeon, *Costumes* Rhona Russell, *Sound* Nicky Moss.

UK Film Council/Scottish Screen/Moviuehouse Entertainment/Matrrix Film/ Bord Scannán na hÉireann/National Lottery-Optimum Releasing. 96 mins. UK/Germany/Ireland. 2003. Rel: 9 April 2004. Cert 15.

Blind Shaft ★★★★
(*Mang jing*)
China, the present. Two ruthless conmen work the deeply corrupt mining system in China in a cold and deadly sting. They rope in a patsy with a promise of a job at a mine, pretend to be his family, then kill him to obtain compensation from the mining operator who pays them off to avoid any safety investigations. It's a reliable plan until their latest patsy engenders a genuine emotional connection that throws them off their game. Can they continue if he also turns out to be the son of a previous victim? Surreptitiously shot with handheld cameras, the film has raw energy of a proper guerrilla film. Li Yang has magically produced both a thumping film noir and an earnest social commentary on the evils of an industry that preys on desperate labour. AK

• *Song Jinming* Qiang Li (as Li Xiang), *Yuan Fengming* Wang Baoqiang, *Tang Zhaoyang* Wang Shuangbao, *Xiao Hong* An Jing, *first boss* Bao Zhenjiang, *Tang Zhaoxia* Sun Wei, *Miss Ma* Zhao Junzhi, *Mamasan* Wang Yining.
• *Dir*, *Screenplay* and *Pro* Li Yang, *Ph* Liu Yonghung, *Art Dir* Yang Jun, *Ed* Li Yang and Karl Riedl, *M*

Yadong Zhang, *Costumes* Wang Xiaoyan, *Sound* Wang Yu.

The Film Library/Tag Splendour Films/ Bronze Age Films-Optimum. 92 mins. Hong Kong. 2003. Rel: 7 November 2003. Cert 15.

Blind Spot: Hitler's Secretary ★★★¹/₂
(*Im toten Winkel: Hitlers Sekretärin*)
This feature length documentary is a testimony, almost a confessional, direct to camera by the late Traudl Junge. As such, it has no cinematic appeal whatever but, even if 90 minutes may seem a bit long save for specialist audiences, what she has to say is remarkable. Taken on as a secretary by Hitler in 1942 when aged 22, she found him a sympathetic employer and a father figure. Cut off from the outside world – she remained in his service right up to his last days in the bunker – she was in a blind spot that denied her a clearer view of the Führer. She may have been an innocent but she was naïve and kept her past a secret. Only in her last years both in a book and in this film did she speak out. You couldn't ask for a more personal view of history. MS

• *With*: Traudl Junge.
• *Dir* André Heller and Othmar Schmiderer, *Pro* Danny Krausz and Kurt Stocker, *Ph Sound* Mr. Schmiderer; *Ed* Daniel Pöhacker

Dor Filmproduction-Columbia Tristar. 90 mins. Austria. 2002. Rel: 26 September 2003. Cert PG.

Bodysong ★★★★
Welcome to a cross-media project done right. Writer-director Simon Pummell, his editor Daniel Goddard and composer Jonny Greenwood (also a member of rock group Radiohead) have collaborated to create a film/website/album dedicated to the human experience, seen through a lens. Arresting clips from documentary archives (some as famous as Dziga Vertov's *Man With a Movie Camera*, others wonderfully obscure) are stitched together to charts life from its beginnings, to childhood, through to maturity, sexual and otherwise. Its perspective then enlarges to a wider view of human society, taking in dark and cruel territory. The frenzy of ideas and images make for a fascinating, if bumpy, ride accompanied by an undulating experimental-rock score. The thin narrative pulse means your attention tends to drift before the sequence wrests you back into the tide. The website is an easier affair, allowing you to delve deeper at your own pace into this stunning, kaleidoscopic experiment on the theme of man. AK

• *Dir* and *Screenplay* Simon Pummell, *Pro* Janine Marmot, *Ex Pro* Robin Gutch, Paul Trijbits and Pat Joseph, *Ed* Daniel Goddard, *M* Jonny Greenwood.

Filmfour/Film Council/Hot Property-Pathé.
81 mins. UK. 2002. Rel: 5 December 2003.
Cert 18.

Bollywood Queen ★¹/₂

If you love the 'mad, bad and beautiful' ways of Bollywood, then you may get a thrill from this cheesy confection. Yet another variation of *Romeo and Juliet*, this colourful musical takes the bright lights of London's East End for its stage and fills it with stereotypes. First-time director Jeremy Wooding knows how to move his camera, but he's less successful in coaxing convincing performances from his cast. Preeya Kalidas (who starred in *Bombay Dreams* on the London stage) plays Geena, a college girl with a part-time job in a sari shop who breaks into song nine times. She talks East End English but sings in Hindi, complete with subtitles, saying things like, 'I'm a Gemini twin in a permanent spin.' When she bumps into Jay, a handsome white lad from Somerset (McAvoy), it's love at first sight because they hover in mid-air. Of course, her family disapproves of the liaison, as does Jay's brother, so there's plenty to sing about. The idea of transposing a Bollywood musical to London is not a bad one, but the film's naiveté and absence of edgy satire makes it an embarrassing joke. JC-W

• *Geena* Preeya Kalidas, *Jay* James McAvoy, *Anil* Ray Panthaki, *Frank* Ian McShane, *Sanjay* Amerjit Deu, *Dean* Ciáran McMenamin, *Dillip* Ronny Jhutti, *Neeta* Karen Shenaz David, *Anjali* Kat Bhathena, *Mother* Lalita Ahmed, *with* Badi Uzzaman, Matt Bardock, Riz Abbasi, Andy Beckwith
• *Dir* Jeremy Wooding, *Pro* Wooding, Michael Lionello Cowan and Jason Piette, *Ex Pro* David Rogers, Alex Marshall, Ash Shah, Zygi Kamasa, Simon Franks and Gary Hamilton, *Line Pro* Tony Arman-Jones, *Screenplay* Wooding and Neil Spencer, *Ph* Jono Smith, *Pro Des* Jeffrey Sherriff, *Ed* Ben Yeates, *M* Steve Beresford; songs by Najma Akhtar; songs performed by Preeya Kalidas, Tina Charles, Lexi Love, SutraSonic, Paul Young, The Dhol Foundation, Something Wonderful, Smoke City, Raj & Pablo, The Dum Dum Project, Ricky Nelson, The Shirelles, Martha Reeves and the Vandellas, etc, *Costumes* Helen Woolfenden.

Arclight Films/Great British Films/Spice Factory/Stretch Limo/Enterprise Films/Dreamfish-Redbus.
89 mins. UK/Australia. 2002. Rel: 17 October 2003.
Cert. PG.

El Bonaerense ★★★¹/₂

This Argentinian drama deals with the familiar theme of police corruption but treats it less as an action piece than as a personal drama centred on character. A man in his thirties with a covered up criminal past trains as a policeman in Buenos Aires. He finds himself part of a force which, through incompetence and lack of control, becomes a breeding ground for laziness and corruption. This is all quite interesting (some officers have privately acknowledged that the portrayal is basically accurate) but the screenplay, which drags in sex in a sub-plot as the leading character becomes involved with a cop who is also a single mother, would benefit from greater insight and detail. We never feel too involved which means that the film although quite good could have been better. MS

• *Zapa* Jorge Román, *Deputy Inspector Gallo* Dario Levy, *Mabel* Mimí Arduh, *Polaco* Hugo Anganuzzi, *Inspector Molinari* Victor Hugo Carrizo, *Zapa's mother* Graciana Chironi, *Uncle Ismael* Roberto Posse.
• *Dir, Pro, Ex Pro* and *Screenplay* Pablo Trapero, *Ph* Guillermo Nieto, *Pro Des* Sebastian Roses, *Ed* Nicolás Goldbart, *M* by Pablo Lescano and Damas Gratis, *Costumes* Marisa Urruti.

Instituto Nacional de Cine y Artes Audiovisuales/Studio Canal-Soda Pictures.
102 mins. Argentina/ Netherlands/France/ Chile. 2002.
Rel: 5 September 2003. Cert 15.

Bon Voyage ★

Despite its distinguished cast, this movie is a disaster. The main cause is that, in telling a tale set in Paris and Bordeaux in 1940, the film tries to have it every which way. Essentially it's a farce centred on a Jewish professor seeking to get heavy water to England for fear it will fall into German hands. But Jean-Paul Rappeneau's film also tries for suspense as though the story were credible and he additionally incorporates a romantic triangle story – will the young hero (Grégori Derangère) see through his manipulative actress lover (Isabelle Adjani) and recognise the affection of a student (Virginie Ledoyen)? No better is the fact that some of the cast understand that farce needs to be played seriously (the wasted Gérard Depardieu) while others (Adjani especially) overplay like mad. A genius named Ernst Lubitsch made a comparable mix work in 1942's *To Be Or Not To Be*, but this achieves nothing beyond its good production values. MS

• *Viviane Denvert* Isabelle Adjani, *Jean-Etienne Beaufort* Gérard Depardieu, *Camille* Virginie Ledoyen, *Raoul* Yvan Attal, *Frédéric* Grégori Derangère, *Kopolski* Jean-Marc Stehlé, *Alex Winckler*

Peter Coyote, *with* Aurore Clément, Xavier de Guillebon, Édith Scob.
• *Dir* Jean-Paul Rappeneau, *Pro* Michèle Pétin and Laurent Pétin, *Screenplay* Jean-Paul Rappeneau and Patrick Modiano, *Ph* Thierry Arbogast, *Pro Des* and *Costumes* Catherine Leterrier, *Ed* Maryline Monthieux, *M* Gabriel Yared.

ARP/France 2 Cinéma/France 3 Cinéma/
Canal Plus-Optimum Releasing.
114 mins. France. 2003. Rel: 14th May 2004. Cert 12A.

The Boy David Story ★★

In the 1970s and 1980s, the late Desmond Wilcox produced a series of BBC documentaries about David Lopez, a Peruvian Indian boy who suffered from terrible facial disfigurement. Fortunately, David was discovered and adopted by Scottish plastic surgeon Ian Jackson. Over the next 25 years, Jackson performed 90 operations on David, painstakingly rebuilding his face. Wilcox's films were widely acclaimed, winning several awards, though his style of presentation has perhaps not aged well. *The Boy David Story* is largely compiled from the original BBC programmes, with some new footage tacked on. Unfortunately, director McCall employs a clumsy narrative structure, compounding his error with soap opera-style commentary. The end result seems superficial and patronising, offering little insight into the real-life protagonists. The new material is perfunctory and ill-judged. David Lopez's extraordinary story deserves better. DO

• *With*: David L. Jackson, Ian Jackson, Marjorie Jackson, Mary Rodriguez, Father Severino, Sister Sita, Mother Amalia.
• *Dir* Alex McCall, *Pro* and *Screenplay* McCall and Desmond Wilcox, *Co-Pro* Terry Chase Chenowith, *Ph* Andrew Dunn, Dennis Borrow, Alex Scott, John McNeil, Dick Johnstone and Chic Cecchini, *Ed* Sarah Böszörményi, *M* Christopher Gunning.

Armac Films/Scottish Screen-Armac Films Dist.
99 mins. UK. 2002. Rel: 12 September 2003. Cert. PG.

Bright Young Things ★¹/₂

Stephen Fry has written four novels, an autobiography, an award-winning play and a musical. He is also a well-known face on both the large and small screen, a popular compere and a ubiquitous presence on the radio. To filmgoers, he is perhaps best known for playing Oscar Wilde, for which he was nominated for a Golden Globe. Of course, he can't do everything. Fry's directorial debut, an all-star adaptation of Evelyn Waugh's *Vile Bodies* (1930), a biting satire of dissolute England in the 1920s, is an over-produced, over-scored and amorphous ensemble devoid of a human centre. Such theatrical stalwarts as Peter O'Toole, Jim

Broadbent and Simon Callow are encouraged to over-act shamelessly, although the younger members of the cast do comport themselves quite well (newcomer Fenella Woolgar is particularly effective as an air-headed flapper). Mysteriously, Fry resorts too often to the prevailing clichés of Waugh terrain (the over-familiar jazz numbers, the mechanical one-liners, the endless, interminable parties) and the result is a flamboyant clutter of banality. Underneath it all, as Waugh intended, there is a frisson of despair, but it's a profoundly depressing experience. JC-W

• *Adam Symes* Stephen Campbell Moore, *Nina Blount* Emily Mortimer, *Agatha* Fenella Woolgar, *Simon Balcairn* James McAvoy, *Miles* Michael Sheen, *Ginger Littlejohn* David Tennant, *Archie* Guy Henry, *Lottie Crump* Julia McKenzie, *Lord Monomark* Dan Aykroyd, *drunk major* Jim Broadbent, *Mrs. Melrose Ape* Stockard Channing, *King of Anatolia* Simon Callow, *Col. Blount* Peter O'Toole, *Chauffeur* Stephen Fry *Father Rothschild* Richard E. Grant, *with* Jim Carter, John Mills, Alec Newman, Bill Paterson, Nigel Planer, Imelda Staunton, Harriet Walter.
• *Dir* and *Screenplay* Stephen Fry, based on the novel *Vile Bodies* by Evelyn Waugh, *Pro* Gina Carter and Miranda Davis, *Ex Pro* Andrew Eaton, Michael Winterbottom, Stephen Fry, Chris Auty, Neil Peplow, Jim Reeve and Steve Robbins, *Co-Pro* Caroline Hewitt, *Ph* Henry Braham, *Pro Des* Michael Howells, *Ed* Alex Mackie, *M* Anne Dudley, *Costumes* Nic Ede.

Revolution Films/Doubting Hall/FilmFour-Icon.
106 mins. UK. 2003. Rel: 28 September 2003. Cert 15.

Brother Bear ★★★

As animation becomes increasingly sophisticated, it's reassuring that Disney can return to its grass roots with such traditional, gimmick-free storytelling. While talking animals and Phil Collins songs may not be to everybody's taste, *Brother Bear* has a simple charm that should appeal to younger viewers. Set in the frozen wastes of Canada, the film focuses on three Inuit brothers, each of whom is entrusted with a special totem designating a human value and its representative animal. Thus Sitka's goal is guidance and his spirit animal an eagle, Denahi's is wisdom and is represented by a wolf. However, when the youngest and most spunky brother, Kenai, is bestowed with a bear-shaped totem representing love, he is frustrated and infuriated. For him, courage is everything and the bear the enemy. But the stars hold a different destiny for Kenai and his literal transformation into a bear paves the way for a new future, both for his people and the wildlife that share their home. Although not visually in the same league as *The Lion King* (nor nearly as entertaining), *Brother Bear* has its eye-catching moments and an eco-friendly message that would make Bambi proud. JC-W

• *Voices:* Kenai Joaquin Phoenix, Koda Jeremy Suarez, Rutt Rick Moranis, Tuke Dave Thomas, Sitka D.B. Sweeny, Denahi Jason Raize, Tug Michael Clarke Duncan, Tanana Joan Copeland, Mabel Estelle Harris, old Denahi Harold Gould.
• *Dir* Aaron Blaise and Robert Walker, *Pro* Chuck Williams, *Assoc Pro* Igor Khait, *Scr* Tab Murphy, Lorne Cameron, David Hoselton, Steve Bencich and Ron J. Friedman, based on a story by Broose Johnson, additional writing by Jeffrey Stepakoff, *Art Dir* Robh Ruppel, *Ed* Tim Mertensm, *M* Mark Mancina and Phil Collins, songs performed by Phil Collins and Tina Turner, *Background stylist* Xiangyuan Jie.

Walt Disney Pictures-Buena Vista.
85 mins. USA. 2003. Rel: 5 December 2003. Cert U.

Buffalo Soldiers ★★★

A blistering black comedy with a stomach-churning undercurrent, *Buffalo Soldiers* is a very dark revision of Sergeant Bilko. Joaquin Phoenix plays Ray Elwood, an amoral opportunist who has opted for three years in the army in lieu of three months' imprisonment. Stationed with the US Army's 317th Supply Battalion near Stuttgart – just prior to the dismantling of the Berlin Wall – Elwood takes huge

liberties with his position as personal secretary to the base commander (an uncharacteristically meek Ed Harris). Confident in his ability to hoodwink his superiors as he `cooks' heroin on base and sells off equipment on the black market, Elwood meets his match when he locks horns with the redoubtable Sgt. Robert Lee (Glenn). In the tradition of *M*A*S*H* and *Kelly's Heroes, Buffalo Soldiers* exploits the US Army for laughs and achieves a degree of credibility as it does so, thanks in large part to Gregor Jordan's authoritative direction. But as the humour dries up in the second half and Elwood's limited charms evaporate, the film throws up some uncomfortable questions, which its glib and sudden recourse to formula cannot justify. JC-W

• *Ray Elwood* Joaquin Phoenix, *Colonel Wallace Berman* Ed Harris, *Sgt. Robert Lee* Scott Glenn, *Robyn Lee* Anna Paquin, *Mrs Berman* Elizabeth McGovern, *General Lancaster* Dean Stockwell, *Knoll* Gabriel Mann, *Stoney* Leon Robinson, *Sgt. Saad* Sheik Mahumd-Bey, *Garcia* Michael Pena, *with* Brian Delate, Glenn Fitzgerald, Amani Gethers, Noah Margetts, Jimmie Ray Weeks.
• *Dir* Gregor Jordan, *Pro* Rainer Grupe and Ariane Moody , *Ex Pro* Paul Webster, James Schamus and Reinard Kloss, *Co-Pro* Chris Thompson, *Co-Ex Pro* James Wilson and Kai May, *Screenplay* Gregor Jordan, Eric Alex Weiss and Nora MacCoby, based on the novel by Robert O'Connor, *Ph* Oliver Stapleton, *Pro Des* Steve Jones-Evans, *Ed* Lee Smith, *M* David Holmes, *Costumes* Odile Dicks Mireaux, *Sound* Martin Muller.

FilmFour/Good Machine/Odeon Pictures/Grosvenor Park/Gorilla Entertainment/Strange Fiction-Pathé.
98 mins. UK/Germany. 2001. Rel: 18 July 2003. Cert 15.

Bugs! ★★★★¹/₂

An IMAX short initially shown outside London, *Bugs!* points up the miracles of creation, the IMAX format and cinema itself. Transporting the viewer into the microcosmic world of the insect, the film is wondrous in its detail, revealing sticky dimensions we couldn't even have dreamed of. Judi Dench lends a sensible gravitas to the story that evolves around the life cycle of a caterpillar dubbed Papilio and a praying mantis called Hierodula. Thankfully, the film eschews a Disneyesque anthropomorphism and refuses to molly-coddle its audience. Indeed, the ending is a bit of a shock, but that's Mother Nature for you – brought into your laps with all the stunning ingenuity of 3-D. JC-W

• *Narrator* Judi Dench.
• *Dir* Mike Slee, *Pro* Phil Streather and Alexandra Ferguson, *Screenplay* Slee and Abby Aron, *Ph* Sean MacLeod Phillips, *Specialist Ph* Peter Parks, *Art Dir*

Left: You're in the army now: Joaquin Phoenix subverts the American dream in Gregor Jordan's cynical, authoritative *Buffalo Soldiers* (from Pathé)

Nigel Pollock, *Ed* Peter Beston, *M* John Lunn, *Sound* Tim Archer.

Principal Large Format/Quest 3-D/
National Lottery, etc-Film Consortium Ltd.
40 mins. UK/Canada/USA. 2003.
Rel: 3 October 2003. Cert U.

Bus 174 ★★★★
(Ônibus 174)

This feature length documentary deals with the hi-jacking of a bus in Rio de Janeiro in 2000 when the passengers were held hostage by a troubled youth. Interviews with those concerned are included here, but the film largely relies on the TV footage of the event which was broadcast live on Brazilian television. This does not always make for good filmmaking and even more importantly one questions the recycling of such footage in which people lost their lives. But doubts are firmly set aside when you realise what José Padilha's film has achieved. It not only raises important points about how the authorities handled this incident, but paints a damning picture of the treatment of the homeless and of inhumane prison conditions that can only aggravate the situation. A valuable and important document. MS

• *With* Captain Batisa, Antonio Werneck, Yvonne Bezerra, Claudia Macumbinha, Captain Pimentel, etc.
• *Dir* José Padilha, *Pro* Padilha and Marcos Prado, *Ph* Cézar Moraes and Marcelo Guru, *Ed* Felipe Lacerda, *M* João Nabuco and Sacha Ambak.

Zazen Produções-Metrodome.
119 mins. Brazil. 2002. Rel: 30 April 2004. Cert 15.

The Butterfly Effect ★★

Right: Ashton Kutcher in Eric Bress and J. Mackye Gruber's *The Butterfly Effect* (from Icon)

Evan Treborn has always had amnesiac blackouts starting in a troubled childhood stained with a full fare of suburban tabloid ugliness that include bullying, molestation, an institutionalised father and gruesome pranks-gone-wrong. Fast forward to his college years and he is a typically screwed up psyche-major studying for a dissertation on memory assimilation. He wonders how his life might have been if only he had chosen differently. Lo and behold, he discovers a magical ability to shift back into his child-self when he reads his old journals, and start making his various wrongs right. But fate is cruel, and as he wakes up to various alternate futures, he is confronted by consequences that he did not predict … Ashton Kutcher leads what could have been an interesting adventure into paranoia. The scenes with the child protagonists are remarkably well acted, as are most of the supporting

performances. But Kutcher looks too much the pretty boy to play a role of the cursed plaything of the gods, and the film's chaotic rush towards its moralistic ending just sticks in the craw. AK

• *Evan Treborn* Ashton Kutcher, *Kayleigh Miller* Amy Smart, *George Miller* Eric Stoltz, *Tommy Miller* William Lee Scott, *Lenny Kagan* Elden Henson, *Thumper* Ethan Suplee, *Andrea* Melora Walters, *Tommy Miller aged 13* Jesse James, *Tommy Miller aged 7* Cameron Bright, *with* Logan Lerman, John Patrick Amedori, Irene Gorovaia, Callum Keith Rennie, John Tierney, Sadie Lawrence.
• *Dir* and *Screenplay* Eric Bress and J. Mackye Gruber, *Pro* Chris Bender, A.J. Dix, Anthony Rhulen and J.C. Spink, *Ex Pro* Toby Emmerich, Richard Brener, Cale Boyter, William Shively, David Krintzman, Jason Goldberg and Ashton Kutcher, *Ph* Matthew F. Leonetti, *Pro Des* Douglas Higgins, *Ed* Peter Amundson, *M* Michael Suby, *Costumes* Carla Hetland.

New Line Cinema/FilmEngine-Icon.
113 mins. USA/Canada. 2003. Rel: 14 April 2004. Cert. 15

C

Cabin Fever ★★★

Of course, anyone who caught Stephen King's *Dreamcatcher* may well suffer a suffocating sense of *déjà vu* here. The basic premise is surprisingly akin: a bunch of young friends move into a cabin for some recreational activity, only to find themselves besieged by bleeding, rabid strangers from the surrounding woodland. But there the similarities end as *Cabin Fever*, made for a fraction of the price, is a far more contained, tighter piece of filmmaking with a healthy sense of its own absurdity. It is, though, extremely derivative, echoing shades of everything from *The Evil Dead* to *The Blair Witch Project*. But it is very well photographed, competently acted and has a few comic twists up its sleeve that will alleviate the nausea produced by its routine dismemberment and disembowelling. It is *extremely* nasty, although its most disturbing scenario is an illustrated anecdote told round a campfire at the beginning of the film. Writer-producer-director Eli Roth obviously has a future and is as baffled as I am by the film's '15' certificate. JC-W

• *Paul* Rider Strong, *Karen* Jordan Ladd, *Jeff* Joey Kern, *Marcy* Cerina Vincent, *Bert* James DeBello, *Old Man Cadwell* Robert Harris, *Tommy* Hal Courtney, *Andy* Tim Parati, *Sheriff* Richard Fullerton, *with* Arie Verveen, Matthew Helms, Gabriel Roth, Adam Roth.
• *Dir* Eli Roth, *Pro* Roth, Lauren Moews, Sam Froelich and Evan Astrowsky, *Ex Pro* Susan Jackson, *Co-Ex Pro* Jeffrey D. Hoffman, *Screenplay* Roth and Randy Pearlstein from the former's story, *Ph* Scott Kevan, *Pro Des* Franco Giacomo-Carbone, *Ed* Ryan Folsey, *M* Nathan Barr and Angelo Badalamenti; songs performed by David Hess, Bo Hess, Jesse Hess, Noah's Rock Stars, Your Mom, Scrappy Hamilton, The Turtlenecks, and Happy Wednesday, *Costumes* Paloma Candelaria, *Make-up FX* Kurtzman, Nicotero and Berger EFX Group.

Black Sky Entertainment/Deer Path Films/DownHome Entertainment/Tonic Films-Redbus.
92 mins. USA. 2002. Rel: 10 October 2003. Cert 15.

The Calcium Kid ★½

Other than the visual nourishment of Orlando Bloom, there's not a whole lot to recommend *The Calcium Kid*. A tired retread of the mockumentary format, the comedy traces the rise to improbable stardom of Jimmy Connelly, a wholesome milkman who happens to be in the wrong place at the right time. It doesn't make much sense that Billy would want to be involved in the brutal world of boxing (he's far happier guiding his milk float around the back streets of Vauxhall), but as a part-time sparrer he breaks the hand of Britain's boxing champ. The joke is that because of Jimmy's devotion to milk,

his bones are unnaturally hard. With the world title-holder on his way from the States, first-time promoter Herbie Bush has no choice but to put Jimmy forward to fight Britain's corner. In spite of the omnipresence of a camera crew recording our hero's rise to fame, the film has the implausible air of a *Carry On Milkman* for the new millennium, complete with comely female extras billed as 'dolly birds'. And the jokes are lame: the promoter doesn't know what 'pugilism' means, while Jimmy quips, 'there's normally a winner in a two-horse race.' Hhmm. JC-W

• *Jimmy Connelly* Orlando Bloom, *Herbie Bush* Omid Djalili, *Stan Parlour* Rafe Spall, *Artie Cohen* Michael Lerner, *Sebastian Gore-Brown* Mark Heap, *Angel* Billie Piper, *Mags* Lyndsey Marshal, *Paddy* David Kelly, *Pat* Ronni Ancona, *Pete Wright* Tamer Hassan, *Jose Mendez* Michael Peña, *with* Frank Harper, Bill Thomas, Anna Wing, Ram John Holder, Frank Bruno, Chris Eubank.
• *Dir* Alex De Rakoff, *Pro* Natascha Wharton, *Ex Pro* Ereic Fellner and Tim Bevan, *Co-Pro* Richard Johns, *Screenplay* De Rakoff, Raymond Friel and Derek Boyle, *Ph* David Dunlap, *Pro Des* Joel Collins, *Ed* Mags Arnold, *M* The Boilerhouse Boys, *Costumes* Sammy Sheldon.

Working Title/Universal/StudioCanal/WT-UIP.
89 mins. UK/USA/France. 2003. Rel: 30 April 2004. Cert 15.

Calendar Girls ★★½

When Angela Baker and Tricia Stewart posed naked for the Women's Institute calendar in 1999 they hoped to raise enough money to buy a sofa. Turning their backs on the conventions of cider-pressing and flower arranging, they caused a stir that ricocheted from the dales of Yorkshire to the streets of London to the boulevards of Hollywood. It is a priceless story of how ordinary women – middle-aged, at that – can make a difference with a little chutzpah and even fewer clothes. A fictionalised version of events – Angela has been turned into Annie and Tricia into Chris – *Calendar Girls* is very strong on story and what a great story it is. Furthermore, director Nigel Cole (*Saving Grace*) has assembled some of the finest actresses that this country can boast. Considering what's on offer, then, it's a shame that *Calendar Girls* doesn't reach the same giddy heights of *The Full Monty* (a fair enough male equivalent). It's not actually a very well made film, there are few too many stock stereotypes and a predictable, trite subplot featuring Penelope Wilton (who is pretty much wasted, here). Patrick Doyle's music is also brash and intrusive and Ashley Rowe's cinematography pedestrian, but that didn't stop the film from becoming a huge hit with the blue-rinse crowd. JC-W

• *Chris* Helen Mirren, *Annie* Julie Walters, *Ruth* Penelope Wilton, *Jessie* Annette Crosbie, *Celia* Celia Imrie, *Cora* Linda Bassett, *Kathy* Georgie Glen, *May* Angela Curran, *Trudy* Rosalind March, *Rod* Ciarán Hinds, *John* John Alderton, *Lawrence* Philip Glenister, *Jem* John-Paul McLeod, *Marie* Geraldine James, *Gaz* Marc Pickering, *Eddie* George Costigan, *Richard* Graham Crowden, *Frank* John Fortune, *Danny* John Sharian, *with* Matt Malloy, Jay Leno, George Costigan.
• *Dir* Nigel Cole, *Pro* Suzanne Mackie and Nick Barton, *Scr* Juliette Towhidi and Tim Firth, *Ph* Ashley Rowe, *Pro Des* Martin Childs, *Ed* Michael Parker, *M* Patrick Doyle, *Costumes* Frances Tempest.

Harbour Pictures/Touchstone Pictures-
Buena Vista International.
108 mins. UK. 2003. Rel 5 September 2003. Cert 12.

Camp ★★★★

Camp is not a great movie. It's a little corny, the acting is a tad iffy, it lacks edge and at times it's even a little soft. But… *Camp* was actually filmed at and inspired by Stagedoor Manor, a summer camp for the performing arts outside New York which once saw Robert Downey Jr, Jennifer Jason Leigh and Natalie Portman take their first steps into the limelight. Todd Graff also went there (he later counselled Downey Jr), before becoming a professional actor (*Five Corners, The Abyss*) and scriptwriter (*Used People, Angie*). Here, he makes his directorial debut and has fashioned an irresistible tale of a group of misfits who find the courage to celebrate their individuality. Featuring a cast of unknowns and non-professionals who look like normal kids (complete with bad skin and unsightly bulges), the film settles into its stride as the various characters get to know each other and discover their potential. Shot on a minuscule budget over 23 days, *Camp* is a passionate paean to the redemptive power of music and is funny, surprising and poignant. A cross between *Fame* and *A Chorus Line*, it is further proof that the film musical is making a sterling comeback. JC-W

• *Vlad* Daniel Letterle, *Ellen* Joanna Chilcoat, *Michael* Robin De Jesus, *Shaun* Steven Cutts, *Spitzer* Vince Rimoldi, *Petie* Kahiry Bess, *Jenna* Tiffany Taylor, *Dee* Sasha Allen, *Jill* Alana Allen, *Fritzi* Anna Kendrick, *Bert* Don Dixon, *himself* Stephen Sondheim.
• *Dir* and *Screenplay* Todd Graff, *Pro* Graff, Katie Roumel, Christine Vachon, Pamela Koffler, Danny DeVito, Michael Shamberg, Stacey Sher and Jonathan Weisgal, *Ex Pro* John Wells, Richard Klubeck, Holly Becker, Caroline Kaplan and Jonathan Sehring, *Ph* Kip Bogdahn, *Pro Des* Dina Goldman, *Ed* Myron Kerstein, *M* Stephen Trask,

M supervisor Linda Cohen; songs performed by Sasha Allen and Steven Cutts, Tiffany Taylor, Daniel Letterle, Alana Allen and Anna Kendrick, Dequina Moore, Tracee Beazer, The Replacements, The Wonder Stuff, Snow Patrol, The Voices of East Harlem, Warren Wiebe, and Oasis, *Costumes* Dawn Weisberg.

IFC Productions/Jersey Films/Killer Films/Laughlin Park
Pictures-Momentum.
114 mins. USA. 2003. Rel 5 September 2003. Cert 12.

Capturing the Friedmans ★★★★★

This marvellously impartial documentary, a first feature by Andrew Jarecki, invites the audience to act as a jury as it assembles testimony regarding accusations brought in 1984 against Arnold Friedman and his son Jesse. Incorporating extracts from old home movies into new footage of comments from family, lawyers, police and others, it is fascinatingly direct about issues surrounding charges of paedophiliac abuse: the hysteria that can be unleashed, people's willingness to regard paedophile tendencies as evidence automatically supporting extreme charges, the possibility of plea bargaining leading to false pleas being given in court and the pressure that exists on witnesses to say what is expected. But, above all, the film illustrates that if justice depends on ascertaining the truth it may be unattainable. All the conflicting evidence is here, a complex jungle which leaves us aware that we can be certain of nothing. Remarkable. MS

• With Arnold Friedman, Elaine Friedman, David Friedman, Seth Friedman, Jesse Friedman, Howard Friedman, etc.
• *Dir* Andrew Jarecki, *Pro* Jarecki and Marc Smerling, *Assoc Pro* Jennifer Rogen, *Ph* Adolfo Doring, *Ed* Richard Hankin, *M* Andrea Morricone.

Magnolia Pictures-Tartan Films.
108 mins. USA. 2003. Rel: 9 April 2004. Cert 15.

Carandiru ★★¹/₂

The harsh outspoken social consciousness embedded in 1981's *Pixote* leads you to feel that you know what to expect from this new film by its director Hector Babenco. After all, this work shows events leading to a real-life tragedy: the massacre in 1992 of inhabitants of São Paulo's over-filled House of Detention following protests against conditions. Instead, this long film plays like a soap opera about the prisoners and one that grows increasingly kitsch in tone. Inevitably the grim climax that follows, a drawn out portrayal of the massacre itself, seems to belong to another film altogether. Prior to that point, we are given a series of stories or situations revolving around the inmates and connected by the comments of the prison's medical officer although portrayed with flashbacks. This figure is clearly based on the man who wrote the book which inspired the film yet he emerges here so thinly drawn as to be a cypher. MS

• *doctor* Luiz Carlos Vasconcelos, *Seo Chico* Milton Gonçalves, *Moacir* Ivan de Almeida, *Highness* Ailton Graça, *Dalva* Maria Luisa Mendonça, *Rosirene* Aida Leiner, *Lula* Dionísio Neto, *Dagger* Milhem Cortaz, *Zico* Wagner Moura, *Deusdete* Caio Blat, *Lady Di* Rodrigo Santoro, *No Way* Gero Camilo.
• *Dir* and *Pro* Hector Babenco, *Screenplay* Babenco, Victor Navas and Fernando Bonassi, based on the book *Carandiru Station* by Drauzio Varella, *Ph* Walter Carvalho, *Pro Des* Clóvis Bueno, *Ed* Mauro Alice, *M* André Abujamra, *Costumes* Cris Camargo, *Sound* Andy Kris.

Sony Pictures Classics/ HB Filmes /Columbia TriStar do Brasil/ Globo Filmes-Columbia Tristar.
145 mins. Brazil/USA. 2003. Rel: 16 April 2004.
Cert 15.

Carnages ★★★¹/₂

Delphine Glaize's first feature won the BFI's Sutherland Trophy in 2002 and does indeed possess an originality that is striking. It's really a mix of stories, six in number, in which different parts of a bull killed in a bullfight in Spain and dispatched to various destinations feature in each tale. The oddity is increased by the range of moods: some of the material is extremely harrowing (there are several scenes of surgery) but other episodes are decidedly playful. The early scenes tend to confuse but then the film settles down and the extent of the material ensures that a long film is never boring. On the other hand, even if awareness of life's fragility lies at the heart of the movie, you feel that ultimately it doesn't all come together as it should. Interesting but not wholly satisfactory.
MS

• *Carlotta* Chiara Mastroianni, *Alicia* Angela Molina, *Betty* Lio, *Jeanne* Lucia Sanchez, *Luc* Bernard Sens, *Rosie* Esther Gorintin, *Lucie* Marilyne Even, *Alexis* Clovis Cornillac, *Jacques* Jacques Gamblin, *Winnie* Raphaëlle Molinier, *Paco* Feodor Atkine.
• *Dir* and *Screenplay* Delphine Gleize, *Pro* Jérôme Dopffer, *Ph* Crystel Fournier, *Art Dir* André Fonsny, *Ed* François Quiqueré, *M* Eric Neveux, *Costumes* Marielle Robaur.

Balthazar Prods/ Need Prods/
Oasis PC/Canal Plus-Tartan Films.
132 mins. France/Belgium/Spain/Switzerland. 2002.
Rel: 12 March 2004.
Cert 15.

The Cat in the Hat ★★¹/₂
(*Dr. Seuss' The Cat in the Hat*)

Dr Suess's classic rhyme-story gets the big-budget Mike Myers treatment. The result is an oversized, overblown, and truly messy production that superficially dazzles but fails to do justice to elegant idiocy of its source material. Myers plays the Cat as a seedy avuncular menace in a tone-deaf performance, while helmer Bo Welch appears to have completely given up the reins to his Special Effects department. The parade of cut-and-paste images blend uncomfortably with a cloying Hollywood-style delivery such that it is impossible to care about the fate of the two children left in the Cat's care. Ultimately misjudged, and a big flop against audience expectations. AK

• *Cat* Mike Myers, *Quinn* Alec Baldwin, *Mom* Kelly Preston, *Sally* Dakota Fanning, *Conrad* Spencer Breslin, *Mrs. Kwan* Amy Hill, *Mr Humberfloob* & *fish* Sean Hayes, *voice of Nevins* Frank Welker, *with* Clint Howard, Paige Hurd, Paris Hilton.
• *Dir* Bo Welch, *Pro* Brian Glazer, *Ex Pro* Eric McLeod, Gregg Taylor, Karen Kehela Sherwood and Maureen Peyrot, *Screenplay* Alec Berg, David Mandel and Jeff Schaeffer, based on the book by Dr. Seuss, *Ph* Emmanuel Lubezki, *Pro Des* Alex McDowell, *Ed* Don Zimmerman, *M* David Newman, *Special makeup effects* Steve Johnson, *Costumes* Rita Ryack.

Universal/DreamWorks/Imagine-UIP.
81 mins. USA. 2003. Rel: 2 April 2004. Cert PG.

The Cat's Meow ★★★¹/₂

There's no obvious reason why this uneven but diverting entertainment should have waited so long for a British release even if it's true that the satirical tone of the opening stretch of this Hollywood tale of 1924 is more engaging that the drama that follows. The piece ultimately centres on a real-life death, one that has always remained somewhat mysterious, but, as scripted by Steven Perros from his play, this treatment lacks depth. Nevertheless with a neat introduction from Elinor Glyn (Joanna Lumley) and a potential romantic triangle at its centre involving the famous newspaper magnate William Randolph Hearst (Edward Herrmann), his mistress the actress Marion Davies (Kirsten Dunst, admirable) and the lascivious Charlie Chaplin (Eddie Izzard unexpectedly but successfully cast), the film is never boring. It could have been better but it pleases. MS

• *Marion Davies* Kirsten Dunst, *Thomas Ince* Cary Elwes, *William Randolph Hearst* Edward Herrmann, *Charlie Chaplin* Eddie Izzard, *Elinor Glyn* Joanna Lumley, *Louella Parsons* Jennifer Tilly, *George Thomas* Victor Slezak, *Margaret Livingston* Claudia Harrison.
• *Dir* Peter Bogdanovich, *Pro* Kim Bieber and Carol

Lewis, *Ex Pro* Mike Paseornek, *Co-Pro* Ernie Barbarash, *Screenplay* Steven Peros, *Ph* Bruno Delbonnel, *Pro Des* Jean-Vincent Puzos, *Ed* Edward G. Norris, *M* Ian Whitcomb; songs performed by Ian Whitcomb and His Bungalow Boys, Clarence Williams' Blue Five, Al Jolson, Eva Taylor, Louis Armstrong, and Kirsten Dunst, *Costumes* Caroline de Vivaise.

Lions Gate Films-Swipe Films.
112 mins. USA. 2001. Rel: 4 June 2004. Cert 15.

Charlie ★¹/₂

Just what the world needed: another bad British gangster movie. This is a fumbled biopic of Charlie Richardson, who ruled the South London underworld during the 1960s, while the Krays took care of business in the East End. Director Needs favours flashbacks and splitscreen, failing to disguise a weak script filled with clichés and stereotypes. It seems that Charlie Richardson went bad because his mean dad gave him a hard time, breaking one of his favourite toys. *Charlie* suffers from confused intentions. While the sentimental depiction of Richardson glamorises gang violence, the numerous torture scenes suggest he wasn't always a charming rogue. The film also argues that Richardson should not have been convicted on the evidence of dodgy witnesses, all of whom ended up in jail. At the same time, their testimony appears to have been 100 per cent accurate. Whatever the case, *Charlie* ends up being criminally dull. DO

• *Charlie Richardson* Luke Goss, *Charlie Richardson Sr* Steven Berkoff, *Richard Waldeck* Leslie Grantham, *Charlie's mum* Anita Dobson, *Jean Le Grange* Nicole Sherwin, *Van Den Berg* Marius Weyers, *Justice Lawson* Antony Carrick, *Eddie Richardson* Langley Kirkwood, *Cyril Green* Mark Arden, *Roy Hall* Tony Longhurst.
• *Dir* and *Screenplay* Malcolm Needs, *Pro* Tim Ireland and Malcolm Needs, *Co-Pro* Tim Lewiston, *Ph* Zoran Veljkovic, *Pro Des* Andrea Christelis, *Ed* Toby Yates and Jeremy Gibbs, *M* Stephen W. Parsons, *Costumes* Diana Cilliers, *Special Effects* Johnny Rafique.

Midas Films-Entertainment.
94 mins. UK. 2004. Rel: 6 February. Cert 18.

Charlie's Angels 2: Full Throttle ★

As eye candy, Cameron Diaz and Lucy Liu must rate pretty high on the ogle scale for hot-blooded males. However, co-producer Drew Barrymore is a sore piece of miscasting, a miscalculation that is highlighted in a particularly embarrassing scene in which she waddles hopelessly in the wake of her

more sprightly co-stars. In fact, as eye candy, *Full Throttle* contains a lot of ill-matched computer shots (that summer deadline just had to be reached), with the best visuals supplied by the girls, including an incredibly hard-bodied Demi Moore as a fallen Angel. Then there's Demi's ex, Bruce Willis, who appears in an early cameo, followed by a slew of other stars, from John Cleese to Jaclyn Smith. It's like it's all one big joke and a host of Hollywood friends have been invited along to look for the punchline. However, a film that thinks it can get by with a wink, a fast cut, a dumb musical cue and another wiggle of Cameron's rear end is sorely mistaken. This is bubblegum entertainment without the bubble. JC-W

• *Natalie Cook* Cameron Diaz, *Dylan Sanders/ Helen Zass* Drew Barrymore, *Alex Munday* Lucy Liu, *Jimmy Bosley* Bernie Mac, *Thin Man* Crispin Glover, *Seamus O'Grady* Justin Theroux, *Ray Carter* Robert Patrick, *Madison Lee* Demi Moore, *Randy Emmers* Rodrigo Santoro, *Pete* Luke Wilson, *Max* Shia LaBeouf, *Mr Munday* John Cleese, *Charles 'Charlie' Townsend* John Forsythe, *with* Matt LeBlanc, Robert Forster, Pink, Eve, Carrie Fisher, Eric Bogosian, Tommy Flanagan, Andrew Wilson; . uncredited: *future Angels* Ashley Olsen and Mary-Kate Olsen, *Kelly Garrett* Jaclyn Smith, *William Rose Bailey* Bruce Willis.
• *Dir* McG (aka Joseph McGinty Nichol), *Pro* Leonard Goldberg, Drew Barrymore and Nancy Juvonen, *Scr* John August, Cormac Wibberley and Marianne Wibberley, based on a story by August, *Ph* Russell Carpenter, *Pro Des* J. Michael Riva, *Ed* Wayne Wahrman, *M* Edward Shearmur.

Columbia Pictures Corporation/Flower Films/Tall Trees Productions/ Wonderland Sound and Vision-Columbia Tristar.
106 mins. USA. 2003. Rel 1 July 2003. Cert 12A.

Cheaper By the Dozen ★

With the honourable exception of *Bowfinger*, Steve Martin seems to be marking time in crass 'remakes' of classic Hollywood comedies. *Cheaper By the Dozen* bears little resemblance to the 1950 original, which starred Clifton Webb as an efficiency expert who treats his large family as a controlled experiment. Martin gives a tired performance as a football coach with twelve deeply unappealing kids. This obnoxious brood undercuts the film's reactionary argument that a high-flying Big City career is no match for rural family bliss. The coarse physical humour – food fights aplenty – is similarly cack-handed. Director Levy merely points his camera and hopes for the best. Even *Father of the Bride 2* had more laughs. DO

• *Tom Baker* Steve Martin, *Kate Baker* Bonnie Hunt,

Nora Baker Piper Perabo, *Charlie Baker* Tom
Welling, *Lorraine Baker* Hilary Duff, *Henry Baker*
Kevin G. Schmidt, *Sarah Baker* Alyson Stoner,
Hank Ashton Kutcher (uncredited), *with* Kevin G.
Schmidt, Alyson Stoner, Jacob Smith, Liliana Mumy,
Morgan York, Forrest Landis, Blake Woodruff, Brent
Kinsman, Shane Kinsman, Paula Marshall, Steven
Anthony Lawrence, Alan Ruck, Richard Jenkins,
Holmes Osborne, Vanessa Bell Calloway, Rex
Linn, Shawn Levy, Regis Philbin, Kelly Ripa,
Wayne Knight.
• *Dir* Shawn Levy, *Pro* Robert Simonds, Michael
Barnathan, Ben Myron, *Co-Pro* Ira Shuman,
Screenplay Sam Harper, Joel Cohen and Alec
Sokolow, story by Craig Titley, based on the book
by Frank Bunker Gilbreth Jr. & Ernestine Gilbreth
Carey, *Ph* Jonathan Brown, *Pro Des* Nina Ruscio,
Ed George Folsey Jr, *M* Christophe Beck,
Costumes Sanja Milkovic Hays.

Fox-Fox.
97 mins. USA. 2003. Rel: 13 February. Cert PG.

Le Chignon d'Olga ★★★★

If the opening of Jérôme Bonnell's first feature recalls
Rohmer, the piece as a whole, engaging and subtle,
suggests an individual new voice. Set in Northern
France in a small town, his film centres on a father
newly widowed and his son and daughter who still
live at home. The son, Julien, may be the most
prominent figure (22-year-old Hubert Benhamdine
is ideally cast) but various friends also have
important roles to play. Well characterised, it could
yet seem lightweight and lacking a firm centre
despite the theme of adjusting to a death. But then
you realise that the various plot threads all invite
speculation on the way we tell lies to one another
from a variety of motives. There's a distinctive view
of human behaviour here which makes Bonnell a
new talent to note and welcome. MS

• *Julien* Hubert Benhamdine, *Alice* Nathalie
Boutefeu, *Gilles* Serge Riaboukine, *Emma* Florence
Loiret Caille, *Basile* Antoine Goldet, *Olga* Delphine
Rollin, *Nicole* Valerie Stroh.
• *Dir* and *Screenplay* Jerome Bonnell, *Pro* Joel Frages
and Elise Jalladeau, *Co-Pro* Arnauld de Battice and
Sylvain Goldberg, *Ph* Pascale Lagriffoul, *Pro Des*
Benoit Bechet, *Ed Costumes* Carole Gerard.

Artcam Intl./StudioCanal France/France 3 Cinéma/Canal
Plus/Centre National de la Cinematographie
Procirep/Studio Image 8-Artifical Eye.
96 mins. France/Belgium. 2002. Rel: 12 September 2003.
Cert. 15.

Citizen Verdict ★¹/₂

The cinematic exploitation of reality TV has almost
become a genre unto itself. However, the casting of
Jerry Springer as the sleazy producer of a Florida-
based TV show (*So Sue Me*) is a bit of a coup. In a
bid to increase ratings, Marty Rockman devises a
new show called *Citizen Verdict*, in which a real-life
criminal will be tried live on television. And, if voted
guilty by the Great American Public, the said
criminal will be executed on pay-per-view (for a
bargain-basement $19.99). Juggling a number of
white-hot potatoes (the public as executioner, the
negation of the due process of law, the glorification
of the death penalty and the manipulation of
evidence), *Citizen Verdict* sets up a tinderbox of
dramatic anticipation. But even with four credited
scriptwriters, it cannot begin to harness the potential
of its concept. Furthermore, the film cops out in the
eleventh hour and its overblown production values
merely neutralise the essence of its message. Pure
trash. JC-W

• *Sam Patterson* Armand Assante, *Bull Tyler* Roy
Scheider, *Marty Rockman* Jerry Springer, *Jessica
Landers* Justine Mitchell, *Ricky Carr* Raffaello
Degruttola, *Larry Grimes* Gideon Emery, *Michael
Krauss* Brett Goldin, *Carlene Osway* Dorette
Potgieter, *TV interviewee* Sheri Schifter.
• *Dir* Philippe Martinez, *Pro* Martinez and Helmut
Breuer, *Line Pro* Luc Campeau, *Ex Pro* Douglas W.
Miller, Juan Montilla Eslava, Ian Burlingham,
Donald A. Barton, Kim Leggatt and Terence S.
Potter, *Co-Pro* Alan Latham, Luc Campeau and
Stéphanie Martinez, *Co-Ex Pro* Karen Alison
Hamilton and Karinne Martinez, *Screenplay* Tony
Clarke, Kristina Hamilton, Philippe Martinez and
Frank Rehwaldt, *Ph* Michael Brierley, *Pro Des* Zack
Grobler, *Ed* Kristina Hamilton, *M* Guy Farley,
Costumes Reza Levy.

Bauer Martinez Studios/Aquarius Film Co./
Exactlord a Lucky 7-Georgia Films.
98 mins. UK/Germany/USA. 2003.
Rel: 12 September 2003. Cert 15.

The Clay Bird ★★★★
(*Matir Moina*)
A film from Bangladesh but set there in the sixties
when it was East Pakistan, this reveals in its creator
Tareque Masud a filmmaker whose deep humanity
prompts thoughts of his idol, Satyajit Ray. In a work
close to autobiography, he tells of a village boy from
a Muslim family. The strict father, something of an
extremist and wary of Hindus, sends the child away
to an Islamic school. What follows shows the boy
learning broader sympathies in this very traditional
institution through friendship with a pupil treated
like an outcast and through admiration for a liberal
teacher. This personal tale takes on extra resonance
by emphasis on the period's political turmoil when
democracy was promised but withheld. This

Right:
Ruby Gets Her Gun:
Renée Zellweger in
her Oscar-winning
performance in
Anthony Minghella's
Cold Mountain
(from BVI)

admirable work is essentially a protest against extremism, and it's only weakness is that it evokes at least three Ray masterpieces without being able to equal them. MS

• *Anu* Nurul Islam Bablu, *Rokon* Russell Farazi, *Kazi* Jayanto Chattopadhyay, *Ayesha* Rokeya Prachy.
• *Dir* Tareque Masud, *Screenplay* Tareque Masud and Catherine Masud, *Ph* Sudheer Palsane, *Art Dir* Kazi Rakib and Sylvain Nahmias, *Ed* Catherine Masud, *M* Moushumi Bhowmik.

Audiovision/MK2 Productions-ICA Projects
98 mins. France/Pakistan/Bangladesh. 2002.
Rel: 4 July 2003.
Cert PG.

Cold Creek Manor ★¹/₂

Most films, even those that fall miserably short of their goal, have some redeeming feature. Be it a choice supporting performance, a wonderful piece of music or the exploration of a hitherto unknown sub-culture, there's usually something. However, there is little to interest anybody in *Cold Creek Manor*, give or take a person of limited brain who has you to acquaint themselves with *Fatal Attraction* or *The Hand That Rocks the Cradle* or *Swimf@n* or... The surprising thing about this mechanical and clumsy thriller is that it is brought to us by Mike Figgis, the garlanded director of *Leaving Las Vegas*. True, Figgis has made several suspect movies, but they've all had their virtues. Which just goes to show how hard it is to pull off a mainstream Hollywood thriller. The story of an urban family who buy an old house in the country and fall out with its previous tenant, *Cold Creek Manor* loses its way as soon as it strays into the countryside. Every nuance is underlined, every twist potholed by irrationality and every scene prompting a violent attack of déjà vu. Still, Stephen Dorff has some very impressive abs...
JC-W

• *Cooper Tilson* Dennis Quaid, *Leah Tilson* Sharon Stone, *Dale Massie* Stephen Dorff, *Ruby* Juliette Lewis, *Kristen Tilson* Kristen Stewart, *Mr Massie* Christopher Plummer, *Jesse Tilson* Ryan Wilson, *Sheriff Ferguson* Dana Eskelson, *with* Simon Reynolds, Kathleen Duborg, Peter Outerbridge.
• *Dir* Mike Figgis, *Pro* Figgis and Annie Stewart, *Ex Pro* Lata Ryan and Richard Jefferies, *Screenplay* Jefferies, *Ph* Declan Quinn, *Pro Des* Leslie Dilley, *Ed* Dylan Tichenor, *M* Mike Figgis; songs performed by George Strait, Hypnogaja, John Porter, and Canned Heat, *Costumes* Marie-Sylvie Deveau.

Touchstone Pictures/Red Mullet-Buena Vista.
119 mins. USA/UK. 2003. Rel: 30 January 2004.
Cert 15.

Cold Mountain ★★★★

Anthony Minghella's sprawling, detailed epic certainly lives up to its name. It's an Everest of a movie and has a cold streak that will chill the marrow of romantics looking for a latter-day *Gone With the Wind*. Adapted from the acclaimed, best-selling novel by Charles Frazier, *Cold Mountain* is an epic love story set during the last stages of the American Civil War. It's a romance based on looks as the genteel Ada Monroe (Kidman) finds herself strangely drawn to the reticent W.P. Inman (Law). Accordingly, the film is composed of imagery that will likely become a part of the cinematic landscape for years to come. Filmed in Romania, North Carolina and South Carolina, the movie cries out for an Oscar for best cinematography (it duly secured a nomination). But then everything about it looks tailor-made for the American Academy. Jude Law establishes his stellar credentials as the taciturn, conflicted Inman and Nicole is radiant as Ada, a preacher's daughter brought up to enhance high society. Yet, for all its many virtues, *Cold Mountain* is never more than A Great Movie. It looks great, it delivers several punches below the waist, but it remains a cinematic spectacle, a melodrama several removes from complex reality. JC-W

• *W.P. Inman* Jude Law, *Ada Monroe* Nicole Kidman, *Ruby Thewes* Renée Zellweger, *Maddy* Eileen Atkins, *Stobrod Thewes* Brendan Gleeson, *Rev. Veasey* Philip Seymour Hoffman, *Sara* Natalie Portman, *Junior* Giovanni Ribisi, *Reverend Monroe* Donald Sutherland, *Teague* Ray Winstone, *Sally Swanger* Kathy Baker, *Esco Swanger* James Gammon, *Bosie*

Charlie Hunnam, *Georgia* Jack White, *Pangle* Ethan Suplee, *Ferry Girl* Jena Malone, *Lila* Melora Walters, *Oakley* Lucas Black, *Shyla* Taryn Manning, *blind man* Tom Aldredge, *doctor* James Rebhorn, *with* Emily Deschanel, Cillian Murphy, Sean Gleeson.
• *Dir* and *Screenplay* Anthony Minghella, based on the book by Charles Frazier, *Pro* Sydney Pollack, William Horberg, Albert Berger and Ron Yerxa, *Ex Pro* Iain Smith, Bob Weinstein, Harvey Weinstein and Bob Osher, *Assoc Pro* Steve E. Andrews and Timothy Bricknell, *Ph* John Seale, *Pro Des* Dante Ferretti, *Ed* Walter Murch, *M* Gabriel Yared, *Exec M Pro* T-Bone Burnett; songs performed by Jack White, Alison Krauss, T-Bone Burnett, Lonnie Carter, Elvis Costello, Walter Jacobs, Bobby Neuwirth, Sting, and Gabriel Yared, *Costumes* Ann Roth and Carlo Poggioli, *Civil War Consultant* Don Troiani.

Miramax Films/Mirage Enterprises/
Bona Fide-Buena Vista International.
152 mins. USA/UK/Romania/Italy. 2003.
Rel: 26 December 2003. Cert 15.

Comandante ★★★

Oliver Stone's documentary feature in which he interviews the 75-year-old Fidel Castro in Cuba provides ample evidence of his filmmaking skill and the editing is admirable, but what function the film serves is open to question. It might be that Stone would claim that his gentle questioning was the price of getting this footage. However, given his beady eye for American politics, it may be that Stone is pro-Castro, at least to the extent of believing that the man is a victim of U.S. propaganda. In any case, the film falls between two stools: those as politically ignorant as myself will need more background information, while those who know much more will be even less accepting of Stone's pussy-footing approach. Interesting, but decidedly unsatisfactory. MS

• *With:* Fidel Castro, Oliver Stone, Juanita Vera, Fidel Castro Jr., Fidel Castro III, Juan Almeida.
• *Dir* Oliver Stone, *Pro* Stone and Fernando Sulichin, *Ex Pro* Jaume Roures, José Ibañez and Alvaro Longoria, *Line Pro* Vincent Joliet, *Orig. idea* Ibañez and Álvaro Longoria, *Ph* Rodrigo Prieto and Carlos Marcovich, *Ed* Alex Marquez, Elisa Bonora, *M* Alberto Iglesias.

Pentagrama Films/ Morena Films/
HBO-Optimum Releasing.
99 mins. Spain/USA. 2003. Rel: 3 October 2003.
Cert PG.

The Company ★★★

Robert Altman surprises his admirers here by showing real flair for presenting dance on screen. Shot on video but utilising the latest high definition techniques, *The Company* not only illustrates Altman's mastery of the 'Scope format but is also visually stunning photographically. The opening credits accompany dancers of the Joffrey Ballet Company of Chicago in Alwin Nikolais's *Tensile Involvement* and show the film at its best. But, despite a credit for 'Story' shared by ex-dancer Neve Campbell (who takes the lead role also) and Barbara Turner, the plot-line is almost non-existent, and you need to turn to *A Chorus Line* for a movie that really captures the highs and lows in the lives of dancers. There are fine moments but the whole is a good deal less satisfactory than some of the parts. MS

• *Ry* Neve Campbell, *Alberto Antonelli* Malcolm McDowell, *Josh* James Franco, *Harriet* Barbara Robertson, *Edouard* William Dick, *Susie* Susie Cusack, *Ry's mother* Marilyn Dodds Frank, *Ry's father* John Lordan.
• *Dir* Robert Altman, *Pro* David Levy, Joshua Astrachan, Neve Campbell, Christine Vachon, Robert Altman and Pamela Koffler, *Ex Pro* Jane Barclay, Sharon Harel, Hannah Leader, John Wells, Roland Pellegrino and Dieter Meyer, *Scr* Barbara Turner, based on a story by Neve Campbell and Barbara Turner, *Ph* Andrew Dunn, *Pro Des* Gary Baugh, *Ed* Geraldine Peroni, *M* Van Dyke Parks; Chopin, Saint-Saëns, JS Bach, Alan Raph and Lee Holdridge, Doug Adams and Russ Gauthier, Richard Rodgers and Lorenz Hart, John Zeretzke, Cesare Pugni and Jean-Baptiste Nadaud, Angelo Badalamenti and David Lynch, Mark O'Connor, Alexander Glazunov, and Alwin Nikolais, *Costumes* Susan Kaufman.

Capitol Films/CP Medien/ Killer Films/
Snow Prods-Pathé.
112 mins. USA/Germany/UK. 2003.
Rel: 7th May 2004. Cert 12A.

La Comunidad ★★★

(Common Wealth)
In technical terms the Spanish director Alex de la Iglesia has never made a better film than this. Furthermore, it exists as a vehicle for that splendid actress Carmen Maura, not an artist to let you down, and carries engaging echoes of Hitchcock. Even so, the attempt to pitch this film half-way between farce and horror proves increasingly uneasy. Maura plays a woman acting for an estate agency in Madrid whose work leads to her locating the hidden lottery winnings of a dead lessee. She wants this money for herself, but discovers that the neighbours are willing to kill for it. If the first half is light-weight yet agreeable, the second in contrast is too stupid to be frightening or exciting but sufficiently schlocky to be

unpleasant. Mackendrick's classic *The Ladykillers* blended somewhat comparable elements beautifully; this film doesn't. MS

• *Julia* Carmen Maura, *Charly* Eduardo Antuña, *Encarna* María Asquerino, *Ricardo* Jesús Bonilla, *Paquita* Marta Fernández Muro, *Hortensia* Paca Gabaldón, *Karina* Ane Gabarain, *Castro* Sancho Gracia, *Emilio* Emilio Gutiérrez Caba, *Dolores* Kiti Manver, *Ramona* Terele Pávez, *Oswaldo* Roberto Perdomo, *Chueca* Manuel Tejada, *Domínguez* Enrique Villén.
• *Dir* Álex de la Iglesia, *Pro* Andrés Vicente Gómez, *Assoc Pro* Marco Gómez, *Screenplay* de la Iglesia and Jorge Guerricaechevarría, *Ph* Kiko de la Rica, *Art Dir* José Luis Arrizabalaga and Biaffra, *Ed* Alejandro Lázaro, *M* Roque Baños, *Costumes* Paco Delgado.

Antena 3 Televisión/Lolafilms/
Vía Digital-Maiden Voyage Pictures.
110 mins. Spain. Rel: 4 July 2003. Cert 15.

Concert for George ★★★¹/₂

Featuring the lookalike son and produced by his daughter, it is no wonder that the concert documentary of George Harrison's memorial concert feels like a family home video. Granted, of course, that his family included as adopted brothers some of the greatest names in rock and roll, including the likes of Sir Eric Clapton, Ringo Starr, Jeff Lynne, Joe Brown, Tom Petty and Michael Palin (if one, like Harrison, considers Monthy Python the Beatles of comedy), and the home happens to include a crowd of thousands in the Royal Albert Hall, present on the night of 29 November 2002, the anniversary of George Harrison's passing. Beyond delivering a storming concert and a feast of old-master virtuosity, the film artlessly constructs an emotional portrait of who George Harrison was to his friends, through the music and intermittent to-camera confessions by those who knew him best. The cumulative effect cannot help but break your heart, just a little. AK

• *As themselves* Paul McCartney, Ringo Starr, Eric Clapton, Tom Petty, Anoushka Shankar, Ravi Shankar, George Harrison, Terry Gilliam, Eric Idle, Terry Jones, Michael Palin, Tom Hanks, Neil Innes, Tessa Niles, Katy Kissoon, Jim Keltner, Jim Horn, Dhani Harrison, Jim Capaldi, Joe Brown, Dave Bronze, Marc Mann, Gary Brooker, Albert Lee, Jools Holland, Andy Fairweather-Low, Ray Cooper.
• *Dir* David Leland, *Pro* Olivia Harrison, John Kamen and Ray Cooper, *Ex Pro* Olivia Harrison and Brian Roylance, *Ph* Chris Menges, *Pro Des* Eve Stewart, *Ed* Claire Ferguson, *M Dir* Eric Clapton.

Warner Music/@radical media-Pathé.
97 mins. UK/Australia/USA. 2003. Rel 10 October 2003. Cert PG.

Confessions of a Teenage Drama Queen ★¹/₂

Manhattan teen queen Lindsay Lohan is transplanted to suburban New Jersey. Needless to say, she finds the culture shock hard to take, especially at her new high school. Lohan is desperate to get back to Manhattan for the farewell gig by her current pop idol, a foul-mouthed British rock star. Can she achieve her impossible dream? Maybe. Thin on plot, *Confessions of a Teenage Drama Queen* is a bog-standard teen comedy. Lohan is an appealing lead, though she had more chance to shine in *Freaky Friday* and *Mean Girls*. If nothing else, the film marks modest progress for British director Sara Sugarman, who perpetrated the appalling *Mad Cows*. DO

• *Lola Cep* Lindsay Lohan, *Stu Wolff* Adam Garcia, *Karen Cep* Glenne Headly, *Ella Gerard* Alison Pill, *Sam* Eli Marienthal, *Miss Baggoli* Carol Kane, *Carla* Megan Fox, *Mrs Gerard* Sheila McCarthy, *Calum* Tom McCamus.
• *Dir* Sara Sugarman, *Pro* Robert Shapiro and Jerry Leider, *Screenplay* Gail Parent, *Ph* Stephen H. Burum, *Pro Des* Leslie McDonald, *Ed* Anita Brandt Burgoyne, *M* Mark Mothersbaugh, *Costumes* David C. Robinson.

Walt Disney Pictures-Buena Vista International.
89 mins. USA/Germany. 2004. Rel: 7th May 2004. Cert. PG.

Confidence ★★★★

This improbable but diverting thriller replete with twists is a genre movie that delivers. A well cast Ed Burns plays a con-man who bites off more than he can chew. That's when he and his associates trick a man out of the money he is carrying unaware that it belongs to a dangerous big time crook named King (Hoffman). Desperate to avoid King's vengeance, the con-man makes a deal with him: he will undertake a big-time con job, one involving a pickpocket (Weisz) who will seduce a bank employee as an essential part of the scheme. Doug Jung's snappy screenplay is relished by the players, and by nobody more than Hoffman as the formidable and bisexual boss man. It's all too preposterous to be memorable, but James Foley's able direction adds to the pleasure making this a fun night out. MS

• *Jake Vig* Edward Burns, *Lily* Rachel Weisz, *Gunther Butan* Andy Garcia, *King* Dustin Hoffman, *Gordo* Paul Giamatti, *Whitworth* Donal Logue, *Manzano* Luis Guzman, *Mile* Brian Van Holt, *Lupus* Franky G, *Travis `Butch'* Morris Chestnut, *Morgan Price* Robert Forster, *with* Ethan Embry, Tommy `Tiny' Lister, John Carroll Lynch, Louis Lombardi, Leland Orser, Robert Pine.

• *Dir* James Foley, *Pro* Marc Butan, Michael Paseornek, Michael Burns and Michael Ohoven, *Ex Pro* Eric Kopeloff, Marco Mehlitz, Eberhard Kayser and Scott Bernstein, *Screenplay* Doug Jung, *Ph* Juan Ruiz-Anchia, *Pro Des* Bill Arnold, *Ed* Stuart Levy, *M Sup* Joel High, *Costumes* Michele Michel.

Lions Gate-Momentum.
98 mins. USA. 2003. Rel: 22 August 2003. Cert 15.

Confidences Trop Intimes ★★★

(*Intimate Strangers*)
Patrice Leconte's latest film suffers from uncertainties of tone as he tells the story of a troubled married woman (Sandrine Bonnaire) seeking out a psychiatrist but ringing the wrong bell and encountering instead a tax adviser (Fabrice Luchini). However, the latter has a sympathetic ear and the woman is attractive which may explain why their confidential meetings continue despite having commenced erroneously. Since the music score and the look of the piece evoke Hitchcock's thrillers, it's a drawback to find that the unlikely premise leads less to a mystery tale than to a love story. The film also dabbles in comedy at times and its conflicting signals undermine the efforts of the lead actors leaving it to the supporting cast (Michel Duchaussey, Hélène Surgère and Anne Brochet) to steal the show in this rather disappointing and drawn-out movie. MS

• *Anna Delambre* Sandrine Bonnaire, *William Faber* Fabrice Luchini, *Dr Monnier* Michel Duchaussoy, *Jeanne* Anne Brochet, *Marc* Gilbert Melki, *Luc* Laurent Gamelon, *Mrs. Mulon* Hélène Surgère.
• *Dir* Patrice Leconte, *Pro* Alain Sarde, *Ex Pro* Christine Gozlan, *Screenplay* Jérôme Tonnerre and Patrice Leconte, *Ph* Eduardo Serra, *Pro Des* Ivan Maussion, *Ed* Joëlle Hache, *M* Pascal Estève, *Costumes* Annie Perier-Bertaux and Sandrine Kerner.

Les Films Alain Sarde/France 3 Cinema/Zoulous Films/Assise Production-Pathé.
104 mins. France. 2003. Rel: 18 June 2004. Cert 15.

Connie and Carla ★★★

Sometimes the sheer force of personality can dismantle the critical faculties of a reviewer. *Connie and Carla*, a crass, clumsy composite of *Some Like it Hot* and *Tootsie*, has a winning streak and the nub of a great idea that retains the interest. After the phenomenal success of her *My Big Fat Greek Wedding*, writer-producer-star Nia Vardalos dug around in her drawer and dragged out this derivative, artless charmer. Obsessed with musical theatre from their early teens, best friends Connie and Carla pursue their dream of a Rita Moreno/Liza Minnelli re-match and joyfully play venues from a school canteen to an airport departure lounge (as if). When they witness a murder perpetrated by a Chicagoan drug lord, they leave town immediately – unwittingly carrying with them a kilo of the latter's cocaine. Hiding out in Los Angeles, they go undercover as drag queens and, for the first time, find a small degree of success… Some wonderful opportunities for real drama are routinely wasted, but there's still a lot to like here. The underused David Duchovny is genuinely charming as a straight guy inexplicably drawn to Connie (as if), Toni Collette is astonishingly persuasive as a man in drag and the musical numbers are fab. In fact, I can't remember the last time that I enjoyed such a bad film so much. JC-W

• *Connie* Nia Vardalos, *Carla* Toni Collette, *Jeff* David Duchovny, *Robert/Peaches* Stephen Spinella, *Lee/N'Cream* Alec Mapa, *Brian/Brianna* Christopher Logan, *Paul* Robert Kaiser, *Stanley* Ian Gomez, *herself* Debbie Reynolds, *Rudy* Robert John Burke.
• *Dir* Michael Lembeck, *Pro* Roger Birnbaum, Gary Barber and Jonathan Glickman, *Ex Pro* Nia Vardalos, Rita Wilson and Peter Safran, *Co- Pro* Warren Carr, *Screenplay* Vardalos, *Ph* Richard Greatrex, *Pro Des* Jasna Stefanovic, *Ed* David Finfer, *M* Randy Edelman, *Costumes* Ruth Myers.

Universal/Spyglass Entertainment/Birnbaum/Barber-UIP.
98 mins. USA. 2004. Rel: 11 June 2004. Cert 12A.

The Cooler ★★

Writer turned director Wayne Kramer relishes the 'Scope screen but behind the visual verve lies less happily a sleazy, violent drama intended to reflect life in Las Vegas. The title role, that of a man employed to cool down gamblers on a winning streak by his mere presence (his own lack of luck is supposed to communicate itself to others), is played by William H. Macy. But using this fine actor – miscast in a role which requires a middle-aged loner to emerge as a figure of romantic appeal – only emphasises that the material is unworthy of him. Alec Baldwin plays the ruthless casino boss who employs him and Maria Bello is the waitress who gets beaten up when she alters the cooler's luck by falling for him. The tale is improbable with sentimental passages at odds with the generally nitty-gritty approach. A distasteful movie. MS

• *Bernie Lootz* William H. Macy, *Natalie Belisario* Maria Bello, *Shelly Kaplow* Alec Baldwin, *Mikey* Shawn Hatosy, *Larry Sokolov* Ron Livingston, *Buddy Stafford* Paul Sorvino, *Charlene* Estella Warren, *Doris* Ellen Greene, *with* M.C. Gainey, Don Scribner, Joey Fatone, Doc Watson.
• *Dir* Wayne Kramer, *Pro* Sean Furst and Michael Pierce, *Ex Pro* Edward R. Pressman, John Schmidt,

Alessandro Camon, Brett Morrison, Robert Gryphon and Joe Madden, *Co-Pro* Elliot Lewis Rosenblatt and Bryan Furst, *Screenplay* Frank Hannah and Wayne Kramer, *Ph* James Whitaker, *Pro Des* Toby Corbett, *Ed* Arthur Coburn, *M* Mark Isham, *Costumes* Kristen M. Burke.

ContentFilm/Gryphon Films/Dog Pond Prods-Tartan Films.
102 mins. USA. 2002. Rel: 18 June 2004.
Cert 15.

Crimson Gold ★★★

(*Talaye sorgh*)
Being a great admirer of Jafar Panahi's film *The Circle*, I had high hopes of this, especially since the screenplay is by another Iranian master, Abbas Kiarostami. But, by beginning with an attempted robbery, a murder and a suicide before going into flashback to reveal the anguish of the man responsible, it seems to promise a highly dramatic work. Instead, it's another example of Iranian minimalism meandering slowly through a series of episodes which, even when quirky and striking, never really cohere to make a satisfactory whole. It may underline the plight of the poor in a city where the rich, not necessarily happy, are to be found. But that's hardly revelatory. The non-professional cast plays with conviction and there are those who regard this as another masterpiece from Iran.
MS

• *Hussein* Hussein Emadeddin, *Ali* Kamyar Sheissi, *the bride* Azita Rayeji, *with* Shahram Vaziri, Pourang Nakhael.
• *Dir, Pro* and *Ed* Jafar Panahi, *Screenplay* Abbas Kiarostami, *Ph* Hossain Jafarian, *Art Dir* Iraj Raminfar, *M* Peyman Yazdanian, *Sound* Masoud Behnam and Laurent Bailly.

Jafar Panahi Prods-ICA Projects.
96 mins. Iran. 2003. Rel: 12 September 2003.
Cert. 12A.

The Cuckoo ★★★¹⁄₂

(*Kukushka*)
Finland, 1944. Veiko, a Finn, is dressed in an SS uniform, chained to a rock, and given a sniper rifle by retreating German soldiers with the instructions to shoot as many Russians as he can before they get to him. By determination and the ingenuity of desperation, he escapes, and runs into the isolated Lapp farm of Anni. He is shocked to discover the presence of a Russian, Ivan, being nursed to health by the vivacious widow, who thanks her gods for the sudden appearance of not one but two strapping young men … The elements of misunderstanding

that drive all war are magnified in this romantic farce about three people blocked by their inability to understand the other's language, who nevertheless stumble along into a modus vivendi, guided by the desolation of their circumstances and the wisdom of a woman of the land. The Lapp woman Anni is the epitome of basic humanity, caring for the two bickering men like a mother over two sons, except that she views them with more than maternal affection. Together, they achieve a dramatic circus that feels more profound that it probably is, thanks in no small to the pungent setting.
AK

• *Veiko* Ville Haapasalo, *Anni* Anni-Kristina Juuso, *Ivan* Psholty Viktor Bychkov.
• *Dir* and *Screenplay* Aleksandr Rogozhkin, *Pro* Sergei Selianov, *Ph* Andrei Zhegalov, *Pro Des* Vladimir Svetozarov, *Ed* Iuliia Rumiantseva, *M* Dmitrii Pavlov.

STV Film Company-Soda Pictures.
103 minutes. Russia. 2002. Rel: 28 November 2003.
Cert 12A.

Cypher ★★

In an alternate, Orwellian America, dull accountant Morgan Sullivan is approached by the multinational Digicorp to become an industrial spy. But the terms of his employment initially appears to have very little to do with espionage. Sullivan's 007 fantasies are interrupted by the appearance of a the sexy Rita Foster, who shows him that something far more sinister is going on … A sub-Philip K. Dick sci-fi thriller, *Cypher* boasts little of the taut atmospherics that made Vincenzo Natali's debut feature *Cube* a cult hit. Almost predictably, the availability of a big-ish budget has leeched the creativity from his vision, and the film draws on stock genre tropes to tell a fairly uninspired story. Jeremy Northam delivers an unconvincingly pat performance as the brainwashed Morgan Sullivan, and Lucy Liu doesn't quite carry off the super spy-bitch role which has, for her, become a self-parody. AK

• *Morgan Sullivan* Jeremy Northam, *Rita* Lucy Liu, *Finster* Nigel Bennett, *Calloway* Timothy Webber, *Vergil Dunn* David Hewlett.
• *Dir* Vincenzo Natali, *Pro* Paul Federbush, Wendy Grean, Casey La Scala and Hunt Lowry, *Assoc Pro* Richard J. Anobile, *Ex Pro* Shebnem Askin, *Screenplay* Brian King, *Ph* Derek Rogers, *Pro Des* Jasna Stefanovich, *Ed* Bert Kish, *M* Michael Andrews, *Costumes* Tamara Winston.

Gaylord Films/Headspace/Pandora Cinema-Pathé
95 mins. USA. 2002. Rel 29 August 2003.
Cert 15.

D

Daddy Day Care ★★★

Eddie Murphy and director Steve Carr team-up again after *Dr. Dolittle 2* to tell the tale of two fathers who lose their jobs and are forced to take their respective sons out of the exclusive Chapman Academy to become stay-at-home dads. Underestimating the demands of professional childcare, the two decide to open their own facility called 'Daddy Day Care'. However, while their methods may be unconventional, their venture is quite the success and, therefore a threat to the Chapman Academy's monopolistic matriarch, the aptly named Mrs Harridan. Fun, if predictable, comedy ensues. Taking a page from *Saturday Night Live* alumnus Adam Sandler, Murphy learns you can never go wrong surrounding yourself with precocious kids. And, truth be told, Khamani Griffin as Murphy's son is the film's most endearing quality. Steve Zahn is always a scene-stealer, and a host of other former *SNL* players including Kevin Nealon, Siobhan Fallon and Laura Kightlinger all make you feel right at home. SWM

• *Charlie Hinton* Eddie Murphy, *Phil* Jeff Garlin, *Marvin* Steve Zahn, *Kim Hinton* Regina King, *Miss Gwyneth Harridan* Anjelica Huston, *Ben Hinton* Khamani Griffin, *Max* Max Burkholder, *Bruce* Kevin Nealon, *Jennifer* Lacey Chabert.
• *Dir* Steve Carr, *Pro* John Davis, Matt Berenson and Wyck Godfrey, *Ex Pro* Joe Roth, Dan Kolsrud and Heidi Santelli, *Screenplay* Geoff Rodkey, *Ph* Steven Poster, *Pro Des* Garreth Stover, *Ed* Christopher Greenbury, *M* David Newman, *Costumes* Ruth Carter.

Revolution/Day Care Prods/Davis Entertainment/Fox-Columbia Tristar.
93 mins. USA. 2003. Rel: 11 July 2003. Cert PG.

Dark Blue ★★★¹/₂

Derived from a James Ellroy story and directed with panache by veteran Ron Shelton, this is comparable to *Narc*, both being police procedurals that look set for near classic status until the last quarter goes seriously awry. This one features the L.A. Special Investigations Squad and weight is provided by placing this tale of police corruption at the time of the riots consequent on the acquittal of white officers accused of beating up Rodney King. Aided by some good acting, especially from Brendan Gleeson as the corrupt chief, this is compelling and exciting stuff. It gains from the audience's uncertainty in predicting the outcome, but then, alas, it derails by going on too long and nose-diving into phoneyness at its climax. MS

• *Eldon Perry* Kurt Russell, *Jack Van Meter* Brendan Gleeson, *Bobby Keough* Scott Speedman, *Beth Williamson* Michael Michele, *Sally Perry* Lolita

Davidovich, *Arthur Holland* Ving Rhames, with Khandi Alexander, Kurupt.
• *Dir* Ron Shelton, *Pro* James Jacks, Sean Daniel, Caldecot Chubb and David Blocker, *Ex Pro* Moritz Borman, Guy East and Nigel Sinclair, *Screenplay* David Ayer, from a story James Ellroy, *Ph* Barry Peterson, *Pro Des* Dennis Washington, *Ed* Paul Seydor, *M* Terence Blanchard, *Costumes* Kathryn Morrison.

MGM/United Artists/Intermedia-Momentum.
119 mins. USA. 2002. Rel: 4 July 2003. Cert 15.

Dawn of the Dead ★★★

George A. Romero's original *Dawn of the Dead* (1978) is a *bona fide* horror classic, making any remake a risky proposition. The new *Dawn* is an effective *de luxe* revamp, despite front-office tampering. The action is largely set within a Milwaukee shopping mall, where nurse Sarah Polley and cop Ving Rhames are among the human survivors fighting off hordes of flesh-eating zombies. Director Snyder has created a slick, efficiently made horror comic that matches the 1978 film for action and gore. What the new version lacks is Romero's satirical touches and dark humour. Promoting the remake, Rhames admitted that the political allegory of the original had been largely sidelined. In fairness, Snyder was constrained by Universal's insistence on an R-rating, resulting in significant re-editing. DO.

• *Ana* Sarah Polley, *Kenneth* Ving Rhames, *Michael* Jake Weber, *Andre* Mekhi Phifer, *Steve* Ty Burrell, *CJ* Michael Kelly, *Terry* Kevin Zegers, *Nicole* Lindy Booth, *Luda* Inna Korobkina.
• *Dir* Zack Snyder, *Pro* Richard Rubinstein, Marc Abraham and Eric Newman, *Ex Pro* Thomas Bliss, Dennis Jones and Armyan Bernstein, *Screenplay* James Gunn, based on screenplay by George Romero, *Ph* Matthew Leonetti, *Pro Des* Andrew Neskoromny, *Ed* Niven Howie, *M* Tyler Bates, *Costumes* Denise Cronenberg, *Special makeup effects* David Leroy Anderson.

Strike Entertainment/New Amsterdam Entertainment-UIP.
100 mins. USA. 2004. Rel: 26 March 2004. Cert 18.

The Day After Tomorrow ★★★★

Helicopters freeze mid-flight, hailstones the size of melons kill Tokyo commuters, giant-hurricanes spread like a rash across the globe … Yea, the end of the world is nigh! Roland 'Independence Day' Emmerich is a specialist at the Hollywood apocalypse, and this is a grand example of how to film the end of civilization as we know it properly. The 'lone voice of reason' this time belongs to scientist Jack Hall, who recognizes early on that the freak weather conditions are signs of a sudden global Ice Age. Naturally, nobody heeds the Cassandra until it is all too late and most of the American coastline has been swallowed by tidal waves. Spectacular, eye-popping special effects come as standard, but the episodic ensemble cast hit their marks well and give the bombastic premise at least a chance of making an emotional connection. AK

• *Professor Jack Hall* Dennis Quaid, *Sam Hall* Jake Gyllenhaal, *Terry Rapson* Ian Holm, *Laura Chapman* Emmy Rossum, *Dr Lucy Hall* Sela Ward, *Jason Evans* Dash Mihok, *Frank Harris* Jay O. Sanders, *Vice President Becker* Kenneth Welsh, *President Blake* Perry King, *Simon* Adrian Lester, *with* Austin Nichols, Nestor Serrano, Tamlyn Tomita, Sheila McCarthy, Arjay Smith, Glenn Plummer.
• *Dir* Roland Emmerich, *Pro* Emmerich and Mark Gordon, *Ex Pro* Stephanie Germain, Ute Emmerich and Kelly Van Horn, *Screenplay* Emmerich and Jeffrey Nachmanoff, *Ph* Ueli Steiger, *Pro Des* Barry Chusid, *Ed* David Brenner, *M* Harald Kloser, *Costumes* Renee April, *Visual effects supervisor* Karen Goulekas.

Centropolis Entertainment/Lions Gate/Mark Gordon Co.-Fox
124 mins. USA. 2004. Rel: 28 May 2004.
Cert 12A.

Dead End ★★★¹/₂

It's Thanksgiving, and a family of bickering middle-class types are en route to a torturous traditional family reunion with Dad at the wheel. But a shortcut-gone-wrong finds them on an endless highway where things start to go very, very wrong … Jean-Baptiste Andrea and Fabrice Canepa are two French filmmakers who had a decent homage to the Twilight Zone which, with some American money and a few good actors, has become a lean, mean horror. Your hackles rise at the first horror ('family road-trip'. Need I say more?) which is an instantly recognisable sketch of filial tension upon which the gorier thrills are built with great élan. The big scares are off-screen, edge-of-sight stuff and are terrifically effective. The acting is first-rate and the cast disintegrate with style as they come to realise the full horror of their predicament. AK

• *Frank Harrington* Ray Wise, *Marion Harrington* Alexandra Holden, *Laura Harrington* Lin Shaye, *Richard Harrington* Mick Cain, *Brad Miller* Billy Asher, *lady in white* Amber Smith, *man in black* Steve Valentine, *doctor* Karen S. Gregan.
• *Dir* and *Screenplay* Jean-Baptiste Andrea and Fabrice Canepa, with additional dialogue by Billy Asher, *Pro* James Huth and Gabriella Stollenwerck, *Ex Pro* Yves Chevalier and James Huth, *Co-Pro* Guy Courtecuisse, *Ph* Alexander Buono, *Pro Des* Bryce

Holtshousen, *Ed* Antoine Vareille, *M* Greg De Belles, *Costumes* Deborah Waknin.

Captain Movies/Sagittaire Films/Studio Canal Plus/3.2.1 Films-Pathé.
83 mins. France. 2003. Rel: 5 December 2003. Cert 15.

Deep Blue ★★★★

A documentary five years in the making, *Deep Blue* is a giddy trip into the unknown. A technically astonishing surveillance of our oceans, the film encompasses every aspect of the sea, from the beaches of Patagonia to the ice flows of the Arctic to the Stygian depths of the ocean floor. Accompanied by a magnificent score by Oscar nominee George Fenton (*Gandhi*, *The Fisher King*) and occasionally punctuated by the mellifluous narration of Michael Gambon, this is a sensorial expedition. A feature-length compendium of moments culled from the BBC's *The Blue Planet*, *Deep Blue* demands to be seen on the big screen. This is very much a visual experience, and whether capturing the might of a tempestuous sea or a jam of marine life just under the surface, the film dumbfounds the eye. Academics may feel a little short-changed, but then *Deep Blue* never aspires to educate. It is as it is: a dazzling, hypnotic, dramatic and trailblazing document of a mysterious, vanishing universe. JC-W

• *Narrator* Michael Gambon.
• *Dir* Andy Byatt and Alastair Fothergill, *Pro* Alix Tidmarsh and Sophokles Tasioulis, *Ex Pro* Stefan Beiten, Andre Sikojev and Nikolaus Weil, *Ed* Martin Elsbury, *M* George Fenton, performed by the Berlin Philharmonic Orchestra.

BBC/Greenlight Media AG-Optimum Releasing.
83 mins. UK/Germany. 2003. Rel: 18 June 2004. Cert PG.

Demonlover ★★★

France's talented writer/director Olivier Assayas has never been so controversial as with this look at the age of the internet. He shows rival corporations using underhand methods to acquire exclusive rights to the latest animated pornography about to become a 3-D sensation. The comment on dehumanising trends of our time is ambitious and the acting good, but the confusions of the plot (claimed by Assayas as deliberate and as an attempt to create a cinema experience not narrative-led) suggest only a traditional noir rather badly told. Technically this movie re-affirms the filmmaker's exceptional skills, but the end result is disappointing all the same. MS

• *Dianede Monx* Connie Nielsen, *Hervé Le Millinec* Charles Berling, *Elise Lipsky* Chloë Sevigny, *Elaine Si Gibril* Gina Gershon, with Jean-Baptiste Malartre,

Dominique Reymond, *Lara Croft* Diana Jones.
• *Dir* and *Screenplay* Olivier Assayas, *Pro* Edouard Weil and Xavier Giannoli, *Ph* Denis Lenoir, *Art Dir* François-Renaud Lebarthe, *Ed* Luc Barnier, *M* Sonic Youth, *Costumes* Anaïs Romand.

TPS Cinéma/Elizabeth Films- ICA Projects.
129 mins. France/Japan/Mexico/USA. 2002.
Rel: 7 May 2004. Cert 18.

The Deserted Station ★★★★
(*Istgah-Matrouk*)
The long opening sequence of a married couple travelling by car may suggest material for a parody of Iranian cinema but this is nevertheless an undervalued film. The surface story finds the couple stranded in an almost deserted town when their car breaks down. This interrupts their pilgrimage in quest of a blessing for the pregnant wife whose previous children were stillborn. A teacher herself, she looks after the town's remaining youngsters while the one man left there, both teacher and local mechanic, departs with her husband to get aid to repair the vehicle. The story-line may be slight, but the location is unfamiliar and striking and the players have presence. Deeper meaning in Iranian films is rarely suggestive of wider, outward-looking themes, but this poetic movie becomes a comment on the haves and have-nots as the wife reaches out to these poor children but can do little for them. In its own way this is a remarkable and rewarding film with a haunting final image. MS

• *Mahtab* Leila Hatami, *Mahmood* Nezam Manouchehri, *Feizollah* Mehran Rajabi, *signal guard* Mahmoud Pak Neeyat.
• *Dir* Alireza Raisian, *Pro* Hossein Zandbaf, *Screenplay* Kambuzia Partovi, from a story by Abbas Kiarostami, *Ph* Mohammad Aladpoush, *Pro Des* Mohsen Shah Ebrahimi, *Ed* Hossein Zandbaf, *M* Peyman Yazdanian.

IFDC/ArtCam International-Soda Pictures.
93 mins. Iran/France/Netherlands. 2003.
Rel: 9 April 2004. No Cert.

Les Diables ★
(*The Devils*)
Mention the valiant lead performance by young Vincent Rottiers and the good photography by Eric Guichard in colour and 'Scope and you have covered all that can be said positively about this risible drama. Over-heated, unconvincing and obscurely motivated, it is the story of Joseph (Rottiers) and Chloe (Adele Haenel coming on as though she were auditioning for an *Exorcist* film). Brought up as siblings in homes and by foster parents, they run away to seek the house of their parents in Marseilles. Chloe in particular clearly needs medical help, but we are meant to sympathise with Joseph's misguided attempts to help her in his own way. *Les Diables* starts out seeming ill-judged and ends by appearing ludicrous. MS

• *Joseph* Vincent Rottiers, *Chloé* Adèle Haenel, *Joseph's mother* Aurélia Petit, *Dr Doran* Jacques Bonnaffé, *Karim* Rochdy Labidi, *Djamel* Galamelah Lagra, *La directrice* Dominique Reymond, *l'homme de la maison* Frédéric Pierrot, *la femme de la maison* Danielle Ambry.
• *Dir* Christophe Ruggia, *Pro* Bertrand Faivre, *Screenplay* Ruggia and Olivier Lorelle, *Ph* Eric Guichard, *Pro Des* Laurent Deroo, *Ed* Tina Baz-Legal, *M* Fowzi Guerdjou, *Costumes* Elsa Rio.

Lazennec/Studio Canal/Arte France Cinéma/
Canal Plus, etc-Gala Film.
105 mins. France/Spain. 2002.
Rel: 9 April 2004. Cert 15.

Dickie Roberts: Former Child Star ★½
Back in the 1970s, child actor Dickie Roberts starred in a sitcom watched by 50 million Americans. Now 35, he works as a car valet at a Hollywood eatery. Offered the chance of a comeback, Roberts decides he needs to experience the normal childhood he never had, even hiring a foster family. Co-produced by Adam Sandler, Dickie Roberts is a puerile, lazy comedy that wastes an intriguing premise. Given the problems faced by many real-life ex-child stars, the film could have been much sharper, while David Spade, who also co-wrote the script, once again proves a charmless screen presence. FYI: Several former child stars appear in cameo roles. Presumably, they're still looking for their own comebacks. DO

• *Dickie Roberts* David Spade, *Grace Finney* Mary McCormack, *Sidney Wernick* Jon Lovitz, *George Finney* Craig Bierko, *Cyndi* Alyssa Milano, *Peggy Roberts* Doris Roberts, *Sam Finney* Scott Terra, *Sally Finney* Jenna Boyd, *Mrs Gertrude* Edie McClurg, *with* Rob Reiner, Leif Garrett, Tom Arnold, Brendan Fraser, Dick Van Patten, Barry Williams, Danny Bonaduce, Corey Feldman, Dustin Diamond, Willie Aames, Gary Coleman, Jeff Conaway, Corey Haim, Florence Henderson, Barry Livingston, Charlene Tilton, etc.
• *Dir* Sam Weisman, *Pro* Adam Sandler and Jack Giarraputo, *Ex Pro* Fred Wolf, *Co-Pro* Blair Breard, *Screenplay* Fred Wolf and David Spade, *Ph* Thomas Ackerman, *Pro Des*: Dina Lipton, *Ed* Roger Bondelli, *M* Chrisophe Beck and Waddy Wachtel, *Costumes*: Lisa Jensen.

Right: Perfect stranger: Nicole Kidman in Lars von Trier's daring, iconoclastic *Dogville* (from Icon)

Paramount/Happy Madison-UIP
98 mins. USA. 2003. Rel: 20 February 2004. Cert 12A.

Dogville ★★★★★

A finely acted stylised masterpiece, this is the best film yet from the erratic Lars von Trier. It may last almost three hours and be presented as on a stage set, but John Hurt's unseen narrator grabs your attention from the outset and the film is riveting throughout. A Preface and eight Chapters show how the inhabitants of Dogville are persuaded to give shelter to a stranger in need (Nicole Kidman) but subsequently manipulate her, use her for their own ends and eventually turn on her as a useful scapegoat. This amounts to a generalised comment on human nature and its American location (chances for fine work by Lauren Bacall and Ben Gazzara among others) is not thematically relevant until the long finale (Chapter 9). Throughout it's a chilling indictment, but once you realise that the character played by James Caan, 'The Big Man', could represent President Bush you are brought to the very edge of your seat. A film accused of being anti-American seems to me to be something very different: anti-Bush. Brilliant. MS

• *Grace* Nicole Kidman, *Tom Edison* Paul Bettany, *Gloria* Harriet Andersson, *Ma Ginger* Lauren Bacall, *the Man With the Big Hat* Jean-Marc Barr, *Mrs Henson* Blair Brown, *the Big Man* James Caan, *Vera* Patricia Clarkson, *Bill Henson* Jeremy Davies, *Jack McKay* Ben Gazzara, *Tom Edison Sr* Philip Baker Hall, *Martha* Siobhan Fallon Hogan, *Ben* Zeljko Ivanek, *the Man in the Coat* Udo Kier, *Olivia* Cleo King, *Jason* Miles Purinton, *Mr Henson* Bill Raymond, *Liz Henson* Chloe Sevigny, *June* Shauna Shim, *Chuck* Stellan Skarsgard, *narrator* John Hurt.
• *Dir* and *Screenplay* Lars von Trier, *Pro* Vibeke Windelovm, *Ex Pro* Peter Aalbaek Jensen, *Co-Pro* Gillian Berrie, Bettina Brokemper, Anja Grafers and Els Vandervorst, *Co-Ex Pro* Lene Borglum, Peter Garde, Lars Jonsson and Marianne Slot, *Line Pro* Jonas Frederiksen, *Ph* Anthony Dod Mantle, *Pro Des*, Peter Grant, *Ed* Molly Malene Stensgaard, *Costumes* Manon Rasmussen, *Sets* Simone Grau, *Light design* Asa Frankenberg.

Zentropa/Filmmek/Entertainments 8 ApS/ Isabella Films, etc-Icon.178 mins. Denmark/Sweden/France/UK/Germany/Finland/Netherlands/Italy/Norway. 2003. Rel: 13 February 2004. Cert 15.

Double Whammy ★★★

Made in 2001 and given a belated release here, Tom DiCillo's New York movie is a black comedy involving policemen, writers and hoodlums. Alas, it doesn't really work because improbabilities of plot acceptable in an exaggerated comedy here clash with elements of distasteful violence that play less like a Tarantino parody then the real thing. Nevertheless, although it's a downhill ride, the opening offers a vintage DiCillo scene as a detective with back problems (Leary) is shown up by a mere child. There's also Elizabeth Hurley well cast as a glamorous chiropractor and the ever-excellent Steve Buscemi registering as Leary's partner forever denying the indicators that suggest he is homosexual. The concept of combining a police thriller with off-beat comedy was never a workable proposition as scripted here, but the cast ensure that this disappointing film is something less than a total write-off. MS

• *Ray Pluto* Denis Leary, *Dr Ann Beamer* Elizabeth Hurley, *Jerry Cubbins* Steve Buscemi, *Juan Benitez* Luis Guzmán, *Lt. Spigot* Victor Argo, *Chick Dimitri* Chris Noth, *Boover* Maurice G. Smith, *Duke* Keith Nobbs, *Cletis* Donald Faison, *Maribel Benitez* Melonie Diaz, *truck driver* Daniel Margotta.
• *Dir* and *Screenplay* Tom DiCillo, *Pro* Larry Katz, David Kronemeyer, Jim Serpico, Marcus Viscidi and Denis Leary, *Ex Pro* Mike Delich and Norm Waitt, *Co-Pro* Meredith Zamsky, *Ph* Robert D. Yeoman, *Pro Des* Michael Shaw, *Ed* Camilla Toniolo, *M* Jim Farmer, *Costumes* Jennifer von Mayrhauser.

Apostle Pictures/Gold Circle Films/Lemon Sky Productions/Myriad Pictures-Winchester. 100 mins. USA. 2001. Rel: 18 July 2003. Cert 15.

Down With Love ★★¹/₂

1950s, New York. Playboy and star magazine writer Catcher Block meets his match in the ultra-smart Barbara Novak, whose book *Down With Love* dares to suggest that women don't need the love of a good man, suggesting (scandalously and to enormous feminine acclaim) that sex-for-its-own-sake is a … no, *the* perfectly rational perspective. But the pampered male society cannot stomach the idea that the goose should be sauced as the gander, and Catcher Block makes it his mission to stop ms. Novak's crusade … As an homage to the culturally iconic films of Rock Hudson and Doris Day, Peyton Reed has covered his bases well. But the prevalent knowingness that subverts just about every scene is fatiguing and unless you are willing to work very hard to squeeze every bit of postmodern referential wit out of what is undeniably a very clever production, very sharply performed, it begins to feel suspiciously schematic and banal. AK

• *Barbara Novak* Renée Zellweger, *Catcher Block* Ewan McGregor, *Vicki Hiller* Sarah Paulson, *Peter McMannus* David Hyde Pierce, *Gladys* Rachel Dratch, *Maurice* Jack Plotnick, *Theodore Banner* Tony Randall, *with* Lynn Collins.
• *Dir* Peyton Reed, *Pro* Bruce Cohen and Dan Jinks, *Ex Pro* Paddy Cullen and Arnon Milchan, *Screenplay* Eve Ahlert & Dennis Drake, *Ph* Jeff Cronenweth, *Pro Des* Andrew Laws, *Ed* Larry Bock, *M* Marc Shaiman, *Costumes* Daniel Orlandi.

Epsilon Motion Pictures/Fox 2000 Pictures/Jinks/Cohen Company/Mediastream III/Regency Enterprises-Fox. 94 mins. USA. 2003. Rel 3: October 2003. Cert 12A.

Dracula: Pages From A Virgin's Diary ★★★¹/₂

Guy Maddin virtually redefines the term choreography in this his first musical film. He has taken a staging by the Royal Winnipeg Ballet retelling the familiar story of Dracula to music from the first two symphonies of Mahler and thought it through afresh in cinematic terms. Maddin's visuals echo silent cinema (the film is in black and white with some tinting and occasional splashes of colour), while movement is as much a matter of the camera's motion and of the editing together of images as it is of the dancers' own steps. The novelty of the first half is strong, but the later scenes fail to build further leaving a certain sense of anti-climax. Nevertheless, as a highly original example of approachable experimental cinema it is worth investigating by Maddin fans and by dance film enthusiasts alike. MS

• *Dracula* Zhang Wei-Qiang, *Lucy* Tara Birtwhistle, *Van Helsing* David Moroni, C. M., *Nina* CindyMarie Small, *Harker* Johnny Wright.
• *Dir* and *Screenplay* Guy Maddin, based on Mark Godden's ballet `Dracula' adapted and choreographed for Canada's Royal Winnipeg Ballet, *Pro* Vonnie Von Helmolt, *Ex Pro* Robert Sherwin, *Co-Pro* Lesley Oswald, *Assoc Pro* Danishka Esterhazy, *Ph* Paul Suderman, *Pro Des* Deanne Rohde, *Art Dir* Deanne Rohde, *Ed* Deco Dawson, *M* Gustav Mahler, *Costumes* Paul Daigle, *Ballet Master* Bruce Mark.

Vonnie Von Helmut Film/Mark Goddin/Guy Maddin/ The Royal Winnipeg Ballet/Dracula Prod.-Metro Tartan. 75 mins. Canada. 2002. Rel: 12 December 2003. Cert 12A.

Dragonflies ★★

(Øyenstikker)
Optimistically compared by some to Polanski's classic *Knife in the Water*, this psychological drama

set in rural Norway certainly centres on three characters, but it soon develops into a tale of unlikely behaviour which grows ever more unbelievable leading to a climax of attempted vengeance so underplanned as to be ludicrous. The start has been promising, but Maria (Maria Bonnevie) is far too intelligent not to react earlier when her partner, Eddie (Kim Bodnia), invites back to their farm a mysterious and disquieting friend (Mikael Persbrandt) to whom he feels obligated. The build-up to the action requires psychological conviction, but the behaviour of the trio is so unpersuasive that, through no fault of the actors, following this tale is a total waste of your time. MS

• *Maria* Maria Bonnevie, *Eddie* Kim Bodnia, *Kullman* Mikael Persbrandt, *Kvinne i leilighet* Tintin Anderzon, *Mann i leilighet* Shanti Roney, *Gutti leilighet* Stasse Soulis, *Butikkeier* Willy Karlsson, *Ekspeditrise* Ulla-Britt Norrman-Olsson, *Sven* Tord Peterson, *Thomas* Thomas Skarpjordet.
• *Dir* Marius Holst, *Pro* Sigve Endresen, *Co-Pro* Håkan Bjerking, *Line Pro* Ørjan Karlsen, *Co-Pro* Aagot Skjeldal, Pål Sletaune, Turid Øversveen and Håkon Øverås, *Screenplay* Nikolaj Frobenius, based on the short story *Natt Til Mørk Morgen* by Ingvar Ambjørnsen, *Ph* John Christian Rosenlund, *Pro Des* Katrin Lea Tag and Lotta Wallin, *Ed* Sophie Hesselberg, *M* Kjetil Bjerkestrand and Magne Furuholmen, *Costumes* Charlotta Gustafsson.

4 1/2 / Motlys-Optimum Releasing.
109 mins. Norway. 2001. Rel: 4 July 2003.
Cert 15.

The Dreamers ★★★¹/₂
Beautifully filmed by Bertolucci and photographer Fabio Cianchetti, this adaptation by Gilbert Adair of his own novel is set in Paris in 1968. The three main characters who become sexually involved (and very graphically so in this '18' certificate movie) are an American (Michael Pitt) and French siblings (Eva Green and Louis Garrel). All three are film enthusiasts and everything here that evokes the year of 'les événements' and the excitement felt for cinema in that decade is terrific. But the other side of the coin is that, save for those content to gaze on unclothed young bodies for their own sake, these self-absorbed characters become tedious company, making it impossible to care about them or their fate. For older cinemagoers the filmmaker's nostalgia for the period is more likely to appeal than his uncritical take on the central trio. MS

• *Matthew* Michael Pitt, *Isabelle* Eva Green, *Théo* Louis Garrel, *father* Robin Renucci, *mother* Anna Chancellor, *Patrick* Florian Cadiou.
• *Dir* Bernardo Bertolucci, *Pro* Jeremy Thomas, *Co-Pro* John Bernard, *Assoc Pro* Hercules Bellville and Peter Watson, *Screenplay* Gilbert Adair, inspired by his novel *The Holy Innocents*, *Ph* Fabio Cianchetti, *Pro Des* Jean Rabasse, *Ed* Jacopo Quadri, *M* Janice Ginsberg; songs performed by Jimi Hendrix, Steve Miller Band, Fred Astaire, Nino Ferrer, The Doors, Michael Pitt, The Platters, Big Brother and The Holding Company, Bob Dylan, Charles Trenet, Françoise Hardy, The Grateful Dead, Edith Piaf, etc, *Costumse* Louise Stjernsward,

Fox Searchlight/HanWay/Recorded Picture Co/Peninsular/Fiction-Fox
114 mins. France/Italy/UK/USA. 2003. Rel: 6 February. Cert 18.

Duplex
See *Our House.*

Elephant ★★★★

A school in Portland, Oregan, is about to become the site of a senseless massacre. Here are the hours that lead to it … Gus Van Sant's disconnected, anti-dramatic, and infuriatingly reserved analysis-by-fiction of the Columbine High School killings follows a series of ordinary happenings at a very ordinary school in a dream-like criss-cross of images and snatched conversations. His 'controversial' move is his complete refusal to indict the two young boys who plan and then perpetrate the massacre as monsters. He also blunts the idea that the usual suspects of violent films, video games or parents are to blame. The film challenges the desperate impulse to easy answers regarding the causes of the tragedy. It really is a masterly piece of work. AK

• *Alex* Alex Frost, *Eric* Eric Deulen, *John McFarland* John Robinson, *Elias* Elias McConnell, *Jordan* Jordan Taylor, *Carrie* Carrie Finklea, *Nicole* Nicole George, *Brittany* Brittany Mountain, *Acadia* Alicia Miles, *Michelle* Kristen Hicks, *Benny* Bennie Dixon, *Nathan* Nathan Tyson, *Mr McFarland* Timothy Bottoms, *Mr Luce* Matt Malloy, *GSA Teacher* Ellis E. Williams.
• *Dir*, *Screenplay* and *Ed* Gus Van Sant, *Pro* Dany Wolf, *Ex Pro* Diane Keaton and Bill Robinson, *Assoc Pro* JT Leroy and Jay Hernandez, *Ph* Harris Savides, *Art Dir* Benjamin Hayden.

HBO Films/Meno Films/Blue Relief/FineLine-Optimum Releasing.
81 mins. USA. 2003. Rel: 30 January 2004. Cert 15.

Elf ★★★★

Buddy is an orphan who crawled one night into Santa's sleigh, and was then adopted by Papa Elf. Years pass, and Buddy, the 6 foot 3 inch adult human-who-thinks-he's-an-elf, is told the truth: His real dad is a jaded publishing executive in Manhattan. Shocked that his father is on the 'Naughty List' Buddy decides to meet his real family, and to spread the Real Christmas Spirit … *Elf* is the kind of star vehicle that the highly underrated Will Ferrell has been waiting for. There is no more gormless, oxen or sincere an idiot who could have done a better job. Naturally, the plot is pure nonsense. It trots out the usual basket of family-movie chestnuts (Will Buddy and his father connect? Will Buddy fall in love with the singing checkout girl played by the remarkable Zooey Deschanel?), Justifiably because it's the genre to be jolly. Jon Favreau helms at a relaxed pace, and successfully balances the wildly overblown delivery of his star with a knowing mood that rescues *Elf* from the cloying sentimentality. AK

• *Buddy* Will Ferrell, *Walter* James Caan, *Jovie* Zooey Deschanel, *Emily* Mary Steenburgen, *Santa Claus* Edward Asner, *Papa Elf* Bob Newhart, *Michael* Daniel Tay, *Gimbels Manager* Faizon Love, *with* Michael Lerner, Andy Richter, Jon Favreau, Peter Dinklage.
• *Dir* Jon Favreau, *Pro* Jon Berg, Todd Komarnicki and Shauna Robertson, *Ex Pro* Jimmy Miller, Julie Wixson Darmody, Toby Emmerich, Kent Alterman and Cale Boyter, *Screenplay* David Berenbaum, *Ph* Greg Gardiner, *Pro Des* Rusty Smith, *Ed* Dan Lebental, *M* John Debney, *Costumes* Laura Jean Shannon, *Visual effects supervisor* Joe Bauer.

Shawn Danielle Productions Ltd./Gold/Miller Productions/Guy Walks into a Bar Productions/ Mosaic Media Group-Entertainment.
95 mins. USA. 2003. Rel: 14 November 2003. Cert PG.

Emile ★★★

Although the use of elaborate colour schemes for different sequences makes this a film for the cinema, Carl Bessai's light-weight tale is one that would be well suited to TV. Even at 95 minutes it seems over-extended, although it presents a narrative working on two levels. In the present a professor (Sir Ian McKellen) returns to his Canadian homeland. He seeks to reach out to the niece he has neglected (Deborah Kara Unger) and to the daughter (Theo Crane) being brought up by her as a single mother. In memory, the professor re-lives the events involving his family from which he had turned away. Echoes of masterpieces (Wild Strawberries, Asquith's The Browning Version) underline how superficial this is by comparison despite the good acting. MS

• *Emile* Ian McKellen, *Nadia/ Nadia's mother* Deborah Kara Unger, *Freddy* Tygh Runyan, *Maria/Nadia, aged 10* Theo Crane, *Carl* Chris William Martin, *Superintendent* Nancy Sivak, *Tom* Ian Tracey, *Alice* Janet Wright, *taxi driver* Frank Borg.
• *Dir* and *Screenplay* Carl Bessai, *Pro* Bessai and Jacquelyn Renner, *Ex Pro* Bessai, Jonathan English and Bjorg Veland, *Ph* Carl Bessai, *Pro Des* Dina Zecchel, *Ed* Julian Clarke, *M* Vincent Mai, *Costumes* Lara Lupish.

Raven West Films/Meltemi Entertainment/BV International/ Helkon SK/Seville Pictures-Redbus.
92 mins. Canada/UK/Norway. 2003. Rel: 21 May 2004. Cert 15.

The Emperor's New Clothes ★★★

Falling between all possible stools, this is a whimsical tale suggesting how Napoleon could have escaped from St. Helena leaving a double in his place. The tone is often humorous, but not sufficiently so to create an effective comedy, while the problems of the emperor as he seeks to get back to Paris lack the edge that would give the piece a sense of adventure. But if anyone could make this odd concept work it is Sir Ian Holm appearing as both emperor and impostor. He never over-plays and every detail of his double performance is a master-class in quality acting. What a pity that the context was not more deserving. MS

• *Napoleon Bonaparte/Eugene Lenormand* Ian Holm, *Nicole Pumpkin* Iben Hjelje, *Dr Lambert* Tim McInnerny, *Gerard* Tom Watson, *Montholon* Nigel Terry, *Bertrand* Hugh Bonneville, *Antommarchi* Murray Melvin, *Marchand* Eddie Marsan, *Sgt Justin Bommel* Clive Russell, *with* George Harris, Chris Langham, Trevor Cooper, Bob Mason, Hayley Carmichael, Tony Vogel, Roger Frost, Moya Brady
• *Dir* Alan Taylor, *Pro* Uberto Pasolini, *Ex Pro* Paul Webster, Hanno Huth and Roberto Cicutto, *Co-Pro* Polly Leys, Marco Valerio Pugini and James Wilson, *Assoc Pro* Kevin Molony, *Screenplay* Molony, Taylor and Herbie Wave, based on the novel *The Death of Napoleon* by Simon Leys, *Ph* Alessio Gelsini Torresi, *Pro Des* Andrea Crisanti, *Ed* Masahiro Hirakubo, *M* Rachel Portman, *Costumes* Sergio Ballo, *dialect coach* Julia Wilson-Dixon.

FilmFour/Redwave Films/Mikado Films/Senator Film/RAI Cinema-Pathé.
106 mins. UK/Italy/Germany. 2003.
Rel: 30 January 2004. Cert PG.

The End of Summer ★★★★

Dating from 1961, Ozu's penultimate film is one of two works of his receiving a belated release here. Another of his family tales and one ranging from humorous detail to a sudden death (a key moment), the film is nevertheless atypical. This is partly because the father figure here, splendidly played by Ganjiro Nakamura, is a striking comic creation very different from the characters portrayed by Chishu Ryu (here seen only in a cameo). But even more crucially there's a bitterness rare in Ozu as he views characters who behave badly and a society increasingly under the influence of the West and losing its traditional character. It's not as moving as the best of Ozu, but it is superior to the other delayed release *Floating Weeds* even if the colour photography is less beautiful. A fascinating work. MS

• *Manbei Kohayagawa* Ganjiro Nakamura, *Akiko Kohayagawa* Seysuko Hara, *Noriko Kohayagawa* Yoko Tsukasa, *Hisao Kohayagawa* Keiju Kobayashi, *Fumiko Kohayagawa* Michiyo Aratama, *Tsuna Sasaki* Chieko Naniwa, *Yanosuke Kitagawa* Daisuke Kato, *sister* Haruko Sugimura, *grandson* Masahiro Shimazu.

• *Dir* Yasujiro Ozu, *Pro* Sanezumi Fujimoto and Masakatsu Kaneko, *Screenplay* Ozu and Takago Noda, *Ph* Asaichi Nakai, *M* Toshiro Mayazumi.

Toho-Artificial Eye.
103 mins. Japan. 1961. Rel: 8 August 2003. Cert. PG.

Eternal Sunshine of the Spotless Mind ★★★

What if you could erase all memory of a bad relationship as easily as removing an embarrassing tattoo? When Joel discovers that he has been thus erased from the mind of his ex, Clem, he does the mature thing and returns the favour. But, in Michel Gondry's rather idealistic lo-sci-fi rom-com, the heart rules the mind and their subconscious minds fight to recall the bonds of their love as it was before familiarity fostered contempt ... Jim Carrey and Kate Winslet, and a strong supporting cast, do a terrific job of selling this complex and boldly experimental production with performances that transcend the basic silliness of the supporting premise. The film plays on three interchanging keys, swapping between the present, the past and the mental landscape of Joel's besieged memories. While Gondry ostensibly colours his story in emotionally negative tones, the essential message is of the power of love to overcome every trial. AK

• *Joel Barish* Jim Carrey, *Clementine Kruczynski* Kate Winslet, *May* Kirsten Dunst, *Stan* Mark Ruffalo, *Patrick* Elijah Wood, *Dr Howard Mierzwiak* Tom Wilkinson, *Carrie* Jane Adams, *with* David Cross, Deirdre O'Connell, Debbon Ayer.
• *Dir* Michael Gondry, *Pro* Steve Golin and Anthony Bergman, *Ex Pro* David Bushness, Charlie Kaufman, Glenn Williamson and Georges Bermann, *Screenplay* Kaufman, from a story by Kaufman, Michael Gondry and Pierre Bismuth, *Ph* Ellen Kuras, *Pro Des* Dan Leigh, *Ed* Valdis Oskarsdottir, *M* Jon Brion; songs performed by Beck, The Willowz, Lata Mangeshkar, Don Nelson, and The Polyphonic Spree, *Costumes* Melissa Toth, *Sound* Eugene Gearty.

Focus Features/Anonymous Content/
This Is That Productions-UIP.
107 mins. USA. 2004. Rel: 30 April, 2004. Cert 15.

Eurotrip ★★★¹/₂

Four college-bound teens hook up for the ultimate dumb Eurorail adventure in this desperately tasteless, but undeniably funny comedy. The gang, made up of earnest Scotty, horny best pal Cooper, and their twin friends Jenny and Jamie, are en route to Germany to allow Scotty to make up (and make out) with his exceedingly hot German email-palm Mieke. Along the way, they are put through the kind

of intentionally sadistic and morally unrestrained comic disaster that you'd expect from the producers of *Road Trip* and *Old School*. The important thing in movies like these is a cast that you continue to like, no matter how debased or humiliated they become. Given that, and the mood to uncritically silly, the only thing to do is to stuff the demands of intellect and hang on for the ride. AK

• *Scotty Thomas* Scott Mechlowicz, *Jenny* Michelle Trachtenberg, *Cooper Harris* Jacob Pitts, *Jamie* Travis Wester, *Mieke* Jessica Boehrs, *Madame Vandersexxx* Lucy Lawless, *Mad Maynard* Vinnie Jones, *creepy*

Italian guy Fred Armisen, *Donny* Matt Damon, *Fiona* Kristin Kreuk, *with* Jeffrey Tambor, Rade Serbedzija, Patrick Malahide.
• *Dir* Jeff Schaffer, *Pro* Daniel Goldberg, Jackie Marcus, Alec Berg and David Mandel, *Ex Pro* Ivan Reitman, Tom Pollick and Joe Medjuck, *Screenplay* Alec Berg, David Mandel and Jeff Schaffer, *Ph* David Eggby, *Pro Des* Allan Starski, *Ed* Roger Bondelli, *M* James L. Venable, *Costumes* Julia Caston.

DreamWorks/Montecito Picture Co/Berg/Mandel/Schaffer-UIP.
92 mins. USA. 2004. Rel: 25 June 2004. Cert 15.

Above: Naked ambition: Travis Webster, Scott Mechlowicz and Jacob Pitts in the cringe-worthy yet oddly beguiling *Eurotrip* (from UIP)

Fear X ★★★

The Danish director Nicolas Winding Refn follows up the powerful Pusher and Bleeder with an American piece which he co-wrote with the late Hubert Selby Jnr. There are excellent things here: the superb use of the 'Scope format, the choice of music, the quality of the photography and a fine cast headed by John Turturro. But, in developing the story of a security guard who becomes obsessed with tracing the killer of his pregnant wife, the piece loses its way. In so far as it reflects the unbalanced mind of its central character it is much less adroit than David Cronenberg's Spider, and it becomes increasingly pretentious and mysterious without investigating the issues thrown up. Not really a success, then, but defiantly individual all the same. MS

• *Harry Cain* John Turturro, *Kate* Deborah Kara Unger, *Lt Peter Northrup* James Remar, *Phil* Stephen McIntyre, *Agent Lawrence* William Allen Young, *Ed* Eugene M. Davis, *diner cop* Mark Houghton, *Claire* Jacqueline Ramel, *prostitute* Amanda Ooms.
• *Dir* Nicolas Winding Refn, *Pro* Henry Danstrup, *Ex Pro* Donald C. Archbold, Joseph Newton Cohen, Gary Phillips, Kenneth D. Plummer, Nadia Redler and Mark Vennis, *Line Pro* Johnny Andersen, *Co-Pro* Aaron Kim Johnston and Rupert Preston, *Screenplay* Winding Refn and Hubert Selby Jr., *Ph* Larry J. Smith, *Pro Des* Peter De Neergaard, *Ed* by Anne Østerud, *M* Brian Eno and J. Peter Schwalm, *Costumes* Darena Snowe, *Visual Effects* Morten Balling, *Flame artist* Lars Bjørn Hansen.

Moviehouse Entertainment/ NWR ApS-Verve Pictures. 91 mins. Denmark/UK/Canada/Norway. 2002. Rel: 26 March 2004. Cert 12A.

50 First Dates ★★★½

Hawaii, the present. A serial Casanova finally falls in love with a girl suffering serial amnesia … Arguably his least juvenile and offensive film since *The Wedding Singer* and *Anger Management*, Adam Sandler reunites with Drew Barrymore in what is really a sweet rom-com tat suffers only slightly from the Happy Madison house-style. The low-brow has been plucked ever so slightly to accommodate the earnest wooing that Sandler's marine biologist pitches in the direction of Barrymore's maid, who has lost her capacity to make new memories due to an accident, and so never remembers having met (and fallen for) Sandler the morning after. It is a premise which makes for lovely sitcom. Previously known as *50 First Kisses*. AK

• *Henry Roth* Adam Sandler, *Lucy Whitmore* Drew Barrymore, *Ula* Rob Schneider, *Doug Whitmore* Sean Astin, *Alexa* Lusia Strus, *Marlin Whitmore* Blake

Clark, *Dr Keats* Dan Aykroyd, *Sue* Amy Hill, *Ten Second Tom* Allen Covert, *Nick* Nephi Pomaikai Brown, *with* Maya Rudolph, Linda Segal.
• *Dir* Peter Segal, *Pro* Jack Giarraputo, Steve Golin and Nancy Juvonen, *Ex Pro* Daniel Lupi, Michael Ewing and M. Jay Roach, *Co-Pro* Larry Kennar and Scott Bankston, *Screenplay* George Wing, *Ph* Jack Green, *Pro Des* Alan Au, *Ed* Jeff Gourson *M* Teddy Castellucci; songs performed by The Mākaha Sons of Ni'ihau, Bob Marley & the Wailers, Toots & the Maytals, Wayne Wonder, Elan, The Flaming Lips, 311, Paul McCartney, No Doubt, English Beat, Seal, The Beach Boys, Wyclef Jean and Eve, Snoop Dogg, Ziggy Marley, Sting, Harve Presnell, Will.I.Am, Fergie, etc, *Costumes* Ellen Lutter, *Spiritual leader* Mark Vannucki.

Columbia Pictures/Happy Madison/Anonymous Content/Flower Films-Columbia Tristar. 99 minutes. USA. 2004. Rel: 9 April 2004. Cert 12A.

The Fighting Temptations ★★

In *Snow Dogs*, Cuba Gooding Jr played a slick urban professional who leaves the big city after being bequeathed a pack of huskies in his mother's will. In *The Fighting Temptations*, Cuba Gooding Jr plays a slick urban professional who leaves the big city after being bequeathed a gospel choir in his aunt's will. Actually, that's not entirely true – Cuba (as advertising executive Darrin Hill) has been left $150,000 on the condition that he can whip the local church choir into shape and win the highly competitive Gospel Explosion competition. Small-town Montecarlo, Georgia, has a very fine choir, thank you, but after a few flip remarks from Darrin, he's just left with a straggle of underperformers. He also offends Beyoncé Knowles (big mistake) and has to draw on all his resources of seduction to get her to sing for him. Beyoncé has an amazing voice and is backed up some real heavyweights here – Faith Evans, Melba Moore, Montell Jordan, The O'Jays – and if you love gospel then the film is a blast. But when the singing stops, Cuba's unrestrained mugging and the formulaic plotting are pretty close to excruciating. JC-W

• *Darrin Hill* Cuba Gooding Jr., *Lilly* Beyoncé Knowles, *Lucius* Mike Epps, *Maryann Hill* Faith Evans, *Miles Smoke* Steve Harvey, *The Rev Lewis* Wendell Pierce, *Paulina* LaTanya Richardson, *Bill* Dave Sheridan, *Alma* Angie Stone, *Nancy* Rue McClanahan, *Bessie* Melba Moore, *Aunt Sally* Ann Nesby, *Homer* Lou Myers, *Scooter* Mickey Jones, *Johnson* Montell Jordan, *Bee-Z Briggs* T-Bone, *Lightfoot* Chris Cole, *Rosa* Lourdes Benedicto, *Mr Fairchild* Dakin Matthews, *Frank* Walter Williams Sr, *Samuel* Eric Nolan Grant, *as themselves* the Rev.

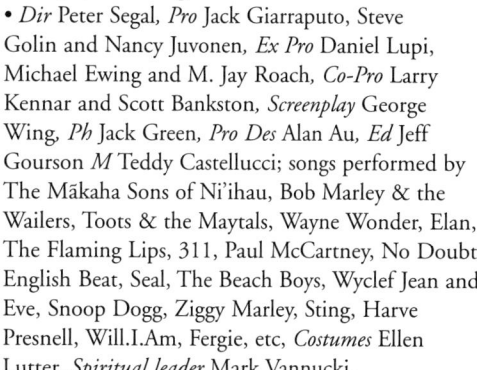

Shirley Caesar, the Blind Boys of Alabama.
• *Dir* Jonathan Lynn, *Screenplay* Elizabeth Hunter and Saladin K. Patterson, *Pro* David Gale, Loretha Jones and Jeff Pollack, *Ex Pro* Van Toffler and Benny Medina, *Co-Pro* Susan Lewis and Momita Sengupta, *Ph* Affonso Beato, *Pro Des* Victoria Paul, *Ed* Paul Hirsch, *M* Jimmy Jam, Terry Lewis and James 'Big Jim' Wright; Chopin; songs performed by Ann Nesby, Faith Evans, Ursula 2000, Lauren Evans, Dr Luke, Dropped, Shawn Kane, Angie Stone, Jimmy Jam, Beyoncé Knowles, LL Cool J and Kandice Love, T. Bone, Mike Epps, The O'Jays, Destiny's Child, Rose Royce, etc, *Exec Music Pro* Jimmy Jam, Terry Lewis, James 'Big Jim' Wright and Loretha Jones, *Costumes* Mary Jane Fort and Tracey A. White.

Paramount/ MTV Films/Handprint Films-UIP.
123 mins. USA. 2003. Rel: 12 December 2003. Cert PG.

Finding Nemo ★★★★★

The biggest box-office hit of the summer, *Finding Nemo* shows that ingenuity and originality can still seduce the public. The fifth feature from Pixar Animation (whose previous credits include *A Bug's Life*, *Toy Story*, *Toy Story 2* and *Monsters, Inc.*), *Finding Nemo* is an aquatic odyssey that is as thrilling as it is beguiling and funny. A widowed clown fish called Marlin (voiced by the inestimable Albert Brooks) brings up his one remaining son, Nemo, single-handedly (he lost his other 399 offspring to a rapacious carnivore). Then, on Nemo's first day of school, the aspiring student swims off to investigate the deeper ocean and is summarily abducted by a scuba diver. Teaming up with a terminally optimistic and forgetful blue tang called Dory (Ellen DeGeneres), Marlin ventures into perilous waters to seek the whereabouts of his missing son. Along the way, Marlin and Dory encounter all sorts of danger and odd characters, including a sea of deadly jellyfish and a Great White who's sworn off eating fish (Barry Humphries). Needless to say the computer animation is astonishingly wonderful, while the witty and inventive script will keep older viewers doubled up. So, something for everyone – peerless entertainment with a miraculous visual punch. JC-W

• *Voices*: *Marlin* Albert Brooks, *Dory* Ellen DeGeneres, *Nemo* Alexander Gould, *Gill* Willem Dafoe, *Bloat* Brad Garrett, *Peach* Allison Janney, *Gurgle* Austin Pendleton, *Bubbles* Stephen Root, *Deb (& Flo)* Vicki Lewis, *Jacques* Joe Ranft, *Nigel* Geoffrey Rush, *Crush* Andrew Stanton, *Coral* Elizabeth Perkins, *Squirt* Nicholas Bird, *Mr Ray* Bob Peterson, *Bruce* Barry Humphries, *Anchor* Eric Bana, *Chum* Bruce Spence, *dentist* Bill Hunter, *Darla* LuLu Ebeling, *Tad* Jordy Ranft, *Pearl* Erica Beck, *Sheldon*

Erik Per Sullivan, *fish school* John Ratzenberger.
• *Dir* Andrew Stanton, *Co-dir* Lee Unkrich, *Pro* Graham Walters, *Ex Pro* John Lasseter, *Screenplay* Andrew Stanton, Bob Peterson and David Reynolds, *Story* Andrew Stanton, *Ph* Sharon Calahan and Jeremy Lasky, *Pro Des* Ralph Eggleston, *Ed* David Ian Salter, *Supervising technical director* Oren Jacob, *Supervising animator* Dylan Brown, *Art Dir* Ricky Vega Nierva, Robin Cooper, Anthony Christov and Randy Berrett, *M* Thomas Newman; 'Beyond the Sea' sung by Robbie Williams, *CG supervisors* Brian Green, Lisa Forssell, Danielle Feinberg, David Eisenmann, Jesse Hollander, Steve May, Michael Fong, Anthony A Apodaca and Michael Lorenzen, *Sound designer* Gary Rydstrom.

Buena Vista Pictures/Pixar Animation Studios-Buena Vista International.
100 mins. USA. 2003. Rel 3 October 2003.
Cert U.

The Five Obstructions ★★★★

(De Fem benspænd)
It may have humour but this is an egghead movie and therefore of specialised appeal. In it Lars von Trier challenges fellow Dane and fellow director Jorgen Leth to re-make five times a short film he created in 1967. Each new version is subject to different conditions regarding style, locations etc. These make the task a challenge, but it's one that stimulates Leth as is apparent when we see the work which resulted. We are also shown part of the original movie, *The Perfect Human*, but, since it is itself an obscure piece, the variations on it require an audience attuned to this kind of filmmaking. Such viewers should find this entertaining, not least in the final section where you have to ask if von Trier is criticising Leth or himself or perhaps both. MS

• *the director/the man* Jørgen Leth, *the obstructor* Lars von Trier, *the producer* Carsten Holst, *the man* Claus Nissen, *the woman* Maiken Algren, *M Rukov, the man* Patrick Bauchau, *the man* Daniel Hernandez Rodriguez, *the woman #1* Jacqueline Arenal, *the woman* Alexandra Vandernoot, *the maid* Marie Dejaer.
• *Dir* Jørgen Leth and Lars von Trier, from an idea by Lars von Trier, based on *The Perfect Human* by Jorgen Leth, *Pro* Carsten Holst, *Ex Pro* Peter Aalbæk Jensen and Vibeke Windeløv, *Ph* Dan Holmberg, *Ed* Camilla Skousen and Morten Højbjerg.

Zentropa Real/Wajnbrosse Productions/Almaz Film Productions/Panic Productions-ICA Projects.
90 mins. Denmark/
Belgium/Switzerland/France/Sweden/Finland/UK/
Norway. 2003. Rel: 7 November 2003.
Cert 15.

Floating Weeds ★★★

(*Ukigusa*)
Fans of the great Japanese director Yasujiro Ozu will no doubt derive much pleasure from this forgotten piece. A remake of Ozu's own silent film A Story of Floating Weeds (1934), it tells the story of a kabuki actor who visits a small island town in Southern Japan. There, he meets up with an old flame and the son who still regards him as an uncle. However, the actor's current mistress is appalled and sets about stirring up the hornet's nest. Painstakingly storyboarded, the film is a paean to subtle, understated drama, where every nuance is loaded with subterranean irony. Lushly photographed by Kazuo Miyagawa (a regular cinematographer of Kurosawa), the film has its moments (in particular a laughable altercation carried out on opposite sides of a rain-pummelled street), but is likely to leave most cinemagoers dozing in their popcorn. It is re-released to coincide with the centenary of Ozu's birth. JC-W

• *Komajuro Arashi, director of the troupe* Ganjiro Nakamura, *Sumiko, his mistress* Machiko Kyô, *Oyoshi, former mistress* Haruko Sugimura, *Kiyoshi, Arashi's son* Hiroshi Kawaguchi, *Kayo, the young actress* Ayako Wakao, *Kimura* Hikaru Hoshi, *Sugiyama* Yosuke Irie.
• *Dir* Yasujiro Ozu, *Pro* Masaichi Nagata, *Screenplay* Ozu and Kôgo Noda, *Ph* Kazuo Miyagawa, *Art Dir* Tomo Shimogawara, *Ed* Toyo Suzuki, *M* Takanori Saitô.

Daiei-Artificial Eye.
119 mins. Japan. 1959. Rel: 1 August 2003. Cert. U.

The Fog of War ★★★★

(*The Fog of War: Eleven Lessons from the Life of Robert S. McNamara*)
Errol Morris is a documentary filmmaker with a distinctive style that extends, as here, to choosing Philip Glass for the music score. Nevertheless, what really counts this time is not the style (occasionally distracting with its almost subliminal edits) but the substance. It is concerned with one-time American Defence Secretary Robert S. McNamara interviewed aged 85 and it provides a survey of his life in his own words and his comments on key issues. In particular there is revealing evidence about the Cuban Missile Crisis and about Vietnam and the misreading of events that led to war. The film itself is clear (and pessimistic) even as it suggests that the complexity and uncertainty of issues in war-time create a fog which makes clear human understanding next to impossible. MS

• With: Robert S. McNamara.
• *Dir* Errol Morris, *Pro* Morris, Michael Williams and Julie Bilson, *Ex Pro* Jack Lechner, Jon Kmen, Frank Scherma, Robert Fernandez, Robert Mayh

and John Sloss, *Ph* Peter Donahue and Robert Chappell, *Pro Des* Ted Bafaloukos and Steve Hardy, *Ed* Karen Schmeer, Doug Abel and Chyld King, *M* Philip Glass, *Sound* Tom Paul.

Sony Pictures Classics/@radical media/SenArt Films/Globe Department Store-Columbia Tristar.
107 mins. USA. 2003. Rel: 2 April 2004. Cert PG.

Food of Love ★¹/₂

Paul Porterfield is a gay 18-year-old music student who falls for concert pianist Richard Kennington. While the feeling proves mutual, Paul is destined for heartbreak. When Richard breaks off the affair, Paul suffers disillusion and a severe attack of cynicism, sleeping with influential older men to advance his career. The narrative structure is odd, shifting the emphasis to Paul's mother (Juliet Stevenson) halfway through, as she struggles to accept her son's sexuality. Working in English for the first time, director Pons fumbles the material and the dialogue is often atrocious. A capable cast are stuck with poorly defined roles, with even Juliet Stevenson acting on autopilot. DO

• *Pamela Porterfield* Juliet Stevenson, *Paul Porterfield* Kevin Bishop, *Richard Kennington* Paul Rhys, *Joseph Mansourian* Allan Corduner, *Izzy* Craig Hill, *Tushi* Leslie Charles, *Diane* Pamela Field, *Teddy* Naím Thomas, *Novotna* Geraldine McEwan, *Waiter* Mingo Ràfols, *Receptionist* Roger Coma, *Gypsy* Pepa López, *Hector* Mauricio De La Cruz.
• *Dir* Ventura Pons, *Pro* Pons, *Ex Pro* Michael Smeaton, Thomas Spieker, *Assoc Pro* Gemma Folch, Monika Ganzenmüller and Petra Schepeler, *Screenplay* Pons, based on the novella *The Page Turner* by David Leavitt, *Ph* Mario Montero, *Pro Des* Aintza Serra, *Ed* Pere Abadal, *M* Carles Cases, *Costumes* María Gil.

42nd Street Productions-Parasol Peccadillo Releasing.
112 mins. Spain/Germany. 2002. Rel: 8 August 2003. Cert 12A.

The Football Factory ★★★★

Nick Love, the writer/director who made a promising feature debut with *Goodbye Charlie Bright*, here confirms that he possesses the filmic skills of a true auteur. Whether or not you like his film is, however, another question. As a study of males of varying ages who participate in football hooliganism and get off on it like taking drugs, the piece convinces and it is well acted. But there is a sense of having your cake and eating it since the film seems to relish the mentality it theoretically exposes while also casting a jaundiced eye on modern Britain. It's easier to admire it as film craft (fine editing and good location work are additional virtues and the rating given is based on this) than to approve its attitudes. MS

• *Tommy Johnson* Danny Dyer, *Billy Bright* Frank Harper, *Rod* Neil Maskell, *Zeberdee* Roland Manookian, *taxi driver* Jamie Foreman, *Milwall Jack* Tamer Hassan, *Old Man Farrell* Dudley Sutton, *with* Anthony Denham, Calum McNab, John Junkin, Sophie Linfield, Kara Tointon.
• *Dir* and *Screenplay* Nick Love, from the book by John King, *Pro* Allan Niblo and James Richardson, *Ex Pro* Robert Blagojevic and Rupert Preston, *Line Pro* Jack Armstrong, *Ph* Damian Bromley, *Pro Des* Paul Burns, *Ed* Stuart Gazzard, *M* Ivor Guest; songs performed by Rennie Pilgrem, Primal Scream, Buzzcocks, Dogzilla, Alabama 3, Death in Vegas, The Jam, etc, *Costumes* Jayne Gregory, *Sound* Keith Marriner.

Vertigo Films/Rockstar Games-Vertigo Films. 90 mins. UK. 2004. Rel: 14 May 2004. Cert 18.

The Four Feathers ★★

A.E.W. Mason's classic *Boy's Own* novel, about one man's redemption during the British Army's 1890s Sudan campaign, was first filmed in 1915. This seventh film version stars the young-and-pretty Ledger, Hudson and Bentley, all offering vital teen-appeal. Casting aside, *The Four Feathers* is a botched attempt to rework Mason's pro-colonial story for the PC age. Given the solid blueprint, the plotting and dialogue are remarkably cack-handed. Even the period detail is often shaky, wasting the big budget production values. The performances are variable, with Ledger a solid action man, Hudson badly miscast and Bentley just hanging around. Despite some lavish action set-pieces, the dull end result is little more than *Young Guns in the Sudan*. FYI: Kapur's original cut supposedly ran three hours. The drastically edited release version suffers from a curtailed narrative and choppy continuity. DO

• *Harry Feversham* Heath Ledger, *Jack Durrance* Wes Bentley, *Ethne Eustace* Kate Hudson, *Abou Fatma* Djimon Hounsou, *Trench* Michael Sheen, *Castelton* Kris Marshall, *Willoughby* Rupert Penry-Jones.
• *Dir* Shekhar Kapur, *Pro* Stanley R. Jaffe, Robert D. Jaffe, Marty Katz and Paul Feldsher, *Ex Pro* Allon Reich and Julie Goldstein, *Screenplay* Michael Schiffer and Hossein Amini, based on the novel by A.E.W. Mason, *Ph* Robert Richardson, *Pro Des* Allan Cameron, *Ed* Steven Rosenblum, *M* James Horner, *Costumes* Ruth Myers.

Paramount/Miramax/Jaffilms-UIP. 130 mins. USA/UK. 2002. Rel: 18 July 2003. Cert 12A.

Freaky Friday ★★★★¹/₂

In terms of family entertainment, it was the novel *Vice Versa* that established body-swapping tales with a child and parent briefly changing places as something of special appeal. This latest contemporary variant is itself a re-make of the 1976 movie of the same title, but, far from being the tired end of the line, Mark Waters's film is the best of all. Admittedly it's a little slow to find its feet, but, once mother (Jamie Lee Curtis) and daughter (Lindsay Lohan) discover that a magic spell has put them inside each other's skins, the film is a delight. The lightness of touch, the admirable pacing and the refusal to labour the inherent moral of the tale (each comes to understand the other better during the transformation) all help. But it's the playing that makes this film a joy three times over: Curtis is perfect, Lohan is perfect and together they make a perfect team. MS

• *Dr Tess Coleman* Jamie Lee Curtis, *Anna* Lindsay Lohan, *Ryan* Mark Harmon, *Grandpa* Harold Gould, *Jake* Chad Michael Murray, *Mr Bates* Stephen Tobolowsky, *Maddie* Christina Vidal, *Harry* Ryan Malgarini, *Stacey Hinkhouse* Julie Gonzalo, *with* Haley Hudson, Rosalind Chao, Willie Garson, Marc McClure, Mary Ellen Trainor, Erica Gimpel.
• *Dir* Mark Waters, *Pro* Andrew Gunn, *Ex Pro* Mario Iscovich, *Co-Po* Ann Marie Sanderlin, *Screenplay* Heather Hach and Leslie Dixon, based on the book by Mary Rodgers, *Ph* Oliver Wood, *Pro Des* Cary White, *Ed* Bruce Green, *M* Rolfe Kent; songs performed by The Turtles, Simple Plan, Ashlee Simpson, American Hi-Fi, Forty Foot Echo, The

Below: Officially a gentleman? Heath Ledger as Feversham in Shekhar Kapur's *The Four Feathers* (from UIP)

Blake Babies, Christina Vidal, Halo Friendlies, Lillix, Lash, Diffuser, The Flaming Lips, Bowling for Soup, Joey Ramone, The Donnas, Damone, Lindsay Lohan, etc, *Costumes* Genevieve Tyrrell.

Walt Disney Pictures/GUNN Films-Buena Vista.
97 mins. USA. 2003. Rel: 19 December 2003. Cert PG.

Freddy vs Jason ★¹/₂
Welcome to the kind of fantasy matchup that is purpose-made for the horror-movie freak who should really know better, but doesn't care. The big-match bill stars Freddy Krueger from the Nightmare on Elm Street franchise, and Jason Vorhees, the hockey-masked, machete wielding killer with a camp counsellor fetish from the Friday the 13ᵗʰ slasher flicks. The story goes that Krueger is in dream limbo and on the verge of exstinction because the kids simply don't scare … I mean, 'care' anymore. In a stroke of genius unworthy even of Dr. Evil, he plans to re-animate Jason and unleash him on the waking world to wreak havoc and start a wave of nightmares that will bring him back to power. Ronny Yu's splatter cred relies on a fetishist's attention to detail, but anything like an intelligent plot has fallen completely off his radar, to be replaced by a series of slasher-freak inside jokes and a ludicrous battle of the titans that confirms the sell-by date for this genre as long gone. AK

• *Freddy Krueger* Robert Englund, *Jason Vorhees* Ken Kirzinger, *Lori* Monica Keena, *Kia* Kelly Rowland, *Will* Jason Ritter, *Carlos* Joshua Mihal, *Linderman* Chris Marquette, *Heather* Odessa Munroe, *Billy* Jake Kaese, *Trey* Jesse Hutch, *Shack* Chris Gauthier, *Tim* James Callahan, *Gibb* Lauren Lee Smith, *Freeburg* Kyle Labine, *Jenny* Katharine Isabelle, *Scott* Lochlyn Munro, *Jacob* Brendan Fletcher, *Lisa Johnson* Lisa Wilcox, *Pamela Voorhees* Paula Shaw, *JD* Gary Chalk, *uncredited* Brian Thompson, Kenneth Tsang.
• *Dir* Ronny Yu, *Pro* Sean S. Cunningham, *Ex Pro* Douglas Curtis, *Assoc Pro* Renee Witt and Robert Shaye, *Screenplay* Damian Shannon, Mark Swift and David S. Goyer, *Ph* Fred Murphy, *Ed* Mark Stevens, *M* Graeme Revell.

New Line Cinema/Cecchi Gori Group Tiger Cinematografica/Avery Pix/Sean S. Cunningham Films/WTC Productions-Entertainment.
97 mins. USA. 2003. Rel: 15 August 2003. Cert 18.

Freeze Frame ★★¹/₂
Set in London and telling a contemporary tale of a man who has escaped a conviction for murder but believes in a paranoid manner that someone will frame him for another crime, this debut feature from John Simpson has the courage of its convictions. A virtually unrecognisable Lee Evans gives himself over to the central role, while the 'Scope visuals play on

the character's determination to be photographed by digital cameras at all times so that he will never be without an alibi. Unfortunately, this novel plot yields to an explanation of the original crime and of other killings which ensue that could hardly be more preposterous. Despite an able cast, this one is only for connoisseurs of thrillers that go over the top, and then some. MS

• *Sean Veil* Lee Evans, *Det. Inspector Emeric* Sean McGinley, *Saul Seger* Ian McNeice *Katie Carter* Rachael Stirling, *Det. Mountjoy* Colin Salmon.
• *Dir* and *Screenplay* John Simpson, *Pro* Michael Casey, *Ex Pro* Martha O'Neill and Brendan McCarthy, *Assoc Pro* Stephen Stewart, Daria Jovivic, Bill Stephens and Mark Thomas, *Ph Ed* Simon Thorne, *Ed* Simon Thorne, *M* Debbie Wiseman, *Costumes* Maggie Donnelly, *Sound* Nicky Moss, *Rain Effects* Robert Gyle.

Universal/Bord Scannán na hÉireann/Irish Film Board/Green Park Films-Verve Pictures.
99 mins. UK/Ireland/USA. 2003. Rel: 4 June 2004. Cert 15.

Fubar ★★
Great title, mediocre film. In a less than attractive district of Calgary, Canada, a documentary filmmaker follows the exploits of Dean and Terry, two deadhead losers with criminal mullets. Childish in the extreme, this unappealing duo drink beer, take drugs, screw around and listen to heavy metal at maximum volume. *Fubar* is yet another 'mocumentary', a form perfected by *This Is Spinal Tap*, only to be reused and abused ever after. Despite good moments, the largely improvised dialogue often falls flat and character development is minimal. While Dean is diagnosed with a cancerous testicle, subsequently removed, there's little suggestion that this deadbeat duo will ever change. Apparently, many of the onscreen participants thought the documentary was for real. FYI: FUBAR is a US military acronym for Fucked Up Beyond All Recognition. DO

• *Dean Murdoch* Paul J. Spence, *Terry Cahill* Dave Lawrence, *Farrel Mitchener* Gordon Skilling, *Trixie Anderson* Tracey Lawrence, *Chastity Anderson* Sage Lawrence, *Rose Murdoch* Rose Martin, *Dr. S.C. Lim* Doctor S.C. Lim, *Ron Miller* Jim Lawrence, *Tron/Troy McRae* Andrew Sparacino.
• *Dir* and *Ph* Michael Dowse, *Pro* Michael Dowse, David Lawrence, Melanie Owen and Paul Spence, *Ex Pro* Marguerite Pigott and Mark Slone, *Screenplay* Michael Dowse, David Lawrence and Paul Spence, *Ed* Jerome Canon and Michael Dowse.

Odeon Films/Busted Tranny/Téléfilm Canada-Momentum.
80 mins. Canada. 2002. Rel: 21 May 2004.
Cert 15.

Game Over: Kasparov and the Machine ★★★¹/₂

The fascination here stems from the material, not from the movie-making. Director Vikram Jayanti's documentary feature is focused on six games of chess played in New York in 1997 by the Russian champion Garry Kasparov in which his opponent was a computer created by IBM and named 'Deep Blue'. When Kasparov lost, the value of IBM shares soared, leaving the loser increasingly worried by moves that he could not credit as having been made by a computer. Had IBM cheated, or was Kasparov a victim of paranoia? You need no knowledge of chess to be intrigued, but it's a pity that the director has over-extended and over-dramatised the material. Worth seeing despite its faults. MS

• *With:* Gary Kasparov, Frederic Friedel, Joel Benjamin, Murray Campbell, Feng Hsuing-Tsu, John Searle, Steven Levy, Owen Williams, Jeff Kisselhof.
• *Dir* Vikram Jayanti, *Pro* Hal Vogel *Ex Pro* Andre Singer, Andy Thomson, Nick Fraser, Paul Trijbits, Tom Perlmutter and Eric Michel, *Ph* Maryse Alberti, *Ed* David Hill, *M* Rob Lane.

World Documentary Fund/UK Film Council New Cinema Fund/ National Film Board of Canada/BBC/Alliance Atlantis-Momentum. 87 mins. UK/Canada. 2003. Rel: 23 January 2004. Cert PG.

Gasoline

See *Benzina*.

Gerry ★★¹/₂

Essentially a piece portraying figures in a landscape, this film from Gus Van Sant offers wide screen images by Harris Savides that are absolutely stunning (in point of fact the wilderness in which the two leading characters get lost is a mix of shots taken in Argentina, Death Valley and Nevada). But, the look of it apart, there's nothing here of the slightest interest. The friends, both called Gerry, who put their lives at risk when they wander off the trail, are played by Matt Damon and Casey Affleck. What could have worked as an allegory plays instead as a literal tale with touches of surrealism about two singularly stupid people whose comments veer between the boring and the pretentious. *Gerry* will appeal only to the director's most avant-garde devotees or to those prepared to give themselves over to finely composed visuals that exist in a dramatic vacuum. MS

• *Gerry* Casey Affleck, *Gerry* Matt Damon.

• *Dir* Gus Van Sant, *Pro* Dany Wolf, *Screenplay* Van Sant, Casey Affleck and Matt Damon, *Ph*, Harris Savides; *Steadicam* Jen Wall, *Ed* Paul Zucker and Lilah Bankier, *M* Arvo Pärt.

My Cactus Inc/ThinkFilm-Pathé. 103 mins. USA. 2002. Rel: 22 August 2003. Cert 15.

Gigli ★

So, here is the turkey that nearly swept the board at this year's Razzies (the insult ceremony that 'rewards' the worst in cinema). In it, Ben Affleck and Jennifer Lopez play (badly) a pair of mobster-types who are thrown into partnership for the kidnapping of a prosecutor's son. I would say more about the plot, but it really would be much more amusing to pillory the script (offensive), the stars (relentless ham-meisters), the co-stars (what were they thinking?), the director (you sold out cheaply, here Mr Brest), and the studio that chose to release what they *must* have realised was destined to be garbage from the very first rushes. *Don't* watch this. AK

• *Larry Gigli* Ben Affleck, *Ricki* Jennifer Lopez, *Brian* Justin Bartha, *Mother* Lainie Kazan, *Robin* Missy Crider, *Starkman* Al Pacino, *Stanley Jacobellis* Christopher Walken, *with* Terrance Camilleri, David Backus.
• *Dir* and *Screenplay* Martin Brest, *Pro* Casey Silver and Martin Brest *Ex Pro* John Hardy, *Ph* Robert Elswit, *Pro Des* Gary Frutkoff, *Ed* Billy Weber and Julie Monroe, *M* John Powell, *Costumes* Michael Kaplan.

Revolution/City Light/Casey Silver Prods-Columbia TriStar 121 mins. USA. 2003. Rel: 26 September 2003. Cert 15.

The Girl Next Door ★★★

What would you do if you discovered the hottie who has the hots for your teenage ass was also a porn star? That it has taken this long for that question to be asked in the context of a teen comedy is, frankly, astounding. The lucky guy is class prez and future leader of America, Matthew Kidman, and the object of mass desire is Danielle. Luke Greenfield openly admits to recycling *Risky Business* (*More Risqué Business* if you like) into a permissive post-millennial, post-internet incarnation where the commercialisation of hardcore sex and recreational Type-A drug use is an embedded aspect of pop culture. The leads are hugely likable and do a smart job of selling the rather convoluted story, while Timothy Olyphant hits a home run as the avuncular pimp/porn producer who stands in the way of true love. AK

• *Matthew Kidman* Emile Hirsch, *Danielle* Elisha Cuthbert, *Kelly* Timothy Olyphant, *Hugo Posh* James Remar, *Eli* Chris Marquette, *Klitz* Paul Dano, *Mr Kidman* Timothy Bottoms, *Mrs Kidman* Donna Bullock, *Samnang* Ulysses Lee, *with* Jacob Young, Brian Kolodziej, Laird Stuart, Richard Fancy.
• *Dir* Luke Greenfield, *Pro* Charles Gordon, Harry Gittes and Marc Sternberg, *Ex Pro* Arnon Milchan and Guy Riedel, *Co-Pro* Richard Wenk, *Screenplay* Stuart Blumberg, David T. Wagner and Brent Goldberg, *Ph* Jamie Anderson, *Pro Des* Stephen Lineweaver, *Ed* Mark Livolsi, *M* Paul Haslinger, *Costumes* Marilyn Vance.

Daybreak/Fox 2000 Pictures/New Regency Pictures/Regency Enterprises-Fox.
109 mins. USA. 2003. Rel: 16 April 2004. Cert 15.

Girl With a Pearl Earring ★★★★

This fictional tale about the maid (Scarlett Johansson) who inspired the married Vermeer (Colin Firth) to one of his most famous paintings is inherently popular in tone. It's the story of a love never to be consummated but immortalised indirectly in art. Such a concept might have yielded an artless movie, but debut director Peter Webber achieves distinction by trusting to a slow pace apt for us to appreciate fully the production design of Ben van Os and the superlative colour photography of Eduardo Serra. It magnificently echoes Dutch paintings and the casting of many supporting roles (Essie Davis, Judy Parfitt, Joanna Scanlan) is exceptionally acute. This approach and the standard of acting (Johansson especially) bring unexpected quality to this material. MS

• *Vermeer* Colin Firth, *Griet* Scarlett Johansson, *Van Ruijven* Tom Wilkinson, *Maria Thins* Judy Parfitt, *Pieter* Cillian Murphy, *Catharina* Essie Davis, *Tanneke* Joanna Scanlan, *Cornelia* Alakina Mann.
• *Dir* Peter Webber, *Pro* Andy Paterson and Anand Tucker, *Ex Pro* Francois Ivernel, Cameron McCracken, Duncan Reid, Tom Ortenberg, Peter Block, Daria Jovicic, Philip Erdoes and Nick Drake, *Co-Pro* Jimmy de Brabant, Matthew T. Gannon and Jason Constantine, *Screenplay* Olivia Hetreed, based on the novel by Tracy Chevalier, *Ph* Eduardo Serra, *Pro Des* Ben van Os, *Ed* Kate Evans, *M* Alexandre Desplat, *Costumes* Dien van Straalen.

Pathé Pictures/Lions Gate/U.K. Film Council/Archer Street/Delux/Inside Track/Film Fund Luxembourg-Pathé.
99 mins. UK/Luxembourg. 2003. Rel: 9 January. Cert 12A.

Gods and Generals ★★

A prequel to *Gettysburg*, the handsome, exciting epic released nine years ago, *Gods and Generals* is a brain-numbing disappointment. Bloated with honourable intentions, it is a four-hour adaptation of Jeff Shaara's novel chronicling the first half of the American Civil War. A lumbering history lesson neatly divided into improbable, theological speeches and underwhelming battle scenes (this is one of the cleanest war movies in recent history), *Gods and Generals* really is a vanity museum piece. The first shock is to see Robert Duvall, now 72, playing the 54-year-old Robert E. Lee. Duvall is one of America's greatest actors, but he looks far too old to lead an army into battle. Still, he's a sight more credible than a lot of the players here, many of whom border on the amateur. The top honours go to Stephen Lang, whose portrayal of the Confederate General Thomas 'Stonewall' Jackson goes some way in relieving the bum-dulling tedium. What is so tragic is that the subject matter is ripe for a fresh cinema epic (Steven Spielberg should really give it a try) and has all the potential to fuel the Great American Film. JC-W

• *Col. Joshua Chamberlain* Jeff Daniels, *General Thomas 'Stonewall' Jackson* Stephen Lang, *General Robert E. Lee* Robert Duvall, *Fanny Chamberlain* Mira Sorvino, *Sgt. 'Buster' Kilrain* Kevin Conway, *Lt. Thomas Chamberlain* C. Thomas Howell, *Jim Lewis* Frankie Faison, *Anna Jackson* Kali Rocha, *Jane Beale* Mia Dillon, *with* John Castle, Jeremy London, William Sanderson, Bruce Boxleitner, Billy Campbell.
• *Dir, Pro* and *Screenplay* Ronald F. Maxwell, from the book by Jeffrey M. Shaara, *Ex Pro* R.E. Turner, Robert Katz, Robert Rehme, Moctesuma Esparza and Mace Neufeld, *Co-Pro* Nick Grillo, *Co-Ex Pro* Ronald G. Smith, *Ph* Kees Van Oostrum, *Pro Des* Michael Z. Hanan, *Ed* Corky Ehlers, *M* John Frizzell and Randy Edelman, *Visual effects* Thomas G. Smith.

Ted Turner Pictures/Antietam Filmworks-Warner.
231 mins. USA. 2002. Rel: 4 July 2003.
Cert 12A.

Good Boy! ★

An envoy from an alien canine race crashes to Earth and befriends an all-American boy, granting him the power to understand all doggie-speech. Between them, they must captain the mutley crew of local pooches in a charade to convince the imperial Greater Dane that dogs on Earth rule, while humans, cats and all other creature drool. Matthew Broderick, Vanessa Redgrave, Carl Reiner and Brittany Murphy are some of the stars who soil themselves in this pandering, clichéd old bone of a family movie, one so desperate to hit all the standard tropes of movies about A Boy And His Dog that it stinks. Films like these are enough to convince me that cat-lovers are onto something when they pick out a dogs panting urge to please as a species fault. AK

• *Mrs Baker* Molly Shannon, *Owen Baker* Liam
Aiken *Mr Baker* Kevin Nealon, *Connie* Brittany
Moldowan.
Voices: Hubble Matthew Broderick, *Barbara Ann*
Delta Burke, *Wilson* Donald Faison, *Nelly* Brittany
Murphy, *Shep* Carl Reiner, *Greater Dane* Vanessa
Redgrave, *Greater Dane's henchmutt* Cheech Marin.
• *Dir* and *Screenplay* John Hoffman, from a story by
Zeke Richardson and John Hoffman, based on the
radio play *Dogs From Outer Space* by Zeke
Richardon, *Pro* Lisa Henson and Kristine Belson,
Ex Pro Stephanie Allain, *Co-Pro* Bill Bannerman,
Ph James Glennon, *Pro Des* Jerry Wanek, *Ed* Craig
P. Herring, *M* Mark Mothersbaugh, *Costumes*
Antonia Bardon.

Jim Henson Productions / Metro-Goldwyn-Mayer
(MGM) / Jim Henson Pictures-Fox
87 mins. USA. 2003. Rel: 19 December 2003. Cert U.

Good Bye Lenin! ★★★¹⁄₂

It is easy to understand how this gentle comedy
has become the most successful German film of all
time. A touching and stylish parable, it threads the
extraordinary social changes of East Germany
through an ingenious story peopled by quirky,
recognisable characters. Just as young Alex Kerner is
arrested while protesting against the Berlin Wall, his
mother, a staunch Socialist, suffers a heart attack and
slips into a coma. Eight months later, during which
time East Germany has become a thriving Capitalist
nation, Frau Kerner awakes. However, her condition
is extremely unstable and the doctors warn that any
excitement could threaten her life. So Alex and his
sister Ariane embark on an elaborate charade to
shield their mother from the escalating reality of a
world dominated by Coca-Cola, Burger King and
the freedom of speech. Recycling old food labels,
handling outdated currency and relaying faux news
bulletins via VCR, Alex and Ariane recreate a bygone
era as their mother lies blissfully unaware in her
bedroom. Strong on charm and comic invention, the
film never ceases to beguile, although its political
sting is probably lost on a non-German audience.
JC-W

• *Alex Kerner* Daniel Brühl, *Christiane Kerner*
Katrin, *Ariane Kerner* Maria Simon, *Lara* Chulpan
Khamatova, *Denis* Florian Lukas, *Rainer* Alexander
Beyer, *Robert Kerner* Burghard Klaussner, *Principal
Dr Klapprath*.Michael Gwisdek.
• *Dir* Wolfgang Becker, *Pro* Stefan Arndt, *Screenplay*
Becker and Bernd Lichtenberg, *Ph* Martin Kukula,
Pro Des Lothar Holler, *Ed* Peter R. Adam, *M* Yann
Tiersen, *Costumes* Aenne Plaumann.

X Filme Creative Pool/WDR/Arte-UGC Films.
121 mins. Germany. 2003. Rel: 25 July 2003. Cert. 15.

The Good Old Naughty Days ★★★★
(Polissons et Galipettes)

How could I rate what is, essentially, a collection of
vintage hardcore pornography this highly? Could it
be for its illuminating revelation on the sexual mores
of the early 1900s? Or is it for the comment on the
human condition given pornography this
sophisticated was being produced from the very
birth of film? Honestly? It is mainly because I never
stopped laughing throughout its modest 69 minutes,
its play-length (ahem) itself another of Michel
Reilhac's jokes. Even as the screening room emptied
of viewers who simply could not stomach the raw
exploitation of the 12 short films that make up
TGOND, which starred prostitutes being serviced by
'friends of the filmmaker' in hilarious disguise; even
when the remarkably game doggy joined in the fun;
even when it really went over every available
boundary of good taste, I found it unfailingly
entertaining, hilarious and shocking. AK

• *Dir* and *Pro* Michel Reilhac, inspired by Pascal
Greggory from an idea by Reilhac and Sébastien
Marnier, *M* Eric Le Guen, *Ed* Olivier Lupczynsky.

Mélange/Lobster-Tartan Films.
69 mins. France. 2002. Rel: 23 April 2004. Cert R18.

Gothika ★★

Gothika is a fancy name for Krapula. A Gothic
thriller with pretensions above its genre, the film
tackles intriguing material with a flatulence of style.
Of course, it doesn't help that Halle Berry utters
lines like, 'I'm not deluded, Pete, I'm possessed' and,
'logic is overrated.' It may not be fair to say so, but
Halle looks far too young and gorgeous to be a
reputable criminal psychologist, particularly one
married to a very fat 53-year-old. Berry is Dr
Miranda Grey, who is treating a Spanish woman
who believes she is possessed by the devil. Along
the way there is a transference of evil and Miranda
herself begins to see dead people (oh, no, not again).
The string section of the orchestra sounds
appropriately nervous, a startled owl makes the
audience jump and all the usual horror clichés
are applied with motorized dexterity. JC-W

• *Dr Miranda Grey* Halle Berry, *Dr Pete Graham*
Robert Downey Jr., *Dr Doug Grey* Charles S.
Dutton, *Sherriff Ryan* John Carroll Lynch, *Phil
Parsons* Bernard Hill, *Chloe Sava* Penélope Cruz,
Teddy Howard Dorian Harewood, *with* Bronwen
Mantel, Kathleen Mackey, Matthew G. Taylor.
• *Dir* Mathieu Kassovitz, *Pro* Joel Silver, Robert
Zemeckis and Susan Levin, *Ex Pro* Steve Richards,
Gary Ungar and Don Carmody, *Screenplay* Sebastian
Gutierrez, *Ph* Matthew Libatique, *Pro Des* Graham
`Grace' Walker, *Ed* Yannick Kergoat, *M* John

Ottman, *Costumes* Kym Barrett.

Warner/Columbia/Dark Castle Entertainment-Columbia. 98 mins. USA. 2003. Rel: 2 April 2004. Cert 15.

Grand Theft Parsons ★★★

In 1973 the singer Gram Parsons died of an overdose but not before he had indicated that he wanted his body to be burnt ceremonially in Joshua Tree National Park. His road manager, Phil Kaufman (Johnny Knoxville), stole the corpse to give effect to his wishes and this film converts the reality into a shaggy dog story as Phil involves an eccentric but innocent hippie (Michael Shannon) in his plans. The duo find themselves pursued by the dead man's father (Robert Forster) and by his former girl-friend (Christina Applegate). The latter, a tiresome character, is in fact fictional and leads the film downhill through several silly contrivances to a misjudged fantasy appearance by the dead singer at

the close. The decline is especially sad because the film is well cast and possesses a warmth and amiability rare in cinema today. Songs by Parsons feature on the track. MS

• *Phil Kaufman* Johnny Knoxville, *Barbara Mansfield* Christina Applegate, *Larry Oster-Berg* Michael Shannon, *Susie* Marley Shelton, *Stanley Parsons* Robert Forster, *Gram Parsons* Gabriel Macht, *with* Jamie McShane, David Caffrey, Mike Shawver, Phil Kaufman.
• *Dir* David Caffrey, *Pro* Frank Mannion, *Ex Pro* Zygi Kamasa, Simon Franks, Matt Candel, Brad Zipper and Jesse Itzler, *Screenplay* Jeremy Drysdale, from a story by Drysdale and David Caffrey, *Ph* Bob Hayes, *Pro Des,* Bryce Elric Holtshousen, *Ed* Mary Finlay and Alan Roberts, *M* Richard G. Mitchell, *Costumes* Sophie De Rakoff Carbonnell.

Swipe Films/Morty-Stevie G Productions-Redbus. 88 mins. UK/USA. 2003. Rel: 19 March 2004. Cert 12A.

Below:
Possessed, not deluded: Criminal psychologist Halle Berry in Mathieu Kassovitz' mechanical *Gothika* (from Columbia TriStar)

The Hard Word ★★★

This Australian heist movie, a directorial debut of some assurance by Scott Roberts, seeks to blend excitement and plot twists with amusing dialogue. It gains from a fine ensemble cast (Guy Pearce has the star billing as one of three criminal brothers but the lesser known Damien Richardson and Joel Edgerton as the siblings are equally strong). However, there's a debit side. Although Rachel Griffiths playing Pearce's unfaithful wife fits the genre, there are unconvincing roles for Kate Atkinson and Rhondda Findleton as women improbably drawn to the other brothers. Furthermore, the last half-hour is even more contrived and implausible than what has gone before. Technically it's a good calling card for Roberts, but the players are good enough to deserve better. MS

• *Dale Twentyman* Guy Pearce, *Carol* Rachel Griffiths, *Shane Twentyman* Joel Edgerton, *Mal Twentyman* Damien Richardson, *Frank Malone* Robert Taylor, *Detective Jack O'Riordan* Paul Sonkkila, *Detective Mick Kelly* Vince Colosimo, *with* Rhondda Findleton, Kate Atkinson, Kim Gyngell, Stephen Whittaker, Ross Daniels, Nash Edgerton.
• *Dir* and *Screenplay* Scott Roberts, *Pro* Al Clark, *Ex Pro* Gareth Jones and Hilary Davis, *Ph* Brian Breheny, *Pro Des* Paddy Reardon, *Ed* Martin Connor, *M* David Thrussell, *Costumes* Terry Ryan.

Metrodome/Alibi Films International/Australian Film Finance Corp./Wildheart-Metrodome.
103 mins. Australia/UK. 2002.
Rel: 12 September 2003. Cert 18.

Harry Potter and the Prisoner of Azkaban ★★★¹/₂

When the notorious wizard Sirius Black escapes from Azkaban prison, Hogwarts Academy is put on high alert. For not only is Black accused of betraying Harry Potter's parents to the evil Voldemort; he has also promised to kill Harry the first chance he gets ... With the exciting talents of Alfonso Cuarón at the reins, the visual and emotional universe of J.K. Rowling's characters have taken a sharp turn to edgier ground. It is a move that well suits the maturing look of its now familiar stars. By far the best of the franchise to date, the film runs at a breathless pace and boasts some handsome photography by Michael Seresin that helps one overlook the less than inspirational lead performances, excepting a cracking right hook by Emma Watson that raised cheers in cinemas the world over. AK

• *Harry Potter* Daniel Radcliffe, *Ron Weasley* Rupert Grint, *Hermione Granger* Emma Watson, *Rubeus Hagrid* Robbie Coltrane, *Albus Dumbledore* Michael Gambon, *Vernon Dursley* Richard Griffiths, *Sirius Black* Gary Oldman, *Professor Snape* Alan Rickman, *Petunia Dursley* Fiona Shaw, *Professor McGonagall* Maggie Smith, *Peter Pettigrew* Timothy Spall, *Professor Lupin* David Thewlis, *Professor Trelawney* Emma Thompson, *Mrs Weasley* Julie Walters, *Draco Malfoy* Tom Felton, *Madame Rosmerta* Julie Christie, *Aunt Marge* Pam Ferris, *Argus Filch* David Bradley, *Dudley Dursley* Harry Melling, *with* Dawn French, Robert Hardy, Chris Rankin, Mark Williams, Paul Whitehouse, Adrian Rawlins, Warwick Davis, Violet Columbus, Freddie Davis, Peter Best.
• *Dir* Alfonso Cuarón, *Pro* David Heyman, Chris Columbus and Mark Radcliffe, *Ex Pro* Michael Barnathan, Callum McDougall and Tanya Seghatchian, *Screenplay* Steve Kloves, based on the novel by J.K. Rowling, *Ph* Michael Seresin, *Pro Des* Stuart Craig, *Ed* Steven Weisberg, *M* John Williams, *Costumes* Jany Temime, *Visual effects supervisors* Roger Guyett and Tim Burke.

Warner/Heyday Films/1492 Pictures-Warner.
141 mins. UK. 2004. Rel: 31 May 2004. Cert PG.

The Haunted Mansion ★★

Like *Pirates of the Caribbean*, *The Haunted Mansion* is modelled on a theme ride from DisneyWorld. Thus, the accent is heavily on the production design and special effects and however wide Eddie Murphy stretches his grin he can't upstage the digital trickery. A fairly loyal homage to the ride, the film falls flat on its own terms, as it is neither very funny nor particularly scary. Murphy plays Jim Evers, an ambitious real estate agent who neglects his family to further his professional ends (much like the eponymous physician he played in *Dr Dolittle*). When Evers suggests to his wife and kids that they stop by a rambling mansion on the first leg of a family weekend, he could never have imagined what lay in store. Of course, the property is haunted, prompting Evers' ten-year-old son to observe, 'I see dead people.' Unfortunately, the script cannot compete with the effects, the banality of the dialogue exemplified when Evers stares at the mansion's front door and says, 'look at the size of those knockers.' JC-W

• *Jim Evers* Eddie Murphy, *Ramsley* Terence Stamp, *Ezra* Wallace Shawn, *Sara Evers* Marsha Thomason, *Madame Leota* Jennifer Tilly, *Master Gracey* Nathaniel Parker, *Emma* Dina Waters, *Michael* Marc John Jeffries, *Megan* Aree Davis, *with* Jim Doughan, Rachel Harris, Deep Roy, Gregg London, Zach Minkoff.
• *Dir* Rob Minkoff, *Pro* Don Hahn and Andrew Gunn, *Ex Pro* Barry Bernardi and Rob Minkoff, *Screenplay* David Berenbaum, based on Walt Disney's Haunted Mansion, *Ph* Remi Adefarasin, *Pro Des*,

John Myhre, *Ed* Priscilla Nedd Friendly and Gregg London, *M* Mark Mancina; 'Grim, Grinning Ghosts' performed by Barenaked Ladies, *Costumes*, Mona May, *Special Makeup Effects* Rick Baker, *Visual effects supervisor* Jay Redd, *Choreographer* Elizabeth Aldrich.

Walt Disney Pictures-Buena Vista.
86 mins. USA. 2003. Rel: 13 February 2004. Cert PG.

Hidalgo ★★★

At the end of the 19th century, the legendary adventurer and his race-winning mustang, Hidalgo, accept a challenge by an imperious Sheikh to race one last time in the 3000 mile trans-Saharan marathon fearfully dubbed 'the Ocean of Fire' …
It has been a year for films about 'The Little Horse Who Could'. With *Seabiscuit* taking the high ground of docu-dramatics, *Hidalgo* races for the populist sweepstakes of legend and fable. But where *Seabiscuit* was all about the horse, *Hidalgo* is all about Viggo Mortensen. The lean, mean, brooding machine hogs the screen like an old school matinee icon, which wouldn't be so bad if he had anything worthwhile to say. By the end of the movie, the audience is damned well convinced that Frank Hopkins is as noble a horseman as ever walked the Earth, thanks in no small part to his Native American heritage. If only it did not seem so much like an extended advertorial for Mortensen's masculinity, one might actually appreciate the epic sweep of the story it meant to tell. AK

• *Frank Hopkins* Viggo Mortensen, *Sheik Riyadh* Omar Sharif, *Lady Anne Davenport* Louise Lombard, *Prince Bin Al Rech* Saïd Taghmaoui, *Jaffa* Peter Mensah, *Buffalo Bill Cody* J.K. Simmons, *Jazira* Zuleikha Robinson, *Aziz* Adam Alexi-Malle, *Katib* Silas Carson, *Annie Oakley* Elizabeth Berridge, *Major Davenport* Malcolm McDowell (uncredited), *with* Floyd Red Crow Westerman, Jerry Hardin, C. Thomas Howell, Philip Sounding Sides, John Prosky, David Midthunder, Mary Ellis.
• *Dir* Joe Johnston, *Pro* Casey Silver, *Ex Pro* Don Zepfel, *Screenplay* John Fusco, *Ph* Shelly Johnson, *Pro Des* Barry Robison, *Ed* Robert Dalva, *M* James Newton Howard, *Costumes* Jeffrey Kurland, *Groom* Cynthia Jane Ruddiman.

Touchstone Pictures-Fox.
136 mins. USA. 2003. Rel: 16 April 2004. Cert 12A.

Historias Minimas ★★★★

(*Minimal Stories*)
In essence three interwoven tales in one, this award-winning film from Patagonia could be described as a road movie since it shows various characters, none too well off, travelling some two hundred miles to reach San Julián. Old Don Justo (Benedictti) is defying his family by doing this but has heard that

the dog which left him three years previously may be found there. A salesman (Lombardo) is taking a specially baked cake for the child of a female customer of his as a means of wooing the mother. María (Bravo) is on her way to take part as a potential prizewinner in a TV show. The non-professional cast play excellently and, if the film is comparatively light-weight, it is also heart-warming, managing a blend of drama and humour without ever being too sentimental or manipulative. MS

• *Roberto* Javier Lombardo, *Don Justo Benedictis* Antonio Benedictti, *María Flores* Javiera Bravo, *Hija de María* Francis Sandoval, *Losa* Carlos Montero, *Fermín* Aníbal Maldonado, *Ana* María Rosa Cianferoni, *Amiga de María* Mariela Díaz, *Julia* Julia Solomonoff, *El mesero* Armando Grimaldi, *César García* César García.
• *Dir* Carlos Sorin, *Pro* Leticia Cristi, *Ex Pro* Martin Bardi, *Screenplay* Pablo Solarz, *Ph* Hugo Colace, *Art Dir* Margarita Jusid, *Ed* Mohamed Rajid.

Guacamole Films/Nirvana Films/
Wanda Visión-Optimum Releasing.
91 mins. Argentina. 2002. Rel: 25th July 2003. Cert 15.

Holes ★★★¹/₂

Adapted from Louis Sachar's award-winning novel for children and young adults, *Holes* is a most engaging and unusual entertainment. Set in parallel time frames and cutting liberally between the two, it builds a satisfying momentum as our young protagonist – Stanley Yelnats – discovers that his current predicament is irrevocably tied to his family's past. Convicted of the theft of a pair of celebrity trainers, Stanley is carted off to Camp Green Lake in Texas where there's no lake, green or otherwise. There is plenty of desert, however, and Stanley and his fellow inmates are forced to dig a hole each day in order to help 'build their character.' As it happens, Stanley is innocent of the misdemeanour for which he is being punished and is actually paying for the 'sin' of his 'no-good-dirty-rotten-pig-stealing great-great-great-grandfather.' Directed at a lively clip by Andrew Davis (*The Fugitive*) and acted with brio by a top-notch cast (Jon Voight in particular has fun consuming the scenery), *Holes* manages to succeed on a number of levels. JC-W

• *the warden* Sigourney Weaver, *Mr Sir* Jon Voight, *Kissin' Kate Barlow* Patricia Arquette, *Dr Pendanski* Tim Blake Nelson, *Stanley Yelnats* Shia LaBeouf, *Stanley's mother* Siobhan Fallon Hogan, *Stanley's father* Henry Winkler, *Madame Zeroni* Eartha Kitt, *Sam* Dulé Hill, *Dector 'Zero' Zeroni* Khleo Thomas, *Squid* Jake M. Smith, *Armpit* Byron Cotton, *X-Ray* Brenden Jefferson, *Magnet* Miguel Castro, *with* Roma Maffia, Ray Baker, Nathan Davis, Bruce

Ramsay, Scott Plank.
• *Dir* Andrew Davis, *Pro* Davis, Mike Medavoy, Teresa Tucker-Davies and Lowell Blank, *Scr* Louis Sachar, based on his novel, *Ph* Stephen St. John, *Pro Des* Maher Ahmad, *Ed* Thomas Nordberg and Jeffrey Wolf, *M* Joel McNeely; songs performed by Eels, Shaggy, Teresa James, Pepé Deluxé, North Mississippi Allstars, Beck, Stephanie Bentley, Eagle-Eye Cherry, Little Axe, Moby, Bessie Jones, Keb' Mo, Sandy Rogers, Dr John, Fiction Plane, etc, *Sound* Bruce Stambler.

Chicago Pacific Entertainment/Phoenix Pictures/Walden Media/Walt Disney Pictures-Buena Vista International. 117 mins. USA. 2003. Rel: 24 October 2003. Cert PG.

Hollywood Homicide ★★★¹/₂

LA, the present. Detective Joe Gavilan is an old dog with bills to pay, hence his daylight moonlighting gig as an LA real estate agent. K.C. Calden is the young pup in this classic odd couple cop partnership, a beautiful young man more interested in his dreams of being the next Marlon Brando than in a police career. Their path to mediocrity is well-paved until a ruthless murder in a hip-hop club tests whether they are made of the right stuff … The hugely entertaining banter between Harrison Ford and Josh Hartnett, coupled with the refreshingly unforced eccentricities of their characters make for a fun, slightly lightweight twist on the LA cop-noir story. While all other elements barely escape their stereotypes, the strong lead performances pulls the movie through. AK

• *Joe Gavilan* Harrison Ford, *K.C. Calden* Josh Hartnett, *Ruby* Lena Olin, *Bernie Macko* Bruce Greenwood, *Sartain* Isaiah Washington, *Cleo* Lolita Davidovich, *Leon* Keith David, *Julius Armas* Percy 'Master P' Miller, *Wasley* Dwight Yoakam, *Jerry Duran* Martin Landau, *Olivia Robidoux* Gladys Knight, *Wanda* Lou Diamond Phillips, *K-RO* Kurupt, aka Ricardo Brown, *with* Eric Idle, Robert Wagner, Master P.
• *Dir* Ron Shelton, *Pro* Shelton and Lou Pitt, *Ex Pro* Joe Roth and David Lester, *Screenplay* Robert Souza and Ron Shelton, *Ph* Barry Peterson, *Pro Des* Jim Bissell, *Ed* Paul Seydor, *M* Alex Wurman, *M Supervisors* Dawn Soler and Kathy Nelson, *Costumes* Bernie Pollack.

Revolution Studios-Columbia Tristar 111 mins. USA. 2003. Rel 29 August 2003. Cert 12A.

Honey ★★

LA, the present. Honey Daniels runs a community dance class and lives for the joys of dancing the night away with her friends after pulling the late shift behind the bar, until a sleazy music video director pulls thrusts her into the Klieg lights of MTV choreography and makes her famous as the hip-hop prancer of choice. Honey uses her big break to draw the community kids away from a life of crime, but when she rebuffs her sponsor's advances, the bubble bursts and she has to find her own way back into the spotlight … Jessica Alba strikes a stunning figure in leotards but that cannot wash over the fact that this is a deeply uninspired rehash of every inner-city dance movie, ever. Mekhi Pfiher injects a bit of class as Alba's straight-walkin' boyfriend, and some of the kids are pretty cute, but this is an exercise in bling, making a weak attempt at soul. AK

• *Honey Daniels* Jessica Alba, *Chaz* Mekhi Phifer, *Gina* Joy Bryant, *Benny* Lil' Romeo, *Michael Ellis* David Moscow, *Mrs Daniels* Lonette McKee, *Raymond* Zachary Isaiah Williams, *Mr Daniels* Anthony Sherwood, *Katrina* Laurie Ann Gibson, *Michael* Marc John Jefferies, *Megan* Aree Davis, *and as themselves*: Missy Elliott, Jadakiss & Sheek, Shawn Desman, Ginuwine, Harmonica Sunbeam, Rodney Jerkins, Silkk, 3rd Storee, Tweet.
• *Dir* Bille Woodruff, *Pro* Marc Platt, Andre Harrell, *Ex Pro* Billy Higgins, *Screenplay* Alonzo Brown and Kim Watson, *Ph* John R. Leonetti, *Pro Des* Jasna Stefanovich, *Ed* Mark Helfrich and Emma E. Hickox, *M* Mervyn Warren, *Costumes* Susan Matheson.

Universal Pictures/Marc Platt/NuAmerica-UIP. 94 mins. USA. 2003. Rel: 12 March 2004. Cert PG.

The Honeymooners ★★¹/₂

With its inept use of hand-held cameras almost guaranteed to hurt the eyes and the botched efforts of writer/director Karl Golden to create a contemporary romantic comedy more raw than glossy, this film is a non-starter. The piece is best when it's most old-fashioned, with excellent performances from Jonathan Byrne as a man who has ditched his bride-to-be and from Alex Reid as the female stranger who agrees to drive him to Donegal after becoming disenchanted with her own married lover. The duo are clearly made for each other, but what might work in a TV slot lasting an hour is stretched out here – first by treading ground and then by playing with the possibility of other resolutions. This latter phase involves the hero in increasingly bad behaviour so that the supposedly happy ending doesn't come across as being that at all. The talented cast deserved better. MS

• *David* Jonathan Byrne, *Claire* Alex Reid, *Fiona* Justine Mitchell, *Peter* Conor Mullen, *Ben* David Nolan, *Larry* Eamon Hunt, *Mary* Briana Corrigan,

Fiona's father Niall O'Brien, *Ray* David Murray, *David's mother* Britta Smith.
• *Dir* and *Screenplay* Karl Golden, *Pro* Martin Brinkler and Martina Niland, *Ex Pro* David Collins, Lucy Darwin and Brendan McCarthy, *Co-Pro* Colin McKeown, *Ph* Darran Tiernan, *Pro Des* Stephen Daly, *Ed* Martin Brinkler, *M* Niall Byrne, *Costumes* Louise Kelly.

The Northern Ireland Film Commission/Samson Films/TV3/The Irish Film Board/Bord Scannán na hÉireann/Utah Films-Verve Pictures.
89 mins. Ireland/UK. 2003. Rel: 30 April 2004. Cert 15.

Hoover Street Revivial ★★★

Sophie Fiennes points her camera at the downtown LA mission of Bishop Noel Jones, a powerful preacher and a force for change in a drug-scarred and crime-ridden LA neighbourhood that is desperate for revival. Fiennes lo-fi images seem to see all but judge nothing, capturing the stories of the congregation with a Spartan aesthetic that invites an open interpretation of her subject. The results are sometimes interesting, and sometimes slack. Nevertheless, the energy inherent in her chosen subject is enough to make the watching worthwhile. AK

• *Dir* Sophie Fiennes, *Ex Pro* Kees Kasander, *Assoc Pro* Senain Kheshgi, *Ph* Blane Davidson, Sophie Fiennes, Daniel Kozman (as Dan Kozman), Jennifer Lane and Benito Strangio, *Ed* Brian Tagg.
• *As himself* Bishop Noel Jones.

Amoeba Film/BBC/Film Council/France 2 Cinéma/ Idéale Audience-Metro Tartan.
104 mins. UK/France. 2002. Rel 4 July 2003. Cert 15.

The Hours of the Day ★★★★

(Las Horas del día)
Whether we need another film about a serial killer is questionable, but this Spanish movie is never exploitative and, rather than using the subject as the basis of a thriller entertainment, it is a compellingly convincing illustration of the theory that the majority of serial killers appear normal and remain unsuspected by their families and friends. Jaime Rosales' film set outside Barcelona simply concentrates on the minutiae of the killer's everyday existence. The precise judgment behind every image can make the film seem distanced, but the subsidiary characters come to vivid life and the killer's compulsions become just another illustration of how difficult it is to know truly another human being. It may not have sufficient new insights to create a masterpiece, but the filming is indeed masterly. MS

• *Abel* Alex Brendemühl, *Tere* Àgata Roca, *Madre* María Antonia Martínez, *Trini* Pape Monsoriu, *Marcos* Vicente Romero, *Carmen* Irene Belza, *María* Anna Sahun, *Taxista* Isabel Rocatti,

señor mayor Armando Aguirre.
• *Dir* Jaime Rosales, *Pro* Rosales, María José Díez and Ricard Figueras, *Ex Pro* María José Díez, *Assoc Pro* José María de Orbe, *Screenplay* Jaime Rosales and Enric Rufas, *Ph* Oscar Durán, *Pro Des* Leo Casamitjana, *Ed* Nino Martínez.

Fresdeval Films/In Vitro Films-ICA Projects.
102 mins. Spain. 2003. Rel: 18 June 2004. Cert 15.

House of a 1000 Corpses ★★¹/₂

A car of college kids wander into the clutches of a seriously deranged family – the kind that accumulate a rusting yard full of cars they never bought – and are picked off in the grand tradition of warped B-movie massacres. The aptly named Rob Zombie exploits every cliché in the Texas Chainsaw slasher movie genre in this twisted, yet affectionate tribute to his love for the genre. The acting ain't much, and the plot is as tried and true as the plague, but the sheer gusto at which he attacks the production (and his victims) counts for something. The art direction is fairly lavish considering the size of the budget and the rudimentary nature of the genre aesthetic, but unless you are *real* fan of this type of cinema (the subversion of the ideal), there ain't much here for you to enjoy. AK

• *Capt Spaulding* Sid Haig, *Otis* Bill Moseley, *Baby Firefly* Sheri Moon, *Mother Firefly* Karen Black, *Stucky* Michael J Pollard, *Jerry Goldsmith* Chris Hardwick, *Denise Willis* Erin Daniels, *Mary Knowles* Jennifer Jostyn, *Bill Hudley* Rainn Wilson, *Lieutenant George Wydell* Tom Towles, *Deputy Steve Naish* Walton Goggins, *Tiny Firefly* Matthew McGrory, *Rufus 'R J' Firefly Jr* Robert Allen Mukes, *Grandpa Hugo* Dennis Fimple, *Don Willis* Harrison Young, *Sheriff Drake Huston* William Bassett, *Ravelli* Irwin Keyes, *Dr. Wolfenstein's Assistant* Rob Zombie (uncredited).
• *Dir* and *Screenplay* Rob Zombie, *Pro* Andy Gould, *Ex Pro* Andy Given and Guy Oseary, *Ph* Tom Richmond and Alex Poppas, *Pro Des* Gregg Gibbs *Art Dir* Michael Krantz, *Ed* Kathryn Himoff, Robert K. Lambert and Sean Lambert, *M* Rob Zombie and Scott Humphrey, *Special makeup effects* Wayne Toth, *Costumes* Amanda Friedland.

Universal Pictures-Metro Tartan
88 mins. USA. 2003. Rel 3 October 2003. Cert 18.

House of Sand and Fog ★★★★

A small house on the San Francisco coast lies at the centre of a bitter duel between a proud Persian migrant and a melancholy recovering alcoholic in a magnificent tragedy based on the award-winning novel by Andre Dubus III. Masterstrokes of casting include Ben Kingsley as Col. Massoud Behrani, who endures the humiliation of menial labour to maintain his family's pride amongst the Persian émigré community, Shohreh Aghdashloo as his haunted wife, and Jennifer Connelly as his sympathetic opponent. Lush lenswork, intricately crafted scenes and first-rate acting all combine to creat heavyweight drama of rare distinction. Justice lies with both sides of the fight, and the only try villain is the stupidity policeman who, in love with Connelly's character, goes too far in pursuit of his lover's interests. AK

• *Kathy Nicolo* Jennifer Connelly, *Massoud Amir Behrani* Ben Kingsley, *Lester Burdon* Ron Eldard, *Connie Walsh* Frances Fisher, *Carol Burdon* Kim Dickens, *Nadi Behrani* Shohreh Aghdashloo, *Esmail Behrani* Jonathan Ahdout, *Soraya Behrani* Navi Rawat, *Lt Alvarez* Carlos Gomez.
• *Dir* Vadim Perelman, *Pro* Perelman and Michael London, *Co-Pro* Jeremiah Samuels and Shawn Lawrence Otto, *Screenplay* Perelman and Shawn Lawrence Otto, based on the novel by Andre Dubus III, *Ph* Roger Deakins, *Pro Des* Maia Javan, *Ed* Lisa Zeno Churgin, *M* James Horner, *Costumes* Hala Bahmet.

DreamWorks-Buena Vista International.
127 mins. USA. 2004. Rel: 27 February 2004. Cert 15.

Hulk ★'/₂

Unless you are a big comics fan, it will be hard for you to fathom the gigantic disappointment that is Ang Lee's adaptation of the genre's biggest hero. Lee has transformed the classic story of a mild-mannered scientist who, thanks to a gamma radiation accident, turns into the most powerful mortal in the Universe when enraged into a family soap opera with aspirations toward Greek tragedy. Even the so-called cutting-edge computer animation, promised to bring the Hulk into visual reality like never before, feels contrived. Eric Bana does a decent job as Dr. Banner, moping with style, while Jenifer Connelly is an unconvincing subject of a Freudian attachment to 'remote men'. Nick Nolte would have been the best actor of the lot, were it not for the serious unintelligibility of his diction. In sum, the movie is a hulking waste of money. AK

• *Bruce Banner* Eric Bana, *Betty Ross* Jennifer Connelly, *General Ross* Sam Elliott, *Talbot* Josh Lucas, *David Banner* Nick Nolte, *young David Banner* Paul Kersey, *Edith Banner* Cara Buono, *Security Guard* Lou Ferrigno, *security suard* Stan Lee, with Todd Tesen, Kevin Rankin, Celia Weston, Michael Kronenberg, David Kronenberg, John Prosky.
• *Dir* Ang Lee, *Pro* Gale Anne Hurd, Avi Arad, James Schamus and Larry Franco, *Ex Pro* Stan Lee and Kevin Feige, *Screenplay* John Turman, Michael France and James Schamus, *story* James Schamus,

based on characters created by Stan Lee and Jack Kirby, *Ph* Frederick Elmes, *Pro Des* Rick Heinrichs, *Ed* Tim Squyres, *M* Danny Elfman, *Costumes* Marit Allen, *Animation supervisor* Colin Brady, *Visual effects supervisor* Dennis Muren, *Special Effects* Industrial Light & Magic (ILM), K.N.B. EFX Group Inc./yU+Co.

Universal Pictures/Marvel Enterprises/Valhalla Motion Pictures/Good Machine-UIP.
138 minutes. USA. 2003. Rel 18 July 2003. Cert 12A.

The Human Stain ★★★'/₂

Much under-valued, this ambitious adaptation of Philip Roth's novel is uneven but very interesting. Not every scene works, and you have to accept that Anthony Hopkins, despite any Welsh intonations, is an American black man who has passed as white for some fifty years. Similarly, the young woman (Kidman) with whom widower Hopkins falls in love lacks distinctive American roots. But if you buy into it you will be rewarded by admirable direction (Benton) and superb images from the late Jean-Yves Escoffier. What's more it combines an examination of a society in which passing as white is a wise career move with a study of reckless sexual impulses (this is the Clinton era). Best of all, Kidman and Hopkins (he especially) convincingly chart the genuine love found unexpectedly by two people whose past prevents them from liking themselves and who, recognising this in each other, can form a healing bond. MS

• *Coleman Silk* Anthony Hopkins, *Faunia Farley* Nicole Kidman, *Lester Farley* Ed Harris, *Nathan Zuckerman* Gary Sinise, *young Coleman* Wentworth Miller, *Steena Paulsson* Jacinda Barrett, *Mr Silk* Harry Lennix. *Nelson Primus* Clark Gregg, *Mrs. Silk* Anna Deavere Smith, *Ernestine* Lizan Mitchell, *Ellie* Kerry Washington, *Iris Silk* Phyllis Newman, *psychologist* Margo Martindale, *Herb Keble* Ron Canada, *young Iris* Mili Avital, *Walter* Danny Blanco Hall, *young Ernestine* Kristen Blevins, *Lisa Silk* Anne Dudek, *Professor Delphine Roux* Mimi Kuzyk, *Louie Borero* John Finn.
• *Dir* Robert Benton, *Pro* Tom Rosenberg, Gary Lucchesi and Scott Steindorff, *Ex Pro* Bob Weinstein, Harvey Weinstein, Ron Bozman, Andre Lamal, Rick Schwartz, Steve Hutensky, Michael Ohoven and Eberhard Kayser. *Co-Pro* Mario Ohoven, *Screenplay* Nicholas Meyer, based on the novel by Philip Roth, *Ph* Jean Yves Escoffier, *Pro Des* David Gropman, *Ed* Christopher Tellefsen, *M* Rachel Portman; Schubert, *M Supervisor* Dondi Bastone; songs performed by Jess Stacy, Woody Herman, Tommy Dorsey, Fred Astaire, The Oscar Peterson Trio, Teddy Wilson, etc, *Costumes* Rita Ryak.

Miramax/Lakeshore/Stone Village/
Cinerenta-Cineepsilon-Buena Vista.
106 mins. USA/Germany. 2003. Rel: 23 January 2004. Cert 18.

I'll Sleep When I'm Dead ★★★¹/₂

Not to be missed by anybody who admires the work of Mike Hodges, this atmospheric drama is seriously uneven but highly distinctive. With tough guy Will (Clive Owen) travelling to London to investigate what drove his brother (Jonathan Rhys Meyers) to suicide and then seeking vengeance, it sounds like a variation of the director's biggest hit, *Get Carter*. But the action is sidelined in favour of an atmospheric existentialist mood piece that could well be acclaimed in France. Unfortunately the splendid Charlotte Rampling is seriously miscast as Will's former lover and the script never really gets to grips with Will's character. Even so, this flawed film is more rewarding than many better ones and Rhys Meyers has never been so good before. MS

• *Will Graham* Clive Owen, *Helen* Charlotte Rampling, *Davey* Jonathan Rhys Meyers, *Boad* Malcolm McDowell, *Turner* Ken Stott, *Mickser* Jamie Foreman, *Mrs Barz* Sylvia Syms, *with* Alexander Morton, Ross Boatman, Mark Hardy.
• *Dir* Mike Hodges, *Pro* Mike Kaplan, Michael Corrente, *Ex Pro* Roger Marino, *Screenplay* Trevor Preston, *Ph* Mike Garfath, *Pro Des* Jon Bunker, *Ed* Paul Carlin, *M* Simon Fisher-Turner, *Costumes* Evangeline Averre.

Revere Pictures/Seven Arts/Will & Co-Lagoon Entertainment.
102 mins. UK/USA. 2003. Rel 30 April 2004. Cert 15.

Imagining Argentina ★★

1970s, Buenos Aires. Christopher Lawrence adaptation of Lawrence Thornton's novel about a theatre director who develops a magical second-sight for the fates of the victims of government-sanctioned kidnappings collapses in a mediocre and tepid magical realist thriller. The blame for this falls dually on Lawrence's fuzzy direction and on his star, Antonio Banderas, who plays Carlos, said theatre director, with such teeth-gritting earnestness that he is impossible to take seriously. Emma Thompson is credible as his journalist wife, kidnapped, then tortured and raped by soldiers for daring to express anti-government opinions in public. The idea for the story may be that the power of imagination will always survive the tyranny of fascism, but against the enormity of the truth, of the thousands killed in Argentina for whose families no answers will ever be given, this is a silly and pathetically insubstantial vehicle for it. AK

• *Carlos* Antonio Banderas, *Cecilia* Emma Thompson, *Victor Madrid* Horacio Flash, *Gustavo Santos* Kuno Becker, *Silvio* Rubén Blades, *Mrs. Sternberg* Claire Bloom, *Esmerelda Palomares* Maria Canals, *Lucia* Vera Czemerinski, *Police* Anthony Diaz-Perez, *Teresa* Leticia Dolera, *Eurydice* Irene Escolar, *General Guzman* Anton Lesser.
• *Dir* and *Screenplay* Christopher Hampton, *Pro* Geoffrey C. Lands, Raúl Outeda, Michael Peyser, Santiago Pozo and Diane Sillan, *Ex Pro* Jose Maria Cunillas, Kirk D'Amico and Isabel Mulá, *Co-Pro* José María Cunillés, *Co-Ex Pro* Lourdes Diaz, Lucas Foster, Jordi Ros and Philip von Alvensleben, *Line Pro* José Luis Escolar, *Ph* Guillermo Navarro, *Pro Des* Barbara Perez-Solero, *Ed* George Akers, *M* George Fenton, *Costumes* Sabina Daigeler.

Multivideo/Arenas Entertainment/Myriad Pictures Inc. /Green Moon Productions/Imagining Argentina Productions Ltd./Tide Rock Entertainment
107 mins. USA/Argentina/Spain/UK. 2003.
Rel: 30 April 2004. Cert 15.

I'm Not Scared ★★★¹/₂
(*Io non ho paura*)
This film version of a popular Italian novel made by the director of *Mediterraneo* shows real cinematic fluency. Furthermore, the first part is compelling as we look at life through the eyes of a ten-year-old (the assured Giuseppe Cristano). The year is 1978, the tone summery, but beneath this outward idyll one finds hints of life's more disturbing elements. This builds up in the second half when the child makes discoveries that should not be revealed to potential viewers in advance. Unfortunately, though, the later stages of the story become less original and also increasingly prone to contrivances and improbabilities. For some the continuing quality of the direction and acting may make up for this, but others will find the last part decidedly unsatisfactory. MS

• *Anna* Aitana Sánchez-Gijón, *Pino* Dino Abbrescia, *Felice* Giorgio Careccia, *Michele* Giuseppe Cristiano, *Pietro* Riccardo Zinna, *Filippo* Mattia Di Pierro, *Barbara* Adriana Conserva, *Teschio* Fabio Tetta, *Sergio* Diego Abatantuono.
• *Dir* Gabriele Salvatores, *Pro* Marizio Totti, Riccardo Tozzi, Giovanna Stabilini and Marco Chimenz, *Screenplay* Niccolò Ammaniti and Francesca Marciano, based on the novel by Ammaniti, *Ph* Italo Petriccione, *Pro Des* Giancarlo Basili, *Ed* Massimo Fiocchi, *M* Pepo Scherman and Ezio Bosso, *Costumes* Patrizia Chericoni and Florence Emir, *Sound* Danilo Moroni.

Colorado Film Production/Cattleya/Alquimia Cinema/The Producers Films/Medusa Film-Buena Vista International.
101 mins. Italy/Spain/UK. 2003.
Rel: 11 June 2004.
Cert 15.

Left: A brave face: Giuseppe Cristiano and Giulia Matturro in Gabriele Salvatores' compelling *I'm Not Scared* (see page 61)

In America ★★★★

New York, the present. The Sullivan family, being Sarah and Johnny plus their two darling kids Ariel and Christy, smuggle themselves into America at the Canadian border and start their new lives as yet another of New York's illegal aliens, in a wreck of an apartment in block that is defined by the phrase 'cheap rent'. But for all the grime and crime, their building is a magical place seen through the eyes of the children, where the most uniquely human denizens of the city dwell … Jim Sheridan's semi-autobiographical family tale is a wonderfully acted indie masterpiece. Each frame is packed with feeling as each member of the family undergoes a spiritual transformation of one degree or another in the process of adapting to the blood-pulse of their new home, and in so doing escape the profound sorrows that pushed them there in the first place. AK

• *Sarah Sullivan* Samantha Morton, *Johnny Sullivan* Paddy Considine, *Mateo* Djimon Hounsou, *Christy Sullivan* Sarah Bolger, *Ariel Sullivan* Emma Bolger, *Papo* Juan Hernandez, *with* Ciaran Cronin, Nick Dunning, Tom Murphy, Molly Glynn.
• *Dir* Jim Sheridan, *Pro* Sheridan and Arthur Lappin, *Co-Pro* Paul Myler, *Line Pro* Meredith Zamsky, *Assoc Pro* Nye Heron, *Screenplay* Sheridan, Naomi Sheridan and Kristen Sheridan, *Ph* Declan Quinn, *Pro Des* Mark Geraghty, *Ed* Naomi Geraghty, *M* Gavin Friday and Maurice Seezer; *also*: John Williams, Puccini, Schubert; songs performed by The Mutts, Bus Stop, The Lovin' Spoonful, Kid Creole & The Coconuts, Damn!, Culture Club,

Lisa Gerard and Pieter Bourke, Sarah Bolger, The Byrds, Andrea Corr, etc, *Costumes* Eimer Ni Mhaoldomhnaigh.

Fox Searchlight/Hell's Kitchen/East of Harlem (UK)-Fox 105 mins. Ireland/UK. 2002. Rel 31 October 2003. Cert 15.

Infernal Affairs ★★★¹/₂
(*Mo Gaan Do*)

Hong Kong, the present. An isolated undercover policeman is forced to play on all sides of a war between a powerful crime-lord and the authorities when a high-level mole in the police threatens to blow his cover ... This polished crime thriller is a prime example of how East Asian cinema has rejuvenated an ailing Hollywood genre. The two male leads are as A-list as they come. Tony Leung and Andy Lau effortlessly dominate the screen as mirror images of each other and both labouring to resolve the morality of their circumstances. The *noir*-ish story is given unexpected depth by feeding on a drama of moral compromises where heroes and villains are sometimes indistinguishable. Scenes that reveal the private lives of the protagonists into the fabric of car chases, gun fights and action set-pieces, add humour and pathos to go with the headrush of exotic East Asian adrenaline. FYI: The film's Chinese title, *Mo-Gaan-Do*, refers to the lowest level of hell in Buddhism.
AK

• *Chan Wing-yan* Tony Leung Chiu-wai, *Insp. Lau Kin-ming* Andy Lau, *Supt. Wong* Anthony Wong, *Hon Sam* Eric Tsang, *Keung* Chapman To, *Insp. B.* Lam Ka-tung, *Insp. Cheung* Ng Ting-yip, *Officer Leung* Wan Chi-keung, *Mary* Sammi Cheng, *Dr. Lee Sum-yee* Kelly Chen, *Younger Lau* Edison Chen, *Younger Chan* Shawn Yue, *May* Elva Hsiao.
• *Dir* Andrew Lau and Alan Mak, *Pro* Nansun Shi and John Chong, *Ex Pro* Andrew Lau, *Screenplay* Alan Mak and Felix Chong, *Ph* Andrew Lau and Lai Yiu-fai, *Ed* Danny Pang and Pang Ching-Hei, *M* Chan Kwong-Wing, *Costumes* Lee Pik-kwan, *Sound* Chin Wing-lai, *Stunt co-ordinator* Dion Lam, *Sound Designer* Kinson Tsang, *Visual Consultant* Christopher Doyle.

Media Asia Films/Basic Pictures-Metro Tartan.
100 mins. Hong Kong. 2002. Rel: 27 February 2004.
Cert 15.

The In-Laws ★★¹/₂
The adjectives 'madcap,' 'riotous' and 'farcical' all apply to this remake of the 1979 comedy of the same name (which starred Peter Falk and Alan Arkin). However, this new romp works best in its quieter moments, particularly at the start when retiring podiatrist Jerry Peyser gets to know the father of his future daughter-in-law. Peyser is a priceless creation, an orderly being who once suffered an anxiety attack watching an airline commercial. Now his daughter is about to be married to the son of a Xerox salesman who would appear to be rich and insane. As it happens, Steve Tobias is an undercover spy and is desperately juggling his schedule to accommodate his son's nuptials. The chemistry between Brooks and Douglas is wonderful stuff, and the supporting cast is above average for this sort of thing, but the plot keeps getting in the way. It's one thing for Tobias to feed Peyser snake for dinner (Peyser: 'My food is still eating!'), it's another to drag him to France to meet a gay arms smuggler. When it's not being silly, *The In-Laws* is actually quite endearing. JC-W

• *Steve Tobias* Michael Douglas, *Jerry Peyser* Albert Brooks, *Angela Harris* Robin Tunney, *Marc Tobias* Ryan Reynolds, *Judy Tobias* Candice Bergen, *Jean-Pierre Thibodoux* David Suchet, *Melissa* Lindsay Sloane, *with* Maria Ricossa, Russell Andrews, KC and the Sunshine Band.
• *Dir* Andrew Fleming, *Pro* Bill Gerber, Elie Samaha, Bill Todman Jr. and Joel Simon, *Ex Pro* Andrew Stevens, Tracee Stanley and Oliver Hengst, *Screenplay* Nat Mauldin and Ed Solomon, based on the screenplay *The In-Laws* by Andrew Bergman, *Ph* Alexander Gruszynski, *Pro Des* Andrew McAlpine, *Ed* Mia Goldman, *M* Jocelyn Pook, *Costumes* Deborah Everton.

Franchise Pictures/ Gerber Pictures-Warner.
98 mins. USA/Germany. 2003. Rel: 10 July 2003.
Cert 12A.

interMission ★★★¹/₂
Uneven but often very good indeed and with its talented cast giving a superb example of ensemble acting, this Irish piece, strongly written by Mark O'Rowe, stitches together a number of story-lines. Most of these are about relationships in trouble, but there's also a central thread in which two youths disenchanted by life are sucked into a criminal's plan to rob a bank. An intercut double climax misfires and the film's anarchic streak is not always welcome – to which reservations one can add some distracting camera-work using digital video. But there's much quality work here, with some great comic scenes and several touching moments. Shirley Henderson, Colm Meaney and David Wilmot are especially good, and Colin Farrell blends in splendidly. This is a film with special appeal for younger audiences, one that captures the tone of the times. MS

• *Lehiff* Colin Farrell, *Sally* Shirley Henderson, *Deirdre* Kelly Macdonald, *Det. Jerry Lynch* Colm Meaney, *John* Cillian Murphy, *Oscar* David Wilmot, *Mick* Brian F. O'Byrne, *Sam* Michael McElhatton, *Noeleen* Deirdre O'Kane, *Maura* Ger Ryan, *Ben* Tom O'Sullivan, *Mr Henderson* Owen Roe, *Phillip* Taylor Molloy, *Karen* Barbara Bergin, *Celia* Ruth McCabe, *with* Kerry Condon, John Rogan, Tom Farrelly, Deirdre Molloy.
• *Dir* John Crowley, *Pro* Alan Moloney, Stephen Woolley and Neil Jordan, *Ex Pro* Jonathan Sehring, Rod Stoneman, Paul Trijbits and Tristan Whalley, *Screenplay* Mark O'Rowe, *Ph* Ryszard Lenczewski, *Pro Des* Tom Conroy, *Ed* Lucia Zuchetti, *M* John Murphy, *Costumes* Lorna Marie Mugan.

Buena Vista/Bórd Scannán na hÉireann /The Irish Film Board/IFC Films/Company of Wolves-Buena Vista.
105 mins. Ireland/UK. 2003. Rel: 28 November 2003.
Cert 18.

Interstella 5555 ★★★¹/₂
(*Interstella 5555: The 5tory of the 5ecret 5tar 5ystem*)
Unlike many other animated features that have reached us this year, this is a work of specialised appeal. Thomas Bangalter and Guy-Manuel de Homem-Christo, the two musicians who go by the name of Daft Punk, approached Japanese animators with a film concept. It was the story of pop musicians from another galaxy kidnapped and brought to Earth by a villainous record company. Deprived of their memories and made to turn out music under another name, will they recover their past and get back to their own planet, and will the

love experienced between two of them conquer? No prizes for guessing the answers. With no dialogue and a consistent visual style not far from Japanese manga, this is really akin to an extended music video and how much audiences will like it depends very much on their response to the sounds of Daft Punk. MS

• *Dir* Kazuhisa Takenôchi, *Pro* Thomas Bangalter, Guy-Manuel De Homem-Christo, *Co-Pro* Cédric Hervet, *Ex Pro* Emmanuel de Buretel, *Screenplay* Thomas Bangalter, Guy-Manuel De Homem-Christo, Cédric Hervet and Daft Punk, *Ph* Fumio Hirokawa and Haruhiko Ishikawa, *Ed* Olivier Gajan and Shigeru Nishiyama, *M* Daft Punk, *Visual Supervisor* Leiji Matsumoto

Virgin Music/Daft Life Ltd/Toei Animation-Soda Pictures.
68 mins. Japan/France. 2003.
Rel: 24 October 2003. Cert PG.

In the Cut ★★★★

Meg Ryan plays a repressed yet romantic college professor and part-time poet who walks in on a fellatio scene which, it later transpires, potentially makes her a key witness to a murder. The police detective in charge, played with perfect ambiguity by Mark Ruffalo, falls in lust with Ryan's character, who

responds like a parched desert to a rainstorm … Jane Campion's fluid revamp of the noir crime thriller is on everyone's lips for all the wrong reasons. True, Meg Ryan finally shrugs off the kooky nice-girl persona that has dogged her since *When Harry Met Sally*, playing a role awash in animal sexuality. But most remarkable is how well it revitalises the form with some truly memorable characters and an inspired visual sense that captures both the scale of the paranoid cityscape and the careless intimacies of its inhabitants. AK

• *Frannie Avery* Meg Ryan, *Det. James Malloy* Mark Ruffalo, *Pauline* Jennifer Jason Leigh, *John Graham* Kevin Bacon (uncredited), *Det. Richard Rodriguez* Nick Damici, *Cornelius Webb* Sharrieff Pugh, *with* Michael Nuccio, Heather Litteer, James Firo.
• *Dir* Jane Campion, *Pro* Laurie Parker and Nicole Kidman, *Ex Pro* François Ivernel and Effie T. Brown, *Scr* Campion and Susanna Moore, based on the latter's novel, *Ph* Dion Beebe, *Pro Des* David Brisbin, *Ed* Alexandre de Franceschi, *M* Hilmar Örn Hilmarsson; songs performed by China Forbes, Martine Girault, Annie Lennox, Diana Krall, Macy Gray, Zap Mama, Dusty Springfield, Nick Damici, etc, *Costumes* Beatrix Aruna Pasztor.

Pathé-Pathé.
118 mins. UK. 2003. Rel 31 October 2003. Cert 18.

Below:
Jane Campion, director of *In the Cut* (from Pathé)

Intolerable Cruelty ★★★

The Coen brothers' queer slant on the classic 60s romantic farce stars George Clooney as masterly divorce lawyer Miles Massey who meets, loves, defeats, and is eventually himself defeated by the money-grabbing Marilyn Rexroth (Catherine Zeta-Jones in glacial mode) … A pre-credit sequence where sleazy TV-producer Geoffrey Rush catches his wife *in flagrante de pool-man* sets the tone for the rest of this bitter-farce. Clooney's non-stop repartee with his sidekick associate and admirer Wrigley (Paul Adelstein) is the star feature of a film that has no lack of distractingly eccentric bit-players. From this perspective, the film's ponderous fog of romance and cupidity is merely a thematic feint, hiding the real thrust of the piece. But, darned if I can work out what that might be apart from a great big poke-in-the-eye for fans of an insipid genre. AK

• *Miles Longfellow Massey* George Clooney, *Marilyn Rexroth* Catherine Zeta-Jones, *Donovan Donaly* Geoffrey Rush, *Gus Petch* Cedric the Entertainer, *Rex Rexroth* Edward Herrmann, *Wrigley* Paul Adelstein, *Freddy Bender* Richard Jenkins, *Howard D. Doyle* Billy Bob Thornton, *Heinz, the Baron Krauss von Espy* Jonathan Hadary, *Herb Myerson* Tom Aldredge, *with* Julia Duffy, Irwin Keyes, Stacey Travis, Royce Applegate, George Ives.
• *Dir* Joel Coen, *Pro* Ethan Coen and Brian Grazer, *Ex Pro* James Jacks and Sean Daniel, *Scr* Robert Ramsey, Matthew Stone, Ethan Coen, Joel Coen, based on a story by Robert Ramsey, Matthew Stone and John Romano, *Ph* Roger Deakins, *Pro Des* Leslie McDonald, *Ed* Roderick Jaynes, *M* Carter Burwell; songs performed by Simon and Garfunkel, Elvis Presley, Melissa Manchester, Daniel May, Edith Piaf, Tom Jones, Big Bill Broonzy, *Costumes* Mary Zophores.

Universal/Imagine/Alphaville-UIP.
100 mins. USA. 2003. Rel 24 October 2003. Cert 12A.

The Italian Job ★★★★

The classic crime caper, starring the British Mini, gets a 21st century revamp. The good news is that it still stars the Mini; the better news is that it makes its own way rather than re-treading old ground. However, like the Mini itself, the film is a little less British than it used to be. This time round, a group of professional American thieves are betrayed by a Judas in their midst after an enormous gold heist in Venice. Years pass, and an opportunity arises for their revenge. Their success, however, depends on the cooperation of the daughter of their late mentor, who happens to work on the other side of law. As Americanisations go, F. Gary Gray's effort isn't bad. He maintains the light-yet-edgy spirit of the original and has cast the film well. Even the usually wooden Mark Wahlberg musters the craft to get through his

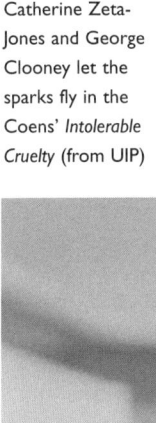

Below: Grievous bodily charm: Catherine Zeta-Jones and George Clooney let the sparks fly in the Coens' *Intolerable Cruelty* (from UIP)

scenes without dropping a clunker. Charlize Theron and Edward Norton are both supremely classy, as usual. But the star turn (in fact, hundreds of turns) belong to the car chases and action sequences, which are elegant, fresh and utterly absorbing. AK

• *Charlie Croker* Mark Wahlberg, *Stella Bridger* Charlize Theron, *Steve Frezelli* Edward Norton, *Lyle* Seth Green, *Handsome Rob* Jason Statham, *Left Ear* Mos Def, *Wrench* Franky G, *John Bridger* Donald Sutherland, *Yevhen* Boris Krutonog, *Mashkov* Olek Krupa, *Skinny* Pete Gawtti, *with* Shawn Fanning, Boris Krutonog, Julie Costello, Kelly Brook.
• *Dir* F. Gary Gray, *Pro* Donald De Line, *Ex Pro* James R. Dyer, Wendy Japhet, Tim Bevan and Eric Fellner, *Screenplay* Donna Powers and Wayne Powers, based on the film script by Troy Kennedy Martin, *Ph* Wally Pfister, *Pro Des* Charles Wood, *Ed* Richard Francis-Bruce and Christopher Rouse, *M* John Powell, *Costumes* Mark Bridges.

Paramount/De Line Pictures-UIP.
110 mins. USA. 2003. Rel 19 September 2003. Cert 12A.

It Runs in the Family ★★

This blatant vanity project boasts three generations of the Douglas clan: Kirk, son Michael and grandson Cameron. The cast also includes Diana Douglas, Kirk's first wife and Michael's mother. The rambling plot has a dysfunctional New York Jewish family

attempting to resolve their various problems and conflicts. Director Schepisi keeps a respectful distance from his cast, bringing little of the edge or bite seen in his earlier work. Now 87, Kirk Douglas remains an imposing screen presence, despite being disabled by a stroke. Bowing to harsh reality, Kirk's character is also a stroke victim. Michael Douglas, whose considerable Hollywood clout got the film made, takes a back seat, perhaps unwilling to compete with his ailing father. Arguably no worse than the treacly *On Golden Pond*, *It Runs in the Family* is just another generation gap tearjerker. A home movie in more ways than one. DO

• *Alex Gromberg* Michael Douglas, *Mitchell Gromberg* Kirk Douglas, *Eli Gromberg* Rory Culkin, *Asher Gromberg* Cameron Douglas, *Evelyn Gromberg* Diana Douglas, *Rebecca Gromberg* Bernadette Peters, *Peg Mahoney* Michelle Monaghan, *Suzie* Sarita Choudhury, *Deb* Annie Golden, *with* Mark Hammer, Audra McDonald, Josh Pais, Kelly Overton, Erik-Anders Nilsson.
• *Dir* Fred Schepisi, *Pro* Michael Douglas, *Ex Pro* Fred Schepisi and Kerry Orent, *Screenplay* Jesse Wigutow, *Ph* Ian Baker, *Pro Des* Patrizia von Brandenstein, *Ed* Kate Williams, *M* Paul Grabowsky, *Costumes* Ellen Mirojnick.

MGM/Buena Vista/Further Films-
Buena Vista International.
109 mins. USA. 2002. Rel: 5 September 2004. Cert 12A.

Above: What's it all about Marky? Mark Wahlberg slips into Michael Caine mode in F. Gary Gray's irresistible *The Italian Job* (from UIP)

Right:
Family on the
run? Kirk Douglas
surrounded by his
theatrical clan
(with Michael
behind him) in Fred
Schepisi's cloying *It
Runs in the Family*
(from BVI)

It's All About Love ★

Despite a promising opening, technical competence
and Joaquin Phoenix in the leading role, this English
language film from Denmark's Thomas Vinterberg is
truly terrible. It's a preposterous futuristic rigmarole
(the year is 2021) in which a world catastrophe is
presaged by New York freezing in summer and
citizens of Uganda uncontrollably levitating. All this
becomes no more than a background concept to
support a story about an ice-skater (Clare Danes)
finding herself so close to death in these
circumstances that her manager wants to replace
her by cloned replicas – a plot foiled by a husband
(Phoenix) all set to divorce her until their love is
reaffirmed. In such a context even a Hitchcockian
set-piece (a mass killing of skating clones) goes for
nothing. Clare Danes gives the impression that she
would rather be acting in another film and who can
blame her?
MS

• *John* Joaquin Phoenix, *Elena* Claire Danes,
Marciello Sean Penn, *Michael* Douglas Henshall,
David Alun Armstrong, *Betsy* Margo Martindale,
Arthur Mark Strong, *Mr Morrison* Geoffrey
Hutchings, *with* Harry Ditson, Teddy Kempner,
Indra Ové.
• *Dir* Thomas Vinterberg, *Pro* Birgitte Hald, *Ex Pro*
Lars Bredo Rahbek, Bo Ehrhardt, Paul Webster and
Peter Aalbaek Jensen, *Co-Pro* Lars Jonsson, Els
Vandervorst and Tomas Eskilsson, *Co-Ex Pro* James
Wilson, *Screenplay* Vinterberg and Mogens Rukov,
Ph Anthony Dod Mantle, *Pro Des* Ben Van Os, *Ed*
Valdis Oskarsdottir, *M* Zbigniew Preisner, *Costumes*
Ellen Lens, *Visual Effects Supervisor* Peter Hjorth,
Ice skating choreography Brad Baudach.

Nimbus Film/FilmFour/Zentropa, etc-Pathé.
103 mins. Denmark/UK/Germany/Italy/Japan/
Sweden/Netherlands/Spain/Switzerland/
Greece/Israel. 2002. Rel: 13 February 2004. Cert 15.

Left: Spirited away: Gotaro Tsunashima and Toni Collette in Sue Brooks' visually distinguished *Japanese Story* (from Tartan Films)

Japanese Story ★★★★

That superb actress Toni Collette has never been better than here (although her supporting role in *The Hours* runs it close). She brings tremendous emotional conviction to this Australian movie in which she appears as a career woman required to cater to the whims of a visiting Japanese (Gotaro Tsunashima) by driving him around. He is a potential business contact of some importance but his desire to see remote desert areas leads to trouble. The tale has occasional improbabilities and some structural problems at the close, but it is visually distinguished, unusual and not to be missed by connoisseurs of acting. Critics were told not to divulge the plot twist and that fact may be read incorrectly as a hint that the piece will transform into a dark thriller. It doesn't. Instead its initial humorous side yields to an effective if unusual love story.
MS

• *Sandy Edwards* Toni Collette, *Tachibana Hiromitsu* Gotaro Tsunashima, *Baird* Matthew Dyktynski, *Mum* Lynette Curran, *Yukiko* Yumiko Tanaka, *Jackie* Kate Atkinson.
• *Dir* Sue Brooks, *Pro* Sue Maslin, *Co-Pro* Brooks and Alison Tilson, *Screenplay* Tilson, *Ph* Ian Baker, *Pro Des* Paddy Reardon, *Ed* Jill Bilcock, *M* Elizabeth Drake, *Costumes* Margot Wilson.

Gecko Films/Showtime Australia/Screen West Inc.-Tartan Films. 105 mins. Australia/UK. 2004. Rel: 4 June 2004. Cert 15.

Jeepers Creepers 2 ★★★¹/₂

Victor Salva's sequel to his surprise sleeper hit is harder, faster and wittier than before. The film is set almost concurrently with the once-in-23-years feeding season of the original film, and focuses on the fate of a high-school basketball team bus on the way home from the State Championships. The victims are whittled away, one-by-one, until the full horror of their predicament descends upon the wide-eyed teenagers. Their only hope lies with the vengeful farmer who has lost his own son to the creature and has transformed his truck into a Creeper-killing wagon of death. A certain level of silliness is granted, but Salva's attention to the smallest detail and his uncanny sense for the rhythm of a creepy scene make for an excellent trashy-movie experience. AK

• *Jack Taggart Sr* Ray Wise, *The Creeper* Jonathan Breck, *Billy Taggart* Shaun Fleming, *Scott Braddock* Eric Nenninger, *Deaundre `Double D' Davis* Garikayi Mutambirwa, *Minxie Hayes* Nicki Aycox, *Andy `Bucky' Buck* Billy Aaron Brown, *Rhonda Truitt* Marieh Delfino, *Chelsea Farmer* Lena Cardwell, *Dante Belasco* Al Santos, *Izzy Bohen* Travis Schiffner, *Kimball 'Big K' Ward* Kasan Butcher, *Jake Spencer* Josh Hammond, *Coach Dwayne Barnes* Tom Tarantini.
• *Dir* and *Screenplay* Victor Salva, *Pro* Tom Luse, *Ex Pro* Francis Ford Coppola, Bobby Rock, Kirk D'Amico and Lucas Foster, *Ph* Don E. FauntLeRoy, *Pro Des* Peter Jamison, *Ed* Ed Marx, *M* Bennett Salvay, *Costumes* Jana Stern, *Visual effects supervisor* Joanthan Rothbart, *Special effects makeup* Brian Penikas.

Myriad Pictures/American Zoetrope-Pathé. 106 mins. USA. 2003. Rel: 23 August 2003. Cert 15.

Right: One from the heart: Jason Biggs tries to keep a handle on Ben Affleck in Kevin Smith's surprisingly touching *Jersey Girl* (from BVI)

Jersey Girl ★★★★

Kevin Smith takes a break from making sarcastic farces to deliver a genuinely substantial family drama of remarkable maturity, considering the source. The film introduces the tough love story of Ollie Trinke, as seen through the eyes of his daughter, the instantly lovable Gertie. Having met the love of his life, the high-flying PR 'flak' Ollie looks perfectly set for an ideal New York yuppie-hood until his beloved wife, Gertrude (played with surprising grace by Jennifer Lopez), suffers an aneurysm in childbirth. The stress of grief and his sudden single-parenthood pushes Ollie over the edge and he loses his job and moves out of Manhattan to start all over again as a street cleaner in his Jersey hometown... Smith has crafted a family film of highly traditional dimensions but styles it with his enviably deft ability to create instantly charming characters that feel real in spite of their disingenuous articulacy. George Carlin is the perfect fatherly foil to Affleck's idealised Everyman, and the rest of the cast practically glows with rom-com humanity. But the indisputable star is newcomer Raquel Castro, a very young actress who has already perfected the art of seducing her audience with no apparent effort. AK

• *Ollie Trinke* Ben Affleck, *Maya* Liv Tyler, *Bart Trinke* George Carlin, *Gertie Trinke* Raquel Castro, *Gertrude Trinke* Jennifer Lopez, *Arthur* Jason Biggs, *Greenie* Stephen Root, *Block* Mike Starr, *Will Smith* Will Smith, *with* Jason Lee, Jason Mewes, Matt Damon.
• *Dir* and *Screenplay* Kevin Smith, *Pro* Scott Mosier, *Ex Pro* Bob Weinstein, Harvey Weinstein and Jonathan Gordon, *Co-Pro* Laura Greenlee, *Ph* Vilmos Zsigmond, *Pro Des* Robert Holtzman, *Ed* Smith and Scott Mosier, *M* James Venable, *Costumes* Juliet Polcsa.

Miramax/View Askew-Buena Vista International. 103 mins. USA. 2004. Rel: 18 June 2004. Cert 12A.

K

Kill Bill Vol. 1/Vol. 2 ★★★★

Hindsight has proved that the best way to watch Tarantino's bloody return to the director's chair five years after *Jackie Brown* is to watch the pair of movies together in a massive, ahem, double-bill. The films follow the story of *The Bride* (also known as Black Mamba, and played magnificently by Uma Thurman), the deadliest of the Deadly Viper Assassination Squad presided over by the eponymous Bill. When she tries to escape the killing into a normal life, the old gang massacres everyone at her wedding and she herself is shot in the head by her old boss, and lover, Bill. But she was not killed. After five years in a coma, she awakes and immediately proceeds to hunt down each of the Deadly Vipers leading up to her final showdown with Bill ... Tarantino has fully abandoned himself to the film geek within and has produced a film that is effectively a high-concept epic love poem to the lurid kung-fu and Yakuza movies and comics he clearly loves way too much. The films is an episodic tirade of genres, styles, mediums (one of the best parts of Vol. 1 is an extended animated sequence), visuals and music. The martial arts and sword-play are so over the top they sometimes achieve orbit. The whole enterprise is kept on course by a script that is consummately witty. That alone is enough to give even this scattered whirlwind of ideas the integrity to hang together well enough to at least be considered a classic, though it fails to match either *Reservoir Dogs* or *Pulp Fiction* for class. AK

Kill Bill Vol. 1

• *The Bride/Black Mamba* Uma Thurman, *O-Ren Ishii/Cottonmouth* Lucy Liu, *Vernita Green/Copperhead* Vivica A. Fox, *Budd/Sidewinder* Michael Madsen, *Elle Driver/California Mountain Snake* Daryl Hannah, *Bill* David Carradine, *Sofie Fatale* Julie Dreyfus, *Buck* Michael Bowen, *Sheriff Earl McGraw* Michael Parks, *Hattori Hanzo* Sonny Chiba, *Go Go Yubari* Chiaki Kuriyama, *Johnny Mo* Gordon Liu.
• *Dir* and *Screenplay* Quentin Tarantino, *Pro* Lawrence Bender, *Ex Pro* Harvey Weinstein, Bob Weinstein and Erica Steinberg, *Ph* Robert Richardson, *Pro Des* Yohei Tanada and David Wasco, *Ed* Sally Menke, *M* RZA; Luis Bacalov, Bernard Herrmann, Al Hirt, Quincy Jones, Ennio Morricone; songs performed by Nancy Sinatra, Charlie Feathers, Isaac Hayes, The 5.6.7.8's, Zamfir, Santa Esmeralda, The Human Beinz, etc, *Costumes* Kumiko Ogawa and Catherine Marie Thomas, *Martial arts adviser* Yuen Wo-Ping, *Fight choreographer* Sonny Chiba, *Anime sequence* Production I.G..

Miramax/A Band Apart/Super Cool ManChu-Buena Vista. 112 mins. USA. 2003. Rel 10 October 2003. Cert 18.

Kill Bill Vol. 2

• *The Bride/Beatrix Kiddo/Black Mamba/Mommy* Uma Thurman, *Bill* aka *Snake Charmer* David Carradine, *Budd* Michael Madsen, *Elle Driver* Daryl Hannah, *Pei Mei* Gordon Liu, *Esteban Vihaio* Michael Parks, *Rev. Harmony* Bo Svenson, *Mrs Harmony* Jeannie Epper, *B.B.* Perla Haney-Jardine, *Rufus* Samuel L. Jackson, *with* Lucy Liu, Vivica A. Fox, Larry Bishop, James Parks, Michael Bowen, The 5.6.7.8's, Sonny Chiba, Julie Dreyfus.
• *Dir* and *Screenplay* Quentin Tarantino, *Pro* Lawrence Bender, *Ex Pro* Harvey Weinstein, Bob Weinstein, Erica Steinberg and E. Bennett Walsh, *Ph* Robert Richardson, *Pro Des* David Wasco and Cao Jui Ping, *Ed* Sally Menke, *M* RZA and Robert Rodriguez; Ennio Morricone, Quincy Jones; songs performed by Johnny Cash, Shivaree, Charlie Feathers, Lole Y Manuel, Malcolm McLaren, Meiko Kaji, etc, *Costumes* Catherine Thomas and Kumiko Ogawa, *Sound* Kerry Carmean-Williams and Dino DiMuro, *Martial arts adviser* Yuen Wo-ping.

Miramax/A Band Apart/China Film Co/The Fourth Film Prod. Co.-Buena Vista International. 136 mins. USA/China. 2004. Rel: 23 April 2004. Cert 18.

Kirikou and the Sorceress ★★★★★

(*Kirikou et la sorcière*)

In a year that has seen several remarkable cartoon features shown in Britain, this is the finest but also the least widely seen. French writer/director Michel Ocelot has brought to the screen a Senegalese folk tale in such a way that, even with the voices dubbed into English (sympathetically in fact), the piece emerges as a work of art rooted in ethnicity. The local elements blend perfectly with a story of universal appeal as a male child, Kirikou, born in an African village bereft of men-folk, sets forth to discover the world and to find ways of challenging the sorceress who threatens his people. A film of genuine charm and splendid imagination, it portrays Kirikou's adventures excitingly, but also offers unforced wisdom advocating understanding over violence in dealing with evil. The colouring is exquisite and the film is unconditionally recommended for children and adults alike. MS

• *Karaba* Antoinette Kellermann, *Uncle* Fezele Mpeka, *the mother* Kombisile Sangweni, *Kirikou* Theo Sebeko, *old man/Viellard* Mabutho 'Kid' Sithole.
• *Dir* and *Screenplay* Michel Ocelot, *Pro* Didier Brunner, Paul Thiltges and Jacques Vercruyssen, *Ed* Dominique Lefèvre, *M* Youssou N'Dour.

Exposure/France 3 Cinéma/Les Armateurs/Monipoly/Odec Kid Cartoons/Trans Europe Film-BFI. 74 mins. France/Belgium/Luxembourg. 1998. Rel: 1 August 2003. Cert: U.

Above: My baby
shot me down:
Uma Thurman in
Tarantino's pulp-
cultural *Kill Bill Vol. 2*
(from BVI)

Kiss of Life ★★¹/₂

An inventiveness in the images and the ability to
show characters who belong convincingly to
everyday life make this a promising feature debut for
Emily Young. It's a misfire all the same. A mother
(Ingeborga Dapkunaite) dies in a road accident but
as a ghost-like spirit she remains the story's central
figure. Her husband (Peter Mullan) returning from
aid work in Croatia and Bosnia is unaware of what
awaits him. He is indeed expecting to discuss with
his neglected wife his failings as a husband and
father due to his idealistic choice of work. We look
for the possibility of some understanding and
reconciliation occurring in the limbo created by the
film, but instead substantial footage is wasted on the
husband's return journey which has no relevance to
the supernatural concept. Mullan and the two child
players cannot save a film that lacks the courage of
its convictions.
MS

• *Helen* Ingeborga Dapkunaite, *John* Peter Mullan,
Pap David Warner, *Kate* Millie Findlay, *Telly*
James E. Martin, *with* Ivan Bijuk, Sonell Dadral,
Natalie Dew, Gemma Jones, Elizabeth Powell,
Heather Tobias.
• *Dir* and *Screenplay* Emily Young, *Pro* Gayle
Griffiths, *Ex Pro* Cat Villiers, Chiara Menage,
Paul Trijbits, David M. Thompson and Bill Allan,
Co-Pro Caroline Benjo, Carole Scotta and Simon
Arnal-Szlovak, *Line Pro* (Croatia) Igor A. Nola, *Assoc
Pro* Christopher Collins, *Ph* Wojciech Szepel, *Pro
Des* Jane Morton, *Ed* David Charap, *M* Matt
Dunkley, *Costumes* Julian Day, *Sound* Simon Gershon.

Film Council/BBC Films/France 3 Cinema/Gimages
Films/Sofica Gimages 6/Baker Street Media Finance/
Take 5/Wild Horses Films/Haut et Court/Autonomous-
Artificial Eye.
86 mins. UK/France/Canada. 2003.
Rel 2 January 2004. Cert 12A.

Kitchen Stories ★★★

(Salmer fra kjøkkenet)

Like another quirky Scandinavian film the splendid *Songs From The Second Floor*, this is a movie blending the humorous and the touching. It's a first feature by Norway's Bent Hamer which traces the friendship that develops between a researcher, Folke, and an elderly Jew, Isak. The latter lives alone and has consented to his movements being studied to assist experts concerned with designing and equipping kitchens. To this end having studied housewives they have now moved on to lone males. The methods are observational and distanced, but gradually Folke and Isak build up a rapport. For my taste the first half is too slow and the humour too slight, but the portrayal of growing friendship is beautifully done and the more affecting for the restraint applied. This idiosyncratic piece is worth investigating by adventurous viewers since many do not share my initial reservations. MS

• *Isak* Joachim Calmeyer, *Folke* Tomas Norstrom, *Grant* Bjorn Floberg, *Malmberg* Reine Brynolfsson. • *Dir* and *Pro* Bent Hamer, *Screenplay* Bent Hamer and Jorgen Bergmark, *Ph* Phlip Ogaard, *Pro Des* Billy Johansson, *Ed* Paul Gengenbach, *M* Hans Mathisen, *Costumes* Karen Fabritius.

IFC Films-ICA Projects.
95 mins. Norway/Sweden. 2003.
Rel: 2 January 2004.
Cert PG.

Krámpack ★★★½

(Nico and Dani)

Although described as a comedy, this Spanish study of adolescence centred on two seventeen year-old youths, Nico (Vilches) and Dani (Ramallo), plays as a drama sufficiently laid back to avoid tipping into melodrama. The boys are best friends staying in the coastal house of Dani's parents who happen to be away, a fact that makes it all the easier to pursue girls. But, as Dani's sexual desires become more apparent, it is clear that it is straight Nico who is the subject of attraction for the young host. The film looks rather dark for a summer tale, but the acting (Ramallo especially) is very good, and at times the film displays both sensitivity and insight. However, these highlights confirm that the rest is acceptable rather than special. The title, incidentally, is a term used to describe mutual masturbation, but the film pushes sexual explicitness only so far. MS

• *Dani* Fernando Ramallo, *Nico* Jordi Vilches, *Elena* Marieta Orozco, *Berta* Esther Nubiola, *Julián* Chisco Amado, *Sonia* Ana Gracia, *Marianne* Myriam Mézières. • *Dir* Cesc Gay, *Pro* Marta Esteban and Gerardo

Herrero, *Ex Pro* Marta Esteban, *Screenplay* Gay and Tómas Aragay, based on the play by Jordi Sánchez, *Ph* Andreu Rebés, *Art Dir* Llorenç Miquel, *Ed* Frank Gutiérrez, *M* Riqui Sabatés, Joan Díaz and Jordi Prats.

Messidor Films/Canal Plus-Peccadillo Pictures.
94 mins. Spain. 2000. Rel: 3 October 2003.
Cert 15.

Kung Phooey! ★

A frustrating and desperate satire, supposedly of the Western view of East Asians through the prism of kung fu movies, the film follows the adventures of a most untypical kung fu hero, played by Michael Chow, on a quest to recover the Ancient Peach from an evil Chinese Madame in San Francisco's Chinatown. The spoofing is broad and low-browed, and what good jokes they make are lost in a flood of bad one. *Kung-Pow: Enter the Fist* did a much better job, and even that was a mediocre effort. AK

• *Art Chew* Michael Chow Man-Kin, *Helen Hu* Joyce Thi Brew, *Master Lock* Jones Chan, *Uncle Wong* Wallace Choy, *Sue Shee* Karena Davis, *Roy Lee* Colman Domingo, *Waymon* Darryl Fong, *Young Helen* Sophie Oda, *Mrs. Herb* Shannon Orrock, *Herb* Ralph Peduto, *One Ton* Fred Salvallon, *Jean-Claude Croissant* Todd Senofonte, *Master Card* John Shin, *Dr Kotzbrocken* Karl-Heinz Teuber. • *Dir, Pro* and *Screenplay* Darryl Fong, *Ex Pro* John Lucasey and Simon Johnson, *Assoc Pro* Michael Chow and Clifford Traiman, *Line Pro* Eric Blyler, *Ph* Cliff Traiman, *Pro Des* and *Costumes* Mulan Chan, *Art Dir* Katho Baer, *Ed* Rick LeCompte and Steven Liu, *M* Ryan Kallas and Kent Carter.

Kung Phooey Prods/Nakota Films/Salvation Films-Mandrake Media.
87 mins. USA. 2002. Rel 24 October 2003.
Cert 12A.

Right: Ealing touch: Ryan Hurst, Tzi Ma, Tom Hanks and J.K. Simmons in the Coens' *The Ladykillers* (from BVI)

The Ladykillers ★★★

Few films have been less eagerly awaited than this Hollywood re-make of Ealing's much loved comedy. Since it's been done by the Coen Brothers as writers and directors, it's nothing like as bad as it might have been. They have opted for blending the tried and true (the original plot-line is followed) with wholly new elements (the setting is Mississippi thus letting in gospel music and turning black the old lady who innocently proves to be more than a match for the team of robbers who take lodgings with her). Apart from J.K. Simmons, whose explosives expert misfires in every sense, the cast, including Tom Hanks and award winner Irma P. Hall as the landlady, all do well. Some broader comic strokes are ineffective and the film unexpectedly works best when closest to the original, but it can't help ending up a pale shadow of the 1955 hit. MS

• *Professor Goldthwait Higginson Dorr PhD* Tom Hanks, *Marva Munson* Irma P. Hall, *Gawain MacSam* Marlon Wayans, *Garth Pancake* J.K. Simmons, *General* Tzi Ma, *Lump* Ryan Hurst, *Mountain Girl* Diane Delano, *Sheriff Wyner* George Wallace, *with* John McConnell, Jason Weaver, Stephen Root.
• *Dir* and *Screenplay* Joel Coen and Ethan Coen, based on the film *The Ladykillers* by William Rose, *Pro* Ethan Coen, Joel Coen, Tom Jacobson, Barry Sonnenfeld and Barry Josephson, *Co-Pro* John Cameron, *Ph* Roger Deakins, *Pro Des* Dennis Glassner, *Ed* Roderick Jaynes, *M* Carter Burwell; Archangelo Corelli, Luigi Boccherini; songs performed by The Soul Stirrers, Rose Stone with The Venice Four, Nappy Roots, Bill Landford and The Landfordaires, Little Brother, Blind Willie Johnson, Donnie McClurkin, Rosewell Sacred Harp Quartet, and Claude Jeter and the Swan Silvertones, *Ex Music Pro* T-Bone Burnett, *Costumes* Mary Zophres, *Sound* Eugene Gearty.

Touchstone Pictures-Buena Vista International. 104 mins. USA. 2004. Rel: 25 June 2004. Cert 15.

The Lady of Musashino ★★★★¹/₂

(*Musashino fujin*)

This is a rarity twice over, being a relatively unknown title by the Japanese master Kenji Mizoguchi and a film from the past (1951) that is not a re-issue but a first-time release in Britain. Characteristically, a strong stoic woman (the splendid Kinuyo Tanaka) is at the heart of it. She's a wife faithful to an undeserving husband, a woman whose sense of honour and family fitness prevents her from consummating the love that develops between her and a cousin. Despite early scenes being set in the last phase of the Second World War, this was made as a contemporary tale and, more convincingly than in the work of Douglas Sirk, a melodramatic plot-line is transformed into a convincing character drama offering social comment. It not only criticises a decadent society morally weak but looks to the future which to have value will need to preserve some of Japan's traditional attitudes. The climax doesn't quite transcend the melodrama but the film is totally fascinating. MS

• *Michiko Akiyama* Kinuyo Tanaka, *Tomiko Ono* Yukiko Todoroki, *Tadao Akiyama* Masayuki Mori, *Tsutomu Miyaji* Akihiko Katayama, *Eiji Ono* Sô Yamamura, *Tamiko Miyaji* Kiyoko Hirai, *Shinzaburo Miyaji* Eitarô Shindô, *Yukiko Ono* Minako Nakamuro, *Narita* Satoshi Nishida, *Takako Sasamoto* Reiki Otani, *maid in the Ono house* Noriko Sengoku, *Eiko* Michiko Tsuyama.
• *Dir* Kenji Mizoguchi, *Pro* Hideo Koi, *Screenplay* Yoshikata Yoda, based on the novel by Shohei Ooka, *Ph* Masao Tamai, *Pro Des* So Matsuyama, *Ed* Ryoji Sakato, *M* Fumio Hayasaka, *Special Effects* Eiji Tsuburaya (uncredited).

Toho-Artificial Eye.
85 mins. Japan. 1951. Rel: 19 December 2003. Cert U.

Lara Croft: Tomb Raider – The Cradle of Life ★★★

The original *Lara Croft: Tomb Raider* was slapdash, witless and one-dimensional, even by the standards of a film based on a video game. Still, it boasted the biggest box-office opening for a movie with a female star and went on to gross almost $300m worldwide. Which shows you how effective a great poster can be. The inevitable sequel is better – but that still doesn't make it a classic. Lara has been bestowed with some romantic interest in the shape of hunky Gerard Butler, the film moves at an agreeable clip under the direction of Jan de Bont (of *Speed* and *Twister* fame) and it all looks terrific. With locations in Greece, Hong Kong, mainland China, Tanzania, Kenya and Bucks, it should damn well dazzle. Here, our Lara races against time to retrieve an ancient orb from the hands of a sadistic megalomaniac (Hinds), who's bent on unearthing the whereabouts of Pandora's Box. Realising her limitations, Lara enlists the help of an old flame (Butler) and sets off across the globe by horseback, jet ski, motorbike, rope, customised Jeep and 'wing' suit. There are some fabulous shots, plenty of cool gadgets, a lot of cartoon violence and a self-deprecating humour that makes the two hours zip by. It's also very silly, but, hey, what do you expect from a video game? JC-W

• *Lara Croft* Angelina Jolie, *Terry Sheridan* Gerard Butler, *Bryce* Noah Taylor, *Jonathan Reiss* Ciarán Hinds, *Kosa* Djimon Hounsou, *Sean* Til Schweiger, *Hillary* Christopher Barrie, *Chen Lo* Simon Yam, *Xien* Terence Yin.
• *Dir* Jan De Bont, *Pro* Lawrence Gordon, Lloyd Levin, *Ex Pro* Jeremy Heath-Smith, *Co-Pro* Louis A. Stroller, *Screenplay* Dean Georgaris, story by Steven E. De Souza, James V. Hart, *Ph* David Tattersall, *Pro Des* Kirk M. Petruccelli, *Ed* Michael Kahn, *M* Alan Silvestri, *Costumes* Lindy Hemming.

Mutual Film Co. & BBC Tele-Munchen Toho-Towa/Lawrence Gordon/Lloyd Levin/ Eidos Interactive-UIP.
117 mins. USA. 2003. Rel: 21 August 2003. Cert 12.

Above: *Jolie de vivre:* Angelina in Jan de Bont's relatively improved *Lara Croft Tomb Raider – The Cradle of Life* (from UIP)

The Last Kiss ★★★★

(*L'Ultimo Bacio*)
Films that are hits in their own country – this one was a box-office triumph in Italy – do not always travel well. Here, however, we have a piece balanced between comedy and drama as adroitly as Mike Leigh at his best. Stefano Accosi is the central character, a man nearing thirty who fears that settling down with his pregnant girl-friend (the splendid Giovanna Mezzogiorno) will stultify his existence. The girl's mother (Stefania Sandrelli) has her own mid-life crisis as she considers making a

break from a marriage that has fallen into routine. Around these figures other lives are glimpsed, but even when his characters behave foolishly writer/director Gabriele Muccino's affection for them remains and it is untainted by sentimentality. This film may not have the makings of a masterpiece but it's an engaging work that sustains its length and newcomer Martina Stella is ravishing. MS

• *Carlo* Stefano Accorsi, *Giulia* Giovanna Mezzogiorno, *Anna* Stefania Sandrelli, *Alberto* Marco Cocci, *Marco* Pierfrancesco Favino, *Livia* Sabrina Impacciatore, *Arianna* Regina Orioli, *Adriano* Giorgio Pasotti, *Veronica* Daniela Piazza, *Paolo* Claudio Santamaria, *Francesca* Martina Stella, *Emilio* Luigi Diberti, *Michele* Piero Natoli.
• *Dir* and *Screenplay* Gabriele Muccino, *Pro* Domenico Procacci, *Ph* Marcello Montarsi, *Pro Des*, Eugenia F. di Napoli, *Ed* Claudio Di Mauro, *M* Paolo Buonvino, *Costumes* Nicoletta Ercole, *Children's Co-ordinator* Oh Baby di R. De Angelis.

Fandango/Medusa Film-Verve Pictures.
115 mins. Italy. 2001. Rel: 27 February 2004. Cert 15.

The Last Samurai ★★★★

1880-ish, Japan. Nathan Algren, legendary soldier and Indian fighter, has drifted into a career as a spokesman for Winchester rifles, a demeaning fate he dulls with a stringent bourbon regime. He agrees to an offer by the Japanese government to train their fledgling army in the art of modern warfare, but is captured in their first skirmish with a rebel samurai warlord, Katsumoto. Thanks to a vision, Algren is kept alive and, thanks to a very Hollywood serendipity, is enough of a natural linguist to learn the tongue of his captors while learning to understand the vision of traditional life that Katsumoto is fighting for … Tom Cruise puts in an admirable performance in what is possible the most impressively balanced action movie he has ever done. Stunning visuals and arresting set-pieces are off-set by some seriously heavyweight thesping, from Cruise and from his Japanese co-stars. The is emotional complexity aplenty, right until to the overplayed heroism that ends the film. AK

• *Captain Nathan Algren* Tom Cruise, *Katsumoto* Ken Watanabe, *Simon Graham* Timothy Spall, *Zebulon Gant* Billy Connolly, *Col. Bagley* Tony Goldwyn, *Ujio* Hiroyuki Sanada, *Omura* Masato Harada, *Taka* Koyuki, *Nobutada* Shin Koyamada, *Silent Samurai* Seizo Fukumoto, *Winchester Rep* William Atherton, *Nakao* Shun Sugata, *Nobutada* Shin Koyamada, *Ambassador Swanbeck* Scott Wilson, *General Hasegawa* Togo Igawa, *Emperor Meiji* Shichinosuke Nakamura.
• *Dir* Edward Zwick, *Pro* Edward Zwick,

Marshall Herskowvitz, Tom Cruise, Paula Wagner, Scott Kroopf and Tom Engelman, *Ex Pro* Ted Field, Richard Solomon, Vincent Ward and Charles Mulvehill, *Assoc Pro* Graham J. Larson, Michael Doven and Yoko Narahashi, *Screenplay* Zwick, John Logan and Marshall Herskovitz, from a story by John Logan, *Ph* John Toll, *Ed* Steven Rosenblum and Victor Dubois, *Pro Des* Lilly Kilvert, *M* Hans Zimmer, *Costumes* Ngila Dickson, *Visual effects supervisor* Jeffrey A. Okun, *Visual effects design and matte paintings* Christov Effects & Design, *Special effects supervisor* Paul Lombardi.

Warner/Radar Pictures/Bedford Falls/Cruise-Wagner-Warner.
154 mins. USA. 2003. Rel: 9 January. Cert 15.

Laurel Canyon ★★★★

With its populace of musicians, actors and artists, Laurel Canyon is to Los Angeles what Greenwich Village is to New York. It is here that Sam and Alex, lovebirds and sombre graduates of Harvard medical school, arrive to start a new life together. He is to work as a resident at a local hospital, she to complete her dissertation on genomics, in particular the reproductive behavioural pattern of the fruitfly. However, neither had anticipated that Sam's mother, a veteran, pot-smoking record producer, would still be in residence at the house she had allocated for them. Sam, who has spent his adult years trying to be anything but his mother's son, is appalled and embarrassed to find her entertaining a British rock band. A good and caring doctor, he has been unable to reconcile himself with the libertine ways of his mother and is afraid what influence she might have on his future wife. Meanwhile, a fellow resident (McElhone) finds herself irresistibly drawn to the troubled young man… A proficient and attractive cast look like they've slipped off some Channel Five soap, but the perceptive dialogue they're handed quickly asserts the film's credibility. This is top-rate, intelligent melodrama, a gripping war film of the domestic kind. JC-W

• *Jane Bentley* Frances McDormand, *Sam Bentley* Christian Bale, *Alex Elliot* Kate Beckinsale, *Ian McKnight* Alessandro Nivola, *Sara* Natascha McElhone, with Louis Knox Barlow, Russell Pollard, Imaad Wasif, Marcia Cholodenko, Daniel Lanois.
• *Dir* and *Screenplay* Lisa Cholodenko, *Pro* Jeffrey Levy-Hinte and Susan A. Stover, *Ex Pro* Scott Ferguson, *Ph* Wally Pfister, *Pro Des* Catherine Hardwicke, *Ed* Amy E. Duddleston, *M* Craig Wedren and Mark Linkous (songs), *Costumes* Cindy Evans.

Sony Picture Classics/Good Machine/Antidote Films-Columbia-Tristar.
103 mins. USA. 2002. Rel: 14 November 2003. Cert 18.

Laws of Attraction ★★

Two warring, high-powered divorce lawyers form
the opposites that attract in this formulaic attempt
to revive the classic Tracey & Hepburn magic in
contemporary guise. As the rumpled rogue, Pierce
Brosnan practically gleams with macho smugness,
while Julianne Moore plays the high-maintenance
prude with fearsome gusto. However, it says a great
deal for the chemistry between them that the best
scenes in the film happen to be the ones nicked by
the supporting actors. Frances Fisher is delightful as
Moore's youthful mother, while Michael Sheen and
Parker Posey whirl across the screen like a pair of
wild children who never learnt the meaning of overacting. But for all that energy, nothing much escape
the sucking bog of schmaltzy lines and an incredibly
overworked plot that sets them on a journey to
Ireland where they fall in drunken wedlock, then
return Stateside where the baffling decision to
'pretend' to be in love is somehow deemed their
best chance of surviving the accidental wedding
gracefully. Of course, love must always triumph.
But that is no excuse for the kind of dialogue that
Sliding Doors director Peter Howitt chooses to end
his film with. Ugh. AK

• *Daniel Rafferty* Pierce Brosnan, *Audrey Woods*
Julianne Moore, *Serena* Parker Posey, *Thorne Jamison*
Michael Sheen, *Sara Miller* Frances Fisher, *Judge
Abramovitz* Nora Dunn, *Leslie* Heather Ann
Nurnberg, *with* Sarah Gilbert, David Kelly.
• *Dir* Peter Howitt, *Pro* David T. Friendly, Marc
Turtletaub, Beau St. Clair, Julie Durk and David
Bergstein, *Ex Pro* Pierce Brosnan, Basil Iwanyk, Bob
Yari, Mark Gordon, Mark Gill, Arthur Lappin, Elie
Samaha, Toby Emmerich, Guy Stodel and Oliver
Hengst, *Screenplay* Aline Brosh McKenna and
Robert Harling, from a story by McKenna, *Ph*
Adrian Biddle, *Pro Des* Charles J.H. Wood, *Ed* Tony
Lawson, *M* Edward Shearmur, *Costumes* Joan Bergin

New Line/Mobius Pictures/Stratus Film
Co./Intermedia/MHF Zweite Academy Film/Initial
Entertainment Group/Deep River/Irish Dreamtime-
Entertainment.
90 mins. USA. 2004. Rel: 7th May 2004. Cert 12A.

The League of Extraordinary Gentlemen ★★

The quantum leap in superhero movies has been
the ability to visually re-create the superheroics
on a scale possible only now with the computing
technology available. Stephen Norrington's
adaptation of Alan Moore and Kevin O'Neill's iconic
graphic novel, which brought together the monsters
and heroes of 19th century literature like Allan
Quartermain, Captain Nemo, Mina Harker (from
Bram Stoker's *Dracula*), Dorain Gray, and Dr. Henry

Jekyll/Mr Hyde to create a Victorian Superfriends,
of sorts, proves that technology is no substitute for
traditional dramatic virtues. In this case, the film is
rushed and so narratively ragged in parts that one
can only be reminded of the rumours of an
exceedingly difficult production with the director on
a permanent feud with his biggest star. So, stunning
photography and graphic design, but otherwise a
mess that betrays some of the smartest source
material a superhero movie could ask for. AK

• *Allan Quatermain* Sean Connery, *Tom Sawyer*
Shane West, *Dorian Gray* Stuart Townsend, *Mina
Harker* Peta Wilson, *Henry Jekyll/Edward Hyde* Jason
Flemyng, *M* Richard Roxburgh, *Captain Nemo*
Naseeruddin Shah, *Rodney Skinner* Tony Curran,
Dante Max Ryan, *Nigel* David Hemmings, *with*
Tom Goodman-Hill, Terry O'Neill, Sylvester
Morand, Andrew Rajan.
• *Dir* Stephen Norrington, *Pro* Don Murphy and
Trevor Albert, *Ex Pro* Sean Connery and Mark
Gordon, *Screenplay* James Dale Robinson, based on
the comic books by Alan Moore and Kevin O'Neill,
Ph Dan Laustsen, *Pro Des* Carol Spier, *Ed* Paul
Rubell, *M* Trevor Jones, *Costumes* Jacqueline West.

20th Century Fox/Mediastream-Fox.
110 mins. USA/Germany. 2003. Rel: 17 October 2003.
Cert 12A.

Le Divorce ★★

Isabel Walker is an all-American girl in Paris, initially
there to support her sister in a sudden divorce from
her French artist-husband. But soon afterwards, she
is seduced by the classic charms of the very wealthy,
very powerful and very married Edgar Cosset …
based on the frisky book by Diane Johnson, the film
is a flat soufflé when it comes to capitalising on the
riches of its source materials. Fine acting abounds
from a name-dropping cast, but the whole is
presented with a reserved temper that frustrates any
chance of a Parisian sizzle. This Franco-American
culture clash has produced something akin to a
low-fat, non-calorie, butter-subsitute croissant. AK

• *Isabel Walker* Kate Hudson, *Roxeanne de Persand*
Naomi Watts, *Maitre Bertram* Jean-Luc Barr,
Suzanne de Persand Leslie Caron, *Margreeve Walker*
Stockard Channing, *Olivia Pace* Glenn Close, *Yves*
Romain Duris, *Piers Janely* Stephen Fry, *Antoine de
Persand* Samuel Labarthe, *Roger Walker* Thomas
Lennon, *Edgar Cosset* Thierry Lhermitte, *Tellman*
Matthew Modine, *Julia Manchevering* Bebe
Neuwirth, *Charles-Henri de Persand* Melvil Poupaud,
Charlotte de Persand Nathalie Richard, *Madame
Florian* Catherine Samie, *Chester Walker* Sam
Waterston, *Magda* Rona Hartner.
• *Dir* James Ivory, *Pro* Ismail Merchant and Michael

Schiffer, *Ex Pro* Ted Field, Scott Kroopf and Erica Huggins, *Co-Pro* Paul Bradley and Richard Hawley, *Scr* Ruth Prawer Jhabvala and James Ivory, based on the novel by Diane Johnson, *Ph* Pierre Lhomme, *Pro Des* Frédéric Bénard, *Ed* John David Allen, *M* Richard Robbins, *Costumes* Carol Ramsey.

Merchant Ivory/Radar Pictures-Fox.
117 mins. USA/ France. 2003. Rel: 19 September 2003.
Cert 12A.

Legally Blonde 2: Red, White & Blonde ★★¹/₂

Spunky pink fashion plate, Elle Woods postpones her impending nuptials to hunky heart throb Luke Wilson in order to go Washington, D.C. and join the staff of Congresswoman Victoria Rudd (Sally Field) to help her pass a bill banning animal testing. Elle seems to have lost a lot of her intellect and education travelling from law school to D.C., but grizzled doorman Bob Newhart is there to coach her through the intricacies of the nation's government. With little of the warmth that made Legally Blonde so enjoyable, Reese Witherspoon still proves that she has what it takes to hold the big screen. Implausible, even ludicrous situations become likable merely for her presence and this not so clever sequel musters a bit of charm despite itself. SWM

• *Elle Woods* Reese Witherspoon, *Congresswoman Victoria Rudd* Sally Field, *Grace Rossiter* Regina King, *Paulette Parcelle* Jennifer Coolidge, *Stanford Marks* Bruce McGill, *Libby Hauser* Dana Ivey, *Reena Gulani* Mary Lynn Rajskub, *Margot* Jessica Cauffiel, *Sid Post* Bob Newhart, *Emmett Richmond* Luke Wilson, *with* Alanna Ubach.
• *Dir* Charles Herman-Wurmfeld, *Pro* Marc Platt and David Nicksay, *Ex Pro* Reese Witherspoon, *Co-Pro* Jennifer Simpson and Steve Traxler, *Screenplay* Kate Kondell, *Story* Eve Ahlert, Dennis Drake and Kate Kondell, based on characters created by Amanda Brown, *Ph* Elliot Davis, *Pro Des* Missy Stewart, *Ed* Peter Teschner, *M* Rolfe Kent, *Costumes* Sophie de Rakoff Carbonell.

MGM/Marc Platt Productions/Type A Films-Fox.
95 mins. USA. 2003. Rel: 1 August 2003. Cert PG.

Leo ★★★

Leo walks a thin line between absurdity and pretension. Any film named after a character from James Joyce's *Ulysses* is asking for trouble. Yet, even in the inexperienced hands of director Mehdi Norowzian (this is his first film), it casts an unusual spell. It is best not to reveal too much, other than to say that it explores some fundamental themes, not least about finding the child that you once were.

Bearing a literary stamp (although based on an original idea), the film unfolds in two parallel strands. Stephen has just been released from prison and finds menial work at a Mississippi diner, run by the gruff and standoffish Vic. Meanwhile, in another corner of the Magnolia state, Mary Bloom is trying to adjust to a new neighbourhood where her husband, an English professor, works. Feeling as isolated as Stephen, she attempts to ingratiate herself into the town's social fabric, but her heart just isn't in it. And, as Stephen attempts to make the most of his new life, Mary imperceptibly destroys everything she holds dear… Beautifully filmed and leisurely paced, *Leo* is a thought-provoking, poetic drama, which exerts an almost dream-like grip. Depending on your nature, you will either find it utterly beguiling or rather unconvincing and silly. JC-W

• *Mary Bloom* Elisabeth Shue, *Stephen* Joseph Fiennes, *Ryan Eames* Justin Chambers, *Caroline* Deborah Kara Unger, *Brynne* Mary Stuart Masterson, *Vic* Sam Shepard, *Horace* Dennis Hopper, *Ben Bloom* Jake Weber, *Louis* James Middleton, *Jack* Don Baker, *Ruth Livingston* Amie Quigley, *Gil* Gil Johnson.
• *Dir* Mehdi Norowzian, *Pro* Erica August, Sara Giles, Jonathan Karlsen and Massy Tadjedin, *Ex Pro* Nik Powell and Derek Roy, *Co-Exec Pro* J. David Williams, *Assoc Pro* Paul Bernard and Amir Yazdi, *Screenplay* Amir Tadjedin and Massy Tadjedin, *Ph* Zubin Mistry, *Pro Des* Stefania Cella, *Ed* Tariq Anwar, *M* Mark Adler, *Costumes* Jacqueline West.

Freewheel International/Joy Films/Scala-UIP.
103 mins. UK/USA. 2002. Rel: 12 March 2004. Cert 15.

The Lizzie Mcguire Movie ★★★

Lizzie McGuire, American Every Teen, goes on a Roman holiday where because of an uncanny likeness she is whisked into the spotlight by a hot young Italian pop-star who needs her to be his new partner at an gong show. But can the gawky American girl transform herself into a suave and sultry Italian diva? Is her middle name *not* Cinderella? Hilary Duff is America's biggest star tweener thanks to the popularity of *Lizzie McGuire*, the TV series. As such, the sitcom-feel of this movie launchpad is to be expected. The film's high production qualities are matched by the wholesome confidence of its star, who is as professional as they come. But the overwhelming whiff of the commercial exploitation of the tweenage market can get more than a little off-putting, particularly for honorary adolescents like myself. AK

• *Lizzie/Isabella* Hilary Duff, *David 'Gordo' Gordon* Adam Lamberg, *Paolo Valisari* Yani Gellman, *Jo McGuire* Hallie Todd, *Sam McGuire* Robert

Carradine, *Matt McGuire* Jake Thomas, *Kate Sanders* Ashlie Brillaut, *Ethan Craft* Clayton Snyder, *Miss Ungermeyer* Alex Borstein.
• *Dir* Jim Fall, *Pro* Stan Rogow, *Screenplay* Susan Estelle Jansen, *Ph* Jerzy Zielinski, *Pro Des* Douglas Higgins, *Ed* Margie Goodspeed, *M* Cliff Eidelman.

Teen Life Prods/Walt Disney-Buena Vista International.
94 mins. USA. 2003. Rel: 29 August 2003.
Cert U.

Looney Tunes: Back in Action ★'/₂

Surely, the whole point of pitting cartoons against human actors is to show the contrast between wacky creatures and flesh-and-blood people? Here, however, the likes of Brendan Fraser and Steve Martin attempt to upstage their two-dimensional counterparts, resulting in face-pulling overkill. In the tradition of *Who Framed Roger Rabbit* and *The Adventures of Rocky and Bullwinkle*, we are thrust into a world in which animated animals interact freely with real-life Equity members, a format which seems to pay greater dividends to the SFX guys than the audience. When VP of Comedy at Warner Bros (Elfman) fires Daffy Duck from the latest Bugs Bunny extravaganza, the babbling bird hooks up with WB security guard DJ Drake (geddit?), who has also just lost his job. As it happens, DJ is the son of legendary movie star Damian Drake, who uses his vaulted position as a cover for international espionage. This might've worked as an extended short, but as a feature it's akin to being screamed at by a pub full of drunk comedians. JC-W

• *DJ Drake/himself/the voices of Tazmanian Devil/Tazmanian She-Devil* Brendan Fraser, *Kate Houghton* Jenna Elfman, *Mr Chairman* Steve Martin, *Damien Drake* Timothy Dalton, *mother* Joan Cusack, *Mr Smith* Bill Goldberg, *Dusty Tails* Heather Locklear, *voice of Bugs Bunny/Daffy Duck/Beaky Buzzard/Sylvester/Mama Bear* Joe Alaskey, *with* Marc Lawrence, Bill McKinney, George Murdock, Ron Perlman, Robert Picardo, Leo Rossi, Vernon G. Wells, Mary Woronov, Dick Miller, Roger Corman, Kevin McCarthy, Matthew Lillard, Allan Graf.
• *Dir* Joe Dante, *Pro* Paula Weinstein and Bernie Goldmann, *Ex Pro* Chris DeFaria and Larry Doyle, *Animation Pro* Allison Abbate, *Screenplay* Doyle, *Ph* Dean Cundey, *Pro Des* Bill Brzeski, *Ed* Marshall Harvey and Rick W. Finney, *M* Jerry Goldsmith, *Special Effects Supervisor* Scott F. Johnston.

Warner/Lonely Film Prods/Baltimore/Spring Creek/Goldmann Pictures-Warner.
90 mins. USA/Germany. 2004.
Rel: 13 February 2004. Cert PG.

The Lord of the Rings: The Return of the King ★★★★

Peter Jackson's conclusion to his truly epic realisation of J.R.R. Tolkien's trilogy is a supremely cinematic experience. Surely, the battle of Pelennor Fields is the most spectacular ever committed to celluloid. The phantasmagorical creatures – the mammoth-like Mûmakil and the screaming, pterodactyl-like Fell Beasts – are jaw-twistingly astounding. The unbounded landscapes, the sound bites of wisdom, the piercing eyes of Cate Blanchett… A production designer's wet dream, *The Return of the King* is the cinematic equivalent of a royal banquet. As a pictorial translation of Tolkien's original, it could hardly be surpassed. Even so, the film is not without its faults. At 201 minutes, it is easily half-an-hour too long (the end refuses to) and it certainly doesn't work as a single movie in its own right. To have a clue as to what's going on in the first thirty minutes, you will have to have seen *The Two Towers* fairly recently. It is a worthy culmination of an extraordinary undertaking, but as an emotional experience it's more likely to leave one with heartburn than a satisfying caffeine buzz. JC-W

• *Frodo Baggins* Elijah Wood, *Gandalf* Ian McKellen, *Arwen* Liv Tyler, *Aragorn* Viggo Mortensen, *Samwise Gamgee* Sean Astin, *Galadriel* Cate Blanchett, *Gimli/voice of Treebeard* John Rhys-Davies, *Theoden* Bernard Hill, *Pippin* Billy Boyd, *Merry* Dominic Monaghan, *Legolas* Orlando Bloom, *Lord Elrond* Hugo Weaving, *Eowyn* Miranda Otto, *Faramir* David Wenham, *Eomer* Karl Urban, *Denethor* John Noble, *Gollum/Smeagol* Andy Serkis, *Bilbo Baggins* Ian Holm, *Boromir* Sean Bean, *Witchking/Gothmog* Lawrence Makoare, *King of the Dead* Paul Norell, *Celeborn* Marton Csokas.
• *Dir* Peter Jackson, *Pro* Jackson, Barrie M. Osborne and Fran Walsh, *Ex Pro* Mark Ordesky, Bob Weinstein, Harvey Weinstein, Robert Shaye and Michael Lynne, *Co-Pro* Rick Porras and Jamie Selkirk, *Screenplay* Jackson, Walsh and Philippa Boyens, based on the book by JRR Tolkien, *Ph* Andrew Lesnie, *Pro Des* Grant Major, *Ed* Jamie Selkirk and Annie Collins, *M* Howard Shore, *Supervising Art Director* Dan Hennah, *Art Directors* Joe Bleakley, Phil Ivey and Simon Bright, *Set Decorators* Dan Hennah and Alan Lee, *Costumes* Ngila Dickson and Richard Taylor, *Visual Effects Supervisor* Jim Rygiel, *Makeup and Hair Designers* Peter Owen and Peter King, *Conceptual Designers* Alan Lee and John Howe, *Stunt Coordinator* George Marshall Ruge.

New Line Cinema/Wingnut Films-Entertainment.
201 mins. USA/New Zealand/Germany. 2003.
Rel: 17 December 2003. Cert 12A.

Lost in Translation ★★★¹/₂

Tokyo, today. Young Charlotte (Scarlett Johansson) meets an older man, Bob Harris (Bill Murray). She is travelling with her husband of two years, a workaholic photographer; he is a film star reduced to making a Japanese commercial for Santori whiskey. These two, each undergoing disillusionment in marriage, find in passing a rapport which they will never forget, even if sympathy and understanding do not build into a love affair. This second feature by Sofia Coppola has been acclaimed by critics. That's justified as regards the superb performances and the expert photography by Lance Acord, but this slow-moving piece is akin to a short story misguidedly extended into a full-length work. It's also the case that the individuality of Tokyo is not caught, but to render it as an anonymous capital city, a modern limbo, may be the intention. MS

• *Bob Harris* Bill Murray, *Charlotte* Scarlett Johansson, *John* Giovanni Ribisi, *Kelly* Anna Faris, *Charlie* Fumihiro Hayashi, *Jazz Singer* Catherine Lambert, *Charlie* Fumihiro Hayashi.
• *Dir* and *Screenplay* Sofia Coppola, *Pro* Ross Katz and Sofia Coppola, *Ex Pro* Francis Ford Coppola and Fred Roos, *Co-Pro* Stephen Schible, *Line Pro* Callum Greene and Kiyoshii Inoue, *Assoc Pro* Mitch Glazer, *Ph* Lance Acord, *Pro Des* Anne Ross, K.K. Barrett, *Ed* Sarah Flack, *M* Brian Reitzell; songs performed by Death in Vegas, Rick James, The Chemical Brothers, Scarlett Johansson, My Bloody Valentine, Kevin Shields, Air, Brian Reitzell, Happy End, Phoenix, Bill Murray, Peaches, The Jesus and Mary Chain, etc, *Costumes* Nancy Steiner.

Focus Features/Tohokushinsha/American Zoetrope/Elemental Films-Momentum.
102 mins. USA/Japan. 2003. Rel: Friday 9 January. Cert 15.

Love Actually ★★★★

With his scripts for *Four Weddings*, *Notting Hill* and *Bridget Jones's Diary*, Richard Curtis has established himself as Britain's leading purveyor of the romantic comedy. Now he has turned director and delivers his starriest, most ambitious project to date, the UK's equivalent to Altman's *Short Cuts* and Paul Thomas Anderson's *Magnolia*. Twenty-two characters, no less, are seduced, battered and disappointed by the innumerable variations of love in a slick, epic and ruthlessly commercial package. Hugh Grant is a funny, befuddled bachelor Prime Minister with a penchant for well-upholstered girls; Liam Neeson a grieving husband who overlooks the romantic needs of his 11-year-old stepson; Colin Firth a cuckolded writer who moves to the south of France to recover his sanity; Laura Linney a shy American unable to express her feelings for a colleague; and so on. The entertainment quotient is so high that you want to forgive the film everything, even its predictable comic set-ups and occasional lapses into utter absurdity. It is wickedly funny, often very moving, and is likely to become a fixture in the British consciousness for years to come. JC-W

• *David, the Prime Minister* Hugh Grant, *Daniel* Liam Neeson, *Jamie* Colin Firth, *Sarah* Laura Linney, *Karen* Emma Thompson, *Harry* Alan Rickman, *Juliet* Keira Knightley, *Natalie* Martine McCutcheon, *Billy Mack* Bill Nighy, *Rufus* Rowan Atkinson, *Mark* Andrew Lincoln, *Peter* Chiwetel Ejiofor, *Joe* Gregor Fisher, *Mia* Heike Makatsch, *Aurelia* Lucia Moniz, *John* Martin Freeman, *Just Judy* Joanna Page, *Colin Frissell* Kris Marshall, *Karl* Rodrigo Santoro, *Carol* Claudia Schiffer *Mia* Heike Makatsh *Joanna Anderson* Olivia Olson, *Tony* Abdul Salis, *Harriet* Shannon Elizabeth, *Carla* Denise Richards, *Jamie's girlfriend* Sienna Guillory, *American President* Billy Bob Thornton, *Carole-Ann, American goddess* Elisha Cuthbert, *with* Thomas Sangster, Lulu Popplewell, Nina Sosanya, Jill Freud, Lynden David Hall, Tim Hatwell, Julia Davis, Edward Hardwicke, Brian Bovell, Richard Hawley, Gillian Barge, Declan Donnelly, Meg Wynn Owen, Jo Whiley, Michael Parkinson, Emma Buckley, Sheila Allen, Ruby Turner, Arturo Venegas.
• *Dir* and *Screenplay* Richard Curtis, *Pro* Tim Bevan, Eric Fellner and Duncan Kenworthy, *Co-Pro* Debra Hayward and Liza Chasin, *Ph* Michael Coulter, *Pro Des* Jim Clay, *Ed* Nick Moore, *M* Craig Armstrong; songs performed by Bill Nighy, Wyclef Jean and Sharissa, Lynden David Hall, Bay City Rollers, Maroon 5, Joni Mitchell, Dido, Olivia Olson, Sugarbabes, Norah Jones, Darlene Love, The Calling, Otis Redding, Texas, The Pointer Sisters, Girls Aloud, Justin Timberlake, Eva Cassidy, Santana, Kelly Clarkson, The Beach Boys, etc, *Costumes* Joanna Johnston, *Choreography* Jonathan Lunn.

Universal Pictures/StudioCanal/Working Title/DNA Films-UIP.
135 mins. UK/USA/France. 2003. Rel: 21 November 2003. Cert 15.

Right: Prime target: Martine McCutcheon in Richard Curtis's entertaining *Love Actually* (from UIP)

Man Dancin' ★

Promoted as the tale of a criminal trying to break with the crime boss who wants him back on his release from jail, this Glasgow-set work is really a religious drama in disguise. Our reformed hero (*EastEnders*' Alex Ferns) transforms a passion play staged by a lovable old priest and ends up persecuted by his former gang boss until he becomes a sacrificial Christ-like victim. Acting and direction could be worse, but there's no conviction whatever in this unlikely story wrapped in a coating of religious propaganda. MS

• *Jimmy Kerrigan* Alex Ferns, *Gabriel Flynn* Tom Georgeson, Kenneth Cranham, *Donnie McGlone* James Cosmo, *Maria* Jenny Foulds, *Terry Kerrigan* Cas Harkins, *Johnny Bus Stop* Tam White, *Flex* Stewart Porter, *Lenny Quinn* Gerald Lepkowski, *Billy Maddison* Ron Donachie.
• *Dir* Norman Stone, *Pro* Ray Marshall, *Ex Pro* Stone, Peter Barber-Fleming and Ray Marshall, *Co-Ex Pro* Christopher Gawor, *Screenplay* Sergio Casci, from an idea by Stone, with additional material from Murray Watts, *Ph* Mike Fox, *Pro Des* Ash Wilkinson, *Ed* Colin Goudie, *M* Colin Towns, *Costumes* Lindsey Davidson and Tommy Hair.

Angel Film Partnership/Jerusalem Prods./Saltire Films/1A Films/Festival Films/The Deo Gloria Trust/Vision Video/Scottish Screen National Lottery Fund-1A Films/Festival Films.
113 mins. UK. 2003. Rel: 20 February 2004. Cert 15.

Man of the Year ★★

Rio de Janeiro is the background for this off-beat tale about a nobody, Máiquel (Benicio), who finds sudden approval through accidentally killing a man who had taunted him about his appearance and who was widely disliked. Having escaped arrest, he finds women pursuing him and offers flooding in to carry out assassinations from those who believe that the original killing had been deliberate. This black comedy finds us being invited to view Máiquel sympathetically, but his own admiration for a racist dentist who hires him makes for uneasy viewing as does dialogue clearly misogynistic. Even if the piece is intended to convey implicit social criticism, it quite fails to make a convincing switch from comedy to moral concern. A repulsive film. MS

• *Maiquel* Murilo Benício, *Cledir* Claudia Abreu, *Érica* Natália Lage, *Dr Carvalho* Jorge Dória, *Silvio* José Wilker, *Seu Humberto* Paulo César Peréio.
• *Dir* José Henrique Fonseca, from the novel *O Matador* by Patricia Melo, *Pro* José Henrique Fonseca, Flávio R. Tambellini and Leonardo Monteiro de Barros, *Screenplay* Rubem Fonseca, *Ph* Breno Silveira, *Pro Des* Toni Vanzolini, *Ed* Sérgio Mekler, *M* Dado Villa-Lobos, *Costumes* Claudia Lopke, *Sound* Tom Paul.

Conspiração Filmes-Optimum.
112 mins. Brazil. 2003. Rel: 29 August 2033. Cert. 15.

The Man Who Sued God ★★

Australia, the present. Billy Connolly plays a retired lawyer who decides to sue the almighty after an insurance company refuses to pay for a lightning-struck fishing boat on the grounds that it was 'and act of God' … As the little guy pitting his wits against the giant insurance company and what could be viewed as the cheekiest get-out clause ever invented, Connolly carries the film along at a reasonably entertaining pace. However, given his larger-than-life reputation, his somewhat muted, rather more family-friendly portrayal of the lawyer-cum-fisherman Steve Myers feels filtered. Given the opportunities to really have a go on a subject laced with potential for the kind of acidic commentary he is capable of, his worldly-wise and avuncular grinning give the sense that the whole enterprise never quite pushes beyond third gear.
AK

• *Steve Myers* Billy Connolly, *Anna Redmond* Judy Davis, *David Myers* Colin Friels, *Gerry Ryan* Bille Brown, *Jules Myers* Wendy Hughes, Les Blair Venn, *Cardinal* Vincent Ball, *Primate* Frank Whitten, *Moderator* Peter Whitford, *Edward Piggot* John Howard.
• *Dir* Mark Joffe, *Pro* Ben Gannon, *Screenplay* Don Watson, *Ph* Peter James, *Pro Des* Luigi Pittorino, *Ed* Peter Barton, *Costumes* Lisa Meagher.

A Gannon Films/Empress Road/Australian Film Finance Corp/The New South Wales Film & Television Office/Showtime Australia/Parasol Pecadillo
102 mins. Australia. 2003. Rel: 22 August 2003. Cert 15.

Married/Unmarried ★★

Originally planned as a theatre piece, this first feature by a playwright who chooses to call himself simply Noli is a dispiriting affair. He's said that he wanted to emulate a European style of filmmaking but his pretentious visuals cannot conceal the fact that the dialogue would only sound at home on the stage. As for his chosen material, he studies two couples with a constant emphasis on sexual detail and on behaviour by all of his characters which renders them unsympathetic (even the women submitting to men who treat them appallingly seem stupid rather than pitiable). Despite a cast who do what they can and some colourful photography that adds to the stylisation, the final credit ('Noli 1') seems more a threat than a promise. MS

• *Paul* Paolo Seganti, *Danny* Ben Daniels, *Amanda* Gina Bellman, *Kim* Kristen McMenamy, *Love* Denis Lavant, *Tanya* Lidija Zovkic, *with* Naomi Sorkin, Gabrielle Richens, Charis Waudby.
• *Dir* and *Screenplay* Noli, *Pro* Jonathan English, Kimberley Barnes and Michael Lionello Cowan, Jason Piette, *Ex Pro* David Rogers and Alex Marshall, *Ph* Paul Sadourian, *Pro Des* Rachel Payne, *Ed* Martin Brinkler, *M* Mark Ryder and C.P. Olins, *Costumes* Suzie Harman.

Fusion International/Meltemi Entertainment/Spice Factory/Great British Films/Enterprise Films-Guerilla Films. 102 mins. UK/USA/Australia. 2001. Rel: 7 May 2004. Cert 18.

Master and Commander: The Far Side of the World ★★★★★

For anybody with a remote interest in 19th century history or maritime conflict, *Master and Commander* is a fascinating and compelling big-screen experience. An amalgamation of story strands plucked from the seafaring novels of Patrick O'Brian, the film is probably the most authentic portrait of life on board a Royal Navy frigate ever committed to celluloid. *Master and Commander* succeeds as a full-bodied enterprise not because of a familiar and manipulative storyline, but because of the minutiae of detail and commitment to atmosphere. From the creak of wood and hemp to the range of nautical instruments, the movie exudes an air of authenticity. It is 1805 and the HMS Surprise has been attacked by a bigger, faster ship, the French *Acheron*. While conventional wisdom suggests that the wounded vessel returns home for repairs, its captain, Jack Aubrey (a commanding Russell Crowe), is determined to out-sail his aggressor and so orders his men to fix their ship at sea. What follows is a compelling log of incident, as Aubrey struggles to retain the respect of his men (including the 12-year-old officer Lord Blakeney), while maintaining his friendship with the on-board surgeon and naturalist Stephen Maturin. JC-W

• *Captain Jack Aubrey* Russell Crowe, *Dr Stephen Maturin* Paul Bettany, *Barrett Bonden* Billy Boyd, *1st Lt Thomas Pullings* James D'Arcy, *Midshipman Hollom* Lee Ingleby, *Joe Plaice* George Innes, *Mr Hogg* Mark Lewis Jones, *2nd Lt. William Mowett* Edward Woodall, *Capt. Howard* Chris Larkin, *Preserved Killick* David Threlfall, *Mr Allen* Robert Pugh, *Calamy* Max Benitz, *Blakeney* Max Pirkis, *with* Jack Randall, Ian Mercer, Tony Dolan.
• *Dir* Peter Weir, *Pro* Weir, Samuel Goldwyn Jr and Duncan Henderson, *Ex Pr* Alan B. Curtiss, *Screenplay* Peter Weir and John Collee, based on the novels by Patrick O'Brian, *Ph* Russell Boyd, *Pro Des* William Sandell, *Ed* Lee Smith, *M* Iva Davies,

Christopher Gordon and Richard Tognetti; Mozart, Vaughan Williams, Corelli, JS Bach, Luigi Boccherini, *Costumes* Wendy Stites, *Sound* Richard King, *Historical consultant* Gordon Laco.

Fox/Universal/ Miramax/Samuel Goldwyn-Fox. 138 mins. USA. 2003. Rel: 21 November 2003. Cert 12A.

Matchstick Men ★★★★

Ridley Scott tries his hand at the grifter-flick, starring Nicolas Cage as a veteran conman who is a bundle of neuroses who is junior-partnered by his exact opposite in Sam Rockwell. Filmed with Scott's usual eye for visual style and an elegant narrative line, the film rides high on Cage's larger-than-life performance, the Griffin brothers' excellent script, and the oodles of naturalism that Alison Lohman brings to her role as Cage's long-lost daughter, who wants desperately to learn Daddy's trade. Essentially a tragic-comedy that blatantly toys with its audience's affections, it is hard to fault Matchstick Men on any technical point, except to say that by the many twists that lead to its melancholy finale it loses the essential heart of a hustler's toolkit … sincerity. AK

• *Roy Waller* Nicolas Cage, *Frank 'Frankie' Mercer* Sam Rockwell, *Angela* Alison Lohman, *Dr Harris Klein* Bruce Altman, *Chuck Frechette* Bruce McGill, *Kathy* Sheila Kelley, *with* Beth Grant, Jenny O'Hara, Steve Eastin.
• *Dir* Ridley Scott, *Pro* Scott, Jack Rapke, Steve Starkey, Sean Bailey and Ted Griffin, *Scr* Nicholas Griffin and Ted Griffin, based on the book by Eric Garcia, *Ph* John Mathieson, *Pro Des* Tom Foden, *Ed* Dody Dorn, *M* Hans Zimmer; Mozart; songs performed by Bobby Darin, Mantovani & His Orchestra, Frank Sinatra, Herb Alpert and The Tijuana Brass, Paige, Kid Rock, George Formby, Roxy Music, Marvin Gaye, Andy Williams, Wayne Newton, Johnny Martinez, etc, *Costumes* Michael Kaplan

Warner/ImageMovers/Scott Free/LivePlanet/ Rickshaw-Warner. 116 mins. USA/UK. 2003. Rel: 19 September 2003. Cert 12A.

The Matrix Revolutions ★★★¹/₂

Picking up immediately where Matrix Reloaded left off, Neo is in a coma, Bane / Smith lies next to him unconscious in the 'real' world; in the Matrix, the viral multiples of Smith grow in strength. And lest we forget the depths of the plight, oceans of metal calamari are bearing down on Zion, the last human city, where every man, woman and child is preparing to make humanity's final stand. It is a hysterically

overloaded scenario that no amount of pseudo-mystical gobbledegook can resolve The final instalment of the Wachowski Brother's 'revolutionary' trilogy mixes fantastical action, space opera plotting, and an embarrassingly pungent wagonload of portentous dialogue with a cavalier attitude towards whatever boundaries of logic remain after the first two films have pushed the series dangerously close to becoming a parody of itself. Nevertheless, there is a great deal to be said for the sheer scale of the spectacle. Wanton destruction and superhuman kung-fu battles never glowed so darkly or looked this good. AK

• *Neo* Keanu Reeves, *Morpheus* Laurence Fishburne, *Trinity* Carrie-Anne Moss, *Agent Smith* Hugo Weaving, *Niobe* Jada Pinkett Smith, *The Oracle* Mary Alice, *Sati* Tanveer K. Atwal, *Persephone* Monica Bellucci, *Bane* Ian Bliss, *Seraph* Collin Chou, *Maggie* Essie Davis, *Zee* Nona Gaye, *Mifune* Nathaniel Lees, *Commander Lock* Harry Lennix, *Link* Harold Perrineau, *The Trainman* Bruce Spence, *The Kid* Clayton Watson, *Rama* Bernard White, *Merovingian* Lambert Wilson, *Ghost* Anthony Wong, *Councillor Hamann* Anthony Zerbe, *with* Kate Beahan, Francine Bell, David Bowers, Robyn Nevin, Gina Torres.
• *Dir* and *Screenplay* Andy Wachowski and Larry Wachowski, *Pro* Joel Silver, *Ex Pro* Andy Wachowski, Larry Wachowski, Grant Hill, Andrew Mason and Bruce Berman, *Ph* Bill Pope, *Pro Des* Owen Paterson, *Ed* Zach Staenberg, *M* Don Davis, *Costumes* Kym Barrett, *Visual effects supervisor* John Gaeta, *Fight choreography* Yuen Wo Ping, *Sanskrit advisor* Andrew Glass.

Warner/Village Roadshow/NPV Entertainment/Silver Pictures-Warner.
129 mins. USA/Australia. 2003. Rel: 5 November 2003. Cert 15.

Ma Vie ★★¹/₂
(aka *Ma Vraie Vie à Rouen*)
This is a tale about a young man (Tavares) given a video camera by his grandmother and the whole film is presented a something shot with this camera – you have been warned! It may look authentic, and it does allow for humour about those obsessed by this hobby, but it soon becomes tiresome. The film has, in effect, been promoted as a work of gay appeal featuring two good-looking young actors in Tavares and Lucas Bonnifait as the hero's best friend. But gay issues only really emerge in the last few minutes and, despite the presence of the admirable Ariane Ascaride in the cast, the other threads of story are so de-dramatized that content runs a poor second to a style which will in any case please very few.
MS

• *Caroline* Ariane Ascaride, *Jonathan* Zaccaï Laurent, *grandmother* Hélène Surgère, *Ludovic* Lucas Bonnifait, *l'homme de la falaise* Frédéric Gorny, *Étienne* Jimmy Tavares, *Madame Langrune* Marcelle Lamy, *with* Nicolas Pontois, Frédéric Sendon, Frédéric Voldman.
• *Dir* Olivier Ducastel and Jacques Martineau, *Pro* Nicolas Blanc, *Screenplay* Ducastel and Jacques Martineau, *Ph* Pierre Milon and Matthieu Poirot-Delpechm, *M* Philippe Miller.

Agat Films & Cie/Canal Plus-Peccadillo Pictures.
105 mins. France. 2002. Rel: 18 July 2003. Cert 15.

Mean Girls ★★★¹/₂
It's hard to keep up, but Lindsay Lohan appears to be the new Hilary Duff-cum-Amanda Bynes-cum-Anne Hathaway. And while we're making comparisons, *Mean Girls* is the new *Heathers*-cum-*Clueless*-cum-fill-in-the-dotted-line. Having said that, this rises above the tide of most high school comedies as it's sharply written, well played and often very funny… Cady Heron is the new girl at North Shore High who, having been brought up in the African bush, thinks she has a keen nose for survival. But the jungle antics of American high school are a whole new ball game and Cady has to learn to adapt in order to survive social apartheid. Adopted by North Shore's two bi-curious outcasts, Cady decides to infiltrate the inner circle of the 'plastics,' the school's teen-bitch royalty. A comic slant on Rosalind Wiseman's serious bestseller, *Queen Bees and Wannabes: Helping Your Daughter Survive Cliques, Gossip, Boyfriends and Other Realities of Adolescence*, *Mean Girls* plays it straight for much of the time and is all the funnier for it. It goes soft near the end, but there are some wonderful performances, not least from Tina Fey who also supplied the screenplay. JC-W

• *Cady Heron* Lindsay Lohan, *Regina* Rachel McAdams, *Ms Norbury* Tina Fey, *Mr Duvall* Tim Meadows, *Mrs George* Amy Poehler, *Betsy* Ana Gasteyer, *Gretchen* Lacey Chabert, *Janis Ian* Lizzy Caplan, *Damian* Daniel Franzese, *Chip* Neil Flynn, *Aaron* Jonathan Bennett.
• *Dir* Mark Waters, *Pro* Lorne Michaels, *Ex Pro* Jill Messick, *Co-Pro* Louise Rosner, *Screenplay* Tina Fey, based on the book by Rosalind Wiseman, *Ph* Daryn Okada, *Pro Des* Cary White, *Ed* Wendy Greene Bricmont, *M* Rolfe Kent, *Costumes* Mary Jane Fort.

Paramount Pictures/Lorne Michaels-UIP.
96 mins. USA. 2004. Rel: 18 June 2004. Cert 12A.

The Medallion ★
Hong Kong, the present. A mysteriously serene Thai boy is the object of mystical desire for a gang of

Above:
A Christmas
Cady: Lindsay
Lohan (right)
and Rachel
McAdams in
the surprise hit
Mean Girls
(from UIP)

villains headed by the improbably arch Snakehead, holding as he does the key to ancient powers including the power to resurrect a dead cop played by Jackie Chan. Too bad he hasn't similar real-world powers to resurrect an entertainment from this messy, unfunny imbroglio that embarrasses all involved. Chan's hyperactive physical clowning is uninspired and the script appears designed to play to all his weaknesses. The UK release disappeared from view almost instantly, for obvious reasons. AK

• *Eddie Yang* Jackie Chan, *Arthur Watson* Lee Evans, *Nicole James* Claire Forlani, *Snakehead* Julian Sands, *Jai* Alex Bao, *Charlotte* Christy Chung, *Commander Hammerstock-Smythe* John Rhys-Davies, *Lester* Anthony Wong.
• *Dir* Gordon Chan, *Pro* Alfred Cheung, *Ex Pro* Jackie Chan, Albert Yeung Sau-Shing and Willie Chan Chi-Keung, *Co-Pro* Candy Leung and Tim Kwok, *Screenplay* Bennett Joshua Davlin, Alfred Cheung, Bey Logan and Paul Wheele, story and original characters by Alfred Cheung, *Ph* Arthur Wong Ngok-Tai, *Pro Des* Joseph C. Nemec II, *Ed* Chan Ki-Hop, *M* Adrian Lee, *Costumes* Grania Preston.

TriStar Pictures/Emperor Multimedia Group/ Golden Port-Columbia TriStar.
88 mins. Hong Kong/USA. 2003.
Rel: 14 November 2003.
Cert PG.

A Mighty Wind ★★¹⁄₂

Christopher Guest, Eugene Levy and the *Spinal Tap* ensemble last treated UK audiences with their magnificently overbred satire 'Best in Show', but passed us over when it came to their follow-up (set in am-dram Americana) 'Waiting for Guffman'. That 'A Mighty Wind' is somehow deemed more audience-friendly that 'Guffman' over here is its own mystery. A gentle rip into the soft underbelly of retro folk music enthusiasts, the style of the film is instantly recognisable as the mockumentary treatment is given to an apparently thriving community of fans who never quite outgrew Flower Power. Premised on the buildup to a tribute concert in memory of a beloved impresario, the cast play their gags straight, but hold back from really going for the jugular. The result is a scatter of entertaining, though not memorable, scenes with a bemusing agenda. And while technically impressive from a musical perspective (Eugene Levy and Catherine O'Hara really do sing well, and Guest actually tours concerts in the US with his screen band, The Folksmen), the point of the humour is blunted by what they claim to be a genuine affection for the music. Which begs the question, why take the piss, if you don't *really* take the piss? AK

• *Jonathan Steinbloom* Bob Balaban, *Lars Olfen* Ed Begley Jr., *Amber Cole* Jennifer Coolidge, *Alan Barrows* Christopher Guest, *Terry Bohner* John Michael Higgins, *Lawrence F. Turpin* Michael Hitchcock, *Mitch Cohen* Eugene Levy, *Laurie Bohner*

Jane Lynch, *Jerry Palter* Michael McKean, *Wally Fenton* Larry Miller, *Mickey Devlin Crabbe* Catherine O'Hara, *Sissy Knox* Parker Posey, *Mark Shubb* Harry Shearer, *Naomi Steinbloom* Deborah Theaker, *Mike LaFontaine* Fred Willard, *George Menschell* Paul Dooley, *Martin Berg* Paul Benedict, *Leonard Crabbe* Jim Piddock, *Elliott Steinbloom* Don Lake, *Mike LaFontaine* Fred Willard, *Shirley Steinbloom* Darlene Kardon, *with* Mary Gross, Laura Harris, Rachael Harris, Christopher Moynihan, Michael Mantell, Bill Cobbs, Diane Baker.
• *Dir* Christopher Guest, *Screenplay* Christopher Guest and Eugene Levy, *Pro* Karen Murphy, *Line Pro* Donna E. Bloom, *Ph* Arlene Donnelly Nelson, *Pro Des* Joseph T. Garrity, *Ed* Robert Leighton, *M* Jeffrey CJ Vanston, songs performed by Christopher Guest, Michael McKean, Harry Shearer, Eugene Levy, Annette O'Toole, Catherine O'Hara, C.J. Vanston, John Michael Higgins, *Costumes* Durinda Wood, *Catheter consultant* Elisha Fiore.

Castle Rock-Warner.
91 mins. USA. 2003. Rel: 16 January 2004. Cert 12A.

Miranda ★

Believe it or not, *Miranda* was developed from a poem. You don't get many of those. Indeed, there are some nice lines in *Miranda*. A Bruce Lee-obsessed sidekick ruminates, 'life's a bitch – and life's got a lot of sisters.' And then John Hurt exclaims that, 'Love – you know it's a myth? It's just an incentive to propagate the species.' *Miranda* is trying to be a sweet, quirky romantic thriller, but its tone is all over the place. Frank represents the film's sweet side, being a gullible librarian who falls for an American beauty played by Christina Ricci. In fact, everybody seems to be falling for Ms Ricci, which is odd as she looks like a chinless Munchkin with unruly eyeballs. Still, the diminutive American star raised the money for this low-budget embarrassment, which at least gave a few English folk some work. As Frank, John Simm is woefully unbelievable, much like the rest of the film. Still, he's better than the smarmy Kyle MacLachlan, who thinks he's in a David Lynch workshop production. JC-W

• *Miranda* Christina Ricci, *Frank* John Simm, *Nailor* Kyle MacLachlan, *Christian* John Hurt, *Rod* Julian Rhind-Tutt, *with* Cavan Clerkin, Matthew Marsh, Pik-Sen Lim.
• *Dir* Marc Munden, *Pro* Laurence Bowen, *Ex Pro* Philip Clarke, Hanno Huth, Robert Jones and Paul Webster, *Co-Pro* Elinor Day, *Screenplay* Rob Young, *Ph* Bill Davis, *Pro Des* Alice Normington, *Ed* Bill Diver, *M* Murray Gold, *Costumes* Michele Clapton.

FilmFour/Film Council/Senator Film/Feelgood Films-Pathé.
92 mins. UK/Germany. 2002. Rel: 7 November 2003. Cert 15.

The Missing ★★¹⁄₂

The hard life of a pioneer-woman is ravaged when her daughter is kidnapped by Apache raiders. Her only hope of rescue comes in the unwelcome form of a father who abandoned her as a child to live with the Indians, and who now returns seeking a redemption she refuses to give … Cate Blanchett and Tommy Lee Jones star in this stylised riff on *The Searchers* directed by mainstream maestro Ron Howard. Sadly, it is a riff without a beat, and all the fabulous long shots and action pieces in Howard's armoury cannot disguise the lack of dramatic rhythm in the film's focus relationship. As father and daughter, Blanchett and Jones miss their marks and leave the audience nothing more than a capable Western that runs too long and says too little. AK

• *Samuel Jones* Tommy Lee Jones, *Maggie Gilkeson* Cate Blanchett, *Lilly Gilkeson* Evan Rachel Wood, *Dot Gilkeson* Jenna Boyd, *Chidin* Eric Schweig, *Brake Baldwin* Aaron Eckhart, *Two Stone* Steve Reevis, *Russell J. Wittick* Ray McKinnon, *Lt Jim Ducharme* Val Kilmer, *Honesco* Simon Baker, *Kayitah* Jay Tavare, *Emiliano* Sergio Calderon, *Sheriff Purdy* Clint Howard, *Anne* Elisabeth Moss, *Isaac Edgerly* Max Perlich, *with* Ramon Frank, Deryle J. Lujan, Rance Howard.
• *Dir* Ron Howard, *Pro* Howard, Brian Grazer and Daniel Ostroff, *Ex Pro* Todd Hallowell and Steve Crystal, *Co-Pro* Thomas Eidson and Sue Berger Ramin, *Assoc Pro* Louisa Velis, Aldric La'auli Porter and Kathleen McGill, *Screenplay* Ken Kaufman, based on the novel *The Last Ride* by Thomas Eidson, *Ph* Salvatore Totino, *Visual consultant* Merideth Boswell, *Ed* Dan Hanley and Mike Hill, *M* James Horner, *Costumes* Julie Weiss, *Sound* Bayard Carey.

Revolution Studios/ Imagine Entertainment-Columbia Tristar.
136 mins. USA. 2003. 27 February 2004. Cert 15.

Mona Lisa Smile ★¹⁄₂

Having stretched her experimental muscles with Steven Soderbergh's smug and pretentious *Full Frontal*, Julia Roberts returns to the mainstream with this American variation of *The Prime of Miss Jean Brodie*. Ms Roberts plays Katherine Watson, a pioneering art teacher from California who's conscripted into the ranks of the austere, blue stocking Wellesley College for young ladies. There, she encounters a variety of eccentrics, from the chintz-loving Nancy Abbey, who teaches poise and leg crossing, to the liberal Amanda Armstrong, who is given her marching orders for distributing contraceptives. Miss Watson herself tries to get her students to think for themselves (she introduces them to a canvas of – shock horror! – Jackson Pollock) but is met with a wall of resistance. From the opening bars of Rachel Portman's gushing score, we are led by the nose down the corridors of predictable cliché as our Julia attempts To Make A Difference. With its filtered light and manicured production design, *Mona Lisa Smile* presents a Cliffs Notes view of art history and is as contrived as Jackson Pollock appeared to be spontaneous. JC-W

• *Katherine Ann Watson* Julia Roberts, *Elizabeth 'Betty' Warren* Kirsten Dunst, *Joan Brandwyn* Julia Stiles, *Giselle Levy* Maggie Gyllenhaal, *Amanda Armstrong* Juliet Stevenson, *Constance 'Connie' Baker* Ginnifer Goodwin, *Professor William J. 'Bill' Dunbar Jr* Dominic West, *Nancy Abbey* Marcia Gay Harden, *Tommy Donegal* Topher Grace, *President Carr* Marian Seldes, *with* John Slattery, Jordan Bridges, Donna Mitchell, Terence Rigby, Tori Amos.
• *Dir* Mike Newell, *Pro* Elaine Goldsmith-Thomas, Deborah Schindler and Paul Schiff, *Ex Pro* Joe Roth, *Screenplay* Lawrence Konner and Mark Rosenthal, *Ph* Anastas N. Michos, *Pro Des* Jane Musky, *Ed* Mick Audsley, *M* Rachel Portman; Mendelssohn, Holst, Berlioz, JS Bach, Saint-Saëns; songs performed by Doris Day, Les Paul and Mary Ford, Perry Como, Celine Dion, Seal, Chris Isaak, Tori Amos, Macy Gray, Nat King Cole, Kelly Rowland, Alison Krauss, Lisa Stansfield, Elton John, Barbra Streisand, etc, *Costumes* Michael Dennison.

Revolution Studios/Red OM Films-Columbia TriStar. 119 mins. USA. 2003. Rel: 12 March 2004. Cert 12.

Monsieur N. ★¹/₂
Exiled to the island of St Helena, in the South Atlantic, Napoleon Bonaparte must contend with his pompous English jailer, Sir Hudson Lowe. So, as the former Emperor of France contemplates a life of confinement, his loyal officers hatch a plan to get him off the island. Largely filmed in South Africa, *Monsieur N.* is pitched somewhere between *Eagle in a Cage* and the more recent *The Emperor's New Clothes*. Philippe Torreton's depressed, if glowering Napoleon has undeniable presence, while Richard E. Grant's enjoyably hammy performance would be more at home in *Carry On… Don't Lose Your Head.* Unfortunately, Manzor's script is neither drama nor thriller, burdened with redundant subplots that stretch the film to two hours. The conspiracy element, involving body switches and suchlike, is more tiresome than intriguing. As a result, *Monsieur N.* seems muddled and unconvincing. DO

• *Napoleon* Philippe Torreton, *Sir Hudson Lowe* Richard E. Grant, *Basil Heathcote* Jay Rodan, *Albine de Montholon* Elsa Zylberstein, *Marshal Bertrand* Roschdy Zem, *Cipriani* Bruno Putzulu, *General Montholon* Stéphane Freiss, *General Gourgaud* Frédéric Pierrot, *Betsy Balcombe* Siobhan Hewlett,

with Peter Sullivan, Stanley Townsend, Igor Skreblin, Bernard Bloch, Christopher Bowen, Michael Culkin.
• *Dir* Antoine de Caunes, *Pro* Marie-Castille Mention-Schaar and Pierre Kubel, *Ex Pro* Teri-Lin Robertson, *Screenplay* Rene Manzor, based on an original idea by Pierre Kubel, *Ph* Pierre Aim, *Pro Des* Patrick Durand, *Ed* Joelle Van Effenterre, *M* Stephan Eicher, *Costumes* Carine Sarfati.

Loma Nasha/Studio Canal/France 3 Cinéma/Scion Films/IMG Prods/Canal Plus/Studio Images 9/France Télévision Images 2-Redbus. 128 mins. France/UK. 2002. Rel: 23 April 2004. Cert. 12A.

Monster ★★★¹/₂
For her role here as the real-life serial killer Aileen Wuornos, Oscar-winner Charlize Theron was made up to look like her. It is remarkable but for those who have seen Nick Broomfield's recent documentary Aileen the impression is of a clever impersonation. In any case the film itself is undistinguished, offering a simplified view of a complex woman. It treats her horrendous yet tragic life as a kind of love story in which Aileen when acting as a prostitute killed several clients for their money in order to build a future with her lesbian lover (Christina Ricci strangely unconvincing). Debutant writer/director Patty Jenkins stresses her indebtedness to movies of the seventies but can't hide the fact that her film is totally overshadowed by the brilliant and moving Boys Don't Cry (1999). That too was a disturbing real-life tale and one with several parallels to this, but it was immeasurably superior. MS

• *Aileen Wuornos* Charlize Theron, *Selby Wall* Christina Ricci, *Thomas* Bruce Dern, *Vincent Corey* Lee Tergesen, *Horton* Scott Wilson, *Donna Tentler* Annie Corley, *Gene* Pruitt Taylor Vince, *with* Marco St John, Marc Macaulay, Tim Ware.
• *Dir* and *Screenplay* Patty Jenkins, *Pro* Charlize Theron, Mark Damon, Clark Peterson, Donald Kushner and Brad Wyman, *Ex Pro* Sammy Lee, Meagan Riley-Grant, Stewart Hall, Andreas Grosch and Andreas Schmid, *Ph* Steven Bernstein, *Pro Des* Edward T. McAvoy, *Ed* Jane Kurson and Arthur Coburn, *M* BT, *Costumes* Rhona Meyers

Media 8/DEJ Prods/K/W Prods/Denver & Delilah Films-Metrodome. 109 mins. USA/Germany. 2003. Rel: 2 April 2004. Cert 18.

The Mother ★★★¹/₂
Making the right choice, the wonderful Anne Reid opted to play the eponymous May in preference to

appearing in *Calendar Girls*. Tackling a difficult subject with frankness but also with understanding, *The Mother* investigates the sexual desires of a woman widowed in her sixties who falls for a much younger man (Daniel Craig). Adding to the complications are the fact that he's not only unhappily married but also involved in an on-off relationship with May's own daughter. The rapport between the lovers is made convincing by Craig as well as by Reid, and Roger Michell's direction is spot-on in capturing contemporary London life. So why not a higher rating? Having portrayed the situation not as a melodrama but as part of everyday life, the writer, Hanif Kureishi, allows the last quarter to sink into improbability. It begins when May draws sketches of her naked lover in a state of arousal and does nothing to ensure that the family won't see them, and carries on from there. But when this film is good it is very, very good and Anne Reid's performance is outstanding. MS

• *May* Anne Reid, *Darren* Daniel Craig, *Bobby* Steven Mackintosh, *Paula* Cathryn Bradshaw, *Bruce* Oliver Ford Davies, *Helen* Anna Wilson Jones, *Toots* Peter Vaughan, *with* Harry Michell, Rosie Michell, Danira Govich, Izabella Telezynska, Carlo Kureishi, Sachin Kureishi.
• *Dir* Roger Michell, *Pro* Kevin Loader, *Ex Pro* David M. Thompson, Tracey Scoffield, Angus Finney and Stephen Evans, *Screenplay* Hanif Kureishi, *Ph* Alwin Kuchler, *Pro Des* Mark Tildesley, *Ed* Nicolas Gaster, *M* Jeremy Sams, *Costumes* Natalie Ward.

BBC Films/Renaissance Films/Free Range Films-Momentum.
112 mins. UK. 2003. Rel: 14 November 2003. Cert. 15.

Mr In-Between ★★★

Photographer-turned-director Paul Sarossy from Canada has retained his eye while making this thriller in Britain. Two themes are combined here. On the one hand, Jon (Howard) has a love affair with the disaffected wife of an old school mate (Tiernan); on the other, we follow the experiences of Jon as a serial killer addicted also to torture who carries out the bidding of a devilish boss known as The Tattooed Man (Calder). Hints of a gay mafia in this connection are offensive, while much of the set-up fails to convince (and it's not helped by glib attempts at psychological depth by name-dropping *Crime And Punishment*). The acting is rather good, but the film is unpleasant and unlikely and the issue of possible redemption, convincingly handled a few years ago in Michael Winterbottom's *Butterfly Kiss*, carries no weight.
MS

• *Jon* Andrew Howard, *Cathy* Geraldine O'Rawe, *Tattooed Man* David Calder, *Mr Basmati* Saeed Jaffrey, *Mr Michaelmas* Clive Russell, *Andy* Andrew Tiernan, *Phil* Mark Benton, *Rickets* Clint Dyer, *priest* Peter Waddington, *dancing woman* Gina Yashere.
• *Dir* Paul Sarossy, *Pro* Adreas Bojohra, Michael Cowan, Yvonne Michael, Jason Piette and Bob Portal, *Ex Pro* Alex Marshall and David Rogers, *Assoc Pro* Adam Betteridge, *Screenplay* Peter Waddington, based on the novel by Neil Cross, *Ph* Haris Zamvarloukos, *Pro Des* Mathew Davies, *Ed* Eddi Hamilton, *M* Jenni Muskett.

Enterprise Films/Great British Films/Phantom Pictures/Spice Factory-Verve Pictures
98 mins. UK. 2003. Rel: 3 October 2003. Cert 15.

My Life Without Me ★★★★★

Who are you? No, really, who are you? It takes a life-challenging event for most of us to even begin to recognise ourselves and Isabel Coixet's perceptive, poetic and profoundly moving film takes a very realistic view of what it means to be human and, briefly, alive. Filmed in a no-frills, pared-down style, *My Life Without Me* shows normal people coping with normal lives, where the prospect of a job can transform the dynamics of a relationship. Ann, 23, is a night janitor at a Vancouver university with two small daughters and a husband she fell in love with at 17. They all live in a trailer parked in the yard belonging to Ann's mother and, in spite of the grey, wet weather and limited amenities, they never complain. This is their reality and they all love each other. But is it enough? One day, Ann decides to change her life and writes down ten goals she is determined to achieve before she dies. Speaking in the second person, she observes, 'you have just discovered that your whole life's been a dream and it's only now that you're waking up…' Written with an acute ear for naturalistic dialogue and kindled with an array of spot-on, intuitive performances, this exceptional Spanish-Canadian co-production might just change your own life. JC-W

• *Ann* Sarah Polley, *Laurie* Amanda Plummer, *Don* Scott Speedman, *Ann, Ann's neighbour* Leonor Watling, *Ann's mother* Deborah Harry, *the hairdresser* Maria de Medeiros, *Lee* Mark Ruffalo, *Dr Thompson* Julian Richings, *Patsy* Kenya Jo Kennedy, *Penny* Jessica Amlee, *Ann's father* Alfred Molina.
• *Dir* and *Screenplay* Isabel Coixet, based on the story *Pretending the Bed is a Raft* by Nanci Kincaid, *Pro* Esther García and Gordon McLennan, *Ex Pro* Pedro Almodóvar, Augustín Almodóvar and Ogden Gavanski, *Line Pro* Jordi Torrent, *Ph* Jean Claude Larrieu, *Pro Des* Carol Lavallee, *Ed* Lisa Jane Robison, *M* Alfonso De Vilallonga; songs performed by Alex Warner, The Langley School Music Project,

Gino Paoli, Omara Portuondo, Blossom Dearie, and Alpha, *Costumes* Katia Stano.

Focus Features/El Deseo/Milestones Prods/
Miss Wasabi-Metrodome.
106 mins. Spain/Canada. 2002.
Rel: 7 November 2003. Cert 15.

Mystic River ★★★★

Boston, the present. Clint Eastwood directs this heavyweight philosophical noir-tragedy about the twisted fate of three neighbourhood buddies, haunted by the childhood kidnap and abuse of one their number by a paedophile policeman. He shows a steady and sympathetic hand, eliciting some startlingly good performances from a cast of skilled veterans, including an Oscar-winning turn by Sean Penn as a criminal clan-leader who goes on a vigilante mission to punish his daughter's killer, with tragic results. The film considers as its themes the long-lived harm to the communal soul that can arise from acts of unspeakable evil, the loyalties and duties of friends, wives and neighbours, and the powerful urge for justice that sometimes overwhelms reason.

The profoundly dark and elegiac tone of the movie demands a bit of work in the watching. In exchange, you'll get one of the most emotionally complex and morally nuanced movies to come out of Hollywood this year. AK

• *Jimmy Markham* Sean Penn, *Dave Boyle* Tim Robbins, *Sean Devine* Kevin Bacon, *Whitey Powers* Laurence Fishburne, *Celeste Boyle* Marcia Gay Harden, *Annabeth Markham* Laura Linney, *Val Savage* Kevin Chapman, *Brendan Harris* Thomas Guiry, *Emily Markham* Emmy Rossum, *Silent Ray Harris* Spencer Treat Clark, *with* Andrew Mackin, Adam Nelson, Robert Wahlberg, Jenny O'Hara, Will Lyman, Susan Willis, Kevin Conway, Eli Wallach.
• *Dir* Clint Eastwood, *Pro* Eastwood, Robert Lorenz and Judie G. Hoyt, *Ex Pro* Bruce Berman, *Screenplay* Brian Helgeland, based on the novel by Dennis Lehane, *Ph* Tom Stern, *Pro Des* Henry Bumstead, *Ed* Joel Cox, *M* Eastwood, *Costumes* Deborah Hopper.

Warner/Village Roadshow/NPV Entertainment/
Malpaso-Warner.
137 mins. USA/Australia. 2003.
Rel: 17 October 2003. Cert 15.

Right: Father of the pride: Sean Penn in his Oscar-winning performance in Clint Eastwood's nuanced, accomplished *Mystic River* (from Warner)

Left: Bushwhacked: Heath Ledger in Gregor Jordan's sombre, disturbing *Ned Kelly* (from UIP)

Ned Kelly ★★★¹/₂

The latest in a long line of films based on Australia's own Robin Hood/Jesse James legend, Gregor Jordan's telling of the story of Ned Kelly features an outstanding cast and lavish period staging that pushes the dramatic threads of the legend to the fore. Aspects of the Ned Kelly legend are almost now stock and trade clichés of folk heroics. Oppressed by the heavy hand of the law, falsely accused of crimes he did not commit, he is compelled into the life of an outlaw who keeps a lookout for the wellbeing of his friends and neighbours. But when the ruthless lawman arrives in the form of Geoffrey Rush's impassive Superintendent Francis Hare, the stakes are raised and Kelly soon raises a challenge to the entire Australian government in his famously dictated note. Heath Ledger carries the weight of a national legend with grim style, supported by a fine cast and an elegantly written script. AK

• *Ned Kelly* Heath Ledger, *Joe Byrne* Orlando Bloom, *Julia Cook* Naomi Watts, *Superintendent Francis Hare* Geoffrey Rush, *Aaron Sherritt* Joel Edgerton, *Mrs Scott* Rachel Griffiths, *Dan Kelly* Laurence Kinlan, *Steve Hart* Philip Barantini, *Fitzpatrick* Kiri Paramore, *Kate Kelly* Kerry Condon, *Grace Kelly* Emily Browning, *Mr Scott* Geoff Morrell, *Premier Berry* Charles 'Bud' Tingwell, *with* Saskia Burmeister, Peter Phelps, Russell Dykstra, Nicholas Bell, Andrew S. Gilbert.
• *Dir* Gregor Jordan, *Pro* Lynda House and Nelson Woss, *Ex Pro* Tim Bevan, Eric Fellner and Tim White, *Co-Pro* Debra Hayward and Liza Chasin, *Line Pro* Catherine Bishop, *Screenplay* John Michael McDonagh, based on the novel *Our Sunshine* by Robert Drewe, *Ph* Oliver Stapleton, *Pro Des* Steven Jones-Evans, *Ed* Jon Gregory, *M* Klaus Badelt, *Costumes* Anna Borghesi.

Universal Pictures/StudioCanal/Working Title/Endymion Films-UIP.
109 mins. Australia/UK/USA/France. 2003.
Rel: 26 September 2003. Cert. 15.

9 Dead Gay Guys ★★★★

This is a film that needs to be taken for what it is: an updated *Carry On* with all the crude sexual frankness of modern alternative comedy. If it's subtlety or sophistication you want, look elsewhere. The story-line concerns two Irish youths servicing older gay men in London and seeking hidden money by tracing the man who may know of its whereabouts, a killer with a willy of only three and a half inches. But the cartoonish plot is only an excuse to be outrageous, and this is done in a manner both lively and knowing about stereotypes. Although some have been offended including homosexuals, this film is never anti-gay, but a work that embraces in its own vulgar way all sexuality. Indeed, by eventually revealing that its two heroes are in reality gay themselves it totally undermines any homophobic response. MS

• *Kenny* Glenn Mulhern, *Byron* Brendan Mackey, *Jeff* Steven Berkoff, *The Queen* Michael Praed, *'Donkey' Dick Clark* Vas Blackwood, *Golders Green* Simon Godley, *Desperate Dwarf* Raymond Griffiths, *Old Nick* Fish, *Jeff's wife* Carol Decker, *the Iron Lady* Karen Sharman, *with* Abdala Keserwani, Leon Herbert, Bill Hayes.
• *Dir* and *Screenplay* Lab Ky Mo, *Pro* Lamia Nayeb-St. Hilaire, *Ex Pro* Amit Barooah, Robert Bevan, Amanda Coombes, Peter Errington, Andrew Melmore and Charlie Savill, *Assoc Pro* Helena Mackenzie and Simon Barnes, *Ph* Damien Elliott, *Pro Des* Nik Callan, *Ed* Chris Blunden and

Jonathan Braman, *M* Stephen W. Parsons, *Costumes* Jane Spicer.

Little Wing Films/9 Films-Guerilla Films. 82 mins. UK. 2002. Rel: 19 September 2003. Cert. 18.

Nói Albinói ★★★

Set in a remote part of Iceland and well cast, writer/director Dagur Kári has produced a first feature of interest. As a tragic-comedy with Nói a bald seventeen year-old as its rebel hero, it carries echoes of such disparate talents as Aki Kaurismäki and David Gordon Green. The youth's disdainful attitude at school and his dreams of persuading his girlfriend to go abroad with him fuel a very slow-moving narrative. Unfortunately, the film never makes it clear if it is to be taken as social comment (we see too little of the community which may offer few prospects for Nói's generation) or as a personal drama (Nói may have been an unwanted child but we need to know more about his background). When the film opts for a conclusion brought about by an act of nature you feel that it has failed to deliver any clear message. MS

• *Nói* Tómas Lemarquis, *Kiddi Beikon* Throstur Leó Gunnarsson, *Íris* Elin Handsóttir.
• *Dir* and *Screenplay* Dagur Kári, *Pro* Philippe Bober, Kim Magnusson, Skuli Fr. Malmqvist, Thorir Snaer Sigurjonsson, *Ph* Rasmus Videbæk, *Pro Des* Jón Steinar Ragnarsson, *Ed* Daniel Dencik, *M* Slowblow, *Costumes* Linda B. Árnadóttir and Tanja Dehmel.

Zik Zak Kvikmyndir-Artificial Eye. 92 mins. Iceland/Germany/UK/Denmark. 2002. Rel: 14 November 2003. Cert. 15.

Northfork ★★★

A newly built dam threatens the dying community of Northfork with the Noah-esque flood, and a team of black-suited men are charged with the removal of the last few stragglers before the valley is filled. Meanwhile, a priest watches over an angelic orphan, who is possibly dreaming of finding a new home with a family of queer travellers who may be searching for a lost angel themselves … The surrealistic strands that tickle the opening scenes grow into a river by then end this a beautifully shot but frustratingly obscure movie. Nick Nolte growls so unintelligibly that his scenes are almost mime dramatics, and it is hard work making any sense of the ragged band of angel-hunters as they bounce through half-finished conversations and non-sequitors. The most entertainment to be got comes from the stories surrounding the movers who must persuade the last eccentrics of Northfork to leave before the flood. AK

• *Father Harlan* Nick Nolte, *Flower Hercules* Daryl Hannah, *Walter O'Brien* James Woods, *Eddie* Peter Coyote, *Happy* Anthony Edwards, *Mr Hope* Kyle MacLachlan, *Willis O'Brien* Mark Polish, *Mrs Hadfield* Claire Forlani, *Irwin* Duel Farnes, *Marvin* Graham Beckel, *Matt* Joshuin Barker, *Arnold* Jon Gries, *Cup of Tea* Robin Sachs, *Cod* Ben Foster, *Mr Stalling* Marshall Bell, *Mrs Hope* Michele Hicks, *with* Douglas Sebern, Rick Overton, Mike Regan.
• *Dir* Michael Polish, *Pro* Mark Polish and Michael Polish, *Ex Pro* Paul F. Mayersohn, James Woods, Anthony Romano, Michel Shane, Janet Jensen and Damon Martin, *Co-Pro* Todd King and Paul Torok, *Co-Ex Pro* Bruce E. Jones, Barbara A. Jones and Gil Amaral, *Screenplay* Mark Polish, Michael Polish, *Ph* M. David Mullen, *Pro Des* Ichelle Spitzig and Del Polish, *Ed* Leo Trombetta, *M* Stuart Matthewman, *Costumes* Danny Glicker, *Oil paintings* Sean Cheetham.

Romano/Shane Prods/ Departure Entertainment/Prohibition Pictures -Metrodome. 103 mins. USA. 2002. Rel: 12 March 2004. Cert. PG.

The Notebook ★★★

Publicised as 'the most romantic movie since *Titanic*', this film is something of a surprise. Made by Nick Cassavetes (son of John, famed champion of independent movies) and starring Ryan Gosling who was brilliant in that disturbing piece *The Believer*, it also finds supporting roles for such admirable artists as Joan Allen, James Garner and (the one thing that is predictable) the director's mother Gena Rowlands. These are not the artists you expect to appear in a love story that is pure Mills and Boon. It's a tale that plays out both in the present and in the 1940s and, despite being over-long, the good performances should ensure that those who like this kind of thing will enjoy it. Others, however, will bemoan the waste of talent. MS

• *Noah Calhoun* Ryan Gosling, *Allie Hamilton* Rachel McAdams, *Duke* James Garner, *Allie Calhoun* Gena Rowlands, *Lon* James Marsden, *Frank Calhoun* Sam Shepard, *Anne Hamilton* Joan Allen *Fin* Kevin Connolly, *John Hamilton* David Thornton, *Martha Shaw* Jamie Anne Brown, *Sarah Tuffington* Heather Wahlquist.
• *Dir* Nick Cassavetes, *Pro* Mark Johnson and Lynn Harris, *Ex Pro* Toby Emmerich and Avram Butch Kaplan, *Scr* Jeremy Leven, *Adaptation* Jan Sardi, based on the novel by Nicholas Sparks, *Ph* Robert Fraisse, *Pro Des* Sarah Knowles, *Ed* Alan Heim, *M* Aaron Zigman, *Costumes* Karyn Wagner.

New Line Cinema/Gran Via-Entertainment. 121 mins. USA. 2004. Rel: 25 June 2004. Cert. 12A.

Octane ★★★

An eye fills the screen. It is closed and upside down and as the eyeball twitches beneath the lid, it resembles a mouth striving to utter some unspeakable truth. Such striking imagery is a hallmark of the British commercials director Marcus Adams, whose first film, *Long Time Dead* (2002), was a minor success. Octane, a thriller that fits loosely in a genre occupied by *Duel*, *Roadkill* and *Jeepers Creepers*, is a suspenseful, visceral feast that preys on our worst fears of the open road. Senga Wilson (Madeleine Stowe) is driving her teenage daughter home and is struggling to stay awake at the wheel. It is night, there is tension in the car and a horrific wreck is holding up traffic. Indeed, it's a highly unpleasant journey and Senga's unease is fuelled by unsettling sights along the road: a child's doll caught under the wheels of a juggernaut, the menacing stares of long-haul truck drivers and a demure couple who seem to be at every rest-stop along the route. What the hell is going on? A lot, as it happens, and Adams pulls out all the stops as Senga's journey spirals into a living nightmare that seems to make no sense. By aligning our heroine's confusion with our own, *Octane* retains its grip on the viewer, making for a stylish, unnerving experience. JC-W

• *Senga* Madeleine Stowe, *recovery man* Norman Reedus, *backpacker* Bijou Phillips, *Nat* Mischa Barton, *'The Father'* Jonathan Rhys-Meyers, *with* Leo Gregory, Gary Parker, Tom Hunsinger.
• *Dir* Marcus Adams, *Pro* Alistair MacLean Clark and Basil Stephens, *Ex Pro* Tim Smith, Carlo Dusi, Melvyn Singer and Bill Allan, *Screenplay* Stephen Volk, *Ph* Robin Vidgeon, *Pro Des* Max Gottlieb, *Ed* Trevor Waite, *M* Orbital, *Costumes* Stewart Meachem.

Four Horseman Films/Random Harvest/Harvest Pictures/Take 4 Partnerships/High Octane-Buena Vista International.
90 mins. UK/Luxembourg. 2003.
Rel: 14 November 2003. Cert 15.

Okay ★★★¹/₂

The title sums it up. This Danish film from Jesper W. Nielsen echoes *Italian for Beginners* in being a tragi-comedy. However, it aims at a slightly darker tone since it turns on a rickety marriage not helped when the wife, Agnethe (Paprika Steen), agrees to take in her terminally ill father (Ole Ernst) who proves a long time a-dying and is a disruptive influence. But will there be time for Agnethe to mend his relationship with her gay brother (Nikolaj Kopernikus), and will the latter donate his sperm to a lesbian couple anxious for a child? Will Agnethe's marriage survive her husband's affair with one of his students? It's all watchable but, compared with the

Left:
Jonathan Rhys-Meyers in Marcus Adams' stylish, unnerving *Octane* (from BVI)

impressive *Open Hearts* (which also stars Paprika Steen), this seems like soap opera, albeit good soap opera. MS

• *Nete* Paprika Steen, *Johannes* Ole Ernst, *Kristian* Troels Lyby, *Martin* Nicolaj Kopernikus, *Katrine, the daughter* Molly Blixt Egelind, *Tanja* Laura Drasbæk, *Trisse* Trine Dyrholm, *Janni* Lotte Merete Andersen, *doctor* Jesper Christensen.
• *Dir* Jesper W Nielsen, *Pro* Peter Bech, *Ex Pro* Mogens Glad, Poul Erik Lindeborg, *Screenplay* Kim Fupz Aakeson, *Ph* Erik Zappon, *Pro Des* Peter De Neergaard, *Ed* Morten Giese, *M* Halfden E, *Costumes* Stine Gudmundsen-Holmgreen and Ingrid Søe.

Bavaria Film/Bech Film-Metropolis Films.
97 mins. Denmark/Norway/Germany. 2002.
Rel: 17 October 2003. Cert 15.

Once Upon a Time in Mexico ★★★¹/₂

Robert Rodriguez's guitar strumming assassin from *El Mariachi* and *Desperado* makes a glorious, gory, and glib comeback in high Technicolor style. Once again, it is revenge that drives his ludicrous killing spree, as he is persuaded by a CIA agent (a cynically cheerful Johnny Depp, who is enjoying a private joke throughout the movie) to kill the General who murdered his wife and daughter. But there is more to this tamale than meets the eye, because the General is also involved in a cross-eyed coup planned by a psychotic cocaine warlord (a beautiful piece of exaggeration by Willem Dafoe). Welcome to the fever season of double-double-cross! Taken with a dash of tequila and salt, Rodriguez's Sergio Leone homage is tons of fun to watch. Cribbing heavily from the Tarantino rule-book (philosophical monologues, yoga-pretzel plotting, cheeky

coincidences, hundreds killed bullet-poisoning …) Rodriguez actually pulls off what must have been the high-concept of his career: 'Sergio Leone does *Pulp Fiction*'. AK

• *El Mariachi* Antonio Banderas, *Carolina* Salma Hayek, *Agent Sands* Johnny Depp, *Billy Chambers* Mickey Rourke, *Ajedrez* Eva Mendes, *Cucuy* Danny Trejo, *Lorenzo* Enrique Iglesias, *Fideo* Marco Leonardi, *Belini* Cheech Marin, *Jorge FBI* Rubén Blades, *Barillo* Willem Dafoe, *president* Pedro Armendáriz.
• *Dir*, *Scr*, *Ph*, *Pro Des*, *Ed* and *M* Robert Rodriguez, *Pro* Rodriguez, Elizabeth Avellán and Carlos Gallardo, *Costumes* Graziela Mazon.

Columbia/Dimension Films/Troublemaker Studios-Buena Vista International.
101 mins. USA. 2003. Rel: 26 September 2003. Cert 15.

One Last Chance ★★★

Like so many British films of late, *One Last Chance* features gangsters, corpses and its fair share of ripe language. But the film's tone is more Local Hero than The Long Good Friday, its droll, laid-back nature recalling the sardonic wit of our Scandinavian

cousins. Indeed, the film happens to be a Scottish-Norwegian co-production (it is produced by one Orjan Karlsen) and is a gentle riot. It opens promisingly as our young hero, Fitz, contemplates the isolation of his existence: 'At Christmas, if you didn't wake up with an erection, chances are you wouldn't have anything to play with.' Fitz grows up and remains in the nowhere town of Tullybridge, dreaming of an escape route. When, finally, his girlfriend convinces him to leave, Fate steps in and delivers a number of unexpected body blows. Whether or not one tunes into the film's comic frequency, it's refreshing to encounter a narrative in which the protagonists travel by bus and where £1,000 still seems like a king's ransom. Previously known as *The Bums' Rush*. JC-W

• *Seany* Kevin McKidd, *Fitz* Jamie Sives, *Nellie* Iain Robertson, *Barbara* Neve McIntosh, *Harry* Jimmy Chisholm, *Fitz's father* Ewan Stewart, *Big John* James Cosmo, *young Fitz* Lewis Kay, *Frankie the Fence* Dougray Scott, *Aunt Jean* Sandy McDade, *with* Rupert Vansittart, Julie Miller, Brian Pettifer, Niall Greig Fulton, Paul Young, William Armour, Jonathan Hackett.
• *Dir* and *Screenplay* Stewart Svaasand, *Pro* Anne Batz, *Ex Pro* Dougray Scott, Steve Robbins and Jim

Reeve, *Co-Pro* Orjan Karlsen and Peter Gallagher, *Ph* Svein Krøvel, *Pro Des* Pat Campbell, *Ed* St John O'Rorke, *M* Donald Shaw, *Costumes* Kate Carin, *Sound* Arne Hansen, *Production accountant* Elizabeth Hurley.

Scottish Screen/Visionview/Momentum Pictures/Glasgow Film Office/Hero Film/National Lottery, etc-Momentum. 96 mins. Scotland/Norway. 2003. Rel: 12 March 2004. Cert 15.

On the Run
See *La Trilogie*

The Order
See *Sin Eater*

Open Range ★★
Somewhere in the West, probably Montana, a small band of free-grazers wander into the avaricious sights of Denton Baxter, an imperious Irish-born rancher who intends to steal their herd, over dead bodies if necessary. At this point Kevin Costner's return into *Dances With Wolves* territory reads like a standard 'little guy versus the big guy' Western. But the film's ambitions go way beyond the generic buildup of cowboy nostalgia that leads finally to a blazing showdown. The film devotes much to the prosaic parts of cowboy existence usually reduced to a few artfully lit campfire scenes. So betwixt the odd action sequence, and clumsy conversation, we are treated to the bitter and mundane particulars of men apparently rationed to a few words a week. The photography is never short of excellent with James Muro debuting strongly behind the lens. But Kevin Costner the director fails the film's potential by being so enamoured with the detail he forgets to sculpt the narrative elegance essential to the genre. AK

• *Bluebonnet `Boss' Spearman* Robert Duvall, *Charles Travis Postewaite* aka *`Charley Waite'* Kevin Costner, *Sue Barlow* Annette Bening, *Denton Baxter* Michael Gambon, *Percy* Michael Jeter, *Button* Diego Luna, *Sheriff Poole* James Russo, *Mose Harrison* Abraham Benrubi, *Doc Walter Barlow* Dean McDermott, *Butler* Kim Coates, *with* Peter McNeill, Julian Richings, Tom Carey.
• *Dir* Kevin Costner, *Pro* Costner, David Valdes and Jake Eberts, *Ex Pro* Armyan Bernstein and Craig Storper, *Screenplay* Craig Storper, based on the novel *The Open Range Men* by Lauran Paine, *Ph* James Muro, *Pro Des* Gae Buckley, *Ed* Michael J. Duthie and Miklos Wright, *M* Michael Kamen, *Costumes* John Bloomfield.

Touchstone Pictures/Cobalt Media Group/Tig-Winchester Entertainment. 138 mins. USA/UK. 2003. Rel: 19 March 2004. Cert. 12A.

Osama ★★★★
Small-scale but satisfying, this is an insider's view of life in Afghanistan during the period of the Taliban rule. The filmmaker Siddiq Barmak has a background in documentary but here uses non-professional players quite splendidly to tell of a family struggling to survive after being deprived of their men-folk by the war. Regulations inhibit this and, when the mother loses her job through a hospital closure, it becomes necessary to send her daughter to work and to pass her off as a boy, Osama, because girls cannot be employed. The early scenes are somewhat uneasily poised between neo-realism and a hint of Eisenstein's grand manner. However, the story increasingly grips as the young heroine, quite marvellously played by Marina Golbahari, finds herself endangered when taken for training by the Taliban who have failed to penetrate her disguise. This fictional tale reflecting recent realities is highly accessible and very worthwhile. MS

• *Osama* Marina Golbahari, *Espandi* Arif Herati, *mother* Zubaida Sahar, *with* Khwaja Nader, Mohamad Aref Harati, Hamida Refah, Gol Rahman Ghorbandi.
• *Dir, Screenplay* and *Ed* Siddiq Barmak, *Pro* Barmak, Julie LeBrocquy and Julia Fraser, *Ph* Ebrahim Ghafuri, *Pro Des* Akbar Meshkini, *M* Mohammad Reza Darwishi, *Sound* Faroukh Fadai and Behreuz Shahamat

Barmak Films/leBrocquy Fraser//NHK-ICA Projects. 83 mins. Afghanistan/Ireland/Japan. 2003. Rel: 13 February 2004. Cert 12A.

The Other Side of the Bed ★★★
For half of its length this escapist comedy from Spain has an agreeable, campish appeal. It concerns two best friends, both married, but with one cheating on the other by having an affair with his wife. Soon other subsidiary characters join in to provide shifting potential couplings, but the film is overlong and drifts in its second part just when a good farce needs to build. The leading players are youngsters whose good looks are part of the film's attraction and this plus the presence of an eccentric detective with bizarre theories about the deaths of Marilyn Monroe and JFK aids the movie even if it cannot cancel out the poor judgment that develops. The film also offers jokey songs but lacks the sophistication displayed in Ozon's comedy with music, *8 Women*. MS

• *Javier* Ernesto Alterio, *Sonia* Paz Vega, *Pedro* Guillermo Toledo, *Paula* Natalia Verbeke, *Rafa* Alberto San Juan, *Pilar* María Esteve, *Sagaz* Ramón Barea.
• *Dir* Emilio Martínez-Lázaro, *Pro* Tomás

Cimadevella and José Antonio Sáinz de Vicuña, *Screenplay* David Serrano, *Ph* Juan Molina Temboury, *Art Dir* Julio Torrecilla, *Ed* Ángel Hernández-Zoido, *M* Roque Baños, *choreography* Pedro Berdayes.

Telespan 2000/Impala-Swipe Films.
108 mins. Spain. 2002. Rel: 23 April 2004. Cert. 15.

Our House ★★★¹/₂

(US title: *Duplex*)

New York, the present. Thinking they have bought the apartment of their dreams, writer Ben Stiller and magazine sub-editor Drew Barrymore move into real estate hell as the elderly biddy upstairs turns out to be the neighbour you wish you could kill … Danny DeVito's comic nightmare of thin walls, leaking pipes and rude intrusions is just the kind of thing to warm the cockles of your mortgage book, possibly to the point of conflagration. Stiller and Barrymore portray the couples descent into dire depression from the machinations of Eileen Essell's Irish hag in broad strokes, milking the udders of the script for every drop of black comedy they can get. As their dream home descends into a house of horrors, it is inevitable that an audience collectively grow to wish painful death upon their tormentors, more gleefully and pungently for every real-life occasion they have come to regret the enforced proximity of urban living. AK

Below: Seeing the light: Drew Barrymore has the first smile in Danny DeVito's *Our House* (from BVI)

• *Alex Rose* Ben Stiller, *Nancy Kendricks* Drew Barrymore, *Mrs Connelly* Eileen Essell, *Kenneth* Harvey Fierstein, *Coop* Justin Theroux, *Officer Dan* Robert Wisdom, *Celine* Amber Valletta, *Chick* James Remar, *Tara* Maya Rudolph, *Ginger* Cheryl Klein, *Jean* Swoosie Kurtz, *Herman* Wallace Shawn, *with* Tracey Walter, John Hamburg, Jenette Goldstein, Christopher Doyle.
• *Dir* Danny DeVito, *Pro* Ben Stiller, Stuart Cornfeld, Jeremy Kramer, Nancy Juvonen and Drew Barrymore, *Ex Pro* Bob Weinstein, Harvey Weinstein, Meryl Poster, Jennifer Wachtell, Richard N. Gladstein and Alan C. Blomquist, *Co-Pro* and *Screenplay* Larry Doyle, *Ph* Anastas N. Michos, *Pro Des* Robin Standefer, *Ed* Lynzee Klingman, *M* David Newman, *Costumes* Joe Aulisi.

Miramax/Red Hour Films/Flower Films-Buena Vista International.
89 mins. USA. 2003. Rel: 30 April 2004. Cert. 12A.

Out of Time ★★¹/₂

Here's a twisty thriller about a detective in Florida investigating two deaths only to find that, as the unsuspecting victim of a con trick, he is himself being set up as the guilty party to whom the evidence seems to point. It might have been good and suspenseful, but Dave Collard's script is so contrived that the situations become unintentionally comic. As tosh goes, it could still be fun, save for one's annoyance that this film wastes the considerable talents of Denzel Washington, the actor playing the cop, and of director Carl Franklin. It's also the case that, despite being publicised as a hot movie, Washington shows not a spark of sexual rapport with Sanaa Lathan who appears in the role of the cop's mistress. MS

• *Matt Lee Whitlock* Denzel Washington, *Alex Diaz Whitlock* Eva Mendes, *Ann Merai Harrison* Sanaa Lathan, *Chris Harrison* Dean Cain, *Chae* John Billingsley, *Tony Dalton* Robert Baker, *Cabot* Alex Carter, *Deputy Baste* Antoni Corone, *Dr Donovan* Nora Dunn.
• *Dir* Carl Franklin, *Pro* Neal H. Moritz and Jesse B'Franklin, *Ex Pro* Kevin Reidy, Jon Berg, Damien Saccani and Alex Gartner, *Assoc Pro* Steve Traxler, Dan Genetti and Gina White, *Screenplay* Dave Collard, *Ph* Theo Van de Sande, *Pro Des* Paul Peters, *Ed* Carole Kravetz Aykanian, *M* Graeme Revell, *Costumes* Sharen Davis

MGM/Original Film/Monarch Pictures-Momentum.
105 mins. USA. 2003. Rel: 26 December 2003.
Cert 12A.

P

Party Monster ★★

New York in the nineties. Michael Alig (Macaulay Culkin proving himself an actor inferior to his brothers) and his friend James St. James (Seth Green in scene-stealing form) create a new night-life cult in the form of parties where drug-taking and outrageous costumes are the most marked features. According to filmmakers Fenton Bailey and Randy Barbato, whose previous work includes *101 Rent Boy* and *Homo High*, this camp movie is 'a sad film all dressed up and ready to party'. While supposedly showing the limits of this life-style, in reality it seems to want to have its cake and eat it. This film is indulgent and superficial and, more surprisingly, somewhat evasive on issues of sexuality. Despite having Christine Vachon as a producer, it's all show and no substance. MS

• *Michael Alig* Macaulay Culkin, *James St. James* Seth Green, *Gitsie* Chloë Sevigny, *Brooke* Natasha Lyonne, *Freez* Justin Hagan, *Angel* Wilson Cruz, *Keoki* Wilmer Valderrama, *Peter Gatien* Dylan McDermott, *Christina* Marilyn Manson, *Elke Alig, Michael's mother* Diana Scarwid, *talk show host* John Stamos.
• *Dir* and *Screenplay* Fenton Bailey and Randy Barbato, from the book *Disco Bloodbath* by James St. James, *Pro* Bailey, Barbato, Jon Marcus, Bradford Simpson and Christine Vachon, *Ex Pro* Wouter Barendrecht, Michael J. Werner, Edward R. Pressman, John Schmidt, Sofia Sondervan and John Wells, *Ph* Teodoro Maniaci, *Pro Des* Andrea Stanley, *Ed* Jeremy Simmons, *M* Jimmy Harry, *Costumes* Michael Wilkinson.

ContentFilm/Fortissimo Film Sales/Killer Films/John Wells/World of Wonder-Metro Tartan.
98 mins. USA/Netherlands. 2003. Rel: 17 October 2003. Cert. 18.

The Passion of Joan of Arc ★★★★★

Amazingly this release print of Dreyer's silent classic represents the first time that this masterpiece has received public screenings in Britain. A film which loses nothing with the passage of time, it justifies one in believing that Falconetti's performance as Joan is the finest by an actress in the entire history of the cinema. The film is also an example of great direction and its concentration on the trial of Joan of Arc shot largely in close-ups achieves an extraordinary intensity. It is convincing historically while also representing a wider comment on the persecution of those who threaten the status quo. But it's essentially Falconetti, a stage actress displaying under Dreyer's guidance a wondrous understanding of screen acting, who, despite making no other appearance on film, raises this one to the heights. Oldies don't come more golden. MS

• *Jeanne* Marie Falconetti, *Bishop Pierre Cauchon* Eugène Silvain, *Jean d'Estivet, Prosecutor* André Berley, *Nicolas Loyseleur* Maurice Schutz, *Jean Massieu* Antonin Artaud, *Jean Lemaître* Michel Simon, *Guillaume Evrard* Jean d'Yd, *Jean Beaupere* Louis Ravet, *Judges* Armand Lurville, Jacques Arnna, Alexandre Mihalesco, Léon Larive.
• *Dir* and *Screenplay* Carl Theodor Dreyer from the novel by Joseph Deteil, *Ph* Rudolph Maté, *Ed* Theodor Dreyer and Marguerite Beaugé, *M* Ole Schmidt, *Costumes* Valentine Hugo.

Société générale des films-Artificial Eye.
110 mins. France. 1927/28. Rel: 18 July 2003. Cert PG.

The Passion of the Christ ★★★★¹/₂

The very title of Mel Gibson's astonishingly powerful film points both to the decision to concentrate on the last phase of Christ's life on earth (from the arrest in the garden of Gethsemane onwards) and to the film's emphasis on suffering. But, far from being an excuse to revel in violence (the scourging, the whipping, the crown of thorns, the crucifixion itself) for its own sake, the film's purpose is to show one man carrying on himself the weight of the sins of the world. His forgiveness of those involved (the film never preaches hatred and the anti-Semitic accusations seem absurd) becomes all the more extraordinary in a movie which gives fresh impact to a familiar story. This is so despite minor errors of judgment (too much slow motion early on, a couple of weak flashbacks). Well acted though it is, the chief credit goes to Gibson whose film, which has proved commercial despite using the Aramaic language and sub-titles, possesses an emotional depth which turns the viewing of this picture into what can only be described as an experience. MS

• *Jesus* Jim Caviezel, *Mary* Maia Morgenstern, *Mary Magdalene* Monica Bellucci, *Satan* Rosalinda Celantano, *Caiphas, the High Priest* Mattia Sbragia, *Pontius Pilate* Hristo Naumov Shopov, *Claudia Procles* Claudia Gerini, *Judas Iscariot* Luca Lionello.
• *Dir* Mel Gibson, *Pro* Gibson, Bruce Davey and Steve McEveety, *Ex Pro* Enzo Sisti, *Screenplay* Gibson and Benedict Fitzgerald, *Ph* Caleb Deschanel, *Pro Des* Francesco Frigeri, *M* John Debney, *Ed* John Wright, *Costume* Maurizio Millenotti, *Special Effects Makeup* Keith Vanderlaan.

Icon-Icon.
126 mins. USA. 2004. Rel: 26 March 2004. Cert 18

Pas sur la Bouche ★★¹/₂

(*Not on the Lips*)
Heartfelt but seriously misjudged, this movie finds the one-time avant-garde artist Alain Resnais using a

resolutely theatrical staging as he films an operetta by André Barde and Maurice Yvain first staged in 1925. Not far from being a French equivalent to *The Boy Friend*, this venture seeks charm through fidelity to the original, but the book offers farce without a single moment of surprise and the splendid Sabine Azéma is sadly miscast in a role that in looks would have suited Charlotte Rampling. But worst of all is the decision to do it with actors who for the most part can't sing and, save for the septet finale to Act II, the piece never takes off since Resnais has no flair for filming musicals despite his love of them. MS

• *Gilberte Valandray* Sabine Azema, *Arlette Poumaillac* Isabelle Nanty, *Huguette Verberie* Audrey Tautou, *Georges Valandray* Pierre Arditi, *Mme Foin* Darry Cowl, *Charley* Jalil Lespert, *Faradel* Daniel Prevost, *Eric Thomson* Lambert Wilson.
• *Dir* and *Screenplay* Alain Resnais, based on the 1925 operetta *Pas sur la bouche* by Andre Barde and Maurice Yvain, *Pro* Bruno Pesery, *Assoc Pro* Ruth Waldburger, *Ph* Renato Berta, *Pro Des* Jacques Saulnier, *Ed* Herve de Luze, *M* Andre Barde and Maurice Yvain, *Costumes* Jackie Budin.

Pathé/Aréna Films /France 2 Cinéma/ France 3 Cinéma/Arcade/Vega Film/Canal Plus/CinéCinéma-Pathé. 116 mins. France/Switzerland. 2003. Rel: 30 April 2004. Cert. PG.

Paycheck ★¹/₂

Michael Jennings (Affleck) is a top-notch reverse engineer in a future where corporations protect trade secrets with a memory-wipe process. He signs on for a whopping $90 million pay day in exchange for three years of his life. But when, in a blink of the camera's eye, he tries to collect on his reward he discovers that he has signed away the money in exchange for a brown envelope with 19 apparently random items … John Woo loses his top-of-the-bill status on this pedestrian re-tread of a Philip K. Dick 'what-if'. Even if we were willing to go along with the gaping plot holes endemic to any Hollywood story of this kind, we remain lumped with Woo's tired 'leather and slo-mo' aesthetic, and a pair of stars with the chemistry of lead. But being a PKD story, the premise *is* intriguing, and parades a movie-friendly range of paranoid sci-fi themes like the idea of predestination on human choices. However, Woo has literally deafened his script to those subtleties amidst the bombast of mass explosions and ridiculously over-the-top battles that suggest at some point during those blanked out years, Jennings also trained at the Bond Academy for Action Heroes. AK

• *Michael Jennings* Ben Affleck, *Jimmy Rethrick* Aaron Eckhart, *Rachel Porter* Uma Thurman, *Shorty* Paul Giamatti, *Wolfe* Colm Feore, *Agent Dodge* Joe

Morton, *Agent Klein* Michael C. Hall, *Attorney General Brown* Peter Friedman, *Rita Dunne* Kathryn Morris, *with* Ivana Milicevic, Christopher Kennedy, Callum Keith Rennie, Steve Wright.
• *Dir* John Woo, *Pro* Jon Davis, Michael Hackett, John Woo and Terence Chang, *Ex Pro* Stratton Leopold and David Solomon, *Co-Pro* Caroline Macaulay and Arthur Anderson, *Screenplay* Dean Georgaris, based on the short story by Philip K. Dick, *Ph* Jeffrey L. Kimball, *Pro Des* William Sandell, *Ed* Kevin Sitt and Christopher Rouse, *M* John Powell, *Costumes* Erica Edell Phillips, *Makeup* Norma Hill-Patton, *Visual effects supervisor* Gregory L. McMurry, *Special effects coordinators* Alfred Di Sarro (USA), Clay Scheirer (Canada), *Visual effects*, CIS Hollywood, Creo Collective, Frantic Films, Pixel Playground, Rising Sun Pictures, *Special visual effects* Sony Pictures Imageworks, *Supervising stunt coordinators* Gregg Smrz (USA), Owen Walstrom (Canada).

Paramount/DreamWorks/Davis Entertainment/ Lion Rock-UIP. 118 mins. USA/Canada. 2003. Rel: 16 January 2004. Cert 12A.

People I Know ★★★

This New York tale, one of sleaze and corruption, centres on a publicist worn down, aging and in decline generally. Since this character is played by Al Pacino whose screen presence remains formidable, the film has its moments (it works best as a star vehicle). But there's nothing memorable either in its treatment or in the material, which involves conniving film stars, untrustworthy politicians and a rather tiresome drug-taking starlet who gets murdered while in the publicist's care. It passes the time but *Sweet Smell of Success* it ain't – nor does it do itself any favours by featuring a wall poster of *The Parallax View*. MS

• *Eli Wurman* Al Pacino, *Victoria Gray* Kim Basinger, *Cary Launer* Ryan O'Neal, *Jilli Hopper* Téa Leoni, *Elliot Sharansky* Richard Schiff, *The Rev. Lyle Blunt* Bill Nunn, *Dr Sandy Napier* Robert Klein, *with* Mark Webber, Peter Gerety, David Marshall Grant, Paulina Porizkova, Rex Reed, Regis Philbin, Joy Philbin, Sophie Dahl, Mr G.
• *Dir* Dan Algrant, *Pro* Michael Nozik, Leslie Urdang and Karen Tenkhoff, *Ex Pro* Robert Redford, Kirk D'Amico and Philip von Alverselben, *Co-Pro* Nellie Nugiel, *Screenplay* John Robin Baitz, *Ph* Peter Deming, *Pro Des* Michael Shaw, *Ed* Suzy Elmiger, *M* Terence Blanchard, *Costumes* David Robinson.

Myriad Pictures/South Fork Pictures/Galena/Greenstreet Films-Momentum. 100 mins. USA/Germany. 2001. Rel: 13 February 2004. Cert 15.

The Perfect Score ★★★

A disparate group of kids congregate around a daring plan to break into the Educational Testing Service and steal the Scholastic Aptitude Test questions, each for their own reasons. Along the way, the film explores the various facets of their socialisation in a superficially cool and cynical manner. Superficial, because under all the clever edits and style-statements Brian Robbin's film is really just another feel-good, morally sound teen caper starring a bunch of nice suburban kids. Scarlett Johansson pouts her magnificent lips through a caricature that one hopes she will never have to revisit, whereas Leonardo Lam makes a scene-stealing British debut as a genius Super-Slacker, who also narrates the tale. AK

• *Anna* Erika Christensen, *Kyle* Chris Evans, *Matty* Bryan Greenberg, *Francesca* Scarlett Johansson, *Desmond* Darius Miles, *Roy* Leonardo Lam, *Desmond's mother* Tyra Ferrell, *Larry* Matthew Lillard, *with* Vanessa Angel, Michael Ryan, Rebecca Robbins.
• *Dir* Brian Robbins, *Pro* Robbins, Roger Birnbaum, Jonathan Glickman and Mike Tollin, *Ex Pro* Donald J. Lee Jr, *Co-Pro* Sharla Sumpter, *Screenplay* Mark Schwahn, Marc Hyman and Jon Zack, *Ph* Clark Mathis, *Pro Des* Jaymes Hinkle, *Ed* Ned Bastille, *M* John Murphy, *Costumes* Melissa Toth.

Paramount/MTV Films-UIP.
93 mins. USA/Germany/Canada. 2004.
Rel: 19 March 2004. Cert. 12A.

Peter Pan ★¹/₂

Directed by the Australian P.J. Hogan, this retelling of J.M. Barrie's oddball classic lacks real magic. Filmed in Australia with American money, *Peter Pan* shows hints of ambition. Wendy is depicted as a girl on the verge of puberty, her vivid dreams and storytelling inviting comparisons with Neil Jordan's much darker *The Company of Wolves*. On the downside, there is little sense of romance or fantasy. The special effects, courtesy of George Lucas' Industrial Light and Magic, are curiously charmless. There are further problems with the casting. While Jason Isaacs is a fair Captain Hook, Richard Briers looks faintly desperate as Smee. Worst of all, Jeremy Sumpter is an unappealing Peter Pan, resembling a refugee from a failed Boy Band or the early rounds of *Pop Idol*. For all its Americanisation of Barrie's story, Disney's 1953 version stills reigns supreme. DO

• *Mr Darling/Captain Hook* Jason Isaacs, *Peter Pan* Jeremy Sumpter, *Wendy Darling* Rachel Hurd-Wood, *Mrs Darling* Olivia Williams, *Tink* Ludivine Sagnier, *Smee* Richard Briers, *Aunt Millicent* Lynn Redgrave, *Sir Edward Quiller Couch* Geoffrey Palmer, *John Darling* Harry Newell, *Michael Darling* Freddie Popplewell, *Slightly* Theodore Chester, *Tootles* Rupert Simonian, *Curly* George Mackay, *Nibs* Harry Eden, *twins* Patrick Gooch, Lachlan Gooch, *Tiger Lily* Carsen Gray, *narrator* Saffron Burrows, *with* Kerry Walker, Bruce Spence, Frank Gallacher, Bill Kerr.
• *Dir* P.J. Hogan, *Pro* Lucy Fisher, Douglas Wick and Patrick McCormick, *Ex Pro* Mohamed Al Fayed,

Below: Missing Neverland: Jeremy Sumpter in P.J. Hogan's less-than-magical *Peter Pan* (from UIP)

Gail Lyon and Jocelyn Moorehouse, *Co-Pro* Gary Adelson, Craig Baumgarten and Stephen Jones, *Co-Exec Pro* Charles Newirth, *Screenplay* Hogan and Michael Goldenberg, based on the original stageplay and books by J.M. Barrie, *Ph* Donald M. McAlpine, *Pro Des* Roger Ford, *Ed* Garth Craven and Michael Kahn, *M* James Newton Howard, *Costumes* Janet Patterson.

Universal/Columbia/Revolution Studios/Allied Stars-UIP
113 mins. USA/UK/Australia. 2003. Rel: 26 December 2003. Cert PG.

Petites Coupures ★★★¹⁄₂
(*Small Cuts*)
From a British perspective, writer/director Pascal Bonitzer increasingly looks like an intelligent also-run in French cinema. Here we have a tragic-comedy about an aging womaniser (Auteuil) who can't control his desires sufficiently to seize a real relationship with the mysterious woman (Scott Thomas) who might have been his salvation. Jean Yanne in his last screen appearance plays Auteuil's Communist uncle and there are various diversions in this well photographed film which certainly doesn't bore. But it doesn't really cohere memorably either, and with Emmanuelle Devos and Ludivine Sagnier also involved one has to say that with a cast of this distinction one expects more than this film delivers. MS

• *Bruno* Daniel Auteuil, *Beatrice* Kristin Scott Thomas, *Nathalie* Ludivine Sagnier, *Mathilde* Pascale Bussieres, *Anne* Catherine Mouchet, *Gaelle* Emmanuelle Devos, *Marie* Dinara Droukarova, *Verekher* Hanns Zischler, *Gerard* Jean Yanne.
• *Dir* Pascal Bonitzer, *Pro* Jean-Michel Rey and Philippe Liegeois, *Screenplay* Pascal Bonitzer and Emmanue Salinger, *Ph* William Lubtchansky, *Pro Des* Emmanuel de Chauvigny, *Ed* Suzanne Koch, *M* John Scott, *Costumes* Pascaline Chavanne.

Rezo/Axiom Films/France 2 Cinéma/Rhone Alpes Cinema-Artificial Eye.
95 mins. UK/France. 2003.
Rel: 29 August 2003.
Cert 15.

Pieces of April ★★★★
An affecting 'Thanksgiving' family movie, more remarkable for being a directorial debut by a novelist and screenwriter, shot entirely on ugly, noisy lo-res digital cameras. The family involved is deeply divided by a lifelong and savage feud between April Burns (an excellent Katie Holmes) and her mother, Joy (an even better Patricia Clarkson). Given the premise, you might expect a Disney-fied pacification, via various saccharine and contrived

accidents of fate. Thankfully, not here. Fate *does* intervene, but in a mean, cruel and vividly believable fashion. The simple power of the story is easily overcomes the technical inadequacies of its medium (the audio track rasps, and several scenes are quite horribly lit). It also checks all the bases of migrant culture and communal support that define the sub-genre of American Thanksgiving films with a fresh perspective, a rarity in itself. It ends beautifully, at once intimate yet artfully reminding the audience that they have been watching a fable, told with an eye fixed on our own cynical times. AK

• *April Burns* Katie Holmes, *Joy Burns* Patricia Clarkson, *Jim Burns* Oliver Platt, *Bobby* Derek Luke, *Beth Burns* Alison Pill, *Timmy Burns* John Gallagher Jr., *Grandma Dottie* Alice Drummond, *Wayne* Sean Hayes, *Latrell* Sisquo.
• *Dir* and *Screenplay* Peter Hedges, *Pro* John Lyons, Gary Winick, Holly Becker and Alexis Alexanian, *Ex Pro* Jonathan Sehring, Caroline Kaplan and John Sloss, *Co-Pro* Lucy Barzun and Lucille Masone Smith, *Assoc Pro* Dianne Dreyer, *Ph* Tami Reiker, *Pro Des* Rick Butler, *Ed* Mark Livolsi, *M* Stephin Merritt; JS Bach; songs performed by The Magnetic Fields, Studio Musicians, The 6ths, and Johnny Sedona, *Costumes* Laura Bauer, *Sound* Aaron Rudelson.

United Artists/IFC Prods/InDigEnt/Kalkaska-Optimum Releasing.
79 mins. USA. 2003. Rel: 20 February 2004.
Cert 12A.

Piglet's Big Movie ★★¹⁄₂
A.A. Milne's pink little pork pie get's his own movie. Visually faithful to the book's original illustrations, the cartoon is directed at the very young, and tells of how Piglet comes to understand that his size is no measure of his importance, by way of a farcical search for his whereabouts by Pooh and gang that recalls their many adventures together via the pages of a scrapbook. Carly Simon's original compositions add a touch of originality to a film that is deeply faithful to the source material, possibly to a fault. AK

• *Voices*: *Piglet* John Fiedler, *Winnie the Pooh/Tigger* Jim Cummings, *Owl* Andre Stojka, *Kanga* Kath Soucie, *Roo* Nikita Hopkins, *Eeyore* Peter Cullen, *Rabbit* Ken Sansom.
• *Dir* Francis Glebas, *Pro* Michelle Pappalardo-Robinson, *Screenplay* Brian Hohlfeld, adapted from and inspired by the works of A.A. Milne, *Art Dir* Fred Warter, *Ed* Ivan Bilancio, *M* Carl Johnson; with songs written and sung by Carly Simon.

Walt Disney Pictures-Buena Vista International.
75 mins. USA. 2003. Rel: 18 July 2003. Cert. U.

Pirates of the Caribbean:
The Curse of the Black Pearl ★★★★

The Caribbean, 1800-ish. Will Turner is rescued from a burning wreck by Governor Weatherby Swann and his daughter Elizabeth. Years pass, and Will is now a square-jawed blacksmith who dreams of fighting pirates. Elizabeth also dreams of pirates, but more in a Freddy Kruger kind of way. She is to wed to a typically wet English noble, when the dashing, mad and faintly camp pirate Jack Sparrow blows into harbour. Unbeknownst to any of them, a mystical beacon calls the dread pirates of the Black Pearl to her little island to wreak havoc and terror, and to recover a cursed gold medallion … Easily the best film ever to be based on a theme park ride, Disneyland's *Pirates of the Caribbean* has been spun into a tale of ghosts and cursed gold doubloons. Disney has taken every cliché we know about pirates and genetically mutated the Errol Flynn swashbuckler into a heavily mascara-ed, playfully rogue-ish Jack Sparrow, (a role that Depp absolutely slays with). Keira Knightley is now officially an A-list starlet, and Orlando Bloom assures himself of at least another year as the teen-magazine cover-boy of choice. Apart from a profoundly disturbing zombie monkey, there is nothing not to like. AK

• *Capt. Jack Sparrow* Johnny Depp, *Barbossa* Geoffrey Rush, *Will Turner* Orlando Bloom, *Elizabeth Swann* Keira Knightley, *Norrington* Jack Davenport, *Gov. Weatherby Swann* Jonathan Pryce, *Pintel* Lee Arenberg, *Ragetti* Mackenzie Crook, *with* Kevin McNally, Zoe Saldana, Treva Etienne, Trevor Goddard.
• *Dir* Gore Verbinski, *Pro* Jerry Bruckheimer, *Ex Pro* Mike Stenson, Chad Oman, Bruce Hendricks and Paul Deason, *Screenplay* Ted Elliott and Terry Rossio, *Story* Ted Elliott, Terry Rossio, Stuart Beattie and Jay Wolpert, *Ph* Dariusz Wolski, *Pro Des* Brian Morris, *Ed* Craig Wood, Stephen Rivkin and Arthur Schmidt, *M* Klaus Badelt *additional M* Ramin Djawadi, James Michael Dooley, Nick Glennie-Smith, Steve Jablonsky, James McKee Smith, Blake Neely, James McKee Smith, Geoff Zanelli and Hans Zimmer, a*mbient music design* Mel Wesson*, Costumes* Penny Rose, *Sets* Larry Dias.

First Mate Productions Inc/Jerry Bruckheimer Films/Walt Disney Pictures-Buena Vista Internation. 143 mins. USA. 2003. Rel: 8 August 2003. Cert 12A.

The Principles of Lust ★★¹/₂

There's some good acting here and writer/director Penny Woolcock seems to know what she wants. Even so, this drama, shot in Sheffield with expert use of the hand-held camera, becomes depressingly inept. It's the story of a single mother (Sienna Guillory) let down by her boy-friend, a would-be

writer (Alec Newman), when he comes under the influence of a new pal (Marc Warren). The latter's uninhibited life-style includes drug-taking, orgies and the promotion of bare-knuckle fighting between kids. Initially this is relatively familiar territory but handled with a sureness of touch and a potent sensuality in the explicit sex scenes. It's the development which really lets the film down with improbable behaviour and contrived set pieces that leave you not caring a damn about any of the characters. MS

• *Paul* Alec Newman, *Juliette* Sienna Guillory, *Billy* Marc Warren, *Hole* Lara Clifton, *Phillip* Julian Barratt, *with* Alexander Popplewell, Gwyne Hollis, Kelli Hollis, Tommy Yates, Skint Eastwood, Mackenzie Crook, Jake Geddes, Fiona Lawrence.
• *Dir* and *Screenplay* Penny Woolcock, based on a novel by Tim Cooke, *Pro* Madonna Baptiste, *Ph* Graham Smith, *Pro Des* Jo Baker, *Ed* Brand Thumim, *M* Andy Cowton, *Costumes* Karen McKinlay-Gunn.

FilmFour/YMPA/Studio of the North/Blast! Films-Pathé. 108 mins. UK. 2003. Rel: 12 March 2004. Cert 18.

Above:
No ugly duckling: Keira Knightley as Elizabeth Swann in *Pirates of the Caribbean: The Curse of the Black Pearl* (from BVI)

Radio ★½

'Radio' is the nickname bestowed on James Robert Kennedy, a retarded lad from the leafy burg of Anderson in South Carolina. He's dubbed 'Radio' because he loves listening to the radio. Yep, this tedious, sentimental and uneventful film is full of such canny wit. *Radio*, the movie, is 'inspired by a true story' and it's hard to be too hard on it. There's another creditable turn from Ed Harris (arguably one of America's most underrated actors) and Debra Winger pops up in her first film role for nine years. Otherwise, there's not much to recommend this self-indulgent fable which strives to win our hearts by piling on the orchestral goo and assaulting us with an array of cheesy reaction shots. A tough high school football coach takes 'Radio' under his wing – much to the surprise of the former's long-suffering wife and neglected daughter and the reproach of the community. Not a lot else happens. However, if you fancy the prospect of Cuba Gooding Jr doing Forrest Gump, then this is definitely for you.
JC-W

• *James Robert 'Radio' Kennedy* Cuba Gooding Jr, *Coach Harold Jones* Ed Harris, *Principal Daniels* Alfre Woodard, *Maggie* S. Epatha Merkerson, *Honeycutt* Brent Sexton, *Linda* Debra Winger, *Johnny* Riley Smith, *Mary Helen Jones* Sarah Drew, *Frank Clay* Chris Mulkey, *Tucker* Patrick Breen.
• *Dir* Michael Tollin, *Pro* Brian Robbins, Michael Tollin and Herbert W. Gains, *Ex Pro* Todd Garner and Caitlin Scanlon, *Screenplay* Mike Rich, based on the Sports Illustrated article *Someone to Lean On* by Gary Smith, *Ph* Don Burgess, *Pro Des* Clay A. Griffith, *Ed* Chris Lebenzon and Harvey Rosenstock, *M* James Horner, *Costumes* Denise Wingate, *Sound* Hector Gika.

Revolution Studios/Tollin/Robbins-Columbia TriStar. 109 mins. USA. 2003. Rel: 14th May 2004. Cert PG.

Raising Victor Vargas ★★★★

Lower East Side, New York, the present. And Victor is caught *in flagrante* with Fat Donna, a tragedy to his reputation as a ladies man. The only way to save face is to land Judy Ramirez, the untouchable neighbourhood beauty who has no time for the juvenile mating habits of the local boys. But Victor brings something the game the others boys do not; his heart and soul … Peter Sollett's portrait of a boy making his crossing into manhood is a handheld, golden-lit vision of authentic feeling. Much of that elusive quality comes from the untrained cast, which Sollett and his partner Eva Vives found on the streets of Lower Manhattan. The entire film is an act of improvisation from the cast, who were not given a script to work from. The romantic heart of the story

that is being told amidst the inner city tableau beats with authenticity. The results are absolutely stunning.
AK

• *Victor Vargas* Victor Rasuk, *'Juicy' Judy Martinez* Judy Marte, *Melonie* Melonie Diaz, *grandmother* Altagarcia Guzman, *Nino Vargas* Sylvestre Rasuk, *Vicky Vargas* Krystal Rodriguez, *Harold* Kevin Rivera, *Carlos* Wilfree Vasquez.
• *Dir* and *Screenplay* Peter Sollett, from a story by Sollett and Eva Vives, *Pro* Sollett, Alain De La Mata, Robin O'Hara and Scott Macaulay, *Ex Pro* Vincent Maraval, *Line Pro* Cate Wilson, *Ph* Tim Orr, *Pro Des* Judy Becker, *Ed* Myron Kerstein, *M* Roy Nathanson and Bill Ware, *Costumes* Jill Newell, *Sound* Steve Borne.

StudioCanal/Forensic Films-Momentum. 87 mins. USA/France. 2002. Rel 19 September 2003. Cert. 15.

The Reckoning ★★½

England; 1380. On the run for murdering his lover's husband, Nicholas foregoes the priesthood to join a troupe of travelling players. When the company arrives at a small town they discover that a local woman, the deaf-and-dumb Martha, has been convicted of the murder of a boy. Believing her to be innocent, the actors concoct a play that dramatises the supposedly true events of the killing… Paul McGuigan, who kicked Paul Bettany into the limelight with *Gangster No. 1*, is a director strong on style and brings both an arresting palette and kinetic energy to this medieval morality tale. However, he is let down by Mark Mills' uneven script (complete with muddy plotting and banal dialogue) and cannot restrain some of the more hammy acting. Previously known as *Morality Play*.
CB

• *Martin* Willem Dafoe, *Nicholas* Paul Bettany, *Sarah* Gina McKee, *Tobias* Brian Cox, *Brother Simon* Damian Ewen Bremner, *Lord Robert de Guise* Vincent Cassel, *Stephen* Simon McBurney, *Straw* Tom Hardy, *Springer* George Wells, *Martha* Elvira Minguez, *with* Matthew MacFadyen, James Cosmo, Mark Benton, Niall Buggy, Luke de Woolfson, Richard Durden, Hamish McColl, Tom Georgeson, Simon Pegg, Heathcote Williams.
• *Dir* Paul McGuigan, *Pro* Caroline Wood, *Ex Pro* Stephen Evans and Angus Finney, *Co-Pro* Denise O'Dell and Sarah Halioua, *Screenplay* Mark Mills, based on the novel *Morality Play* by Barry Unsworth, *Ph* Peter Sova, *Pro Des* Andrew McAlpine, *Ed* Andrew Hulme, *M* Adrian Lee and Mark Mancina, *Costumes* Yvonne Blake.

Renaissance Films/KanZaman/MDA Films-Entertainment.
109 mins. UK/Spain. 2001. Rel: 4 June 2004. Cert 15.

Re-Inventing Eddie ★★★

Made in 2001, this film by Jim Doyle derived from a play has, sadly, not lost its topicality. The central figure in this tale set in the north west of England is a father (Lynch) who finds himself being investigated under the belief that he might have sexually abused his daughter. His responses to this express his outrage over the implied accusation, but are both ill-advised and believable until a late stage when credibility is left behind. The film also makes the mistake of echoing *Alfie* in having the lead character speak directly to the audience, the hope being that some lighter touches will make the film less grim. These errors of judgment are regrettable because *Re-Inventing Eddie* has important things to say and the cast is a strong one. John Lynch, in particular, is excellent. MS

• *Eddie Harris* John Lynch, *Jeanie Harris* Geraldine Somerville, *Cliff* John Thomson, *Dougie* Ian Mercer, *Donald* John McCardle, *Sheila* Judith Barker, *Katie Harris* Lauren Cook, *Billy Harris* Ben Thompson, *with* Sidney Livingstone, Joan Oliver, Diana Fairfax. • *Dir* Jim Doyle, *Pro* Jonny Boston, Ian Brady and Elaine Grainger, *Ex Pro* David Rogers, *Screenplay* Doyle and Ian Brady, based on the play *One Fine Day* by Dennis Lumborg, *Ph* Damian Bromley, *Pro Des* Sue Booth, *Ed* Andy Loftus, *M* Mark Thomas, *Costumes* Nadine Hindi.

BBG Pictures/Great British Films/Enterprise Films-Guerrilla Films.
94 mins. UK. 2001. Rel: 17 May 2004. Cert 15.

Respiro ★★¹/₂

Despite its intriguingly different setting – the island of Lampedusa off the coast of Sicily – this film suffers from the director's ill-judged screenplay. It's weak in shaping, lacking in depth and muddled. Emanuele Crialese's story takes place in a fishing community where wife and mother Grazia (Golino) is either a free spirit or just plain dotty. The former assumption although often suggested is undermined if she really needs medical care as her jealous husband believes. When she goes into hiding aided by her 13 year-old son but not caring a damn about

Below: Stark staring: Ivan Dobronravov in Andrei Zvyagintsev's impressive if downbeat *The Return* (from UGC Films UK)

his younger brother's feelings despite planting evidence to suggest that she has drowned, you might well question her sanity. Similarly most audiences will be left questioning the final scene unusually obscure in its meaning. MS

• *Grazia* Valeria Golino, *Pietro* Vincenzo Amato, *Pasquale* Francesco Casisa, *Marinella* Veronica D'Agostino, *Filippo* Filippo Pucillo, *Nonna* Emma Loffredo, *Pier Luigi* Elio Germano, *Olivier* Avy Marciano.
• *Dir* and *Screenplay* Emanuele Crialese, *Pro* Domenico Procacci, *Ph* Fabio Zamarion, *Art Dir* Beatrice Scarpato, *Ed* Didier Ranz, *M* John Surman.

Eurimages/Fandango/Les Films des Tournelles/Medusa Produzione/Roissy Films/ Rouse Films/TPS Cinéma / Telepiù-Tartan Films.
95 mins. Italy/France. 2002. Rel: 8 August 2003. Cert 12.

The Return ★★★
(*Vozvraschenie*)
The first half of this highly praised Russia film is indeed impressive as we watch two brothers (one in his mid-teens, the other slightly younger) reacting to the return of their father who had been absent for years. For whatever reason, the father proves to be a tough disciplinarian, but his motives may not be bad. Unfortunately, we never know because neither his background nor the reason for his absence is ever clarified.
If the film seeks to be a social, political or even religious fable as well as a personal tale, then it stands a poor second to Pavel Chukhrai's 1997 film *The Thief*. The downbeat second half is both drawn out and elusive, but the performances are splendid. Tragically the older child actor Vladimir Garin died just after completion of the filming. MS

• *Andrei* Vladimir Garin, *Ivan* Ivan Dobronravov, *father* Konstantin Lavronenko, *mother* Natalia Vdovina, *grandmother* Galina Popova.
• *Dir* Andrei Zvyagintsev, *Pro* Dmitri Lesnevsky, *Ex Pro* Elena Kokaleva, *Screenplay* Vladimir Moiseenko and Alexandre Novototsky, *Ph* Mikhail Krichman, *Pro Des* Janna Pakhomova, *Ed* Vladimir Mogilevsky, *M* Andrei Dergachev, *Costumes* Anna Barthuly.

Ren Film/Nikola Film-UGC Films UK.
110 mins. Russia. 2003. Rel: 25 June 2004. Cert 12A.

Riders
See *Steal*.

Rivers and Tides ★★★★
(*Rivers and Tides: Andy Goldsworthy Working with Time*)
Given a sadly limited release here, this fascinating documentary features the unorthodox sculptor Andy Goldsworthy who, based in Dumfriesshire, travels the world. New York State and France are visited as we view him at work taking natural elements (stones, leaves, wood, ice) and making constructs out of doors that will be reclaimed by nature (he refers to them as being transformed rather than destroyed). The film's lack of structure is a decided weakness, but Goldsworthy explains his aims with clarity and an admirable honesty that allows him to own up to misjudgments. He is a natural communicator and a delight. You can well understand why this film has become a cult hit in America with Thomas Reidelsheimer proving an ideal director and photographer for this material. His poetic sense is a perfect match for Goldsworthy's art. MS

• *With*: Andy Goldsworthy.
• *Dir, Screenplay, Ph* and *Ed* Thomas Riedelsheimer, *Pro* Annedore von Donop, *M* Fred Firth.

Mediopolis Berlin/Westdeutscher Rundfunk/arte-ICA Projects.
90 mins. Germany. 2001. Rel: 4 July 2003. Cert U.

Roger Dodger ★★★★
Manhattan, the present. Cynical, smooth-talking, predatory and louche – Roger Swanson is everything his 16 year-old nephew Nick thinks he wants to be. But when Nick shows up unannounced at Roger's workplace, little does he realise that he is about to witness the destruction in one night of the façade that Roger has spent so many years varnishing to such brittle perfection ... Dylan Kidd's smart and pungent indie film grooves mightily on Campbell Scott's supremely poised performance in the title role. Easily steering wide of the caricature he could have been, Scott constantly hints at the remains of a soul underneath his character's reptilian carapace, which makes his decline and fall all the more affecting, and lends credulity to the upbeat ending. AK

• *Roger Swanson* Campbell Scott, *Nick* Jesse Eisenberg, *Joyce* Isabella Rossellini, *Andrea* Elizabeth Berkley, *Sophie* Jennifer Beals, *Donna* Mina Badie, *Donovan* Ben Shenkman.
• *Dir* and *Screenplay* Dylan Kidd, *Pro* Kidd, Anne Chaisson and George VanBuskirk, *Ph* Joaquin Baca-Asay, *Pro Des* Stephen Beatrice, *Ed* Andy Kier, *M* Craig Wedren.

Holedigger Films-Optimum.
104 mins. USA. 2002. Rel: 15 August 2003. Cert 15.

Rugrats Go Wild ★★★

The third *Rugrats* movie delivers the goods without being in any way memorable. This time out, everyone's favourite animated babies join forces with *The Wild Thornberries*, another hit cartoon show from the Nickelodeon channel. The desert island rescue plot provides a solid backdrop for the succession of gags and a commendable eco-friendly message. *Rugrats Go Wild* also features 'Odorama', a gimmick previously used for *The Scent of Mystery* and John Waters' less fragrant *Polyester* (viewers could obtain scratch'n'sniff cards with a series of numbered smells; when a number appears onscreen, the appropriate odour is unleashed). Even without the smells, *Rugrats Go Wild* is accomplished, fast-paced family entertainment. That said, the numerous film references – including *Gone With The Wind*, *Titanic*, *Planet of the Apes* and even *Tea and Sympathy* – will be lost on most children. However, guardians obliged to sit through it may appreciate the extra laugh or two.
DO

• *Voices: Spike* Bruce Willis, *Siri* Chrissie Hynde, *Tommy Pickles* E.G. Daily, *Chuckie Finster* Nancy Cartwright, *Phil DeVille/Lil DeVille/Betty DeVille* Kath Soucie, *Angelica Pickles* Cheryl Chase, *Sir Nigel Thornberry* Tim Curry, *Debbie Thornberry* Danielle Harris, *Marianne Thornberry* Jodi Carlisle, *Eliza Thornberry* Lacey Chabert, *Donnie Thornberry* Michael Balzary (aka Flea), *Didi Pickles* Melanie Chartoff, *Stu Pickles* Jack Riley, *Darwin* Tom Kane, *Charlotte Pickles* Tress MacNeille, *Dil Pickles* Tara Strong, *with* Michael Bell, Julia Kato, Phil Proctor, Cree Summer, Dionne Quan.
• *Dir* Norton Virgien and John Eng, *Pro* Arlene Klasky and Gabor Csupo, *Ex Pro* Albie Hecht, Julia Pistor, Eryk Casemiro and Hal Waite, *Co-Pro* Tracy Kramer, Terry Thoren and Patrick Stapleton, *Screenplay* Kate Boutilier, *Pro Des* Dima Malanitchev, *Ed* John Bryant and Kimberly Rettberg, *M* Mark Mothersbaugh.

Nickelodeon Movies/Klasky Csupo-UIP.
80 minutes. USA. 2003. Rel: 8 August 2003.
Cert U.

Runaway Jury ★★★★

John Grisham's illustrious career on the cinematic page all but curled up to die with the bland and sombre *The Chamber*. In that 1996 turkey Gene Hackman salvaged all that was left of the film with a biting performance as a boorish bigot. Now the actor is back as another nasty piece of work in the best-selling author's corrosive look at legal injustice in this slick, breathless page-turner. Hackman plays Rankin Fitch, a ruthless jury consultant whose amoral grandstanding is confirmed by such statements as,

'trials are too important to be left to juries.' In this instance, a gun manufacturer is on the stand for an office-shooting spree that has left eleven people dead. The corporation, which makes an annual $200m in sales, could lose their coat in this landmark case, so Fitch's asking fee of $20m to swing the verdict should be chicken feed. How Fitch utilises illegal surveillance and common intimidation to get his results makes for fascinating viewing, but there are other foxes in the chicken coop and no agenda is as straightforward as it seems. With its multi-layered ideologies, narrative U-turns and juicy performances (Dustin Hoffman steals the film as a principled lawyer), *Runaway Jury* is grand, old-fashioned entertainment.
JC-W

• *Nick Easter* John Cusack, *Rankin Fitch* Gene Hackman, *Wendall Rohr* Dustin Hoffman, *Marlee* Rachel Weisz, *Durwood Cable* Bruce Davison, *Judge Harkin* Bruce McGill, *Lawrence Green* Jeremy Piven, *Doyle* Nick Searcy, *Garland Jankle* Stanley Anderson, *Frank Herrera* Cliff Curtis, *Janovich* Nestor Serrano, *Lamb* Leland Orser, *Vanessa Lembeck* Jennifer Beals, *Herman Grimes* Gerry Bamman, *Celeste Wood* Joanna Going, *Lonnie Shaver* Bill Nunn, *Loreen Duke* Juanita Jennings, *Amanda Monroe* Marguerite Moreau, *Stella Jullic* Nora Dunn, *Eddie Weese* Guy Torry, *Millie Dupree* Rusty Schwimmer, *with* Orlando Jones, Gary Grubbs, Henry Darrow, Celia Weston, Ed Nelson, and Dylan McDermott (*uncredited*).
• *Dir* Gary Fleder, *Pro* Arnon Milchan, Gary Fleder and Christopher Mankiewicz, *Ex Pro* Jeffrey Downer, *Screenplay* Brian Koppelman, David Levien, Rick Cleveland and Matthew Chapman, based on the novel by John Grisham, *Ph* Robert Elswit, *Pro Des* Nelson Coates, *Ed* William Steinkamp, *M* Christopher Young, *M Supervisor* Peter Afterman, *Costumes* Abigail Murray, *Sound* Wylie Stateman.

Regency Enterprises/New Regency-Fox.
127 mins. USA. 2003. Rel: 16 January 2004.
Cert 12A.

The Rundown
See *Welcome to the Jungle*.

The Saddest Music in the World

★★★

As camp as can be, Guy Maddin's idiosyncratic film blends a complex story of family friction, much of it pure melodrama, with preparations for a competition in Winnipeg in 1933 to find the saddest music in the world. This pre-Eurovision event with countries going head to head (Serbia vs. Scotland, anyone?) is run by Lady Port-Huntley (Isabella Rossellini), an amputee. As so often with Maddin, the visual style echoes silent cinema (the greater part of the piece is photographed in black and white too). As an oddity, musical or otherwise, the film is unlike anything else and, in truth, assessment of it is entirely a reflection of personal taste. It's certainly true to itself. MS

• *Chester Kent* Mark McKinney, *Lady Port-Huntly* Isabella Rossellini, *Narcissa* Maria de Medeiros, *Fyodor* David Fox, *Roderick/Gavrillo* Ross McMillan. • *Dir* Guy Maddin, *Pro* Niv Fichman and Jody Shapiro, *Screenplay* Guy Maddin and George Toles, from a original screenplay by Kazuo Ishiguro, *Ph* Luc Montpellier, *Pro Des* Matthew Davies, *Ed* David Wharnsby, *M* Christopher Dedrick.

Rhombus Media/ Buffalo Gal Pictures/
Ego Film Arts-Soda Pictures.
100 mins. Canada. 2003. Rel: 7th May 2004. Cert 15.

The Safety of Objects ★★½

Jake Train has fallen in love with his sister's doll, Tani. Jake's father, Jim, is so defined by his job that he's become a stranger in his own household. And across the spread of manicured lawns, Jim and Jake's neighbours are wrestling with their own imperfect lives, clinging to the material objects – inanimate or otherwise – that authenticate their existence. Collated from seven short stories by A.M. Homes, *The Safety of Objects* offers a number of keen observations and a few surprises. There are also some beautifully calibrated, low-key performances from a cast of largely intelligent actors. However, the tenuous link that connects the various tales never feels less than contrived, acting more as a ligature than a bridge. Consequently, the drama of one story (such as the abduction of a child) tends to intrude on the nuance of another, resulting in a fractured mosaic that is entirely alienating. There's much to chew on here, but the film's lack of narrative momentum acts against it. JC-W

• *Esther Gold* Glenn Close, *Jim Train* Dermot Mulroney, *Julie Gold* Jessica Campbell, *Annette Jennings* Patricia Clarkson, *Paul Gold* Joshua Jackson, *Susan Train* Moira Kelly, *Howard Gold* Robert Klein, *Randy* Timothy Olyphant, *Sam Jennings* Kristen Stewart, *Helen Christianson* Mary Kay Place, *Jake Train* Alex House.
• *Dir* and *Screenplay* Rose Troche, based on the book of stories by A.M. Homes, *Pro* Dorothy Berwin and Christine Vachon, *Ex Pro* Stephen Evans, Angus Finney, Jody Patton and Pamela Koffler, *Co-Pro* Troche and Eric Robison, *Assoc Pro* Jon Marcus and Sophie Janson, *Ph* Enrique Chediak, *Pro Des* Andrea Stanley, *Ed* Geraldine Peroni, *M* Emboznik, Barb Morrison, Charles Nieland and Nance Nieland, *Costumes* Laura Jean Shannon.

Renaissance Films/Clear Blue Sky Prods/Infilm/Killer Films-Entertainment.
121 mins. USA/UK. 2001. Rel 15 August 2003. Cert 15.

Scary Movie 3 ★★★

As long as audiences keep flocking to certain films, so the rearguard of Hollywood will continue lampooning them. And if something like *Scary Movie 3* can gross $50m in one weekend, they are going to be arriving with greater frequency. This time the comically abused are predominantly *Signs* and *The Ring*, with a battery of sideswipes aimed at *8 Mile*, *The Others* and *The Sixth Sense*. With David Zucker (*Airplane!*, *The Naked Gun*) taking over the helm from *Scary Movie* regular Keenen Ivory Wayans, the comic bar has been raised and the third outing is a pleasing improvement on the last. Pamela Anderson, with gratuitous cleavage, plays a dumb blonde who is worried about 'that' video. No, not the Pam and Tommy Lee video, the one that kills anyone who watches it. Meanwhile, a white farm boy wants to be a black rapper (although his Eminem/KKK hood proves to be a disadvantage), while his farm has the letters ATTACK HERE carved into the cornfield. It's hard to diss a comedy that provides so many belly laughs, even if there are more misfires, but this should go down nicely after a pizza and two or five beers. JC-W

• *Cindy Campbell* Anna Faris, *Mahalik* Anthony Anderson, *President Harris* Leslie Nielsen, *Trooper Champlin* Camryn Manheim, *George* Simon Rex, *The Architect* George Carlin, *Aunt ShaNeequa/The Oracle* Queen Latifah, *Orpheus* Eddie Griffin, *Annie* Denise Richards, *John Wilson* D.L. Hughley, *Agent Thompson* Ja Rule, *Ross Giggins* Jeremy Piven, *Brenda Weeks* Regina Hall, *Tom* Charlie Sheen, *Tabitha* Marny Eng, *Carson Ward* Tim Stack, *as themselves* Pamela Anderson, Jenny McCarthy, Elaine and Diane Klimaszewski, Simon Cowell, Fat Joe, Master P, Macy Gray, Method Man, Redman, Raekwon, The RZA, U-God.
• *Dir* David Zucker, *Pro* Robert K. Weiss, *Ex Pro* Bob Weinstein, Harvey Weinstein, Andrew Rona and Brad Weston, *Co-Pro* Grace Gilroy, *Screenplay* Craig Mazin and Pat Proft, based on characters

Film Review 2004-2005 **103**

created by Shawn Wayans, Marlon Wayans, Buddy Johnson, Phil Beauman, Jason Friedberg and Aaron Seltzer, *Ph* Mark Irwin, *Pro Des* William Elliot, *Ed* Malcolm Campbell and Jon Poll, *M* James L. Venable, *Costumes* Carol Ramsey, *Makeup* L. Taylor Roberts, *Visual f/x supervisor* Stuart Robertson, *Stunt coordinator* Jacob Rupp, *Choreographer* Viktoria Langton.

Dimension Films/Brad Grey Pictures-Buena Vista. 84 mins. USA. 2003. Rel: 23 January 2004. Cert 15.

School of Rock ★★★★★

In years to come, this could rank as important a film about rock 'n' roll as *Woodstock*, *Quadrophenia* and *Almost Famous*. It's also very, very funny and should appeal equally to jaded rock anoraks and their musically ignorant offspring. Jack Black, who played the Righteous Brothers enthusiast in *High Fidelity* and is one half of the metal/comedy duo Tenacious D, finds his stride as Dewey Finn, an impecunious rock fanatic who sleeps on his best friend's floor and pollutes his mind with unfounded dreams of rock stardom. He then impersonates his friend to land a substitute teaching post at the very proper Horace Green Elementary School. With no concept of discipline or academic protocol, Dewey instils his bemused students with his passion for rock music, forming an unlikely rock band in the process. Black's energy and innate comic persona coupled with a canny script by Mike White (who also plays Black's best friend), makes for high octane entertainment that turns the template of *Dead Poets Society* on its head. The kids are also wonderfully cast, retaining their sedate demeanour even when approximating the musical attack of The Who and Black Sabbath. JC-W

• *Dewey Finn* Jack Black, *Rosalie Mullins* Joan Cusack, *Ned Schneebly* Mike White, *Patti Di Marco* Sarah Silverman, *Theo* Adam Pacal, *Zack* Joey Gaydos Jr., *Tomika* Maryam Hassan, *Freddy* Kevin Clark, *Katie* Rebecca Brown, *Lawrence* Robert Tsai, *with* Jordan-Claire Green, Veronica Afflerbach, Miranda Cosgrove, Angelo Massagli, Kevin Clark, Caitlin Hale, Cole Hawkins, Brian Falduto, James Hosey, Aleisha Allen, Zachary Infante, Rebecca Brown, Jaclyn Neidenthal, Suzzanne Douglas, Kate McGregor-Stewart, Tim Hopper, Nicky Katt, MacIntyre Dixon.
• *Dir* Richard Linklater, *Pro* Scott Rudin, *Ex Pro* Steve Nicolaides and Scott Aversano, *Screenplay* Mike White, *Ph* Rogier Stoffers, *Pro Des* Jeremy Conway, *Ed* Sandra Adair, *M* Craig Wedren; Joaquín Rodrigo; songs performed by No Vacancy, The Clash, Kiss, Cream, The Doors, AC/DC, The Who, Jonathan Richman & The Modern Lovers, The Ramones, Metallica, The Darkness, Led Zeppelin,

The Black Keys, Stevie Nicks, T. Rex, David Bowie, Wylde Ratttz, The Velvet Underground, Jack Black, etc, *Costumes* Karen Patch.

Paramount/MFP Munich/New Century-UIP. 108 mins. USA/Germany. 2003. Rel: 6 February. Cert PG.

Scooby Doo 2: Monsters Unleashed ★★

Granted, Matthew Lillard is a dead ringer for Shaggy. Also granted, the CGI Scooby is pretty funny. However, the sequel to last year's smash hit is pretty dull stuff. The story tries hard to inject a sense of danger to the iconic cartoon series when the world turns against the ghost-busting gang after the big opening of a museum exhibit dedicated to their pursuits goes horribly wrong. But the jokes are uninspired, feeling very much like lazy rehashes of the first film, and we begin to realise there are serious limitations on how far you can go with characters that are as firmly embedded into the cultural consciousness as the Scooby Doo gang. Great CGI and a couple of cool action scenes, but a few big gulps do not a spring hit make. AK

• *Fred* Freddie Prinze Jr., *Daphne* Sarah Michelle Gellar, *Shaggy* Matthew Lillard, *Velma* Linda Cardellini, *Patrick Wisely* Seth Green, *Old Man Wickles* Peter Boyle, *Jacobo* Tim Blake Nelson, *Heather Jasper-Howe* Alicia Silverstone, *voice of Scooby-Doo* Neil Fanning, *himself* Pat O'Brien, *himself* Ruben Studdard, *chauffeur* Bill Meilen, *Ned* Zahf Paroo, *with* Christopher Gauthier, Bradley Gosnell, Stephen E. Miller, Karin Konoval.
• *Dir* Raja Gosnell, *Pro* Charles Roven and Richard Suckle, *Ex Pro* Brent O'Connor, Kelley Smith-Wait and Joseph Barbera, *Co-Pro* James Gunn and Alan G. Glazer, *Screenplay* James Gunn, based on characters created by Hanna-Barbera Prods, *Ph* Oliver Wood, *Pro Des* Bill Boes; *Ed* Kent Beyda, *M* David Newman; songs performed by Clay Aiken, Wild Cherry, Puffy Ami Yumi, Apache Indian, Bad Manners, Big Brovaz, 2 Unlimited, Matthew Lillard and Neil Fanning, New Radicals, Bon Jovi, Bowling for Soup, MxPx, Ruben Studdard, Simple Plan, Patrick Nuo, etc, *Costumes* Leesa Evans, *Visual Effects* Peter Crosman.

Warner/Mosaic Media Group-Warner. 92 mins. USA. 2004. Rel: 2 April 2004. Cert PG.

Seabiscuit ★★★★

In the depths of America's Depression, a grieving automobile tycoon, an obsolete cowboy and an oversized jockey fall into orbit around one of the greatest legends in equine racing history, a pint-sized Hercules named Seabiscuit … A reverential and melodramatic retelling of an epic but true story, the movie distils the historical liquor of hope, tragedy and triumph into a more believable chain of events than in fact occurred. Even against the factual record, it is barely credible that the runt of a pedigreed sire, abused and denigrated throughout its raising, could become the greatest racehorse in America's history, bearing the weight of a washed up, half-blind, oversized jockey, and beating all comers in to set a showdown with a thundering stallion, aptly called War Admiral. The film is strongest when it frees itself from the documentary backgrounding of the Depression Era, intermittently delivered in sonorous narrative, and runs with the idea that it is ultimately a story about the regenerative power of faith, belief and a heroic little horse. AK

• *Red Pollard* Tobey Maguire, *Charles Howard* Jeff Bridges, *Tom Smith* Chris Cooper, *Marcela Howard* Elizabeth Banks, *'Tick Tock' McGlaughlin* William H. Macy, *George Woolf* Gary Stevens, *with* Ed Lauter, Eddie Jones, Sam Bottoms.
• *Dir* and *Screenplay* Gary Ross, based on the book by Laura Hillenbrand, *Pro* Kathleen Kennedy, Frank Marshall, Gary Ross and Jane Sindell, *Ex Pro* Gary Barber, Roger Birnbaum, Tobey Maguire, Allison Thomas and Robin Bissell, *Co-Pro* Patricia Churchill, *Ph* John Schwartzman, *Pro Des* Jeannine Claudia Oppewall, *Ed* William Goldenberg, *M* Randy Newman, *Costumes* Judianna Makovsky.

Universal/DreamWorks/Spyglass Entertainment/Larger Than Life/Kennedy/Marshall-Buena Vista.
141 mins. USA. 2003. Rel: 31 October 2003. Cert PG.

Secondhand Lions ★★★¹/₂

Texas, 1960-ish. 15 year-old Walter is dumped on the rickety doorstep of his two ornery uncles by his selfish, tramp of a mom en route to her further adventures in LA. Neither party much likes being landed with the other, but by way of any movie so deeply doused in Norman Rockwellian imagery, they eventually become a family that grows to include an old circus lion kept as a pet … A mostly delightful story that works well on the gruff chemistry between Robert Duvall and Michael Caine, and on the boyish adventure-story flashbacks of their youthful fighting years, Tim McCanlies' loving trip into cinematic nostalgia would have been so much better without the manipulative arm-twisting that forces us to love his characters as much as he does without giving us the option of taking another road. AK

• *Garth McCann* Michael Caine, *Hubbard 'Hub' McCann* Robert Duvall, *Walter* Haley Joel Osment, *Stan* Nicky Katt, *Mae* Kyra Sedgwick, *Princess Jasmine* Emmanuelle Vaugier, *young Hub* Christian Kane, *young Garth* Kevin Michael Haberer, *adult Walter* Josh Lucas, *with* Eric Balfour, Adrian Pasdar, George Haynes, Eugene Osment.
• *Dir* and *Screenplay* Tim McCanlies, *Pro* David Kirschner, Scott Ross and Carey Sienega, *Ex Pro* Cayle Boyter, Janis Rothbard Chaskin, Kevin Cooper, Mark Kaufman and Karen Loop, *Co-Pro* Amy Sayres, *Ph* Jack N. Green, *Pro Des* David J. Bomba, *Ed* David Moritz, *M* Patrick Doyle, *Costumes* Gary Jones.

New Line Cinema/Digital Domain-Entertainment.
108 mins. USA. 2003. Rel: 24 October 2003. Cert PG.

Right: Horse sense: Tobey Maguire overcomes incredible odds in Gary Ross's inspirational *Seabiscuit* (from BVI)

Secret Window ★★

In yet another underwhelming adaptation of a Stephen King story, Johnny Depp tics his way through a performance as best-selling author Mort Rainey, who is kicked out of his home after a messy separation with his wife, blocked on his latest book, and is confronted by an aggressive, drawling amateur scribbler with accusations of plagiarism. No wonder he looks like an unmade bed. While every indication suggests that the film intends to a complex and intellectual psycho-thriller, the fact is that it is an obvious collection of B-grade noir clichés that have been stretched to a movie-length when it would probably have made a decent 30 minute short. AK

• *Mort Rainey* Johnny Depp, *John Shooter* John Turturro, *Amy Rainey* Maria Bello, *Ted Miner* Timothy Hutton, *Ken Karsch* Charles S. Dutton, *Sheriff Dave Newsome* Len Cariou, *with* Joan Heney, John Dunn Hill, Vlasta Vrana, Bronwen Mantel.
• *Dir* and *Screenplay* David Koepp, based on the novella *Secret Window, Secret Garden* by Stephen King, *Pro* Gavin Polone, *Ex Pro* Ezra Swerdlow, *Ph* Fred Murphy, *M* Philip Glass, *Pro Des* Howard Cummings, *Ed* Jill Savitt, *Costumes* Odette Gadoury, *Sound* Tim Chau.

Columbia/Pariah-Columbia TriStar.
95 mins. USA. 2004. Rel: 30 April 2004. Cert 12A.

Sex is Comedy ★★★★

Although this is less intense than most films by France's Catherine Breillat, the title should not be taken as indicating that you will find great laughs here. What you do get is a kind of self-portrait as a woman filmmaker (Parillaud) deals with the problems of shooting a film akin to Breillat's own *A Ma Soeur*. It covers not only the temperament displayed by the actors, but the difficulties of handling sex scenes due to be played out between players who dislike each other. Things are further complicated by the responses of the male lead, simultaneously nervous of the shoot but excited by it. Grégoire Colin's performance plays up to this unflattering portrait admirably, but the film's main interest is for anyone fascinated by Breillat's work. Those who see her dramas as criticising male dominance in sexual relationships will be intrigued to find that here her alter ego seems to gain sexual stimulation vicariously through the power she exercises as a filmmaker. MS

• *Jeanne* Anne Parillaud, *the actor* Grégoire Colin, *the actress* Roxane Mesquida, *Leo, the first assistant* Ashley Wanninger, *Willy* Dominique Colladant, Bart Binnema, Yves Osmu, Elisabete Piecho, Francis Seleck, Diane Scapa, Ana Lorena, Claire Monatte, Arnaldo Junior.

• *Dir* and *Screenplay* Catherine Breillat, *Pro* Jean-Francois Lepetit and António da Cunha Telles, *Ph* Laurent Macheul, *Pro Des* Frédérique Belvaux, *Ed* Pascale Chavance, *Costumes* Frédérique Belvaux.

CB (Catherine Breillat) Films/Canal Plus/Centre National de la Cinématographie/Flach Film/France Télévision Images 2-Artificial Eye.
94 mins. France/Portugal. 2003.
Rel 25 July 2003. Cert 18.

Sex Lives of the Potato Men ★

Slobbish Brummies Dave and Ferris deliver potatoes to chip chops across the West Midlands, chasing local skirt along the way. But can their mission to have sex with as many women as possible bring them true happiness? It's difficult to imagine how a film with that premise and that title could have a) received such a generous slice of Lottery money and b) managed not to be very funny, but *Sex Lives of the Potato Men* achieves the impossible on both counts. The most notorious film of the year is offensive not because it's so prurient (although there is some jaw-droppingly filthy dialogue) but because it fundamentally fails to deliver. Not a laugh. Not a nipple. This was never going to launch a new wave of smutty blockbusters, but it might have found some kind of an audience if writer/director Andy Humphries had had the courage of his convictions. MH

• *Dave* Johnny Vegas, *Ferris* Mackenzie Crook, *Jeremy* Mark Gatiss, *Tolly* Dominic Coleman, *Joan* Kate Robbins, *Ruth* Lucy Davis, *chip shop girl* Helen Latham, *Poppy* Nicola Reynolds, *Shelley* Julia Davis, *Joan's mum* Evie Garratt *with* Barry Aird, Laurence Inman, Adrian Chiles.
• *Dir* and *Screenplay* Andy Humphries, *Pro* Christine Grayford, Graham Grayford, Cass Marks and Anita Overland, *Ex Pro* Nigel Green and Robert Jones, *Ph* Andy Collins, *Pro Des* Patrick Lyndon Standford and Adam Zoltowski, *Ed* Guy Bensley, *Costumes* Natalie Ward.

Devotion Films-Entertainment.
83 mins. UK. 2004. Rel: 20 February 2004. Cert 18.

The Shape of Things ★★★½

Nerdy collegiate Adam meets anarchic artist Evelyn as she is just about to deface a museum sculpture for the sin of a plaster fig-leaf covering its modesty and falls heavily for her spirited beauty. Their unlikely romance develops a creepingly unhealthy vibe as Evelyn chips away at his conventionality, transforming Adam into an magazine ideal of masculinity. Adam's friends, also a dysfunctional couple, try to warn him to be careful of Evelyn's temptations but he will heed them only too late … Neil LaBute's film of his stage-play maintains its original formalism and its bitter edge. Paul Rudd and Rachel Weisz make impressive leads, rounding out their characters well against the thunder of inevitability inherent in LaBute's script. The analytical atmosphere is typical LaBute and makes for a claustrophobic chamber piece on themes of sexual cruelty and the deluded justifications of 'art'. AK

• *Jenny* Gretchen Mol, *Adam* Paul Rudd, *Evelyn* Rachel Weisz, *Philip* Frederick Weller.
• *Dir* and *Screenplay* Neil LaBute, based on his stage play, *Pro* LaBute, Gail Mutrux, Philip Steuer and Rachel Weisz, *Ex Pro* Tim Bevan and Eric Fellner, *Ph* James L. Carter, *Pro Des Costumes* Lynette Meyer, *Ed* Joel Plotch, *M* Elvis Costello, *Costumes* Lynette Meyer.

Focus Features/StudioCanal/Working Title/
Pretty Pictures-Momentum.
97 mins. USA/France/UK. 2003.
Rel: 28 November 2003. Cert 15.

Shattered Glass ★★

Stephen Glass is the youngest writer on the staff of a prestige magazine *The New Republic*, which tagline boasts itself 'The In-Flight Magazine of Air Force 1'. But his ambitions lead him to plagiarize and invent the content of the human interest stories which make him the staff darling. The film explores the seedy purgatory that the journalist (nervously played by Hayden Christensen in a type-breaking choice of

role) finds himself in when another magazine begins to chip away at his work. Charting the disintegration of a born liar like Stephen Glass makes for uncomfortable watching. But when the star character is this creepy, shifty, deluded and manipulative, even the most outraged audience will find his decline and denouement a painful and frankly unrewarding spectacle. AK

• *Stephen Glass* Hayden Christensen, *Charles 'Chuck' Lane* Peter Sarsgaard, *Caitlin Avey* Chloë Sevigny, *Andie Fox* Rosario Dawson, *Amy Brand* Melanie Lynskey, *Michael Kelly* Hank Azaria, *Adam Penenberg* Steve Zahn, *Kambiz* Cas Anvar, *with* Mark Blum, Simone-Elise Girard, Luke Kirby, Ted Kotcheff, Caroline Goodall.
• *Dir* and *Screenplay* Billy Ray, from the *Vanity Fair* article by Buzz Bissinger, *Pro* Craig Baumgarten, Adam Merims, Tove Christensen and Gaye Hirsch, *Ex Pro* Tom Cruise, Paula Wagner, Michael Paseornek and Tom Ortenberg, *Ph* Mandy Walker, *Pro Des* François Séguin, *Ed* Jeffrey Ford, *M* Mychael Danna, *Costumes* Renée April.

Lions Gate/Cruise/Wagner-Icon.
94 mins. USA/Canada. 2003. Rel: 14th May 2004.
Cert 12A.

Shaun of the Dead ★★★★

London, the present. When the zombie apocalypse strikes, what is an ordinary, lager drinking, dead-end job holding bloke to do? Possibly the funniest rom-zom-com to come from the UK since *Carry On Screaming* (and I stretch the comparison, as I don't

Right:
Gut feelings: Simon Pegg contemplates the future in Edgar Wright's cheap and brilliant *Shaun of the Dead* (from UIP)

really recall many zombies in that camp classic), Simon Pegg and Edgar Wright have struck upon a killer of a concept and gleefully lead a cast of instantly recognizable British underachievers through a delightful comic romp. The question above is posed to Shaun, who wakes up after a heavy night consoling himself over the loss of his girlfriend Liz, to discover that London has been overrun by zombies. Proper zombies, too, who shuffle and bite and roll their eyes with the kind of conviction they teach at RADA. He plans to drive through the shambling masses to save his girlfriend, her flatmates, his mother and her boyfriend, and seek refuge in his local pub like any sensible person would. The comedy that ensues is cheap, piss-taking slapstick, uneven in parts, and actually quite brilliant. AK

• *Shaun* Simon Pegg, *Liz* Kate Ashfield, *Dianne* Lucy Davis, *Ed* Nick Frost, *David* Dylan Moran, *Philip* Bill Nighy, *Barbara* Penelope Wilton, *Yvonne* Jessica Stevenson, *Pete* Peter Serafinowicz, *Noel* Rafe Spall, *Declan* Martin Freeman, *with* Nicola Cunningham, Sonell Dadral, Trisha Goddard, David Park, Carol Barnes, Vernon Kay, Julia Deakin, Matt Lucas, Keith Chegwin.
• *Dir* Edgar Wright, *Pro* Nira Park, *Ex Pro* Tim Bevan, Eric Fellner, Natascha Wharton, James Wilson and Alison Owen, *Screenplay* Wright and Simon Pegg, *Ph* David M. Dunlap, *Pro Des* Marcus Rowland, *Ed* Chris Dickens, *M* Daniel Mudford and Pete Woodhead, *Costumes* Annie Hardinge, *Special Effects Supervisor* Paul Dunn, *Zombie/Prosthetics Make-Up* Stuart Conran, *Choreographer* Litza Bixtier.

Universal Pictures/StudioCanal/Working Title/WT/ Big Talk Prods-UIP.
97 mins. UK/USA/France. 2004.
Rel: 9 April 2004. Cert 15.

Shoreditch ★★¹/₂

Switching back and forth neatly enough between 1939 and the present day, this drama of London's East End centres on an inherited property once a jazz club where human remains are found in a blocked-up cellar. Whose body is it and what drove him to suicide? A promising concept is severely let down by writing which prevents the characters from coming to life and by the inept way in which a mystery tale is turned into a quasi-musical – indeed inept is too mild a word when Joely Richardson interrupts the action to tackle songs made famous by Billie Holiday. Malcolm Needs was writer, producer and director so despite his technical competence he must carry the blame. MS

• *Butterfly* Joely Richardson, *Thomas Hickman* Shane Richie, *Albert Challis* Glen Murphy, *Jenson Thackery*

John Standing, *Maisie Hickman* Natasha Wightman, *Karl* Jonathan Coy, *Tom Hickman* Adam Ross, *Chad* Brian Bovell, *guest singer* Dane Bowers, *William Nicholls* Joe Shaw, *with* Claire Tyler, Douglas McFerran, Jacqueline Dankworth, Hugh Cecil, Peter Howitt.
• *Dir, Pro* and *Screenplay* Malcolm Needs, *Ex Pro* Shane Richie and Terence S. Potter, *Co-Pro* Alan Latham and Tim Lewiston, *Line Pro* Tricia Cooklin, *Ph* Zoran Veljkovic, *Pro Des* Andrea Christelis, Johnny Hawkins and Tracy Ann-Baines, *Ed* Henry Richardson, *M* Rick Taylor and Steve Brown; songs performed by Elton John, Wet Wet Wet, Beverley Clark, *Costumes* Marcia Stanton.

Aquarius Film Co./Mother Meighan Prods/Movietrack Pictures-Georgia Films.
100 mins. UK. 2002. Rel: 28 November 2003. Cert 15.

A Silence Between Two Thoughts
★★★
(*Sokaate beine do feks*)
This appropriately solemn and minimalistic movie from Iran made by the writer/director who gave us *Secret Ballot* gained notoriety when the Iranian authorities confiscated the negatives leaving only a digital original as the basis for prints. Set in a remote village, it works best as an almost Beckettian abstraction about people serving a regime that seems to promise change. Such a man is the central figure, an executioner expected to marry a victim who would have died at his hands but for a reprieve arising from the belief that an executed virgin will go to heaven. For two thirds of its length this anguished, heart-felt film rewards those prepared to give themselves to it, but the last third becomes more diffuse, less clear in intent and perched uneasily between confusing reality and a parable of indefinite meaning. It's powerful and frustrating in equal measure. MS

• *young woman* Maryam Moghaddam, *executioner* Kamalan Narouii.
• *Dir, Pro, Screenplay* and *Ed* Babak Payami, *Ph* Farzad Jodat, *Pro Des* Payami and Jodat, *Ed* Jafar Panahi and Babak Karimi.

Payam Films & Sharmshir-Artificial Eye.
95 mins. Iran/Switzerland. 2003.
Rel: 11 June 2004. No Cert.

Silent Grace ★★★★
(*The Follower*)
While ignoring wider issues about the IRA, Maeve Murphy's promising first feature has unexpected qualities. Her aim is to use a fictional but believable story to record an actuality, namely that women

prisoners, fighting for the right to be given political status and protesting at inhuman prison conditions, were involved in hunger strikes in Armagh in 1980 and 1981. Women are accordingly central to the drama and are both well played and well characterised. David Katznelson's photography brings cinematic flair to bear hiding the stage origins of the piece and Murphy by refusing to demonise such figures as the prison governor ensures that *Silent Grace* comes across as humane rather than narrowly political. Not everyone will be drawn to such material but in its modest way this is very well done. MS

• *Eileen* Orla Brady, *Aine Quinn* Cathleen Bradley, *Margaret* Cara Seymour, *Geraldine* Dawn Bradfield, *Cunningham* Connor Mullen, *Father McGarry* Robert Newman, Carol Scanlon, *Peter, IRA man* Patrick Bergin, *Roisin* Maeve Murphy.
• *Dir* and *Screenplay* Maeve Murphy, inspired by the play *Now and At the Hour of Our Death* by Murphy in collaboration with Trouble & Strife, *Pro* Maeve Murphy and Deirdre McMahon, *Ex Pro* Nigel-Warren Green, Marie Louise Queally, Gerry McColgan and Rod Stoneman, *Ph* David Katznelson, *Pro Des* Nicole Moroney, *Ed* Breege Rowley, *M* Kila and Jimmy Smyth, *Costumes* Soutra Gilmore.

Follower Films/Irish Screen/Crimson Films-Guerilla Films.
86 mins. Ireland/UK. 2001. Rel: 13 February 2004. Cert 15.

Sinbad: Legend of the Seven Seas
★★★

Considering the track record of DreamWorks' animation department (*Antz, Chicken Run, Shrek, Spirit: Stallion of the Cimarron*), the company's seventh cartoon is a tad disappointing. Boasting a stellar voice cast and a powerful narrative arc, *Sinbad* really should have held its own with the likes of Disney's *Aladdin* and *Mulan*. As it is, it's a traditionally animated saga freely juggling Greek and Roman mythology, with Sinbad himself plucked from the *Arabian Nights*. While folklorists may bridle at such artistic liberties, the story is this saga's strongest suit – there's nothing so involving as the reformation of a rogue. Although blandly voiced by Brad Pitt and given the physical characteristics of a cubist painting, Sinbad is, after all, our hero. When he's framed for the theft of the Book of Peace by Eris, the goddess of chaos, he is sentenced to death by the elders of Syracuse. Believing in his innocence, Sinbad's childhood friend Proteus offers to take his place and is given ten days to live while Sinbad gets the book back. But Sinbad couldn't care less and sets

off to Fiji to enjoy some R & R. Hell, he even attempts to seduce Marina, Proteus's fiancée. Where the film truly succeeds is in its spectacular backdrops and high-octane action, superbly engineered by state-of-the-art computer technology. Younger kids should be captivated. JC-W

• *Voices: Sinbad* Brad Pitt, *Marina* Catherine Zeta-Jones, *Eris* Michelle Pfeiffer, *Proteus* Joseph Fiennes, *Kale* Dennis Haysbert, *Dymas* Timothy West, *Rat* Adriano Giannini.
• *Dir* Tim Johnson and Patrick Gilmore, *Pro* Mireille Soria and Jeffrey Katzenberg, *Screenplay* John Logan, *Pro Des* Raymond Zibach, *Ed* Tom Finan, *M* Harry Gregson-Williams, *Animation supervisor* Kristof Serrand.

DreamWorks-UIP.
86 mins. USA. 2003. Rel: 25 July 2003. Cert. U.

Since Otar Left ★★½
(Depuis qu'Otar est parti...)
Three actresses headed by the wonderful 90-year-old Esther Gorintin are well cast here to represent three generations of a family living in Tbilisi. Furthermore, Julie Bertuccelli, making her feature debut, has a gift for atmospheric location shooting and for evoking mood through acute observation of faces. So far, so very good, but it astounds me that most critics seem to have accepted the credibility of the story-line as the old lady is kept in ignorance of the death in Paris of the son she dotes on, Otar. In *Good Bye, Lenin!* a comparable notion was made persuasive, but here the situation is allowed to build in ways that become increasingly unlikely. Long before the end, I had ceased to believe a word of it, and when that happens not even an excellent cast can save the day.
MS

• *Eka* Esther Gorintin, *Marina* Nino Khomassouridze, *Ada* Dinara Droukarova, *Tenguiz* Temour Kalandadze, *Roussiko* Roussoudan Bolkvadze, *Alexi* Sacha Sarichvili, *Niko* Douta Skhirtladze, *the Berber* Abdallah Moundy.
• *Dir* Julie Bertuccelli, *Pro* Yaël Fogiel, *Co-Pro* Diana Elbaum, *Assoc Pro* Laetitia Gonzalez, *Screenplay* Julie Bertuccelli, Roger Bohbot and Bernard Renucci, *Ph* Christophe Pollock, *Pro Des* Emmanuel de Chauvigny, *Ed* Emmanuelle Castro *M* Antoine Duhamel, Dato Evgenidze and Arvo Pärt, *Costumes* Nathalie Raoul.

Entre Chien et Loup/Canal Plus/Les Films du Poisson/Studio 99/arte France Cinéma-Optimum Releasing.
103 mins. France/Belgium/Georgia. 2003. Rel: 4 June 2004. Cert 15.

Sin Eater ★¹/₂

(US title: *The Order*)

Alex, a renegade priest investigating the mysterious death of his mentor comes across the legend of the Sin Eater, a being of heresy who 'consumes' a dying mortal's sins thereby bypassing the inconvenience of excommunication. It comes to light amidst some deeply murky plotting that Alex is the Sin Eater's chosen successor. Cue a dense barrage of religious mumbo-jumbo and stock special effects that barely makes sense to anyone who hasn't already left the cinema for the sheer banality of Brian Helgeland's direction. A complete waste of a decent cast and about $40 million. AK

• *Alex Bernier* Heath Ledger, *Mara Sinclair* Shannyn Sossamon, *Thomas Garrett* Mark Addy, *William Eden* Benno Fürmann, *Cardinal Driscoll* Peter Weller, *Dominic* Francesco Carnelutti, *with* Mattia Sbragia, Richard Bremmer, Steve Toussaint, Seeta Indrani (uncredited).
• *Dir* and *Screenplay* Brian Helgeland, *Pro* Helgeland and Craig Baumgarten, Brian, *Ex Pro* Michael Kuhn and Thomas M. Hammel, *Co-Pro* Giovanni Lovatelli, *Ph* Nicola Pecorini, *Pro Des* Miljen Kreka Kljakovi, *Ed* Kevin Stitt, *M* David Torn, *Costumes* Caroline Harris, *Visual Effects* Nathan McGuinness.

Fox/Baumgarten Merims-Fox.
102 mins. USA/Germany. 2003.
Rel: 12 September 2004. Cert 15.

The Singing Detective ★★

Dennis Potter had always enjoyed an uneasy alliance with the cinema. One of the most innovative, courageous and compelling writers in the history of British television, Potter carved his name into the public conscience with *Blue Remembered Hills*, *Pennies From Heaven* and *Lipstick on Your Collar*, while many of his other works were withdrawn or banned (ie *Blackeyes*, *Brimstone and Treacle*, *Son of Man*). The BBC's *The Singing Detective* prompted a record number of complaints, thanks largely to a scene involving some bucolic bonking between Alison Steadman and Patrick Malahide. The film version, based on an adaptation Potter wrote shortly before his death in 1991, has the action transferred to America and throws in allusions to Aids and President Bush. The format, however, remains largely the same: a writer of cheap detective novels, Dan Dark, is in hospital suffering from a disfiguring skin disease (psoriatric arthropathy). While under the influence of heavy medication, a musical evolves from his muddled brain, combining elements of a lamentable screenplay adaptation of the eponymous novel, the hospital staff and his own domestic war zone. Wilfully artificial and discombobulated, the film is by turns farcical, unpleasant, sleazy, narcissistic and wordy. Very Dennis Potter, in fact. JC-W

• *Dan Dark* Robert Downey Jr, *Nicola/Nina/blonde* Robin Wright Penn, *Dr Gibbon* Mel Gibson, *Mark Binney* Jeremy Northam, *Nurse Mills* Katie Holmes, *first hood* Adrien Brody, *second hood* Jon Polito, *Betty Dark/hooker* Carla Gugino, *skin specialist* Saul Rubinek, *Chief of Staff* Alfre Woodard, *with* Amy Aquino, David Dorfman, Eddie Jones, Clyde Kusatsu.
• *Dir* Keith Gordon, *Pro* Mel Gibson, Steven Haft and Bruce Davey, *Ex Pro* Stan Wlodkowski, *Co-Pro* Jane Potter, Sarah Potter and Robert Potter, *Screenplay* Dennis Potter, based on his TV miniseries, *Ph* Tom Richmond, *Pro Des* Patricia Norris, *Ed* Jeff Wishengrad, *M super* Ken Weiss; songs performed by The Viscounts, Patti Page, Gene Vincent, Danny & the Juniors, The Chordettes, Tommy Edwards, Johnny Ray, Bobby Helms, The Coasters, Big Joe Turner, Eddie Cochran, Conway Twitty, The Kalin Twins, and Robert Downey Jr., *Choreographers* Jaqui Landrum and Bill Landrum, *Makeup* Greg Cannom and Keith Vanderlaan.

Icon Prods/Haft Entertainment-Icon.
109 mins. USA. 2003. Rel: 14 November 2003. Cert 15.

Small Cuts

See *Petites Coupures*.

Something's Gotta Give ★¹/₂

Diane Keaton and Jack Nicholson have suffered a serious lapse in judgment allowing themselves to be humiliated for cheap hyuks in this drippy, inane and pandering comedy about an old ladies man who falls into an unlikely Hampton romance with his young lover's Germaine Greer-ish playwright of a mother. As Harry Sanborn, Nicholson plays priest to the church of Hugh Hefner as a super-successful (and mysteriously virile) aging playboy constantly on the prowl for youthful beauties. Set aside the sleazy parallels to real life, and it still feels weird to see him cavorting with the delectable Amanda Peet. While wrinkles and sexuality may not be mutually exclusive, this particular vista pushes credulity to its limits. Keaton is wonderful but her talents are wasted on a story that holds few surprises. Everything up to and including her final act of vengeance that leads the film to its big twist feels contrived, and that makes for bad comedy. AK

• *Harry Sanborn* Jack Nicholson, *Erica Barry* Diane Keaton, *Julian Mercer* Keanu Reeves, *Zoe Barry* Frances McDormand, *Marin* Amanda Peet, *Leo* Jon Favreau, *Dave* Paul Michael Glaser, *Dr Martinez* Rachel Ticotin, *with* Lorraine Nicholson, KaDee

Strickland, Leslie Upson.
• *Dir* and *Screenplay* Nancy Meyers, *Pro* Bruce A. Block and Nancy Meyers, *Co-pro* Suzanne Farwell, *Ph* Michael Bullhaus, *Pro Des* Jon Hutman, *Ed* Joe Hutshing, *M* Hans Zimmer, *Costumes* Suzanne McCabe.

Columbia/Warner/Waverly Films-Warner.
128 mins. USA. 2003. Rel: 6 February. Cert 12A

Son Frère ★★★★

(*His Brother*)
The fact that I am easily distressed by the atmosphere of hospitals explains why I got no pleasure at all from Patrice Chéreau's grim drama about two brothers despite some fine acting. Bruno Todeschini is the older sibling who relies on his gay brother (Eric Caravaca) when he realises that due to a blood disease he has only a short time to live. You can't dismiss the film as having no positive side because it's about the way in which this situation revitalises the long buried affection that the brothers felt in childhood. Furthermore, it's admirably unsentimental and wholly authentic in capturing the tone of hospital life. It's therefore right that the rating should reflect the quality of this achievement rather than the fact that I found watching it a burden. MS

• *Thomas* Bruno Todeschini, *Luc* Éric Caravaca, *Claire* Nathalie Boutefeu, *Head Doctor* Catherine Ferran, *Vincent* Sylvain Jacques, *Mother* Antoinette Moya, *Manuel* Robinson Stevenin, *Father* Fred Ulysse.
• *Dir* Patrice Chéreau, *Pro* Joseph Strub, *Screenplay* Chéreau and Anne-Louise Trividic, from the novel by Philippe Besson, *Ph* Eric Gautier, *Ed* Francois Gedigier, *M* `Sleep' sung by Marianne Faithful, *Costumes* Caroline de Vivaise.

ARTE France/Azor Films/Love Streams/Canal Plus-Parasol Peccadillo Releasing.
92 mins. France. 2003. Rel: 20 February, 2004. Cert 15.

Song For a Raggy Boy ★★★¹/₂

Arriving just two weeks after *The Passion of the Christ*, *Song for a Raggy Boy* added more gasoline to the fires of Catholic indignation. Another example of how mankind has suffered in the name of God, this is a male riposte to last year's award-winning *The Magdalene Sisters*. Like the former film, *Raggy Boy* is set in an Irish religious institution for young offenders. In this instance, it's an Irish Reformatory School for Boys and the time is 1939. Returning from the Spanish Civil War in a state of shock, lay teacher William Franklin takes a post at St Jude's against the wishes of the local bishop. Here, he finds his young students virtually illiterate and is appalled by the corporal punishment doled out by the head prefect, Brother John. Loosely adapted from Patrick Galvin's autobiographical novel, the film drew gasps at the press screening, an indication of the strength of its subject matter. A damning indictment of what has been tolerated under the umbrella of the Catholic Church, *Raggy Boy* would have been a perfect film had Brother John been allowed an iota of contrition. As it is, the character's one-dimensional evil belongs to a lesser project. JC-W

• *William Franklin* Aidan Quinn, *Brother John* Iain Glenn, *Brother Mac* Marc Warren, *Brother Tom* Dudley Sutton, *Father Damian* Alan Devlin, *Brother Whelan* Stuart Graham, *Liam Mercier* John Travers, *Patrick Delaney* Chris Newman, with Andrew Simpson, Mark Butler, Bernard Manning, Samuel Bright.
• *Dir* Aisling Walsh, *Pro* Tristan Orpen Lynch, Dominic Wright, John McDonnell and Kevin Byron Murphy, *Ex Pro* Michael Lunderskov and Andrés Vicente Gomez, *Co-Pro*, Gillian Barrie and Peter Garde, *Assoc Pro* Will Machin, *Screenplay* Walsh, Byron Murphy and Patrick Galvin, *Ph* Peter Robertson, *Pro Des* John Hand, *Ed* Bryan Oates, *M* Richard Blackford, *Costumes* Allison Byrne.

Lolafilms/Subotica Entertainment/Moviefan (Denmark)/Zoma (UK)/Bord Scannán na hÉireann/Danish Film Institute-Winchester Films.
97 mins. Ireland/Denmark/Spain/UK. 2003. Rel: 9 April 2004. Cert 15.

Spare Parts ★★★

(*Rezervni deli*)
With such films as *In This World* and *Lilya 4-Ever* tackling the theme of illegal immigrants and achieving remarkable intensity in the process, this Slovenian drama is overshadowed despite the sincerity of its concern. The central characters here are two men who carry on this trade. Their involvement may be less a matter of choice than a desperate need to make a living in a town where unemployment is rife but their plight is less involving than that of the refugees they transport to the border with Italy. The locations if drab are unfamiliar and neither the main situation not the various sub-plots are sentimentalised. It's an honest film, but ultimately more depressing than tragic in its effect. MS

• *Ludvik Zajc* Peter Musevski, *Rudi* Aljosa Kovacic, *Rajc* Primoz Petkovsek, *Drago* Valter Dragan, *Angela* Aleksandra Balmazovic, *Geri* Vladimir Vlaskalic, *Ilinka* Verica Nedeska.
• *Dir* and *Screenplay* Damjan Kozole, *Pro* Danijel Hocevar, *Ph* Radislav Jovanov-Gonzo, *Art Dir* Ursa

Loboda, *M* Igor Leonardi, *Ed* Andrija Zafranovic, *Costumes* Sabina Buzdon.

Emotionfilm/RTV Slovenia-Soda Pictures.
87 mins. Slovenia. 2003. Rel: 12 March 2004. Cert 15..

Spellbound ★★★

Any doubts about an American National Spelling Bee providing too little of interest to sustain a feature length documentary can be set aside. My audience applauded loudly at the end, having frequently laughed with delight and experienced the suspense as the kids taking part vie with one another. This appears to be what the filmmaker wanted. It's fine, unless you share my view (possibly a minority one) that the parents encouraging such participation are submitting their children to strains and stresses which could become traumatic in pursuit of a debased notion of education (the event is essentially competitive, spelling correctly takes precedence over knowing the meaning of words, the contest is shown on TV and the winner has a year of promotion as a celebrity). Director Jeff Blitz is also happy to mock relatives who appear. It's well made, but for me it epitomises the worst aspects of American life. MS

• *With*: Harry Altman, Angela Arenivar, Ted Brigham, April DeGideo, Neil Kadakia, Nupur Lala, Emily Stagg, Ashley White.
• *Dir* and *Ph* Jeff Blitz, *Pro* Blitz and Sean Welch, *Ed* Yana Gorskaya, *M* Daniel Hulsizer.

Blitz/Welch/The Pacific Pioneer Fund-Tartan Films.
96 mins. USA. 2002. Rel: 10 October 2003. Cert U.

Spirited Away ★★★★¹/₂
(Sen To Chihiro No Kamikakushi)
Chihiro is sulking about a move to the country her parents have foisted upon her. Along the way, they stop to visit an abandoned summer amusement park. To their surprise, they find a table laden with delicious food with no attendants to charge them for the eating. Against her warnings, her parents gorge themselves, while Chihiro notices strange eyes staring at her from the shadows … so begins a classic of animated cinema by the maestro Hayao Miyazaki. Released in the original Japanese with subtitles, and also with American voiceovers, *Spirited Away* is a contemplative, fabulous, intricate and dazzling presentation that confirms the creator of *Princess Mononoke* as a giant in the art. The story of how Chihiro learns to survive in a land of ghosts and demons, always seeking a means to rescue her family, and teaching herself to be brave is something of a cross between *Alice in Wonderland* and *The Wizard of Oz*, albeit with enough of the mystical East to confound any attempt at easy moralising. AK

• *Voices*: *Chihiro* Daveigh Chase, *Yubaba/Zeniba* Suzanne Pleshette, *Haku* Jason Marsden, *Lin* Susan Egan, *Kamaji* David Ogden Stiers, *Chihiro's mother* Lauren Holly, *Chihiro's father* Michael Chiklis, *assistant manager* John Ratzenberger, *Boh (baby)* Tara Strong.
• *Dir* Hayao Miyazaki, *Director of the American version*, Kirk Wise, *American Pro* Donald W. Ernst, *Chief Ex Pro* Yasuyoshi Tokuma, *American Ex Pro* John Lasseter, *Screenplay* Hayao Miyazaki, *English-language adaptation* Cindy Davis Hewitt and Donald H. Hewitt, *M* Joe Hisaishi.

Tokuma Shoten/Studio Ghibli/Nippon Television Network/Dentsu/Buena Vista Home Entertainment/Tohokushinsha Film/Mitsubishi Commercial Affairs-Optimum Releasing.
125 mins. Japan. 2001. Rel: 12 September 2003. Cert PG.

Spring, Summer, Autumn, Winter… and Spring ★★★★
(Bom yeoreum gaeul gyeoul geurigo bom)
This beautiful and highly original film from Korea views life from a Buddhist perspective and, as the title hints, tells its story in five sections, the last however being merely a coda. More unexpectedly, although the seasons are followed in sequence, the events depicted are not those of one year but show instead a boy growing up as a monk. The main setting is a shrine floating on a pond where an old monk trains the youth who, on reaching adulthood, is tempted sexually by a sick girl whose mother has brought her to the monastery. Not all the details are equally persuasive and certain scenes will be more meaningful to those already well versed in Buddhist rituals, but there's real artistry here and we have never seen a film like it. The last shot is perfectly chosen. MS

• *old monk* Oh Young-Su, *adult monk* Kim Ki-Duk, *young adult monk* Kim Young-Min, *boy monk* Seo Jae Kyung, *girl* Ha Yeo Jin, *child monk* Kim Jong Ho, *girl's mother* Kim Jung Young, *Detective Ji* Ji Dae Han, *Detective Choi* Choi Min, *baby's mother* Park Ji A, *baby* Song Min Young.
• *Dir, Screenplay* and *Ed* Kim Ki-Duk, *Pro* Lee Seung-Jae, *Ex Pro* Chung Soma, *Ph* Back Don-Hyun, *Pro Des* Stefan Schönberg, *M* Bark Ji-Woong, *Art Dir* Oh Sang-Man.

Korea Pictures /LJ Film/Pandora Film-Tartan Films.
102 mins. South Korea/Germany. 2003.
Rel: 14th May 2004. Cert 15.

Spun ★★★★
Uptown slacker Ross (Jason Schwartzman) launches

himself into an amphetamine-fuelled odyssey when a buy at his local dealer segues into a three-day speed binge led by the whims of the backroom pharmacist called 'The Cook' and his brittle nymphomaniac girlfriend Nikki. Ex-heavy metallist and music video wunderkind Jonas Akerlund has produced a perfect companion piece to cinema's other great drug odysseys *Fear and Loathing in Las Vegas*, *Trainspotting*, and *Requiem for a Dream*. Like them, *Spun* flourishes every editing and narrative trick it can think of to simulate an addled state of mind. Pulsing music, stutter edits, bleached palettes and wonky camera angles combine with precise artistry and awesome performances from a brattish cast (notable exceptions being a unrecognisably wasted Mickey Rourke and a camped up, vamped up Eric Roberts). Topped with perfectly surreal sequences like an animated sex-fantasy ripped straight from an adolescent wet dream, and a patriotic-parody where Mickey Rourke reinterprets the 'Ask not what your country can do for you' speech in the filthiest terms, *Spun* is seriously and authentically impressive. AK

• *Ross* Jason Schwartzman, *Spider Mike* John Leguizamo, *Cookie* Mena Suvari, *Frisbee* Patrick Fugit, *Nikki* Britanny Murphy, *the Cook* Mickey Rourke, *April Love* Cookie Hunter, *neighbour* Deborah Harry, *Amy* Charlotte Ayanna, *the Man* Eric Roberts, *doctor* Billy Corgan, *bartender* Ron Jeremy, *with* Peter Stormare, Alexis Arquette, Larry Drake, Tony Kaye.
• *Dir* and *Ed* Jonas Åkerlund, *Pro* Chris Hanley, Fernando Sulichin, Timothy Wayne Peternel and Danny Vinik, *Exec Pro* Mark Boone Junior, Yves Chevalier, Nicola Doring, Kiki Miyake, Mark Mower, Bradford L. Schlei and Ash R. Shah, *Assoc Pro* Rita Dagher, Chris Fisher and Clark McCutchen, *Co-Pro* Will De Los Santos, David Hillary, Thierry Klemniuk, Vincent Maraval and Creighton Vero, *Screenplay* De Los Santos and Vero, *Ph* Eric Broms, *Pro Des* Richard Lassalle, *M* Billy Corgan; Mozart; songs performed by Ozzy Osbourne, T Rex, The Djali Zwan, Mötley Crüe, Blonde from Fargo, Satyricon, The Leather Nun, Paula, Yes, Blues Traveler, Donovan Leitch, Phantom Planet, Soundtrack of Our Lives, *Costumes* 'B', *Sound* Eric Thorsell.

Silver Nitrate/Amuse Pictures/Little Magic Films/Saggitaire-Pathé. 101 mins. USA/UK/France. 2002. Rel: 28 November 2003. Cert 18.

Spy Kids 3D: Game Over ★

… or, preferably, *Spy Kids 3-D: Joke Franchise Finally Over*. This disastrously messy and mindless swamp of gimmickry has the one merit of sounding the box-office death-knell of this deeply irritating teen-Bond adventures. The idea this time is that the

'retired' and jaded Juni Cortez is persuaded to return to the OSS for one final mission, which involves entering a video game, progressing through its levels, rescuing his sister Carmen, and then confronting the evil mastermind who plans to use the mind-control elements of the video game to, mua-haha, take over the world! Desperately bad acting and weak direction suggest that Rodriguez should have just owned up to the profit-incentive and sold this as a video game from the get-go. AK

• *Gregorio Cortez* Antonio Banderas, *Ingrid Cortez* Carla Gugino, *Carmen Cortez* Alexa Vega, *Juni Cortez* Daryl Sabara, *Grandfather* Ricardo Montalban, *Grandmother* Holland Taylor, *Toymaker* Sylvester Stallone, *Cesca Giggles* Salma Hayek, *Donnagon Giggles* Mike Judge, *Felix Gumm* Cheech Marin, *Alexander Minion* Tony Shalhoub, *Dinky Winks* Bill Paxton, *Devlin* George Clooney, *the Guy* Elijah Wood, *with* Steve Buscemi, Alan Cumming, Danny Trejo, Emily Osment, Matt O'Leary.
• *Dir, Screenplay, Ph, Ed, Pro Des* and *M*, Robert Rodriguez, *Pro* Rodriguez and Elizabeth Avellan, *Costumes* Nina Proctor, *Special Effects Supervisor* Jason Gustafson, *Visual Effects Supervisor* Rodriguez, Daniel Leduc and Stuart T Maschwitz.

Dimension/Los Hooligans Prods/Troublemaker Studios-Buena Vista. 84 mins. USA. 2003. Rel: 1 August 2003. Cert U.

Standing in the Shadows of Motown
★★★¹/₂
(*Standing in the Shadows of Motown: The Story of the Funk Brothers*)
Although not in the same league as *Buena Vista Social Club*, Paul Justman's musical documentary will appeal to fans of Motown. It has the laudable objective of acclaiming The Funk Brothers who, providing key backings, nevertheless lost out in terms of fame to the artists they accompanied, artists ranging from Marvin Gaye to The Supremes and from The Temptations to Martha and the Vandellas. Old footage is combined with fresh observations that don't always get to grips with the downside of the story, and some favourite songs are virtually passed over. However, the many new cover versions that do feature are splendid, aided by Justman's lively direction and enthusiastic performances. When the film is at its best, the music pours red hot off the screen. MS

• *Dir* Paul Justman, *Pro* Sandy Passman, Allan Slutsky and Paul Justman, *Screenplay* Walter Dallas and Ntozake Shange, based on the book by Allan Slutsky, *Ph* Doug Milsome and Lon Stratton, *Ed* Anne Erikson.
• *Narrator* Andre Braugher, *With*: Jack Ashford, Bob Babbitt, Johnny Griffith, Joe Hunter, Uriel

Jones, Joe Messina and Eddie Willis (the Funk Brothers); Joan Osborne, Gerald Levert, Meshell Ndegeocello, Bootsy Collins, Ben Harper, Chaka Khan, Montell Jordan, Tom Scott, Richard Allan.

Rimshot-Tartan Films.
108 mins. USA. 2003. Rel: 10 October 2003. Cert 12A.

Starsky & Hutch ★★★

Unlike *Charlie's Angels*, *Mission: Impossible* and even *The Brady Bunch Movie*, this big-screen adaptation of a hit TV show is not an update. In fact, the best thing about it is its unerring satire of the 1970s. Thus, Dave Starsky batters out his reports on a typewriter and the cops communicate via chunky, cumbersome walkie-talkies. And let's not forget the soundtrack, a glorious collection of golden oldies from the likes of The Carpenters, Chicago, Judy Collins, Barry Manilow and, in an unforgettable moment, Owen Wilson – as Hutch – delivering a cover of David Soul's 'Don't Give Up On Us'. Viewers over 40 will undoubtedly get the most out of the movie, although there are gags galore for every generation. Best friends Wilson and Ben Stiller exude an effortless camaraderie (this is their sixth film together) and accentuate the touchy-touchy veiled homosexuality of the undercover cops. Starsky is even having a hard time escaping the influence of his mother, 'one of the best cops the force has ever seen.' This is not the funniest film of the year, but it's sublime, pleasantly innocuous escapism. JC-W

• *David Starsky* Ben Stiller, *Ken 'Hutch' Hutchinson* Owen Wilson, *Reese Feldman* Vince Vaughn, *Huggy Bear* Snoop Dogg, *Captain Doby* Fred Williamson, *Kitty* Juliette Lewis, *Kevin* Jason Bateman, *Holly* Amy Smart, *Manetti* Chris Penn, *Staci* Carmen Electra, *with* Brande Roderick, Molly Sims, Terry Crews, Richard Edson, Paul Michael Glaser, David Soul, *Big Earl* Will Ferrell (uncredited).
• *Dir* Todd Phillips, *Pro* William Blinn, Stuart Cornfeld, Akiva Goldsman, Tony Ludwig and Alan Riche, *Ex Pro* Gilbert Adler, *Assoc Pro* Scott Budnick and David A. Siegel, *Screenplay* Phillips, John O'Brien and Scot Armstrong, from a story by O'Brien and Stevie Long, based on characters created by William Blinn, *Ph* Barry Peterson, *Pro Des* Edward Verreaux, *Ed* Leslie Jones, *M* Theodore Shapiro; songs performed by Barry Manilow, Chicago, Jackson 5, Ground Hog, The Band, Maxine Nightingale, KC & The Sunshine Band, Bill Withers, Judy Collins, The Carpenters, Edwin Starr, Eric Clapton, Average White Band, Aerosmith, Owen Wilson, etc, *Costumes* Louise Mingenbach.

Dimension Films/Warner/Red Hour-Buena Vista International.
100 mins. USA. 2004. Rel: 12 March 2004. Cert 15.

The Statement ★★★

Brian Moore's novel, adapted here by Ronald Harwood, tells of the tracking down decades later of a man who in occupied France in 1944 had executed

Left: Retro chick: Owen Wilson and Ben Stiller admire a respondent's candour in Todd Phillips' agreeable *Starsky & Hutch* (from BVI)

Jews as ordered by his Nazi superiors. Potentially the material is rich indeed: the role of the Catholic Church in protecting this man, a believer; the issues that surround justice delayed (is the man in question properly to be regarded as the man he was over fifty years ago and therefore responsible for these ancient actions?); the conflict inside a man who prays for forgiveness but kills again when assassins seek to eliminate him. Allow for the use of English actors in parts that call for players of other nationalities and one must acknowledge that Michael Caine in the key role together with Tilda Swinton and Jeremy Northam play well. But the screenplay sidelines all the really interesting questions to turn this into what is essentially no more than a routine thriller. Sadly, the film also marks the last appearance of Sir Alan Bates appearing in a cameo role. MS

• *Pierre Brossard* Michael Caine, *Anne Marie Livi* Tilda Swinton, *Roux* Jeremy Northam, *Bertier* Alan Bates, *Nicole* Charlotte Rampling, *Old Man* John Neville, *Pochon* Ciarán Hinds, *Commissaire Vionnet* Frank Finlay, *Le Moyne* William Hutt, *David* Matt Craven, *Michael* Noam Jenkins, *Cholet* Peter Wight, *Cardinal of Lyon* Malcolm Sinclair, *Patrice* Colin Salmon, *Dom Andre* David De Keyser, *with* John Boswall, Edward Petherbridge, Christian Erikson.
• *Dir* Norman Jewison, *Pro* Robert Lantos and Norman Jewison, *Ex Pro* David M. Thompson, Mark Musselman, Jason Piette and Michael Cowan, *Co-Pro* Sandra Cunningham, Yannick Bernard and Robyn Slovo, *Assoc Pro* Julia Rosenberg, *Scr* Ronald Harwood, based on the novel by Brian Moore, *Ph* Kevin Jewison, *Pro Des* Jean Rabasse, *Ed* Stephen Rivkin and Andrew S. Eisen, *M* Normand Corbeil, *Costumes* Carine Sarfati, *Sound* Bruce Carwardine.

Serendipity Point Films/Odessa Films/ Company Pictures/ Astral Media/ Téléfilm Canada/Corus Entertainment/Sony Pictures Classics/BBC Films-Momentum. 119 mins. Canada/UK/France/USA. 2003. Rel: 27 February 2004. Cert 12A.

The Station Agent ★★★★¹/₂

Finbar McBride is fanatical about trains. He works in a model train shop, reads books about trains and watches home movies devoted to trains. However, unlike his fellow enthusiasts, he is not a train-chaser – that is, a fan who films trains while driving alongside them. Finbar cannot do this because he cannot drive. And Finbar cannot drive because he is just four-foot five-inches tall. When he inherits an abandoned train depot in a deserted corner of New Jersey, Finbar sees this as a perfect opportunity to shut himself off from society and pursue his one abiding interest. But the dwarf hadn't reckoned on the intervention of a neighbouring snack vendor and a local woman who unintentionally runs him off the

road – *twice*… A film about a dwarf doesn't exactly sound like an enticing prospect, but *The Station Agent* is a little gem. Unusual, humane, touching and totally credible, it deservedly won the Best Drama, Screenplay and Performance prizes at the Sundance festival. Delicately observed, the film works because it never overplays its hand and because Peter Dinklage as Finbar brings such a surprising dignity, charisma and irony to a difficult part. JC-W

• *Finbar 'Fin' McBride* Peter Dinklage, *Olivia Harris* Patricia Clarkson, *Joe Oramas* Bobby Cannavale, *Cleo* Raven Goodwin, *Henry Styles* Paul Benjamin, *Emily* Michelle Williams, *Carl* Josh Pais, *David* John Slattery.
• *Dir* and *Screenplay* Tom McCarthy, *Pro* Mary Kane Skalski, Robert May and Kathryn Tucker, *Ph* Oliver Bokelberg, *Pro Des* John Paino, *Ed* Tom McArdle, *M* Stephen Trask; songs performed by Sourcerer, Danielle Howle and the Tantrums, Ed Burleson, Six Going On Seven, Alice Stuart, Fetish, and Klear, *Costumes* Jeanne DuPont, *Sound* Paul Hsu.

SenArt Films/Next Wednesday/Miramax-Buena Vista International. 89 mins. USA. 2003. Rel: 26 March 2004. Cert 15.

Steal ★★★¹/₂
(US title: *Riders*)

Had director Gérard Pirès made *Steal* in his native French – à la his action-packed, international hit *Taxi* (1998) – then it could well have stood alongside the very best work of his colleague and compatriot Luc Besson (think *Subway*, *Nikita*). As it is, *Steal* is a cheeky, ingenious and breathless caper that is destined to be re-made by Hollywood in the near future (but with none of its camp flourish or raw charm). Set in Montreal, the film wastes no time in supplying the action, opening in the middle of a bank heist in which four goofy and attractive thieves make off with $300,000 on rollerblades. However, this is just the debut in a string of increasingly audacious robberies in which our engaging anti-heroes repeatedly up the ante (for a start, the cocky ringleader beds the female cop on his case!). The stunts are jaw dropping, the protagonists suitably sexy and some of the acting fabulously bad. Steven Berkoff as a sadistic Southern preacher (in Montreal?) wins the prize for worst performance of the year. The B movie is back with a vengeance. JC-W

• *Slim* Stephen Dorff, *Det. Karen Svenson* Natasha Henstridge, *Lt. Jake McGruder* Bruce Payne, *Surtayne* Steven Berkoff, *Otis* Clé Bennett, *Alex* Karen Cliché, *Frank* Steven McCarthy, *Lou Pandelis* Alain Goulem.
• *Dir* Gérard Pirès *Pro* Éric Altmeyer, Nicolas Altmeyer, Michael Lionello Cowan, Claude Léger

and Jason Piette, *Ex Pro* John Fremes and Jonathan Vanger, *Co-Pro* Michael Cowan, Claie Léger and Jason Piette, *Screenplay* Mark Ezra, *Ph* Tetsuo Nagata, *Pro Des* Guy Lalande, *Ed* Véronique Lange, *M* Andy Gray; songs performed by Fatboy Slim, Motorhead, I Mobster, Marilyn Manson, David Holmes, etc, *Costumes* Daniel Fortin.

Transfilm/Mandarin/Spice Factory/Future Film Financing/Téléfilm Canada-Redbus.
84 mins. Canada/France/UK. 2002.
Rel 21 November 2003. Cert 15.

Strange Gardens ★
(*Effroyables Jardins*)
A candidate for the year's worst film, Jean Becker's movie is a travesty of Michel Quint's popular novella. It retains the story of a child learning of his father's experiences in occupied France and of his indebtedness to a German guard who had once been a clown. However, the film fails to reveal that the German in question was Bernhard Wicki who became a filmmaker of note, chooses to sentimentalise the emotional side of the story and, in addition to playing around with the plot, incorporates large doses of comedy so silly that they make the tale unbelievable. Absolutely awful and without a single redeeming feature. MS

• *Jacques Pouzay* Jacques Villeret, *André Desingy* André Dussollier, *Thierry Plaisance* Thierry Lhermitte, *Emile* Benoît Magimel, *Marie Gerbier* Suzanne Flon, *Louise* Isabelle Candelier, *Bernt* Bernie Collins, *Lucien* Damien Jouillerot.
• *Dir* Jean Becker, *Pro* Louis Becker, *Screenplay* Becker, Jean Cosmos and Guillaume Laurent, based on the novel by Michel Quint, *Ph* Jean-Marie Dreujou, *Pro Des* Therese Ripaud and Bruno Margery, *Ed* Jacques Witta, *M* Zbigniew Preisner, *Costumes* Sylvie de Segonzac.

Louis Becker/UGC/ICE3/UGC Images /France 2 Cinéma/ France 3 Cinéma/Canal Plus-MatCine.
97 mins. France. 2003 Rel: 16 April 2004. Cert 15.

Stuck On You ★★★
Co-directors Bobby and Peter Farrelly have made fun of the obese (in *Shallow Hal*), the schizophrenic (*Me, Myself & Irene*) and the mentally challenged (*Dumb and Dumber*). Until now, though, they have never poked fun at brothers. Once again trading on their highly un-PC ridicule of freaks, oddballs and bigots, the Farrellys work through our hang-ups and prejudice through humour. Here we have Damon and Kinnear as total opposites, albeit conjoined at birth (they share a liver). While Walt Tenor picks up the babes and dreams of a Hollywood career, Bob

Tenor hasn't had sex in five years and is happy flipping burgers. Then one day Bob consents to Walt trying his luck as a movie star in California – even if being his brother's stunt double is a pointless idea… Swapping their erstwhile scatalogical edge for a grosser kind of sentimentality, the Farrellys still can't help being funny. Packing their ludicrous scenario with genuinely outrageous characters and sharp dialogue (girl: 'Can I ask you a personal question?'; Walt: 'Nine inches'), the Farrellys have produced a highly amusing diversion. While it fails to scale the same comic heights as *There's Something About Mary*, *Stuck On You* has many priceless moments. JC-W

• *Bob Tenor* Matt Damon, *Walt Tenor* Greg Kinnear, *April* Eva Mendes, *May* Wen Yann Shih, *herself* Cher, *Morty O'Reilly* Seymour Cassel, *Mimmy* Pat Crawford Brown, *Rocket* Ray 'Rocket' Valliere, *Tommy* Tommy Songin, *Moe* Terence Bernie Hines, *Howard* Jackie Flynn, *himself* Griffin Dunne, *with* Bridget Tobin, Michael Callan, Jessica Cauffiel, Lin Shaye, Googy Gress, Jay Leno, Sergio Garcia, Luke Wilson, Rhona Mitra, Adam Shankman, Mary Murphy, Michael Murphy, Meryl Streep, Frankie Muniz.
• *Dir Scr* Bobby Farrelly and Peter Farrelly, from a story by Charles B. Wessler, Bennett Yellin, Peter Farrelly and Bobby Farrelly, *Pro* Bradley Thomas, Charles. B. Wessler, Bobby Farrelly and Peter Farrelly, *Ex Pro* Marc S. Fischer, *Assoc Pro and Asst. Dir* Hal Joseph Olofsson, *Ph* Dan Mindel, *Pro Des* Sidney J. Bartholomew Jr., *Ed* Christopher Greenbury and Dave Terman, *M* songs performed by The Pixies, Randy Weeks, Jimi Hendrix, Unbusted, Starbuck, Andy Williams, Kings of Leon, The Tigers, Cher, Billy Goodrum, Ben Taylor Band, Peter Yorn, The Rolling Stones, Buva, Gilbert O'Sullivan, Bread, The Weather Girls, Reba Schappell, etc, *Costumes* Deena Appel, *Makeup effects designer* Tony Gardner, *Choreographer* Adam Shankman.

Fox/Conundrum Entertainment/Charles B. Wessler-Fox.
118 mins. USA. 2003. Rel: 2 January 2004. Cert 12A.

Suddenly ★★
A minimalist drama in the vein of Jim Jarmusch's 1984 classic *Stranger Than Paradise*, *Suddenly* certainly has its charms. Shot in black-and-white on the streets of Buenos Aires, it introduces us to the plump, lonely Marcia as she eats in front of her TV and works long hours in a lingerie shop. Her life is one of total inconsequence until, walking down the street, she is accosted by two young women who invite her to have sex with them. Refusing to take 'no' for an answer, the would-be lesbians escort Marcia to a fast-food joint at knife-point. They then hijack a taxi and take Marcia on a journey that will transform her life… Wilfully drab in its appearance

and composed of long, static shots, Diego Lerman's debut feature reminds one of the more experimental ventures of the 1960s from Europe. But here there is a sexual frisson which, while initially arresting, drifts into aimlessness around the halfway mark. JC-W

• *Marcia* Tatiana Saphir, *Mao* Carla Crespo, *Lenine* Verónica Hassan, *Blanca* Beatriz Thibaudin, *Delia* Maria Merlino, Felipe Ferrante Marks, *Ramona* Ana Maria Martinez Susana.
• *Dir* Diego Lerman, *Ex Pro* Lerman, *Assoc Pro* Lita Stantic, *Screenplay* Lerman and Maria Meira, *Ph* Luciano Zito and Diego del Piano, *Art Dir* Mauro Doporto and Luciana Kohn, *Ed* Benjamin Avila and Alberto Ponce, *M* Juan Ignacio Bouscayrol, *Costumes* Constanza Piaerpaoli.

Lisa Stantic Prods/Nylon Cine/Incaa/Hubert Bals Fund-Tartan Films.
92 mins. Argentina/Netherlands. 2002.
Rel: 13 February 2004. Cert 15.

Suzie Gold ★★¹/₂
In a noisy Jewish home in North London, a 23 year-old Jewish princess Suzie Gold is forced to choose between the perfect (and don't he know it) Jewish suitor Anthony Silver and the charming Chelsea-loving Gentile, Gregory ... Ric Cantor's sweet and lively rom-com never strays far from a familiar milieu of Jewish stereotypes, and seems satisfied to sprinkle a series of modest laughs over a thoroughly well-ridden path, where *My Big Fat Greek Wedding* and other migrant-family stories like it. American actress Summer Phoenix does at least provide an attractive focus and plays her crises of decision with a dash of style. AK

• *Suzie Gold* Summer Phoenix, *Darren* Leo Gregory, *Irving Gold* Stanley Townsend, *Barbara Gold* Rebecca Front, *Joyce Spencer* Frances Barber, *Anthony Silver* Iddo Goldberg, *Sadie* Miriam Karlin, *Julius* Leon Lissek, *Debbie Levine* Sophie Winkleman, *Sophie Gold* Ariana Fraval, *Toby Gold* Gem Souleyman, *with* Gwyneth Strong, Steve Jameson, Harriet Thorpe, Claudia Winkleman, Rachel Stevens, Kevin Bishop, Max Gold, Lorelei King, Doreen Mantle.
• *Dir* Ric Cantor, *Pro* Rebecca Green, *Ex Pro* Francois Ivernel and Cameron McCracken, *Co-Pro* Matthew T. Garnon, *Screenplay* Ric Cantor, Carry Franklin and Lisa Ratner, from a story by Rebecca Green, *Ph* Daf Hobson, *Pro Des* Amanda McArthur, *Ed* Michael Ellis, *M* Chris Elliott, *Costumes* Stephanie Collie.

Pathé Pictures/Sky Movies /UK Film Council/Isle of Man Film Commission/Inside Track Films/Green Wolf Films/National Lottery/UK Film Council-Pathé.
93 mins. UK. 2003. Rel: 5 March 2004. Cert 15.

S.W.A.T. ★★★
Having played a crack CIA trainee in *The Recruit*, Colin Farrell now dons flak jacket and combat trousers to play a SWAT tenderfoot. This time he's under the command of renegade, ass-kicking commander Dan 'Hondo' Harrelson and more than proves he's up to the task. Updated from the 1975-76 TV series (which starred Steve Forrest and Robert Urich), *S.W.A.T.* is a typically adrenaline-fuelled, MTV-styled actioner with the accent on heavy metal music, fast cuts and loud bangs. And, considering the controversy generated by the TV series (it was criticised for being one of the most violent show of the Seventies), the film version is surprisingly bloodless, even PC (there's even a female Latino SWAT officer thrown in for good measure). Still, in spite of a flabby mid-section (which looks like a costly recruitment ad), *S.W.A.T.* has more than its fair share of suspense and boasts a terrifically exciting finale. For the record, S.W.A.T. stands for Special Weapons and Tactics and is the abbreviation applied to an elite, military-style police unit trained to tackle highly volatile situations. So there.
JC-W

• *Sgt. Dan 'Hondo' Harrelson* Samuel L. Jackson , *Jim Street* Colin Farrell , *Chris Sanchez* Michelle Rodriguez , *Deacon 'Deke' Kaye* James Todd Smith aka LL Cool J, *T. J. McCabe* Josh Charles, *Brian Gamble* Jeremy Renner, *Michael Boxer* Brian Van Holt, *Alex Montel* Olivier Martinez , *Deacon's father* Rod Perry, *truck driver* Steve Forrest, *with* Larry Pointdexter, Denis Arndt, Lucinda Jenney, E. Roger Mitchell, Jay Acovone, Reed Diamond, *handsome man* Clark Johnson, Tricia Kelly, Neil H. Moritz, *Lara* Ashley Scott, Jeffrey Wincott.
• *Dir* Clark Johnson, *Pro* Neal H. Moritz, Chris Lee and Dan Halsted, *Screenplay* David Ayer and David McKenna, based on a story by Ron Mita and Jim McClain, *Ph* Gabriel Beristain, *Pro Des* Mayne Berke, *Ed* Michael Tronick, *M* Elliot Goldenthal; songs performed by Barry De Vorzon, The Rolling Stones, Thicke, Linkin Park, Buppy, Sammy Davis Jr., Jane's Addiction, Apollo Four Forty, Sam Roberts, Hot Action Cop, etc, *Costumes* Christopher Lawrence *Sound* Cameron Frankley.

Columbia Pictures/Original Film/Camelot Pictures-Columbia TriStar.
117 mins. USA. 2003. Rel: 4 December 2003. Cert 12A.

Swimming Pool ★★★
Partly in English and partly sub-titled, François Ozon's latest is thoroughly enjoyable for much of its length. Charlotte Rampling, on excellent form once again, plays an author of detective stories who, fighting writer's block, takes up residence in the French country house of her publisher. There she

Left: Halcyon daze: Ludivine Sagnier in François Ozon's masterfully calibrated *Swimming Pool* (from UGC Films)

encounters his daughter (Ludivine Sagnier) whose flaunting of her sexuality as she brings back men to the house irritates the writer but also arouses her jealousy. More sexually explicit than you might expect from its '15' certificate, this offers vivid characterisations and food for thought as well as much amusement. But then the tale develops into a totally unbelievable murder drama with added pretentiousness that goes beyond the notion that what we have seen could be in the author's imagination. The final section of this film is a mess and wills surely leave most viewers puzzled and dissatisfied. MS

• *Sarah Morton* Charlotte Rampling, *Julie* Ludivine Sagnier, *John Bosload* Charles Dance, *Marcel* Marc Fayolle, *Franck* Jean-Marie Lamour, *Marcel's daughter* Mireille Mosse.
• *Dir* François Ozon, *Pro* Olivier Delbosc and Marc Missonnier, *Co-Pro* Timothy Burrill, *Line Pro* Christine de Jekel, *Screenplay* Ozon and Emmanuele Bernheim, *Ph* Yorick Le Saux, *Pro Des* Wouter Zoon, *Ed* Monica Coleman, *M* Philippe Rombi, *Costumes* Pascaline Chavanne.

Fidelite/France 2 Cinéma/Gimages Films/Foz/Headforce/Canal Plus-UGC Films.
103 mins. France/UK. 2003. Rel: 22 August 2004. Cert. 15.

Sylvia ★★★¹/₂

Christine Jeffs, the brilliant director of the New Zealand movie *Rain*, confirms her visual skills in this biopic about the poet Sylvia Plath. However, given the conflicting views that exist over the role of Plath's husband and fellow poet Ted Hughes in the events that led to the breakdown of their marriage and to Plath's suicide, the script sidesteps. It tries to take a middle line as the story of a couple deeply in love yet mismatched and offers scarcely any background material on Plath, who had twice attempted suicide before she met Hughes. This failure to investigate in depth is unfortunate because Gwyneth Paltrow and Daniel Craig give commendable performances. They are well supported by (among others) Blythe Danner and Sir Michael Gambon. MS

• *Sylvia Plath* Gwyneth Paltrow, *Ted Hughes* Daniel Craig, *Al Alvarez* Jared Harris, *Assia Wevill* Amira Casar, *David Wevill* Andrew Havill, *Tom Hadley-Clarke* Sam Troughton, *Doreen* Lucy Davenport, *Michael Boddy* Antony Strachan, *Aurelia Plath* Blythe Danner, *Professor Thomas* Michael Gambon, *with* David Birkin, Alison Bruce, Julian Firth, Jeremy Fowlds.
• *Dir* Christine Jeffs, *Pro* Alison Owen, *Ex Pro* David M. Thompson, Tracey Scoffield, Robert Jones, Jane Barclay and Sharon Harel, *Co-Pro* Neris Thomas, *Line Pro* Mary Richards, *Assoc Pro* Phil Rymer, *Screenplay* John Brownlow, *Ph* John Toon, *Pro Des* Maria Djurkovic, *Ed* Tariq Anwar, *M* Gabriel Yared, *Costumes* Sandy Powell.

BBC Films/Capitol Films/U.K. Film Council/ Focus Features/Ruby Films-Icon.
114 mins. UK/USA. 2003. Rel: 30 January 2004. Cert 15.

Taking Lives ★★★

A serial killer is on the loose and the absurdly attractive Angelina Jolie is on his case. She is Special Agent Illeana Scott, an aloof, committed FBI 'profiler' who lies in the graves of the deceased so as to better enter the mindset of the killer. He likes to tear away the faces of his victims, cut off their hands and then take on their identity, even going so far as to pay their taxes. Owing an obvious debt to *Se7en* (even the opening credits pay homage to the 1995 thriller), *Taking Lives* is strong on atmosphere and has some clever tricks up its sleeve. Even so, the film ultimately falls foul of the genre's ludicrous formula and the last third spirals into jaw-dropping implausibility. Still, Ms Jolie is one of the most watchable stars on the planet and is worth the price of admission alone. JC-W

• *Special Agent Illeana Scott* Angelina Jolie, *James Costa* Ethan Hawke, *Hart* Kiefer Sutherland, *Paquette* Olivier Martinez, *Leclair* Tchéky Karyo, *Duval* Jean-Hugues Anglade, *Mrs Asher* Gena Rowlands, *young Asher* Paul Dano, *with* Justin Chatwin, Billy Two Rivers, Marie-Josée Croze, Andy Bradshaw, David Eisner
• *Dir* D.J. Caruso, *Pro* Mark Canton and Bernie Goldmann, *Ex Pro* Bruce Berman, Dana Goldberg and David Heyman, *Co-Pro* Alan C. Blomquist and Anna DeRoy, *Assoc Pro* Josette Perrotta, *Screenplay* Jon Bokenkamp, from the novel by Michael Pye, *Ph* Amir Mokri, *Pro Des* Tom Southwell, *Ed* Anne V. Coates, *M* Philip Glass, *Costumes* Marie-Sylvie Deveau, *Sound* Craig Henighan.

Below: Intermezzo: Harvey Keitel and Stellan Skarsgård in István Szabó's artificial *Taking Sides* (from Guerilla Films)

Warner/Village Roadshow/Atmosphere Entertainment-Warner.
102 mins. USA/Australia. 2004.
Rel: 23 April 2004. Cert 15.

Taking Sides ★★¹/₂

(*Der Fall Furtwängler*)
Not without echoes of his greatest film, *Mephisto*, István Szabó's latest work deals with the great conductor Wilhelm Furtwängler whose career was undermined by his electing to stay in Germany during the Nazi period and becoming an artist functioning through Hitler's approval. As a means of keeping art before the people, was his decision justified, whether or not it enabled him to give help to Jews who approached him (as to which there was conflicting evidence)? It's fascinating material, but this is taken from Ronald Harwood's play and it remains wholly artificial, while the superficial writing (evidenced also in cipher-like subsidiary characters) results in too little serious investigation of the issues and too much emphasis falling on the conductor's interrogator, a philistine army major from America. Harvey Keitel and Stellan Skarsgård are fine as these two men, but they are let down by Harwood's screenplay while repeated footage from Belsen is used obscenely. MS

• *Maj. Steve Arnold* Harvey Keitel, *Wilhelm Furtwängler* Stellan Skarsgård , *Lt. David Wills* Moritz Bleibtreu , *Emmi Straube* Birgit Minichmayr, *Helmuth Rode* Ulrich Tukur, *Rudolf Werner* Hanns

Zischler, *with* Frank Leboeuf, R. Lee Ermey, Oleg Tabakov.
• *Dir* István Szabó, *Pro* Yves Pasquier, *Ex Pro* Rainer Mockert, Rainer Schaper, Jacques Rousseau, Maureen McCabe, Jeremy Isaacs and Michael von Wolkenstein, *Screenplay* Ronald Harwood, based on his play, *Ph* Lajos Koltai, *Pro Des* Ken Adam, *Ed* Sylvie Landra, *M* Beethoven, Bruckner, Schubert, *M Supervisor* Ulrich Trimborn, *Costumes* Györgyi Szakács.

MBP/Maecenas Film/Paladin Production/Studio Babelsberg/Little Bear Enterprise Films/France 2 Cinéma/Canal Plus/Jeremy Isaacs Productions/ TwanPix/The Spice Factory-Guerilla Films. 111 mins. Germany/France/UK/Austria. 2001. Rel: 21 November 2003. Cert 15.

Tattoo ★★★¹/₂
Berlin, the bleak and techno-loving present. A young officer is pressed into partnership by a scarred veteran to investigate a series of gruesome murders that appear linked to the work of a legendary Japanese tattoo-artist … Robert Schwentke's stylish monochrome palate and driving pace cover a multitude of sins, including an improbable plot and coarse shock tactics. As odd-couple partners, August Diehl and Christian Redl pay strict homage to the guiding cop-show conventions, adding another echo to David Fincher's *Se7en*, of which there are many. Ultimately a success of style over substance, it deserves a greater sense of logic to match the quality of the acting. AK

• *Marc Schrader* August Diehl, *Detective Minks* Christian Redl, *Maya Kroner* Nadeshda Brennicke, *Frank Schoubya* Johan Leysen, *Dix* Faith Cevikkollu, *Inspector Roth* Monica Bleibtreu, *Meltem* Ilknur Bahadir, *Marie Minks* Jasmin Schwiers.
• *Dir* and *Screenplay* Robert Schwentke, *Pro* Roman Kuhn and Jan Hinter, *Ex Pro* Jens W. Meyer, *Line Pro* Verena Herfurth, *Ph* Jan Fehse, *Pro Des* Josef Sanktjohanser, *Ed* Peter Przygodda, *M* Martin Todsharow, *Costumes* Peri De Bragança, *Sound* André Bendocchi-Alves, *Tattoo and Body Artist* Alexander Boyko, *Special effects makeup* Henrik Scheib, *Special effects prosthetics* Georg Korpás.

StudioCanal/ Lounge Entertainment/B.A. Produktion-Metro Tartan. 108 mins. Germany. 2002. Rel: 5 December 2003. Cert 18.

Tears of the Sun ★★
Bruce Willis pulls on the grimace of duty to play the Navy Seal team leader sent into the midst of an African civil war (read: horrific massacre of innocents) to rescue an American doctor at a remote Christian mission. The mission aims to extract her, and only her, to a safe border. But when she refuses to abandon the villagers in her charge, he is forced to choose between duty and conscience … Antoine Fuqua's simplistic military fantasy can at least claim the foresight to cast the gorgeous Monica Bellucci as the noble doctor, giving some credence to the moral battle Willis has to fight (who could deny those lips? Seriously.) His sharply choreographed action sequences, and impressively gruesome SFX deserve commendation. However, the adolescent preachiness that embeds itself into almost every spoken line is just offensive to anyone of reasonable intelligence. The clear bright lines separating the good guys from the bad guys is an artefact of a misinformed cinematic past and it belittles the truths of the story to trot out an arthritic justification for machine-gun diplomacy. Previously known as *Man of War*. AK

• *Lieut. A. K. Waters* Bruce Willis, *Dr. Lena Kendricks* Monica Bellucci, *James 'Red' Atkins* Cole Hauser, *Ellis 'Zee' Pettigrew* Eamonn Walker, *Michael 'Slo' Slowenski* Nick Chinlund, *Sister Grace* Fionnula Flanagan, *Col. Idris Sadick* Malick Bowens, *Capt. Bill Rhodes* Tom Skerritt, *Patience* Akosua Busia.
• *Dir* Antoine Fuqua, *Pro* Michael Lobell, Arnold Rifkin and Ian Bryce, *Screenplay* Alex Lasker and Patrick Cirillo, *Ph* Mauro Fiore and Larry Blanford, *Pro Des* Naomi Shohan, *Art Dir* David Lazan, *Ed* Conrad Buff, *M* Hans Zimmer, *additional M* James Michael Dooley, Lisa Gerrard and Steve Jablonsky, *ambient M* Mel Wesson, *Costumes* Marlene Stewart.

Cheyenne Enterprises/Michael Lobell Productions/Revolution Studios-Columbia TriStar. 121 mins. USA. 2003. Rel: 12 September 2003. Cert 15.

Ten Minutes Older – The Cello ★★¹/₂
Ten Minutes Older – The Trumpet ★★★★
Fifteen directors were asked to contribute featurettes of about ten minutes each on the broad theme of visions of time. Eight are seen in *The Cello* and seven in *The Trumpet*, these designations merely indicating which unseen musical instrument accompanies the brief visuals that link the individual sections. It may be chance that one of these compilations is so clearly superior to the other – or it could be taken as a matter of taste, for much of *The Cello* is close to avant-garde cinema. Figgis contributes one of his tedious split-screen experiments, Bertolucci draws on an obscure Indian fable, Schlondörff philosophises without depth and Godard doodles characteristically. Szabó's drama makes pitifully little impact, while Menzel's observation on the aging of Rudolf Hrusinsk_ will mean most to those who know the actor. Radford may please sci-fi fans,

however, and Denis offers an intriguing discussion between a girl and a philosopher. This last echoes Godard's *Vivre Sa Vie* but is overshadowed by it. In contrast in *The Trumpet* almost everything works. Least good are Jarmusch's study of a star (Chloe Sevigny) failing to find relaxation during a work break and Chen Kaige's parable about the past becoming lost to the present, rather whimsical but better than his recent features. For the rest there are contrasted pleasures: high drama from Wenders, a clever documentary take by Spike Lee on the disputed Florida vote in the last American Presidential election, Herzog in ethnographic mode, a tragi-comedy that is quintessential Aki Kaurismäki in miniature and, best of all, a poetic black and white study from Victor Erice. His piece is no longer than the rest, but without dialogue it uses a birth in 1940 in the Basque countryside to create a homage to silent cinema, a reflection on the dangers which surround the individual in a troubled world and a celebration of life. MS

Ten Minutes Older – The Cello
• *Pro* Nicolas McClintock, Nigel Thomas and Ulrich Felsberg, *Ed* Peter Christelis, *M* Paul Englishby.

About Time 2
• *With*: Mark Long, Alexandra Staden, Dominic West.
• *Dir* and *Screenplay* Mike Figgis, *Ph* Mike Figgis, Danny Cohen, Lucy Bristow, Albert Kodagolian and Kirstin McMahon, *Pro Des* Michael Howells,
• *Costumes* Dinah Collins, *Sound* Nigel Heath, James Feltham and Mark Tucker.

One Moment
• *With*: Rudolf Hrusinsky.
• *Dir* and *Scr* Jiri Menzel, *Ed* Zdenek Patocka, *M* Leos Janacek.

Ten Minutes After
• *With*: Ildiko Bansagi, Gabor Mate.
• *Dir* and *Screenplay* Istvan Szabo, *Ph* Lajos Koltai, *Pro Des* Zsuzsa Borvendeg, *Ed* Zsuzsa Csakany, *Costumes* Zsuzsa Stenger and Sandor Csajbok, *Sound* Istvan Sipos.

Histoire d'eaux
• *With*: Amit Arroz, Valeria Bruni Tadeschi.
• *Dir* and *Screenplay* Bernardo Bertolucci, *Ph* Fabio Cianchetti, *Ed*, Jacopo Quadri, *Pro Des* Metka Kosak, *Costumes* Louise Stjvernsward, sound, Tommaso Quattrini

Towards Nancy
• *With*: Jean-Luc Nancy, Ana Samardzija, Alex Descas.
• *Dir* and *Screenplay* Claire Denis, *Ph* Agnes Godard,

Ed Emmanuelle Pencalet, *M* Brice Leboucq, *Sound* Jean-Louis Ughetto, Paulin Sagna

The Enlightenment
• *With*: Bibiana Beglau, Irm Hermann, Mario Irrek, Toks Korner
• *Dir* Volker Schlondorff, *Screenplay* Max Frye, based on *Confessions* by St. Augustinus, *Ph* Tilman Buttner and Andreas Hofer, *Pro Des* Claus-Jurgen Pfeiffer, *Ed* Peter Przygodda and Oliver Weiss, *Costumes* Aenne Plaumann.

Addicted To The Stars
• *With*: Daniel Craig, Charles Simon, Roland Gift, Branka Katic, Claire Adamson.
• *Dir* and *Screenplay* Michael Radford, *Ph* Pascal Rabaud, *Pro Des* Christina Moore, *Ed* Lucia Zucchetti, *M* Jocelyn Pook, *Costumes* Jany Temime

In the Darkness of Time
• *Dir* Jean-Luc Godard, *Screenplay* Anne-Marie Mieville, *Ph* Julien Hirsch, *M* Arvo Part, *Sound* Francois Musy.

London Road Sales/Odyssey Films/Matador Pictures/Road Movies/AtomFilms-Blue Dolphin. 106 mins. Germany/UK/USA. 2002. Rel: 12 December 2003. Cert. 15.

Ten Minutes Older – The Trumpet
• *Pro* Nicolas McClintock, Nigel Thomas and Ulrich Felsberg, *Ex Pro* Ulrich Felsberg, *Ed* Peter Christelis, *M* Paul Englishby.

Dogs Have No Hell
• *With*: Kati Outinen, Markku Peltola, Sulevi Peltola, etc.
• *Dir, Pro, Screenplay* and *Ed* Aki Kaurismäki, *Ph* Timo Salminen and Olli Varja, *Set Design* Markku Pätilä.

Lifeline
• *With*: Ana Sofia Llaño, Pelayo Suarez, Celia Poo, etc.
• *Dir* and *Screenplay* Victor Erice, *Ph* Ángel Luis Fernández, *Art Dir* Javier Manpaso, *Ed* Julia Juaniz.

Ten Thousand Years Older
• *With*: Werner Herzog, Tari, Wapu
• *Dir* and *Screenplay* Werner Herzog, *Pro* Lucki Stipetic, *Ph* Vicente Ríos, *Ed* Joe Bini.

Int. Trailer. Night
• *With*: Chloë Sevigny, Matt Malloy, Susan Blackwell, Liana Pai, Mike Hyde, Jamie Hector.
• *Dir* and *Screenplay* Jim Jarmusch, *Pro* Cecilia Kate Roque, *Ph* Frederick Elmes, Ed Jay Rabinowitz, *Costumes* John Dunn, *Sound* Chic Ciccolini III.

Twelve Miles to Trona
• *With:* Charles Esten, Amber Tamblyn,
Wim Wenders, etc
• *Dir* Wim Wenders, *Pro* Samson Mücke, *Line Pro* Pascal
Leister, *Ph* Phedon Papamichael, *Ed* Mathilde Bonnefroy.

We Wuz Robbed
• *With:* Michael Feldman, Nick Baldick,
Mike Whouley, etc.
• *Dir* and *Pro* Spike Lee, *Ph* Chris Norr,
Ed Barry Alexander Brown.

100 Flowers Hidden Deep
• *With:* Feng Yuanzheng, Gen Le, Li Qiang,
Zhang Jin, Wang Shujun, Feng Feng.
• *Dir* Chen Kaige, *Pro* Chen Hong, *Screenplay*
Zhang Tan, *Ph* Yang Shu, *Pro Des* Cao Jiuping
and Liu Luyi, *Ed* Li Fang, *M* Zhao Lin.

London Road Sales/Odyssey Films/Matador
Pictures/Road Movies/AtomFilms-Blue Dolphin.
92 mins. Germany/UK/USA. 2002. Rel: 3 October 2003.
Cert. 15.

Terminator 3: Rise of the Machines
★★★★

In the present tense, John Connor is a haunted
youth fleeing the prophecies of his late mother
and the knowledge of the apocalypse that could be,
living 'off the grid' just in case ... Well, the feared
eventuality arrives in the form of the T-X, as super-
duped a cyborg assassin as the fevered minds of
a perennially teenaged Terminator fan can devise,
looking very good in her tight leathers.
Schwarzeneggar also makes an impressive return as
a T-1000 sent to protect Connor from her deadly
intentions. Cue a $175 million, big-budget, all-out,
fire and lighting celebrity cyborg deathmatch that
barely pauses for breath. Jonathon Mostow cleverly
chooses not to mess with a winning formula and
gives the panting fans exactly what they were waiting
for; bigger and bolder, brighter and more buxom.
Oh, yes, it's all about Kristanna Loken's utter superiority
against the faintly German efficiency of Arnie's heavy
metal model. A smart twist that turns the expected
finale on its head caps off what may be the last in a
majestic franchise, now that its star has gone to fight
even greater terrors in Californian politics. AK

• *Terminator* Arnold Schwarzenegger, *John Connor*
Nick Stahl, *Kate Brewster* Claire Danes, *T-X*
Kristanna Loken, *Robert Brewster* David Andrews.
• *Dir* Jonathan Mostow, *Pro* Mario F Kassar, Andrew
G. Vajna, Joel B. Michael, Hal Lieberman and Colin
Wilson, *Ex Pro* Moritz Borman, Guy East, Nigel
Sinclair, Gale Anne Hurd, *Screenplay* John Brancato
and Michael Ferris, based on a story by John
Brancato, Michael Ferris and Tedi Sarafian, *Ph* Don

Burgess, *Pro Des* Jeff Mann, *Ed* Neil Travis and
Nicolas De Toth, *M* Marco Beltrami, *Costumes* April
Ferry, *Makeup/animatronic effects supervisor* Stan
Winston.

C-2 Pictures/Intermedia Films/IMF Internationale
Medien und Film GmbH & Co. Produktions
KG/Mostow/Lieberman Productions-Columbia Tristar.
108 mins. USA/Germany/UK. 2003. Rel 1 August 2003.
Cert 12A.

The Texas Chainshaw Massacre ★★¹/₂
August, 1973, Travis County, Texas. Five not-so-
bright young things pick up a lone hitchhiker on
their way home from a long weekend in Mexico ...
so begins the original *Texas Chainsaw Massacre*,
made in 1974 by a passionate and untried crew of
film students and portfolio makers. The slick new
Hollywood version of their now classic scenario has
been styled by the pyrotechnic producer Michael
Bay, under the direction of music video and
commercials specialist Marcus Nispel. Nispel sails
close to the original premise, with key scenes set
up as near duplicates. The money is well spent on
spookier locations, deadlier props and on set reeking
with in-hospitality. The audience is slammed with
sharply imaged tortures of Leatherface's victims.
Against all expectation, this Hollywood version of a
cult B-movie classic is sharp enough, hard enough,
and clever enough to stand alone, spreading the
timeless moral that one should never, ever, stop for
any bleeding thing when driving through the
remote, inbred hinterlands of rural America. AK

• *Erin Hardesty* Jessica Biel, *Morgan* Jonathan Tucker,
Pepper Harrington Erica Leerhsen, *Andy* Mike Vogel,
Kemper Hardesty Eric Balfour, *Thomas Hewitt*
Andrew Bryniarski, *Sheriff Hoyt* R. Lee Ermey,
Jedidiah Sawyer David Dorfman, *teenage
girl* Lauren German, *Old Monty* Terrence Evans,
Luda May Marietta Marich, *Henrietta Sawyer*
Heather Kafka, *the tea lady* Kathy Lamkin, *Big
Rig Bob* Brad Leland, *Clerk* Mamie Meek,
narrator John Larroquette.
• *Dir* Marcus Nispel, *Pro* Michael Bay and Mike
Fleiss, *Ex Pro* Ted Field, Jeff Allard, Guy Stodel,
Brad Fuller and Andrew Form, *Co-Pro* Tobe Hooper
and Kim Henkel, *Screenplay* Scott Kosar, *Ph* Daniel
Pearl, *Pro Des* Greg Blair, *Art Dir* Scott Gallagher,
Ed Glen Scantlebury, *M* Steve Jablonsky; 'Seet
Home Salabama' performed by Lynyrd Skynyrd,
Costumes Bobbie Mannix, *Makeup Effects* Scott
Stoddard and Gregory Nicotero, *Visual Effects
Supervisor* Jason Schugardt and Nathan McGuinness.

Focus Features/Radar Pictures/Platinum Dunes/Next
Entertainment-Entertainment.
98 mins. USA. 2003. Rel 31 October 2003. Cert 18.

thirteen ★★★¹/₂

Director and co-writer Catherine Hardwicke's debut comes in the shape of a powerfully affecting portrait of a lovely teenage girl whose rush towards womanhood is turned to tragedy by the unwholesome influence of a Machiavellian girlfriend. Evan Rachel Wood produces an unforgettable performance as Tracy, who transforms seemingly overnight into a sexualised Lolita, both thrilled and terrified at her new powers, to be part of the school's cool clique of bad girls. Petty thievery, drugs and dangerous seductions ensue, prompted by the subtle manipulations of her new 'pal' Evie, whose flashing dark eyes mask a girl grown old before her time. Part-tragedy, part-cautionary, and part autobiography (Nikki Reed, the actress playing Evie, is credited as co-writer) the film highlights the seismic shifts in Tracy's behaviour with a highly-keyed, confrontational realism that stays a long time in the mind. AK

• *Melanie* Holly Hunter, *Tracy* Evan Rachel Wood, *Evie Zamora* Nikki Reed, *Brady* Jeremy Sisto, *Mason* Brady Corbett, *Brooke* Deborah Kara Unger, *Luke* Kip Pardue, *Birdie* Sarah Clarke, *Travis* D.W. Moffett, *Noel* Vanessa Anne Hudgens, *Astrid* Jenicka Carey, *Rafa* Ulysses Estrada.
• *Dir* Catherine Hardwicke, *Pro* Jeffrey Levy-Hinte and Michael London, *Ex Pro* Tim Bevan, Eric Fellner, Liza Chasin and Holly Hunter, *Co-pro* Rosemary Marks, *Screenplay* Hardwicke and Nikki Reed *Ph* Elliot Davis, *Ed* Nancy Richardson, *Pro Des* Carol Strober, *M* Mark Mothersbaugh; songs performed by Malé, Carmen Rizzo, Eddie Baytos, DJ Assault, The Like, Katy Rose, The Freshmaka, Youth Brigade, Iffy, Clinic, Mark Mothersbaugh, Kinky, The Tormentos, Orlando Brown, Javá Benson and Mo- McRae, Charles Duckworth Jr, Liz Phair, Anet, Imperial Teen, Supervision, The Folk Implosion, and MC 900 Foot Jesus, *Costumes* Cindy Evans.

UniversalPictures/StudioCanal/Michael London Prods/Working Title/Antidote Films-UIP. 100 mins. USA/UK. 2003. Rel: 5 December 2003. Cert 18.

This Is Not a Love Song ★★★

Released from prison after serving a term for theft, Spike is met by his friend Heaton. They then head for the countryside in a stolen car but run out of petrol. Seeking help at a nearby farm, Heaton is mistaken for a burglar and is locked in a shed by the owner. In an ensuing fracas, Spike accidentally kills the farmer's daughter and so he and Heaton flee for their lives… Built round an actors' workshop (much in the way that Mike Leigh creates his films), Simon Beaufoy's screenplay evolved from the interaction of the protagonists. Thus, the story takes second place to the characters, the former feeling a little contrived at times, but the look and atmosphere of the film more than makes up for this. Amazingly, the production was shot in two weeks utilising a DV camera and goes down in history as Britain's very first 'e-premiere,' being simultaneously released in cinemas and shown on-line. A good start. CB

• *Spike* Michael Colgan, *Heaton* Kenny Glenaan, *Mr Bellamy* David Bradley, *Arthur* John Henshaw, *William* Adam Pepper, *Gerry* Keri Arnold.
• *Dir* Bille Eltringham, *Pro* Mark Blaney, *Ex Pro* Simon Beaufoy, Kate Ogborn and Paul Trijbits, *Screenplay* Beaufoy, *Ph* Robbie Ryan, *Pro Des* Jo Henson, *Ed* Ewa J Lind, *M* Adrian Johnston, *Costumes* Claire Anderson.

Soda Pictures/Film Council Development Fund/Footprint Films/Longfellow Prods/Strange Dog-Soda Pictures. 91 mins. UK. 2002. Rel: 5 September 2003. Cert. 18.

The Three Marias ★★★

(*As Tres Marias*)
The most unusual feature of this Brazilian film is that it offers star roles to no less than four able actresses. Three of them play the Marias of the title, the daughters of a widow (the fourth leading role) who sends them out to find ways of exacting revenge for the deaths of their father and brothers. Those killings had been arranged by a jealous suitor twice spurned by the mother and she, believing in an eye for an eye, requires her three Marias to bring about the demise of this man and of his sons. Such material despite its improbabilities could have made an agreeably exciting thriller but, competently made though it is, this emerges as a film which both relishes the violence of the tale and then hypocritically ends up by lamenting lives given over to killing. MS

• *Filomena Capadócio* Marieta Severo, *Maria Francisca* Julia Lemmertz, *Maria Rosa* Maria Luiza Mendonca, *Maria Pia* Luiza Mariani, *Firmino Santos* Guerra Carlos Vereza, *Zé das Cobras* Enrique Diaz, *Chief Tenório* Tuca Andrada, *Jesuíno Cruz* Wagner Moura, *Catrevagem* Lazaro Ramos, *Arcanjo Santos Guerra* Fabio Limma, *José Tranquilo Santos Guerra* Cassiano Carneiro.
• *Dir* Aluizio Abranches, *Pro* Aluizio Abranches and Eva Mariani, *Ex Pro* Bill Castro, *Assoc Pro* Vieri Razzini and Cesare Petrillo, *Screenplay* Heitor Dhalia and Wilson Freire, *Ph* Marcelo Durst, *Pro Des* Bruno Schmidt, *Ed* Aluizio Abranches and Karen Harley, *M* André Abujamra.

BR/Lama Filmes/Teodora Film/Quanta-Gala. 88 mins. Brazil/Italy/The Netherlands. 2003. Rel: 30 January 2004. Cert 15.

Timeline ★

The Michael Crichton bandwagon rolls ever onward, each chunky bestseller snapped up by Hollywood. *Timeline* must count as one of the worst, a risible combination of science fiction and historical epic. A group of young and glamorous archeologists lose their professor through a wormhole in the space-time continuum. Mounting a rescue mission, they end up in fourteenth century Dordogne, where the English and French armies are hacking each other to pieces. It's the Hundred Years War and our intrepid heroes must help the gallant French win a crucial victory. A civilian spin on *The Final Countdown* and the Japanese *Timeslip*, *Timeline* scores only on unintentional laughs. While director Donner can deliver the goods, he comes badly unstuck here. And it's typical of *Timeline*'s sloppy script that our heroes are instant experts with medieval weapons, fighting off hostile soldiers with ease.
DO

• *Chris Johnston* Paul Walker, *Kate Ericson* Frances O'Connor, *Andre Marek* Gerard Butler, *Professor Johnston* Billy Connolly, *Robert Doniger* David Thewlis, *Lady Claire* Anna Friel, *Frank Gordon* Neal McDonough, *Steven Kramer* Matt Craven, *Josh Stern* Ethan Embry, *Lord Oliver* Michael Sheen, *Lord Arnaut* Lambert Wilson, *De Kere* Marton Czokas, *Francois Dontelle* Rossif Sutherland.
• *Dir* Richard Donner, *Pro* Richard Donner, Lauren Shuler Donner and Jim Van Wyck, *Ex Pro* Gary Levinsohn, Michael Ovitz and Don Granger, *Co-Pro* Michael Aguilar and Kevin De La Noy, *Assoc Pro* Derek Hoffman and Brian Read, *Ph* Caleb Deschanel, *Screenplay* Jeff Maguire and George Nolfi, based on the novel by Michael Crichton, *Pro Des* Daniel T. Dorrance, *Ed* Richard Marks *M* Eliot Goldenthal and Brian Tyler, *Costumes* Jenny Bevan.

Paramount/ Mutual Film Company/Cobalt Media Group-Entertainment.
115 mins. USA. 2003. Rel: 5 December 2003. Cert 12A.

Time of the Wolf ★★★★

France, in an alternate future. A mother and two children are set adrift when their escape to the country is brutally terminated by the murder of her husband. The facts are vague but we come to understand that the world is approaching apocalypse, society has collapsed, and a long dark night is about to descend … Isabelle Huppert leads the cast in Michael Haneke's latest rasp at the mores of the comfy middle-classes. They join forces again after *The Piano Teacher*, in a film that shamelessly showcases Haneke's bold, auteurist style. Layers of commentary ripple through the film, but strongest is the sense that we are being treated to a brute and unvarnished vision of the refugee experience, shown through the lens of a very urbane, Western European family. Not that Haneke plays things so simply, and other interpretations are available of his minimalist narrative. Whatever the interpretation, the film remains a gripping poem by a master of simple form that promises to both upset and ultimately uplift an audience, granted a capacity for Haneke's brutal ethics. AK

• *Anne* Isabelle Huppert, *Eva Laurent* Anaïs Demoustier, *Ben Laurent* Lucas Biscombe, *Mr Azoulay* Maurice Benichou, *Thomas Brandt* Patrice Chereau, *Lise Brandt* Beatrice Dalle, *Georges* Daniel Duval, *Mrs Axoulay* Maryline Even, *Koslowski* Olivier Gourmet, *Arina* Rona Hartner, *Nathalie Azoulay* Florence Loiret-Caille, *Bea* Brigitte Rouan, *policeman* Branko Sanarovski, *young runaway* Hakim Taleb, *Jean* Thierry Van Werveke.

Below: Time running out: Michael Haneke's harrowing *Time of the Wolf* (from Artificial Eye)

• *Dir* and *Screenplay* Michael Haneke, *Pro* Margaret Menegoz and Veit Heiduschka, *Ex Pro* Michael Katz and Margaret Menegoz, *Co-Pro* Michael Weber, *Ph* Jurgen Jurges, *Art Dir* Christoph Kanter, *Ed* Monika Willi and Nadine Muse, *Costumes,* Lisy Christl.

Les Films du Losange/Wega Film/Bavaria Film/France 3 Cinéma /Arte France Cinéma/Centre National de la Cinematogrpahie/Canal Plus/Eurimages-Artificial Eye. 113 mins. France/Austria/Germany. 2003. Rel: 17 October 2003. Cert 15

Together ★★★★★

(aka *Together With You/Ha ni zai yi qi*)
A cook from the outskirts of Shanghai, Liu Cheng wants nothing but the best for his son, Xiaochun. Since the death of his mother, Xiaochun has evolved into a phenomenally talented violinist and so Cheng takes him to Beijing in the hope of finding a tutor. Xiaochun, now thirteen, plays to celebrate the memory of his mother (who was a violinist) but also wants to please his father. Being poor, Cheng hopes that his son will achieve fame and fortune, so Xiaochun goes along with his father's wishes… With its exquisite cinematography and sublime soundtrack (combining traditional Chinese music with the glorious sound of Bruch and Tchaikovsky), *Together* immediately appeals to the senses. But beneath this there is a far more powerful and subtle work at play as the great Chinese director Chen Kaige explores the bonds of family vis-à-vis the changes in China since the Cultural Revolution. What emerges is a truly humanist story in which the obvious is kept at bay, shored up by some unexpected twists in the narrative. FYI: Young Tang Yun, who plays Xiaochun, is himself a violinist, although he's dubbed by the real-life prodigy Li Chuanyun (who makes a cameo as an incompetent student!).
JC-W

• *Liu Cheng* Liu Peiqi, *Lili* Chen Hong, *Professor Jiang* Wang Zhiwen, *Professor Yu* Chen Kaige, *Xiaochun* Tang Yun, *Lili's lover* Cheng Qian, *Debao* Liu Bing, *Mrs Yu* Kim Hairi.
• *Dir* Chen Kaige, *Pro* Ton Gang and Chen Hong, *Ex Pro* Yang Buting, Yan Xiaming, Chen Kaige and Li Bolun, *Screenplay* Chen Kaige and Xue Xiaolu, *Ph* Kim Hyungkoo, *Pro Des* Cao Jiuping and Liu Luyi, *M* Zhao Lin, *Costumes* Hah Yongsoo, *Sound* Wang Danrong, *violin solos* Li Chuanyun.

Fourth Prod. Co. of China Film/Century Hero Film Investment/China Movie Channel/21st Century Shengkai-Momentum Pictures. 118 mins. China/South Korea. 2002. Rel: 12 December 2003. Cert. PG.

Tooth ★

It's not until you see a movie as inept as *Tooth* that you realise how difficult it is to get a children's film right. After such gifts from Hollywood as *Finding Nemo*, *Tooth* limps into the arena like an artless, unruly street urchin. Set in America but obviously shot in Britain (the English accents, rolling meadows and overcast skies rather give the game away), the film is a fairy tale for very young children with very little brain. A Tooth Fairy, on a whim, dumps the entire treasury of Fairytopia under the pillow of a little girl, thus stopping Christmas in its tracks. As the girl and her brother lose all concept of the value of money, a dastardly reporter from The Sceptical Examiner (Enfield) turns up for the scoop of the century. Acted, edited and scored with amateurish incompetence, the film showcases the likes of Stephen Fry and Richard E. Grant turning up for their standard fee, while only Phyllida Law – as an embittered Fairy Godmother – retains any sense of dignity and professionalism. JC-W

• *Plug* Harry Enfield, *The Extractor* Vinnie Jones, *Pedro* Stephen Fry, *voice of Rabbit* Jim Broadbent, *Dad* Tim Dutton, *Mom* Sally Phillips, *Bon Bon* Jerry Hall, *Jarvis Jarvis* Richard E. Grant, *Mrs Claus* Phyllida Law, *Tooth* Yasmin Paige, *ancient fairy* Anna Wing, *bitter fairy* Elizabeth McKechnie, *Tolly* Maisie Preston, *Tom* Rory Copus, *New Recruit* Lily Atkinson, *Bulldozer* Patrick Monckton, *store cashier* Craig Parkinson, *Stutter Fairy* Georgina Terry, *Bully Boy* Leagh Conwell, *himself* Santa Claus, *with* Paul Sarony, Roy Holder.
• *Dir* and *Screenplay* Edouard Nammour, *Pro* Susie Brooks-Smith, Simon Franks and Zygi Kamasa, *Ex Pro* Adam Betteridge and David Rogers, *Additional Script Material* Piers Fletcher, Simon Franks and Zygi Kamasa, *Ph* Clive Tickner, *Pro Des* James Merifield, *Ed* Alan Strachan, *M* Guy Fletcher, *Costumes* Howard Burden.

Archangel Filmworks/Redbus Pictures/Great British Films-Redbus. 91 mins. UK. 2003. Rel: 13 February 2004. Cert U.

Torque ★★★¹/₂

2 Daft, 2 Dubious. That should have been the tagline for this fabulously unapologetic, wheelspinning mecha-fanboy frenzy. Starring a swooningly modelicious Martin Henderson as Cary Ford, a cross between *Mad Max*, Vin Diesel and a Tommy Hilfiger fashion catalogue. Our all-American hero (who hails from New Zealand, by the way) returns from exile in Bangkok to the mean streets of Cali to clear his name and settle old scores with a 'Hell's Angels' poster boy called Henry James. All for the love, naturally, of a beautiful woman in the shape of Money Mazur's character, Shane. AK

• *Cary Ford* Martin Henderson, *Trey Wallace* Ice Cube, *Shane* Monet Mazur, *McPherson* Adam Scott, *Henry* Matt Schulze, *China* Jaime Pressly, *Luther* Max Beesley, *Dalton* Jay Hernandez, *Val* Will Yun Lee, *Junior* Fredo Starr, *Henderson* Justina Machado, *Sheriff Barnes* John Doe.
• *Dir* Joseph Kahn, *Pro* Neal H. Moritz and Brad Luff, *Ex Pro* Mike Rachmil, Graham Burke and Bruce Berman, *Co-Pro* Greg Tharp, *Screenplay* Matt Johnson, *Ph* Peter Levy, *Pro Des* Peter J. Hampton, *Ed* Howard E. Smith and David Blackburn, *M* Trevor Rabin, *Costumes* Elisabetta Beraldo.

Warner/Village Roadshow-Warner.
84 mins. US/Australia. 2004. Rel: 12 January 2004. Cert 15.

Touching the Void ★★★¹⁄₂

Joe Simpson and Simon Yates almost lost their lives conquering the virgin West Face of the 21,200-foot Siula Grande. Descending from the summit, Simpson falls and shatters his leg horribly. Without any hope of rescue, Yates attempts to lower his partner down the face of the mountain to safety, until an accident forces Yates into a dreadful choice … A pair of arrogant young mountaineers, a mythical Peruvian mountain and a hellish blizzard are all you need to lay a bloody test of human endurance. Kevin MacDonald, Oscared for *One Day in September*, recreates the harrowing true-life drama of these mountaineers with actors playing their parts, intercut with first-person interviews with Yates and Simpson. The film's unrelenting grip on your attention is almost as stunning as the adventure it recounts and the landscape the tragic drama was played on. AK

• *As themselves*: Joe Simpson, Simon Yates, *Joe Simpson* Brendan Mackey *Simon Yates* Nicholas Aaron.
• *Dir* Kevin Macdonald, based on the book by Joe Simpson, *Pro* John Smithson, *Co-Pro* Sue Summers, *Ph* Mike Eley, *Ed* Justine Wright, *M* Alex Heffes and Bevan Smith.

Darlow Smithon Prods/FilmFour/Pathé/UK Film Council-Pathé
106 mins. UK. 2003. Rel 12 December 2003. Cert 15.

Triggermen ★★★

Chicago provides the unexpected setting for a tale about two Brits played by Neil Morrissey and Adrian Dunbar. These two are mistaken for hit men and try to profit from the situation by taking the money without firing the gun and then getting the girl (Claire Forlani). Portraying a crime boss, Pete Postlethwaite succeeds in slipping in a convincing

touch of human feeling, but this complex crime thriller mainly played for laughs is as a whole light-weight, pretty stupid and reasonably diverting. It's more watchable than most critics suggested, although completely forgettable. However, director John Bradshaw's knowing approach emphasising film techniques (circling cameras, freeze frames and speeded-up shots) does convey to the audience some of the fun that he was clearly having. MS

• *Pete Maynard* Neil Morrisey, *Terry Malloy* Donnie Wahlberg, *Andy Jarrett* Adrian Dunbar, *Emma Cutler* Claire Forlani, *Ben Cutler* Pete Postlethwaite, *Penny Archer* Amanda Plummer, *Tommy O'Brian* Michael Rapaport, *Jazzer* Saul Rubinek, *hobo* Mark Thomas.
• *Dir* John Bradshaw, *Screenplay* Tony Johnston, *Pro* Deborah Kiss, Sabine Mueller and Mark Thomas, *Ex Pro* John Gillespie, Klaus Rettig and Gerhard Schmidt, *Co-Pro* Tony Johnston and Paul Weber, *Ph* Barry Stone, *Pro Des* Tim Boyd, *Ed* Lisa Grootenboer, *M* Terence M. Gowan and Blair Packham, *Costumes* Kimberly Ann Rush.

First Look Media/ International West Pictures// Now Entertainment/Gemini Film-Winchester Film.
96 mins. Canada/Germany. 2001. Rel: 26 December 2003. Cert 15.

La Trilogie ★★★¹⁄₂

The scale of ambition behind Lucas Belvaux's trilogy of interconnecting films is humbling. The Belgian multi-hyphenate's series of three films share a cast of characters over a three-day period, but are engineered into a narrative kaleidoscope. Belvaux says he eventually made four films; the chase thriller *Trilogie 1: On The Run*, the romantic farce *Trilogie 2: An Amazing Couple*, the dramatic character study *Trilogie 3: After Life*, and the larger celluloid canvas created by each individual viewer's interpretation of the set, influenced by the order in which she experiences them. So far, so pretentious. Thankfully, Belvaux's experimentalism is supported by consistently arresting and exciting performances from a commited cast. That the films escape non-sequitors or plain boringness is astounding in itself. The confidence with which Belvaux plays with alternate perspectives and tonal changes is impressive. Nevertheless, one must damn by partial praise. While each film represents fine work, they do not quite match the ambitions of their conception. The first film is the strongest; a lean thriller told behind the eyes of Bruno (played by Belvaux), a moral psychopath who justifies his actions with a deadly socialist agenda. After an explosive prison escape he goes on the run from the law but remains determined to wage a terrorist war against capitalism, along the way searching for the informer who ratted him out. The subsequent parts of his

Trilogie, however, are flabby by comparison. The romantic farce of *An Amazing Couple* chews a little too enthusiastically on a slim rib of misplaced suspicions, whereas the dark drama of *After Life* loses pace halfway through and marches the audience through the pain of an ailing marriage scarred by moral corruption, a drug dependency and the raw feeling of a difficult commitment to love. AK

• *Agnes Manise* Dominique Blanc, *Pascal Manise* Gilbert Melki, *Cécile Coste* Ornella Muti, *Jeanne Rivet* Catherine Frot, *Alain Costes* François Morel, *Claire* Valérie Mairesse, *Jaquillat* Patrick Descamps, *Bruno Le Roux (*aka *Pierre)* Lucas Belvaux, *Louise* Raphaele Godin, *Jeanne's son* Élie Belvaux.

One: On The Run ★★★'/₂
(Cavale)

• *Dir* and *Screenplay* Lucas Belvaux, *Pro* Patrick Sobelman, *Ex Pro* Diana Elbaun, *Ph* Pierre Milon, *Pro Des* Frederique Belvaux, *Ed* Ludo Troch, *M* Riccardo Del Fra, *Costumes* Cecile Cotton, *Sound* Christian Monheim.

114 mins. France/Belgium. 2002.
Rel 14 November 2003. Cert. 15.

Two: An Amazing Couple ★★'/₂
(Un couple épatant)

• *Dir* and *Screenplay* Lucas Belvaux, *Pro* Patrick Sobelman, *Ex Pro* Diana Elbaun, *Ph* Pierre Milon, *Pro Des* Frederique Belvaux, *Ed* Valerie Loiseleux, *M* Riccardo Del Fra, *Costumes* Cecile Cotton, *Sound* Christian Monheim.

97 mins. France/Belgium 2002.
Rel 28 November 2003. Cert PG.

Three: Après la vie ★★'/₂
(After Life)

• *Dir* and *Screenplay* Lucas Belvaux, *Pro* Patrick Sobelman and Diana Elbaun, *Ph* Pierre Milon, *Pro Des* Frédérique Belvaux, *Ed* Danielle Anezin, *M* Riccardo Del Fra, *Costumes* Cecile Cotton, *Sound* Christian Monheim.

Agat Films & Cie and Entre Chien et Loup/Rhône-Alps Cinéma/RTBF/Canal Plus-Metro Tartan.
120 mins. France/Belgium. 2002.
Rel 5 December 2003. Cert PG.

Troy ★★★'/₂

Inspired by the *Iliad* and the *Voyages of Odysseus*, Wolfgang Peterson's sprawling, elaborate, star-filled epic arrived in waves of hype wild enough to sink the proverbial thousand ships. A cast drawn from the Hollywood heavens included Brad Pitt as a fabulously buff and brooding Achilles, Peter O'Toole as King Priam, Orlando Bloom as the poetically built Paris, whose elopement with Helen, wife of Menelaus, ignited the legendary siege of Troy … For all the expensive sets and the cast-of-thousands air about the production, it never lives up to the weight of the epics it takes for its inspiration. Fair enough, the sheer grandeur, the inflated heroics, and the thundering theatricality of the actors do pin you back in your seat, sometimes with genuine excitement as for the duel between Hector and Achilles. But without the emotional complexity to do justice to the power of the epic myths portrayed, it finds itself wanting for substance to match. AK

• *Achilles* Brad Pitt, *Hector* Eric Bana, *Paris* Orlando Bloom, *Helen* Diane Kruger, *Agamemnon* Brian Cox, *Odysseus* Sean Bean, *Menelaus* Brendan Gleeson, *Priam* Peter O'Toole, *Briseis* Rose Byrne, *Thetis* Julie Christie, *Andromache* Saffron Burrows, *Nestor* John Shrapnel, *Patroclus* Garrett Hedlund, *Ajax* Tyler Mane, *Triopas* Julian Glover, *with* James Cosmo, Nigel Terry, Vincent Regan, Trevor Eve, Siri Svegler, Ken Bones.
• *Dir* Wolfgang Petersen, *Pro* Petersen, Diana Rathbun and Colin Wilson, *Co-Pro* Winston Azzopardi, *Screenplay* David Benioff, inspired by *The Iliad* by Homer, *Ph* Roger Pratt, *Pro Des* Nigel Phelps, *Art Dir* Julian Ashby, Jon Billington, Andy Nicholson and Adam O'Neill, *Ed* Peter Honess, *M* James Horner, *Costumes* Bob Ringwood.

Radiant/Plan B-Warner.
163 mins. USA/UK/Malta. 2004.
Rel: 14th May 2004. Cert 15.

21 Grams ★★★

The Mexican director Alejandro González Iñárritu made an international impact with his award-winning *Amores Perros* three years ago. Hinged around a fatal car accident, it threaded the story of three disparate characters through an elliptical, time-jumping narrative. Iñárritu is a supremely cinematic talent and with his second film he builds on his early promise. While working in a foreign language (American), he has elicited extraordinarily naked performances from his stellar trio and with a stripped-down, documentary style he commands our attention. Hinged around a fatal car accident, *21 Grams* threads the story of three disparate characters through an elliptical, time-jumping narrative. However, the film demands enormous patience from the viewer, as there are few hints where, exactly, the story is in its temporal compass. Because of this, it is hard to connect emotionally with the characters and

the film becomes the equivalent of a rather accomplished freak show. Sean Penn is dying and vomits a lot. Naomi Watts drinks too much, takes coke and lets snot hang out of her nose. Benicio Del Toro sprouts the word of the Lord and looks a phenomenal mess. Around this, provocative ideas sprout like herbal weeds. A film largely about dying, the title refers to the fact at the moment of death we lose 21 grams in weight. Heavy. JC-W

• *Paul Rivers* Sean Penn, *Jack Jordan* Benicio Del Toro, *Cristina Peck* Naomi Watts, *Mary Rivers* Charlotte Gainsbourg, *Marianne Jordan* Melissa Leo, *Claudia Williams* Clea DuVall, *Michael* Danny Huston, *Brown* Paul Calderon, *with* Annie Corley, John Rubinstein, Eddie Marsan.
• *Dir* Alejandro González Iñárritu, *Pro* Alejandro González Iñárritu and Robert Salerno, *Ex Pro* Ted Hope, *Screenplay* Guillermo Arriaga, *Ph* Rodrigo Prieto, *Pro Des* Brigitte Broch, *Ed* Stephen Mirrione, *M* Gustavo Santaolalla, *Costumes* Marlene Stewart.

Focus Features/This is That/Y Prods/Mediana Prods-Icon. 124 mins. USA/Germany. 2003. Rel: 5 March 2004. Cert 15.

The Twilight Samurai ★★★★

Famous in Japan for his commercially orientated movies, the veteran director Yoji Yamada is on firm ground here with this traditional samurai tale. Its hero (Hiroyuki Sanada, an actor with presence)

is a low ranking samurai dismissively given the nickname which supplies the film's title. His adventures, some willed and some forced upon him, provide the action highlights (the climactic confrontation is particularly well done), and there's a further plot-line involving the girl he loves while feeling that his status makes him unworthy of her. The use of a female narrator and the stress on the hero's home-life are welcome and unexpected features. This may be a bit overlong and cannot equal the best of Kurosawa, but it honours cinema's classic approach to samurai tales in a way that this year's *Zatoichi* does not. MS

• *Seibei Iguchi* Hiroyuki Sanada, *Tomoe Iinuma* Rie Miyazawa, *Toyotaro Koda* Ren Ôsugi, *Chobei Kutsaka* Nenji Kobayashi, *Michinojo Iinuma* Mitsuru Fukikoshi, *Naota* Hiroshi Kanbe, *Zenemon Yogo* Min Tanaka, *Ito Iguchi* Erina Hashiguchi, *Kayana Iguchi* Miki Ito.
• *Dir* Yoji Yamada, *Pro* Shigehiro Nakagawa, Hiroshi Fukasawa and Ichiro Yamamoto, *Screenplay* Yamada and Yoshitaka Asama, based on three novels (*Twilight Seibei, Sukehachi the Beggar, Record of a Bamboo Sword*) by Shuhei Fujisawa, *Ph* Mutsuo Naganuma, *Pro Des* Mitsuo Degawa, *Ed* Iwao Ishii, *M* Isao Tomita, *Costumes* Kazuko Kurosawa, *Choreography* Hiroshi Kuze.

Nippon TV Network/Sumitomo Corp./ Hakuhodo Inc-Tartan Films. 129 mins. Japan. 2002. Rel: 15 April 2004. Cert 12A

Above: The weight of life: Melissa Leo in Alejandro González Iñárritu's provocative, naked *21 Grams* (from Icon)

Under the Tuscan Sun ★★

A woman whose marriage has broken down due to her husband's infidelity travels from San Francisco to Tuscany to build a new life. Through the casting of the talented Diane Lane in this role the film achieves emotional conviction at the outset and thus leads us to expect something better than the tosh that follows. It may look nice (and Christophe Beck's music score is above average for this kind of movie) but this becomes a romantic comedy that deals exclusively in clichés. These include a youthful romance as a sub-plot, a silly character role for Lindsay Duncan and a young Italian admirer for our leading character. Can he be trusted? Maybe not. Will the film have a happy ending? You bet. Since Lane's presence promises more, you end up totally dissatisfied with this load of rubbish. MS

• *Frances Mayes* Diane Lane, *Patti* Sandra Oh, *Katherine* Lindsay Duncan, *Marcello* Raoul Bova, *Signor Martini* Vincenzo Riotta, *Chiara* Guilia Steigerwalt, *Pawel* Pawel Szajda, *with* Mario Monicelli, David Sutcliffe, Kate Walsh, Don McManus, Matt Salinger, Elden Henson, Jack Kehler, Jeffrey Jones.
• *Dir* and *Screenplay* Audrey Wells, based on the book by Frances Mayes, *Pro* Wells and Tom Sternberg, *Ex Pro* Laura Fattori, Sandy Kroopf and Mark Gill, *Ph* Geoffrey Simpson, *Pro Des* Stephen McCabe, *Ed* Andrew Marcus and Arthur Coburn, *M* Christophe Beck, *Costumes* Nicolette Ercole.

Touchstone Pictures/Timnick Films/Blue Gardenia-Buena Vista International.
112 mins. USA. 2003. Rel: 26 March 2004. Cert 12A.

Underworld ★★

In the far-flung future, the centuries-old war between werewolves (Lycans) and vampires has spilled into the open and mere mortal Michael has fallen into the line of fire. Yes, in this future, the supernaturals rely as much on firearms and natty gadgetry as on fangs and claws. Sleek vampire assassin Selene becomes curious about the Lycans' interest in Michael and takes him under her, er, wing, and embroils him into the convoluted aristocratic feud between the two species ... The film quite shameless mines the growing genre fanbase for this kind of post-*Buffy* dreck, not least by stuffing the delicious Kate Beckinsale in the tightest leathers imaginable. It never escapes from the scent of ridicule, which grows deeply odorous the more seriously it takes itself. Still, it is a fanciable aesthetic with some neat stunt-work. One can only hope the sequel (on its way in 2005) makes good on the hope of a decent franchise. AK

• *Selene* Kate Beckinsale, *Michael Corvin* Scott Speedman, *Viktor* Bill Nighy, *Lucian* Michael Sheen, *Kraven* Shane Brolly, *Singe* Erwin Leder, *Kahn* Robbie Gee, *Erika* Sophia Myles, *Dr Adam* Wentworth Miller, *Raze* Kevin Grevioux.
• *Dir* Len Wiseman, *Pro* Tom Rosenberg, Gary Lucchesi and Richard Wright, *Ex Pro* Skip Williamson, Henry Winterstein, Terry A. McKay, James McQuaide and Robert Bernacchi, *Screenplay* Danny McBride, *story* Kevin Grevioux, Len Wiseman and Danny McBride, *Ph* Tony Pierce-Roberts, *Pro Des* Bruton Jones, *Ed* Martin Hunter, *M* Paul Haslinger; songs performed by Renholder, David Bowie, A Perfect Circle, The Damning Well, and Puscifer, *Costumes* Wendy Partridge.

Lakeshore Entertainment/Screen Gems/Subterranean Prods/Underworld Produktions-Entertainment.
121 mins. UK/Germany/Hungary/USA. Rel 19 September 2003. Cert 15.

Unknown Pleasures ★★★¹/₂

This Chinese movie shot in Shanxi Province looks magnificent –a considerable feat since it was filmed on digital video. Filmmaker Jia Zhang-Ke, who uses sound intelligently and has a real feel for creating a sense of space around his characters, again concentrates in this film on the lives of young people. Two friends and the girl who attracts both of them are central here and lack of faith in the future is emphasised. For much of the time Jia's rather distanced style is balanced by tension, but this and the film's momentum vanish in the last half hour (the most menacing character disappears from the tale and an incompetent bank robber just seems too silly). Uneven but interesting and always distinctive. MS

• *Qiao Qiao* Zhao Tao, *Bin Bin* Zhao Wei Wei, *Xiao Ji* Wu Qiong, *Yuan Yuan* Zhou Qing Feng, *Xiao Wu* Wang Hong Wei, *Bin Bin's mother* Bai Ru, *Xiao Ji's father* Liu Xi An.
• *Dir* and *Screenplay* Jia Zhang Ke, *Pro* Shozo Ichiyama and Li Kit Ming, *Ph* Yu Lik Wai, *Pro Des* Liang Jiang Dong, *Ed* Chow Keung.

E-Pictures/Hu Tong Communications/Lumen Films/Office Kitano/T-Mark-Artificial Eye.
113 mins. South Korea/France/Japan/China. 2002. Rel: 11 July 2003. Cert 12A.

Uptown Girls ★¹/₂

For Uptown think Upper West Side Manhattan, the reserve of the materially advantaged, fashion-obsessed and cultured elite. It is here that you will find Molly Gunn, a sweet kid who has been protected from the real world by the wallet of her father, a legendary rock star and guitarist. However, her father has joined Jimi Hendrix, George Harrison and Mickey Finn in the great pop arena of the sky and the family lawyer has run off with all her savings. Forced to earn a living, Molly is faced with the task of nannying for an eight-year-old rich kid who is every bit as spoilt as herself. The difference is that little Ray (the priceless Dakota Fanning, from *I Am Sam* and *Trapped*) lost her childhood when her father succumbed to a coma, whereas Molly retreated into her inner child when her dad died. And so we have a high-concept comedy in which two spoilt rich kids must come to terms with life – and each other – through their differences. If that sounds mechanical and manipulative you haven't heard the half of it. Packed with broad stereotypes, cereal packet homilies and a soundtrack that jostles for centre stage, *Uptown Girls* is the sort of movie that gives Hollywood a bad name. JC-W

• *Molly Gunn* Brittany Murphy, *Ray Schleine* Dakota Fanning, *Ingrid* Marley Shelton, *Huey* Donald Faison, *Neal Fox* Jesse Spencer, *Mr McConkey* Austin Pendleton, *Roma Schleine* Heather Locklear, *himself* Fisher Stevens, *with* Reed Birney, Polly Adams, Carmen Electra, Duncan Sheik, Edward Hibbert.
• *Dir* Boaz Yakin, *Pro* John Penotti, Fisher Stevens and Allison Jacobs, *Ex Pro* Yakin, Joe Caracciolo Jr. and Tim Williams, *Co-Ex Pro* Gary Winick and Vicki Cherkas, *Screenplay* Julia Dahl, Mo Ogrodnik and Lisa Davidowitz, based on a story by Allison Jacobs, *Ph* Michael Ballhaus, *Pro Des* Kalina Ivanov, *Ed* David Ray, *M* Joel McNeely, *Costumes* Sarah Edwards.

MGM/GreeneStreet Films-Fox.
92 mins. USA. 2003. Rel: 5 March 2004. Cert 12A.

Uzak ★★★¹/₂

(*Distant*)
Every inch an art-house movie, this multiple prize-winner from Turkey offers atmospheric photography from the director himself. The use of sound is equally skilled, but in making a film about boredom and isolation in contemporary life Nuri Bilge Ceylan asks a lot of his audience without always providing sufficient rewards. It's the story of a country cousin arriving in Istanbul desperate for work and of the older relative, a photographer, who despite his own loneliness fails to take this opportunity to connect. Not without humour yet very slow moving and with limited background detail to involve us with the characters, it's closer to Angelopoulos than to the neo-realism of De Sica and bleaker than Ozu. Well acted and more dramatically effective in its second half, it's certainly of interest for serious film-goers, but something of an endurance test too. MS

• *Mahmut* Muzaffer Ozdemir, *Yusuf* Mehmet Emin Toprak, *Nazan* Zuhal Gencer Erkaya, *lover* Nazan Kirilmis, *janitor* Feridun Doc, *mother* Fatma Ceylan, *young girl* Ebru Ceylan.
• *Dir, Pro, Screenplay* and *Ph* Nuri Bilge Ceylan, *Line Pro* Feridun Koc, *Pro Des* Ebru Ceylan, *Ed* Ayhan Ergursel and N.B. Ceylan, *M* Mozart.

NBC Film/Hubert Bals Fund-Artificial Eye.
110 mins. Turkey/The Netherlands. 2003.
Rel: 28 May 2004. Cert 15.

Valentíin ★★★★¹/₂

1960-ish, Buenos Aires, Argentina. Valentin is an excruciatingly cute, precociously smart nine year-old boy who lives with his mad grandmother in the shabbier part of town. He dreams of becoming Argentina's first astronaut, and of a happy family life. Abandoned by his mother at age three, he is practically an orphan as his absent father lives like a bachelor playboy. Valentin's frustrations come to a head when his grandmother falls ill. Valentin realises he can only rely on himself if his dreams are to come true … Set against an age of revolutions flagged by space launches, portable tape recorders and a dramatic eulogy for Che Guevera, Alejandro Agresti has constructed a deeply moving portrayal of an unusual child's heroic attempt at piecing together a model for happiness from the sad wreckage of his dysfunctional family. Rodrigo Noya is simply edible as Valentin, who narrates the story and appears in almost every scene, while Alejandro Agresti, playing Valentin's father, joins his excellent supporting cast who each contribute to the enormous cache of authentic character that brings this reportedly autobiographical film to life. AK

• *grandmother* Carmen Maura, *Valentín* Rodrigo Noya, *Leticia* Julieta Cardinale, *Uncle Chiche* Jean Pierre Noher, *Rufo* Mex Urtizberea, *Father* Alejandro Agresti, *Dr Galaburri* Carlos Roffe, *Priest* Fabian Vena
• *Dir* and *Screenplay* Alejandro Agresti, *Pro* Laurens Geels and Thierry Forte, *Ph* Jose Luis Cajaraville, *Pro Des* Floris Vos, *Ed* Alejandro Brodersohn, *M* Paul M. van Bruggen, *Costumes* Marisa Urruti, *Sound* Fernando Soldevilla.

First Floor Features-Metrodome.
82 mins. Netherlands/Argentina/France/Spain/Italy. 2002.
Rel: 27 February 2004. Cert PG.

Van Helsing ★★¹/₂

Imagine the biggest B-movie monster bunfight ever, lavishly computered via stae of the art CGI animation, and featuring the kind of squint-eyed over-plotting that gets so involved with its narrative

one-upmanship as to totally confuse all but the most committed genre fanatics. Stephen *The Mummy* Sommers has made a movie just like that. Hugh Jackman plays Gabriel Van Helsing, a supernatural bounty hunter ostensibly in the employment of the church, tasked to hunt all manner of nasties. The film builds up in frantic, jerky steps via *Dr. Jekyll & Mr Hyde* and Frankenstein's Monster to an encounter with Dracula and his brides. Along the way, he picks up a medieval incarnation of James Bond's 'Q' and the last surviving member of an ancient family dedicated to battling vampires, played by Kate Beckinsale in tourniquet leathers. It truly is mayhem, and Jackman projects an air of seriousness which unhelpfully counteracts the natural lean of the film towards the wry camp pun. In all, a fast-moving feast for the eyes but little else. AK

• *Gabriel Van Helsing* Hugh Jackman, *Anna Valerious* Kate Beckinsale, *Count Dracula* Richard Roxburgh, *Carl* David Wenham, *Frankenstein's Monster* Shuler Hensley, *Aleera* Elena Anaya, *Velkan Valerious* Will Kemp, *Igor* Kevin J. O'Connnor, *with* Alun Armstrong, Samuel West, Robbie Coltrane.
• *Dir* and *Screenplay* Stephen Sommers, *Pro* Sommers and Bob Ducsay, *Ex Pro* Sam Mercer, *Ph* Allen Daviau, *Pro Des* Allan Cameron, *Ed* Bob Ducsay and Kelly Matsumoto, *M* Alan Silvestri, *Costumes* Gabriella Pescucci.

Universal Pictures/Sommers Co-UIP.
132 mins. USA. 2004. Rel: 7th May 2004. Cert 12A.

Vendredi Soir ★

For me (but not for all) this was the worst film released in 2003. It deals with a one night stand that occurs in Paris between strangers caught up in an exceptional traffic jam caused by a transport strike. Before they meet we've already had over a quarter of an hour in the jam (no more interesting than the reality would be) and of the woman (Lemercier) we know only that she is just about to move in with her boy friend. Of the man (Lindon) we learn nothing. One stylised sequence is cleverly shot to fit music by Shostakovich, but who cares? Claire Denis as director hides the fact that this was originally a novel, but neither The Woman nor The Man (they have names but just as well might not have) arouses the slightest interest in this viewer. MS

• *Laure* Valérie Lemercier, *Jean* Vincent Lindon, *Marie* Hélène de Saint Père, *woman in the pizzeria* Hélène Fillieres, *girl playing pinball* Florence Loiret Caille.
• *Dir* Claire Denis, *Pro* Bruno Pesery, *Screenplay* Denis and Emmanuèlle Berheim, *Ph* Agnès Godard, *Pro Des* Katia Wyszkop, *Ed* Nelly Quettier, *M* Dickon Hinchliffe.

Right: Paper chase: The consummate Cate Blanchett as *Veronica Guerin* (from BVI)

Arena Films/Canal Plus/Centre National de la Cinématographie/France 2 Cinéma/France Télévision Images-Tartan Films.
86 mins. France. 2002. Rel: 22 August 2003. Cert 15.

Veronica Guerin ★★★★

Sadly undervalued by many British critics, this latest telling of the story of Dublin journalist Veronica Guerin whose exposés of drug dealers cost her her life is a powerful work. Admittedly the grandiose coda is a mistake, but for the most part this is exciting and never exploitative. In the title role the splendid Cate Blanchett gives what may well be her best performance ever. This is a mainstream movie tackling a more serious subject than usual rather than an art house picture but, judged on its own terms, it works very well. Director Schumacher provides a model of how to make the most of a location without holding up the pace. MS

• *Veronica Guerin* Cate Blanchett, *John Gilligan* Gerard McSorley, *John 'The Coach' Traynor* Ciaran Hinds, *Bernadette Guerin* Brenda Fricker, *Graham Turley* Barry Barnes, *Holland* Joe Hanley, *Bowden* David Murray, *Peter 'Fatso' Mitchell* David Herlihy, *Gerry 'The Monk' Hutch* Alan Devine, *Martin 'The General' Cahill* Gerry O'Brien, *Chris Mulligan* Don Wycherley, *Cathal Guerin* Simon O'Driscoll, *Brian Meahan* Paudge Beehan, *Spanky McSpank* Colin Farrell, *with* Karl Shiels, Barry McEvoy.
• *Dir* Joel Schumacher, *Pro* Bruckheimer, *Ex Pro* Chad Oman, Mike Stenson and Ned Dowd, *Screenplay* Carol Doyle and Mary Agnes Donoghue, *Ph* Brendan Galvin, *Pro Des* Nathan Crowley, *Ed* David Gamble, *M* Harry Gregson-Williams, *Costumes* Joan Bergin.

Touchstone Pictures/Jerry Bruckheimer Films-Buena Vista International.
98 mins. USA/Ireland/UK. 2003.

Waiting for Happiness ★★★★

(*Heremakono En attendant le bonheur*)
Coming from Mauritania, this film by Abderrahmane Sissako has the appeal of novelty, but even more importantly it is a work revealing a highly individual poetic sensibility. Be it through composition, colour tones or texture, the images as photographed by Jacques Besse are memorable, but neither the beauty nor the strangeness of occasional semi-surreal touches interfere with the film's sense of reality. The players are non-professionals and the film explores life in a small coastal village where some people live but rather more, especially if young, are passing through to find education and opportunities abroad. More details about the situation of some of these individuals would help since, distractingly, we are sometimes left asking questions. But if this weakness means that the film is less than a masterpiece, it is certainly striking and in its blend of the poetic and the documentary it finds a voice of its own. MS

• *Khatra* Khatra Ould Abder Kader, *Maata* Maata Ould Mohamed Abeid, *Adballah* Mohamed Mahmoud Ould Mohamed, *Nana* Nana Diakité *Soukeyna, the mother* Fatimetou Mint Ahmeda, *Makan* Makanfing Dabo, *Tchu* Santha Leng.
• *Dir* and *Screenplay* Abderrahmane Sissako, *Pro* Nicolas Royer and Maji-da Abdi, *Ex Pro* Guillaume de Seille, *Ph* Jacques Besse, *Art Dir* Laurent Cavero and Joseph Kpobly, *Ed* Nadia Ben Rachid, *M* Oumou Sangare.

ARTE France/Duo Films-Artificial Eye
95 mins. France/Switzerland/Netherlands/Czech Republic. 2002. Rel: 24 October 2003. Cert U.

Welcome to the Jungle ★★¹/₂

(US title: *The Rundown*)
The Rock plays the bounty hunter Beck, who is the kind of morally bound he-man that will give his mark the chance to surrender with fair warning before he proceeds to kung-fu his sorry ass six ways to Sunday. His plan to quit is headed off by an offer by his 'fixer' to clear his debts in exchange for one final 'rundown', to collect a wayward son with Indiana-Jones-fever from the jungles of South America … Dwayne Douglas Johnson aka pro-wrestling's favourite son 'The Rock' has demonstrated an impressive ability to fill the screen with real movie star presence. Following his Conan-style adventures in *The Scorpion King* with this, a totally formulaic action-film that is exactly the kind of film Schwarzeneggar would have made in the late early 90s. Fantastic fight choreography, some halfway amusing one-liners, and Christopher Walken doing his usual creepy baddie job on autopilot make for a film that is at least as good an example of the genre as you would expect, but no more. AK

• *Beck* The Rock, *Travis Walker* Seann William Scott, *Mariana* Rosario Dawson, *Hatcher* Christopher Walken, *Declan* Ewen Bremner, *Harvey* Jon Gries, *Walker* William Lucking, *Manito* Ernie Reyes Jr., *Swenson* Stuart Wilson, *with* Dennis Keiffer, Garrett Warren, Stephen Bishop, Arnold Schwarzenegger (uncredited).
• *Dir* Peter Berg, *Pro* Kevin Misher, Marc Abraham and Karen Glasser, *Ex Pro* Vince McMahon and Ric Kidney, *Screenplay* R.J. Stewart and James Vanderbilt, *Ph* Tobias Schliessler, *Pro Des* Tom Duffield, *Ed* Richard Pearson, *M* Harry Gregson-Williams, *Costumes* Louise Mingenbach.

Universal/Columbia/WWE Films/Misher Films/Strike Entertainment-Columbia TriStar.
104 mins. USA. 2003. Rel: 24 March 2004. Cert 12.

Whale Rider ★★★★★

Creating an aura of haunting beauty, screenwriter/director Niki Caro weaves a spell as poignant and as powerful as the Maori legend she brings to modern life. This is the story of 11-year-old Paikea 'Pai' Apirana who, although a girl, is the spiritual heir to her Ngati Porou tribe. However, her grandfather Koro, the local custodian of his people's centuries-old culture, cannot see the truth that dances magically in front of him. Indeed, he bequeaths his leadership to the son of another… Filmed quite naturally in and around the seaside village of Whangara, *Whale Rider* captures the very essence of the omnipresent clash between traditional values and the modern world without ever using a heavy hand. Keisha Castle-Hughes as Pai is mesmerizing, nothing less than perfect. And Rawiri Paratene as Koro seems to personify the film's entire conflict in his weathered face. It is simply the best film I have seen all year. SWM

• *Pai Kea* Keisha Castle-Hughes, *Koro* Rawiri Paratene, *Nanny Flowers* Vicky Haughton, *Porourangi* Cliff Curtis, *Uncle Rawiri* Grant Noa, *Hemi* Mana Taumaunu.
• *Dir* and *Screenplay* Niki Caro, based on the novel by Witi Ihimaera, *Pro* Tim Sanders, John Barnett and Frank Hubner, *Ex Pro* Bill Gavin and Linda Goldstein Knowlton, *Co-Pro* Reinhard Brundig, *Ph* Leon Narbey, *Pro Des* Grant Major, *Ed* David Coulson *M* Lisa Gerrard, *Costume* Kristy Cameron.

New Zealand Film Commission/New Zealand Film Production Fund/New Zealand On Air/South Pacific Pictures/ApolloMedia/Pandora Film-Icon.
102 mins. New Zealand/Germany. 2002. Rel: 11 July 2003. Cert PG.

What a Girl Wants ★★

Singly parented Daphne Reynolds decides to track down her long lost father, who romantically flung a little more than he realised 17 years ago when he ended a shortlived marriage to her mother in Morocco. When she discovers that her missing dad is the ludicrously posh Lord Henry Dashwood, on the verge of complete social calcification in the form of a Parliamentary career and a socialite marriage, she does what any normal Bohemian-raised teenage girl in her position must, that is to turn his world upside down … Formulaic down to its trans-Atlantic roots, the film plays to every single fantasy wish you can imagine, feeding the Cinderella dreams of teenage girls with shameless gluttony. One to avoid by anyone without a multiple subscriptions to magazines dedicated to shirtless cover shots of Colin Farrell and Orlando Bloom. AK

• *Daphne Reynolds* Amanda Bynes, *Henry Dashwood* Colin Firth, *Libby Reynolds* Kelly Preston, *Jocelyn Dashwood* Eileen Atkins, *Glynnis Payne* Anna Chancellor, *Alistair Payne* Jonathan Pryce, *with* Sylvia Syms, Oliver James, Christina Cole.
• *Dir* Dennie Gordon, *Pro* Denise Di Novi, Bill Gerber and Hunt Lowry, *Ex Pro* E.K. Gaylord II, Alison Greenspan and Casey La Scala, *Screenplay* Jenny Bicks and Elizabeth Chandler; based on the play and screenplay *The Reluctant Debutante* by William Douglas Home, *Ph* Andrew Dunn, *Pro Des* Michael Carlin, *Art Dir* Karen Wakefield, *Ed* Charles McClelland, *M* Rupert Gregson-Williams; songs performed by Leslie Mills, Meredith Brooks, The Clash, Oliver James, Holly Valance, Craig David, etc, *Costumes* Shay Cunliffe.

Warner/Gaylord Films/Di Novi Pictures/Gerber Pictures-Warner.
105 mins. USA. 2003. Rel 8 August 2003. Cert PG.

White Oleander ★★¹/₂

Set in sunny Los Angeles, *White Oleander* follows the troubled adolescence of 14-year-old Astrid Magnussen, whose artist mother Ingrid receives a life sentence for murdering her unfaithful lover, Barry. Forced to endure a series of orphanages and foster homes, Astrid learns about life the hard way. Her foster mothers include Starr, an ex-stripper turned religious fanatic, Claire, a depressed actress, and Rena, a hippie street trader, all of whom have problems of their own. Meanwhile, Astrid's mother remains a malevolent influence. Well acted, by and large, *White Oleander* moves at a brisk pace, with much use of hand-held camera. The script is less convincing, lacking depth and character development. The original novel's indictment of the foster care system is also toned down, while the film builds to the obligatory upbeat ending. DO

• *Ingrid Magnussen* Michelle Pfeiffer, *Claire Richards* Renée Zellweger, *Starr* Robin Wright Penn, *Astrid Magnussen* Alison Lohman, *Barry Kolker* Billy Connolly, *Paul Trout* Patrick Fugit, *Ray* Cole Hauser, *Mark Richards* Noah Wyle, *Rena* Svetlana Efremova, *with* Amy Aquino, John Billingsley, Taryn Manning, Kali Rocha, Stephen Root, Liz Stauber, Biff Yeager.
• *Dir* Peter Kosminsky, *Pro* John Wells and Hunt Lowry, *Ex Pro* Kristin Harms, Stacy Cohen, E.K. Gaylord II and Patrick Markey, *Screenplay* Mary Agnes Donoghue, based on the novel by Janet Fitch, *Ph* Elliot Davis, *Pro Des* Donald Graham Burt, *Ed* Chris Ridsdale, *M* Thomas Newman, *Costumes* Susie De Santo.

Warner/Pandora-Red Bus.
109 mins. USA. 2002. Rel: 19 September 2003. Cert. 12A.

The Whole Ten Yards ★¹/₂

Bruce Willis and Matthew Perry are reunited for this redundant sequel to *The Whole Nine Yards*, a less than earth-shattering comedy. Retired hitman Jimmy the Tulip is called back into action when Hungarian gangsters kidnap his friend's wife. Albeit fast moving and competently acted, *The Whole Ten Yards* still feels like a pointless rehash. The main jokes involve impotence and foul-mouthed girl scouts. Big deal. The more tasteless elements, such as Jimmy's kill-crazy wife, are sunk by the general lack of flair. *Friends* star Matthew Perry has yet to prove himself on the big screen. Bruce Willis is capable of much better. DO

• *Jimmy `The Tulip' Tudeski* Bruce Willis, *Oz Oseransky* Matthew Perry, *Jill* Amanda Peet, *Cynthia* Natasha Henstridge, *Lazlo* Kevin Pollak, *Strabo* Frank Collison, *Zevo* Johnny Messner.
• *Dir* Howard Deutch, *Pro* Elie Samaha, Arnold Rifkin, David Willis and Allan Kaufman, *Ex Pro* Andrew Stevens, Tracee Stanley, David Bergstein and Oliver Hengst, *Screenplay* George Gallo, based on characters created by Mitchell Kapner, *Ph* Neil Roach, *Pro Des* Virginia Randolph-Weaver, *Ed* Seth Flaum, *M* John Debney, *Costumes* Rudy Dillon.

Franchise Pictures/Cheyenne Enterprises/
Zweite Academy Film-Warner.
99 mins. USA. 2004. Rel: 18 June 2004. Cert PG.

Wilbur (Wants To Kill Himself) ★★

Denmark's Lone Scherfig comes unstuck with this tragi-comedy set in Glasgow, She has a fine cast and is not thrown by making her first feature in English, but her endeavour to push to extremes the elements of comedy and drama so admirably blended in

2001's *Italian for Beginners* just doesn't work. It's a tale of two brothers attracted to the same girl, Alice, a single mother (Shirley Henderson). The film has potential for black comedy through the brother (Jamie Sives) fixated on suicide but far from adept at it. Equally there's tragedy in the fate of the other brother (Adrian Rawlins) dying of cancer. But to succeed tragi-comedy requires sufficient reality for disbelief to be suspended. That's not achieved here, be it Alice entering the dying man's bed in hospital or the bookshop gag about a customer wanting a book by Kipling and being persuaded to take instead one about pickling!
MS

• *Wilbur* Jamie Sives, *Harbour* Adrian Rawlins, *Alice* Shirley Henderson, *Mary* Lisa McKinlay, *Dr Horst* Mads Mikkelsen, *Moira* Julia Davis, *Sophie* Susan Vidler.
• *Dir* Lone Scherfig, *Pro* Sisse Graum Olsen, *Ex Pro* Peter Aalbeck Jensen, *Co-Pro* Gillian Berrie, *Scr* Lone Scherfig and Anders Thomas Jensen, *Ph* Jorgen Johansson, *Screenplay* Scherfig and Anders Thomas Jensen, *Pro Des* Jette Lehmann, *Ed* Gerd Tjur, *M* Joachim Holbek.

Zentropa Entertainment 6/Scottish Screen/Sigma Films/TV2/Danmark)/Glasgow Film Office, etc-Icon. 109 mins. Denmark/UK/Norway/France. 2003. Rel: 5 December 2003. Cert 15.

Win a Date With Ted Hamilton!
★★★¹/₂

Supermarket checkout girl Rosalee Futch has had a humungous crush on hunky movie idol Tad Hamilton for as long as she can remember. When she wins a date to spend the evening with him in Los Angeles, she cannot believe her luck. Surprised that his blind date is actually young and pretty, serial bachelor Tad Hamilton invites her back to his house. To his disbelief, she refuses to stay and he drives her back to her hotel. Nobody has ever spurned his advances before and Tad Hamilton can't get Rosalee Futch out of his mind… Now, let's get one thing straight. *Win a Date With Tad Hamilton!* is not art. It's a predictable, by-the-numbers teen romance positioned squarely at the popcorn populace. But then there are bad teen romances and good ones, and this certainly falls into the latter category. From the director of the original *Legally Blonde*, *Tad Hamilton* sets up its 'high concept' nicely and then pushes all the right buttons with considerable dexterity. This is a cute set-up and the film makes the most of its winning formula. In its favour, there is a star-making turn from Topher Grace as Rosalee's cynical, silent admirer and a screenplay that refuses to plump for the obvious. JC-W

• *Rosalee Futch* Kate Bosworth, *Pete Monash* Topher Grace, *Tad Hamilton* Josh Duhamel, *Richard Levy the Driven* Nathan Lane, *Richard Levy the Shameless* Sean Hayes, *Henry Futch* Gary Cole, *Cathy Feely* Ginnifer Goodwin, *Angelica* Kathryn Hahn, *with* Octavia Spencer, Amy Smart, Stephen Tobolowsky, Jay Underwood, Patrick O'Brien.
• *Dir* Robert Luketic, *Pro* Douglas Wick and Lucy Fisher, *Ex Pro* William S. Beasley and Gail Lyon, *Screenplay* Victor Levin, *Ph* Peter Collister, *Pro Des* Missy Stewart, *Ed* Scott Hill, *M* Edward Shearmur, *Costumes* Catherine Adair.

Lucy Fisher/Douglas Wick /UIP. 96 mins. USA. 2004.Rel: 23 April 2004. Cert PG.

Winged Migration ★★★★
The French star Jacques Perrin has in recent years turned his attention to producing nature films, the amazing *Microcosmos* being the best known. Now he is director too for this world-wide study of birds and their migratory patterns. As before, the aim is to create something of a film poem rather than a work of detailed information. The music by Bruno Coulais may not be to everyone's taste, but it helps to cement the diverse images which, despite the more limited subject-matter this time, make for a truly stunning impact. The new wonders of the latest camera equipment take us back to the age-old wonders of nature. An awesome experience.
MS

• *Narrator* Jacques Perrin.
• *Dir* Jacques Perrin, *Pro* Perrin and Christophe Barratier, *Screenplay* Perrin and Stéphane Durand, *Ph* Ollie Barbe, Michael Benjamin, Sylvie Carcedo-Dreujou, Laurent Charbonnier, Luc Drion, Laurent Fleutot, Philippe Garguil, Dominique Gentil, Bernard Lutic, Thierry Machado, Stéphane Martin, Fabrice Moindrot, Ernst Sasse, Michael Terrasse and Thierry Thomas, *Pro Des* Régis Nicolino, *Ed* Marie-Josèphe Yoyotte, *M* Bruno Coulais.

Bac Films/Centre National de la Cinématographie/ France 2 Cinéma/France 3 Cinéma /Canal Plus, etc-89 mins. France. 2003. Rel: 5 September 2003. Cert U.

Wonderland ★★★
1981, Los Angeles. The legendarily endowed porn star, John Holmes, is the central figure in a Rashomon-style split narrative surrounding bloody multiple murders at an apartment block in L.A., rumoured to be at the behest of nightclub supreme and sneering thug Eddie Nash … Siping deeply of the cup of late-70s nostalgia, James Cox flushes the

screen with the vintaged glare of the disco era in its afterlife. The cast is a sample group of medallion-wearing, free-loving, post-hippie bikers and groovers who are high on love, life and a lot of drugs. Val Kilmer plays the role of a dissipated celebrity very well (one wonders why) with Kate Bosworth providing the film's one symbol of hope and innocence. It adds up to a distractingly pungent and entertaining melange of images, chopped and cut to the rhythms of an MTV music video. However, the weight of its 'based on the true story' claims burden the film with a duty to objectivity it should not have. After being told the various versions of truth from the perspective of various key players, it aims to give its own final version in a move that cheapens the whole enterprise with the pretension of truth.
AK

• *John C. Holmes* Val Kilmer, *Dawn Schiller* Kate Bosworth, *Sharon Holmes* Lisa Kudrow, *Ron Launius* Josh Lucas, *Billy Deverell* Tim Blake Nelson, *David Lind* Dylan McDermott, *Susan Launius* Christina Applegate, *Eddie Nash* Eric Bogosian, *Louis Cruz* Franky G, *Bill Ward* M.C. Gainey, *Sam Nico* Ted Levine, *Greg Diles* Faizon Love, *with* Carrie Fisher, Janeane Garofalo, Natasha Gregson Wagner, Michael Pitt, Chris Ellis, Paris Hilton.
• *Dir* James Cox, *Pro* Holly Wiersma and Michael Paseornek, *Ex Pro* Tom Ortenberg, Peter Block, Marc Butan, Michael Burns, Julie Yorn, Peter Kleidman, Randall Emmett and George Furla, *Screenplay* James Cox, Captain Mauzner, Todd Samovitz and D. Loriston Scott, *Ph* Michael Grady, *Pro Des* Franco-Giacomo Carbone, *Ed* Jeff McEvoy, *M* Cliff Martinez; tracks perofrmed by Wes Cunningham, Bad Company, Roxy Music, Free, T. Rex, The Cars, Funkadelic, Ted Nugent, Three Dog Night, Terry Reid, Duran Duran, Iggy and The Stooges, Patti Smith, Bob Dylan, Billy Joel, Lou Reed, Joan Jett, Jonathan Davis, Robert Palmer, Gordon Lightfoot, Leon Russell and The Shelter People, and Dobie Grey, *Costumes* Maryam Malakour, *Technical Advis* Bob Chinn.

Lions Gate Films-Tartan Films.
104 mins. USA. 2003. Rel: 7th May 2004.
Cert 18.

Wondrous Oblivion ★★★★

This immensely appealing film seems to echo *Bend It Like Beckham* but is less escapist and was in any case conceived before it. Paul Morrison's movie is set in 1960 (full marks for period detail) and features a Jewish family living in South London who find that their new neighbours are from Jamaica. Emily Woof is the Jewish mother and Delroy Lindo the Jamaican father, while Sam Smith and Leonie Elliott have key roles as the children of the respective families who

share a youthful enthusiasm for cricket. The film is not faultless and the feel-good ending is perhaps a pity. But there's humour and humanity here and a popular appeal which does not involve playing down the issue of racial tension until those last moments. The film is even brave enough to show how one set of outsiders, Jewish, may become compromised over the help and understanding they ought to show for another such group, Jamaicans.
MS

• *Dennis Samuels* Delroy Lindo, *Ruth Wiseman* Emily Woof, *Victor Wiseman* Stanley Townsend, *David Wiseman* Sam Smith, *Grace Samuels* Angela Wynter, *Judy Samuels* Leonie Elliott, *Dorothy Samuels* Naomi Simpson, *Mr Pugh* Jo Stone-Fewings, *Garry Sobers* Gary McDonald, *with* Leagh Conwell, Dominic Barklem, Yasmin Paige, Richard Ashton, Anni Domingo, Barry Davis, Jon Rumney, Frank Mills, Sophie Walker, Julia Ford, Bill Wallis.
• *Dir* and *Screenplay* Paul Morrison, *Pro* Jonny Persey, *Ex Pro* Michael Kuhn and Kevin Loader, *Co-Pro* David Kosse and Lesley Stewart, *Assoc Pro* Stewart Le Marechal, *Ph* Nina Kellgren, *Pro Des* Eve Stewart, *Ed* David Freeman, *M* Ilona Sekacz, Costumes Anushia Nieradzik.

N1/APT-Momentum Pictures.
105 mins. UK/Germany. 2003. Rel: 23 April 2004.
Cert PG.

XX/XY ★★★¹/₂

If the recent *Igby Goes Down* and *Roger Dodger* both owed rather too much to the superior work of Whit Stillman, Austin Chick's Manhattan movie has a voice of its own. Unusually for a film written and directed by a man, its view of sexual relationships tends to present issues from a female perspective. The more overt novelty is that, after introducing us to three students in its first third, it jumps forward some ten years to see how their lives have developed. A would-be filmmaker, Coles (Mark Ruffalo), has ended up in advertising, one of his youthful girl friends (Kathleen Robertson) has married and the other (Maya Stange), although engaged, now finds her old attraction for Coles re-ignited despite his having a live-in girl friend (Petra Wright). The acting, especially from the actresses is fine, but somehow we never care quite enough for the film to leave a lasting impression. MS

• *Coles Burroughs* Mark Ruffalo, *Thea* Kathleen Robertson, *Sam* Maya Stange, *Claire* Petra Wright, *Sid* Kel O'Neill, *Miles* David Thornton.
• *Dir* and *Screenplay* Austin Chick, *Pro* Mitchell B. Robbins, Isen Robbins and Aimee Schoof, *Ex Pro* Mitchell B. Robbins, *Ph* Uta Briesewitz, *Pro Des* Judy Becker, *Ed* William A. Anderson, *M* The Insects, *Costumes* Sarah Beers, *Sound* Bob Hein.

Robbins Entertainment/Intrinsic Value/Natural Nylon/7th Floor-Optimum Releasing.
91 mins. USA. 2001. Rel: 24 October 2003. Cert 15

You Got Served ★¹/₂

In a world of hip-hop dance-offs (think of *8 Mile*'s rap battles, now add leg warmers and breakdancing) in an underground club where the winner of audience acclaim walks away with cash, best pals Elgin and David are joint leaders of winningest crew around. But losing the challenge pot to a middle-class, Orange County crew leaves them broke, forcing them to run errands for a local mobster. When Elgin leaves David hanging on one such gig, the consequences cause the break-up of the Crew just as they are about to compete in the biggest tourney of their young lives … Watch this movie strictly for the dancing, which is seriously impressive and displays an acrobatic athleticism that makes Michael Jackson look like the 98-pound weakling he really is. On all other fronts, the film is a hilarious failure. AK

• *Elgin* Marques Houston, *David* Omari Grandberry, *Rico* Jarell Houston, *Vick* DeMario Thornton, *Rashaan* Dreux Frederic, *Liyah* Jennifer Freeman, *herself* Lil' Kim, *Emerald* Michael 'Bear' Taliferro, *Beautifull* Meagan Good, *Mr. Rad* Steve Harvey, *Wade* Christopher Jones, *herself* Alani 'La La' Vasquez, *Lil' Saint* Malcolm David Kelley, *Grandma* Esther Scott.
• *Dir* and *Screenplay* Christopher B. Stokes, *Pro* Marcus Morton, Cassius Vernon Weathersby and Billy Pollina, *Ex Pro* Ketrina 'Taz' Askew and Max Gousse, *Ph* David Hennings, *Pro Des* Maxine Shepard, *Ed* Earl Watson, *M* Tyler Bates, *Costumes* Ca-Trece Mas'sey, *Choreographers* Dave Scott and Shane Sparks.

Left: Lap of honour: Ewan McGregor and Emily Mortimer in David Mackenzie's atmospheric *Young Adam* (from Warner)

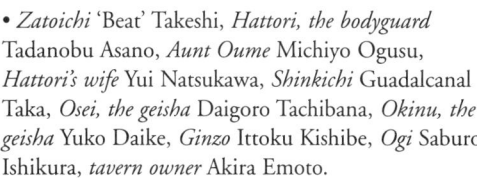

Screen Gems/The Ultimate Group Films/Melee
Entertainment-Columbia TriStar.
94 mins. USA. 2004. Rel: 25 June 2004. Cert PG.

Young Adam ★★★★

The cult novel by Scottish writer Alexander Trocchi
appeared in 1961 and now reaches the screen. Its
anti-hero is a selfish young man in pursuit of sex
(Ewan McGregor). He misleads an older woman
(Tilda Swinton) who is prepared to ditch her
husband for him and, amongst other relationships,
he has been involved with a girl (Emily Mortimer)
who subsequently drowned and for whose death he
was half responsible. As the drama unfolds we may
find the characters unappealing, but we wait to see
whether or not the central figure will attain concern
for others. The acting is splendid, the photography
by Giles Nuttgens in 'Scope and colour brilliant, the
music score by David Byrne admirable and the
setting (canals near Glasgow in the 1950s) superbly
atmospheric. In short, even if the material has
limitations, this second feature from David
Mackenzie reveals him to be a front rank filmmaker.
MS

• *Joe Taylor* Ewan McGregor, *Ella Gault* Tilda
Swinton, *Les Gault* Peter Mullan, *Cathie Dimly*
Emily Mortimer, *Jim Gault* Jack McElhone, *Gwen*
Therese Bradley, *Daniel Gordon* Ewan Stewart, *Bill*
Stuart McQuarrie, *Connie* Pauline Turner, *Bob*
M'bussi Alan Cooke, *Sam* Rory McCann, with
• *Dir* and *Screenplay* David Mackenzie, based on the
novel by Alexander Trocchi, *Pro* Jeremy Thomas,
Co-Pro Alexandra Stone, Nick O'Hagan and Jim
Reeve, *Assoc Pro* Peter Watson, Stephan Mallmann
and Gillian Berrie, *Ph* Giles Nuttgens, *Pro Des*
Laurence Dorman, *Ed* Colin Monie, *M* David
Byrne, *Costumes* Jacqueline Durran.

StudioCanal/Recorded Picture Co/HanWay Films/Film
Council/Scottish Screen/Sveno Media-Warner.
98 mins. UK/France. 2003. Rel: 26 September 2003.
Cert 18.

Zatoichi ★★★

Takeshi Kitano's latest is technically as accomplished
as anything he has done. Every frame is deftly
composed, the soundtrack superb and the editing
(by the director himself) spot on. But, while Kitano
claims that his first samurai movie is a tribute to
Kurosawa and the likes of *Seven Samurai*, the film
jettisons moral drama, social comment and concern
for characters in favour of something else entirely.
Featuring a brilliant blind swordsman (Takeshi in
the titular role) and involving courageous resistance
to exploitative villains as well as a revenge theme and
some comic relief for contrast, the tale could be told

traditionally. Instead, the film offers a postmodern take on it all, highly stylised to be
sure but featuring extreme blood-letting as
the centre of interest throughout. My rating
seeks to do the impossible – to reconcile the
quality of the work done and my repugnance
due to the film being nothing but a celebration
of violence. MS

• *Zatoichi* 'Beat' Takeshi, *Hattori, the bodyguard*
Tadanobu Asano, *Aunt Oume* Michiyo Ogusu,
Hattori's wife Yui Natsukawa, *Shinkichi* Guadalcanal
Taka, *Osei, the geisha* Daigoro Tachibana, *Okinu, the*
geisha Yuko Daike, *Ginzo* Ittoku Kishibe, *Ogi* Saburo
Ishikura, *tavern owner* Akira Emoto.
• *Dir* and *Screenplay* Takeshi Kitano, based on a
short story by Kan Shimozawa, *Pro* Masayuki Mori
and Tsunehisa Saito, *Ex Pro* Chieko Saito. *Co-Pro*
Masanori Sanada and Takio Yoshida, *Ph* Katsumi
Yanagijima, *Pro Des* Norihiro Isoda, *Ed* Kitano and
Yoshinori Ota, *M* Keiichi Suzuki, *Costume Supervisor*
Yohji Yamamoto, *Costumes* Kazuko Kurosawa,
Choreography The Stripes.

Bandai Visual/Tokyo FM/Dentsu/TV Asahi/Saito
Entertainment/Office Kitano-Artifical Eye.
115 mins. Japan. 2003. Rel: 19 March 2004. Cert 18.

Right:
Sword of justice: 'Beat'
Takeshi in Takeshi
Kitano's compelling
and delightfully
idiosyncratic *Zatoichi*
(from Artificial Eye)

Video and DVD Releases

A selection of films released direct to video/DVD in the UK between July 2002 and June 2003 by Daniel O'Brien

Alien Hunter

A lively science fiction thriller, starring James Spader as an expert on extraterrestrial phenomena. A NASA research team stationed at the South Pole are puzzled by a strange signal emanating from deep in the ice. Before anyone can say *The Thing*, it's clear they're dealing with an alien presence. Naturally, they call in troubleshooter Spader, known as 'The Alien Hunter'. One of the scientists is a former lover, adding a sexual *frisson* to the proceedings. With a nod to *Alien*, the signal turns out to be a warning, Spader realising that the earth is probably doomed. Derivative in the extreme, *Alien Hunter* is an enjoyable excursion into apocalyptic s-f fantasy. While Spader's role is hardly a stretch, he provides the film with a solid centre. *Note*: The black-and-white expedition footage is taken from John Carpenter's *The Thing*.
Directed by Ron Krauss.
Columbia TriStar. November 2003. Cert 15.

The Anniversary Party

Written and directed by Alan Cumming and Jennifer Jason Leigh, who also star, this showbiz drama is an intriguing curiosity. Shot over 19 days, on digital video, *The Anniversary Party* is literally a Hollywood home movie, filmed entirely at a Los Angeles residence. Cumming and Leigh also recruited their celebrity friends, including Kevin Kline and Gwyneth Paltrow, for supporting roles. The plot centres on married couple Joe (Cumming), a successful novelist, and Sally (Leigh), a struggling actress. After six years together, their relationship is on the rocks (again). When Joe makes a deal to adapt and direct

the film version of his latest book, he gives the lead to Sally's old rival, Skye (Paltrow). He also invites her to their anniversary party. Can Joe and Sally's marriage survive their contrasting fortunes and his crass insensitivity? Cumming and Leigh's direction is more assured than their script, which lacks structure and focus. At times, *The Anniversary Party* is reminiscent of both Robert Altman and Woody Allen on an off day. The film is carried mainly by the performances, especially the underused Parker Posey. While some may dismiss *The Anniversary Party* as a self-indulgent vanity project, the end result is well worth a look. Also starring: Jennifer Beals, Phoebe Cates (Mrs Kevin Kline) and most of the Kline children.
Entertainment In Video. June 2004. Cert 18.

Beethoven's 5th

The *Beethoven* franchise keeps on going, this time without Judge Reinhold, who starred in parts 3 and 4. With a nod to continuity, the story features one member of the Newton family, daughter Sarah (Daveigh Chase), who goes to stay with her Uncle Freddy. As always, the St Bernard dog is the star attraction. The thin storyline includes a ghost subplot, though the supernatural element is kept family-safe. Any resemblance to *Scooby Doo* is of course coincidental. If nothing else, the film gives gainful employment to veteran character actors Tom Poston, Katherine Helmond and Clint 'Brother of Ron' Howard, one-time child star of *Gentle Ben*. The supporting cast includes John Larroquette, who provided the opening narration for the original *Texas Chain Saw Massacre*.
Direcetd by Mark Griffiths.

Universal Pictures. May 2004. Cert U.

Belly of the Beast

Steven Seagal's career has been in steady decline since the glory days of the *Under Siege* movies and his kitsch masterpiece *On Deadly Ground*. This slick action movie marks a return to form, following a string of dud vehicles. Seagal found a decent director in the shape of Tony Ching Siu Tung, a Hong Kong action specialist. Ching has worked on a number of classic Hong Kong movies, notably *Dangerous Encounter – 1st Kind*, *Peking Opera Blues*, *A Chinese Ghost Story*, *The Killer*, *Swordsman II*, *Dragon Gate Inn*, *Heroic Trio* and *Shaolin Soccer*. While *Belly of the Beast* is hardly in the same league, the film at least delivers the goods. Seagal plays Jake Hopper, a former CIA agent who swings back into action when his daughter is kidnapped by terrorists. While the plot is just a retread of Schwarzenegger's *Commando* (1985), Ching Siu Tung keeps the action spectacular, his trademark wirework well in evidence. Seagal is obviously doubled for some shots – possibly a reflection of the star's advancing years?
Columbia TriStar. February 2004. Cert 15.

Bloody Streetz

A standard tale of vengeance and redemption, set against a backdrop of New York's gang warfare. Gano Grills stars as Black, an assassin-for-hire who questions his chosen profession after an innocent man is killed. Despite the nods to John Woo's 'heroic bloodshed' epics, and even *Macbeth*, *Bloody Streetz* is strictly to formula. Black's tragic past – his young son was murdered – doesn't make him an

interesting character.
Directed by Gerald Barclay.
MIA. May 2004. Cert 15.

City of Ghosts

Matt Dillon's debut as a writer-director flopped in US cinemas. Nevertheless, the film has many admirers. Dillon also stars, as New York criminal Jimmy, who flees the country with the law on his tail. Arriving in Cambodia, Jimmy hooks up with old partner Marvin (James Caan), who owes him serious money. Jimmy's hopes for an easy life are shattered when Marvin falls foul of the Russian mafia. Or so it seems… Favouring atmosphere over action, Dillon lets the pace drag at times. The end result, though often striking, is neither thriller nor character study. The high calibre supporting cast includes Gerard Depardieu, as an eccentric bartender, and Stellan Skarsgard. Unfortunately, leading lady Natasha McElhone is wasted as Dillon's implausible love interest. Highpoint: James Caan's Karaoke number, performed in fluent Cambodian.
MGM. January 2004.
Cert 15.

Crime Spree

Written and directed by Brad Mirman, this curious comedy-thriller is surprisingly successful. A band of incompetent French crooks, led by Gerard Depardieu, arrive in Chicago to carry out a jewel heist. Needless to say, things go wrong, the gang running foul of the Mob, the FBI and the local boyz 'n' the hood. While the tone is uneven, veering from farce to harsh violence, *Crime Spree* avoids the usual comedy-caper pitfalls, despite some weak plotting. Harvey Keitel gives an entertaining performance as Chicago's head *Mafioso*. Also starring: Richard Bohringer and French pop legend Johnny Hallyday.
DEJ Productions. April 2004.
Cert 15.

Derailed

Another year, another Jean-Claude Van Damme movie. Filmed in Bulgaria, this plodding Euro-thriller borrows heavily from *The Cassandra Crossing* and *Under Siege 2*, featuring a train, a deadly virus and the inevitable terrorists. Van Damme plays a government agent dealing with the virus, the bad guys and his own family, who sneak on board for a surprise party. Director Bob Misiorowski handles the action with little flair or even efficiency. The special effects are unusually poor, notably the terrible model shots of the speeding train. *Derailed* appears to have suffered post-production problems, with choppy editing and blatant continuity errors. Even die-hard Van Damme fans were not impressed by this effort.
Columbia TriStar. August 2003. Cert 15.

The Dominatrix

While 'erotic thrillers' rarely deliver on either count, this low budget drama is modestly effective. Jade (Grace Kosaka) is an upmarket dominatrix who relishes the power and control of her profession. By contrast, Grace's personal life is a mess; her best friend is terminally ill and her lesbian lover has tired of their empty relationship. When a routine bondage session turns nasty, Jade is forced to reconsider her way of life. Kosaka gives a strong performance and director Neil Coombs offers some atmospheric visuals.
MIA. February 2004. Cert 18.

Double Tap

An effective action movie, *Double Tap* stars the late, great Leslie Cheung, one of Hong Kong cinema's true superstars. Cheung plays Rick, a hired assassin who works for thrills, not money. Director Law Chi Leung stages some strong set-pieces, notably the climactic shoot-outs in a shopping mall and cinema. A fine example of the 'heroic bloodshed' genre.

MIA. February 2004. Cert 18.

Double Vision

Touted as Taiwan's answer to *Se7en*, this stylish thriller compares favourably with David Fincher's gothic-*noir* hit. Produced, directed and co-written by Chen Kuo Fu, *Double Vision* was backed by US major Columbia, allowing for a big budget, by local standards. Columbia's faith was justified, the film proving a smash hit in Taiwan and other Asian territories. *Double Vision* stars Hong Kong leading man Tony Leung Ka Fai, whose distinguished credits include *Dragon Gate Inn* (1992) and *Ashes of Time* (1994). His best known English-language film is *The Lover* (1992), a pretentious 'erotic' drama. With an eye to the international market, *Double Vision* co-stars David Morse, a fine US character actor seen in *Twelve Monkeys*, *The Long Kiss Goodnight* and *The Green Mile*. The premise is straightforward: a Taiwanese cop (Leung) teams up with an FBI agent (Morse) to investigate a series of bizarre murders. The culture and personality clashes are well handled, Leung's cop dealing with troubles of his own. Demonstrating a firm grasp of character and narrative, Chen Kuo Fu also makes good use of the wide-screen format. There are imaginative touches throughout and at least one major plot twist. The grisly murders are based on the five Taoist hells, the killer seeking immortality through the ritual 'sacrifices'.
Note: Contrary to some reports, this is the complete version of the film, rather than the edited US print, toned down for an 'R' rating.
Columbia TriStar. January 2004. Cert 18.

Dracula

This TV version of Bram Stoker's novel, updated to the present day, has its moments. Jonathan Harker is now an American investment banker, making a

killing on East European properties. He accepts a commission from the mysterious Vlad Teppes (Patrick Bergin), only to regret it. Reasonably faithful to Stoker's book, the film is more effective than Hammer's two modern-day Draculas, *Dracula AD 1972* (1972) and *The Satanic Rites of Dracula* (1973). On the downside, Patrick Bergin is not in the same league as Bela Lugosi, Christopher Lee, Frank Langella or even Gary Oldman. The supporting cast includes Italian actor Giancarlo Giannini, the ill-fated policeman in *Hannibal*. Filmed in Hungary.
Directed by Roger Young.
Anchor Bay UK. April 2004. Cert 12.

Empire

Victor (John Leguizamo) is a South Bronx drug dealer looking to go 'legit'. Introduced to Jack (Peter Sarsgaard), a Wall Street investment banker, he's offered a business deal that will solve all his problems. Or will it…? Written and directed by Franc Reyes, this indie drugs drama is disappointingly clichéd, with a predictable twist ending. Inevitably, Victor finds it hard to leave his old life – and old gang – behind, and Jack is hardly a trustworthy partner, his real motives unclear. Co-star Denise Richards marks time as the token love interest. Former Bond Girl Richards could do with another cult movie like *Starship Troopers*, *Wild Things* or *Drop Dead Gorgeous*. *Empire* isn't it.
Also starring: Isabella Rossellini, Sonia Braga.
Universal Pictures. October 2003. Cert 15.

Fear of the Dark

This derivative horror movie stars Kevin Zegers, who appeared in the spooky hits *Wrong Turn* and *Dawn of the Dead*. A nine-year-old boy suffers from *achluophobia*, literally fear of darkness. His parents and older brother don't realise that this fear is

well founded: evil really does lurk in the shadows. Needless to say, there's soon a power cut. Director K.C. Bascombe does little of interest with the material, inviting unfavourable comparisons with *The Sixth Sense*. The briefly-glimpsed monsters are quite impressive.
High Fliers. October 2003. Cert 15.

Femme Fatale

Brian De Palma's erotic thriller flopped in the US, hence the belated UK premiere on video/DVD. Arguably no worse than *Mission to Mars* (2000), *Femme Fatale* is probably only for De Palma completists, offering style but little sense. Ex-model Rebecca Romijn-Stamos stars as a former jewel thief who takes ruthless measures to hide her criminal past. Made with French money, the film attempts some European chic, the story kicking off at the Cannes Film Festival. Always an erratic, and derivative, craftsman, De Palma has made several fine films, notably the underrated *Blow Out* (1981). Having 'borrowed' freely from Alfred Hitchcock and Michelangelo Antonioni, he now seems reduced to copying himself. The kinky jack boots and coy lesbianism recall *Body Double* (1983), a *Vertigo* rip-off with tame soft-porn imagery. De Palma also has problems with Stamos, best known as Mystique, the shape-shifting mutant in the *X Men* films. Attractive and uninhibited, Stamos lacks the experience and screen presence to carry the film. Co-stars Antonio Banderas and Peter Coyote do what they can with underwritten roles. The supporting cast includes Gregg Henry, who played the duplicitous villain in *Body Double*.
Note: *Femme Fatale* was originally to star Uma Thurman, who left the film after becoming pregnant. Cynics might suggest that she also took another look at the script.
Warner Home Video. June 2004. Cert 15.

Flashback

Promoted as Germany's answer to *Scream*, this stylish, gory thriller has more in common with the work of Dario Argento. Jeanette (Valeria Niehaus) witnesses her parents being murdered by a transvestite with a sickle. Ten years later, she leaves the care of a mental hospital, hoping to start a new life as a French teacher. Then the murders begin again… Directed by Michael Karen, *Flashback* delivers the goods, despite some familiar ingredients. Based on a screenplay by Hammer veteran Jimmy Sangster, *Flashback* is reminiscent of Sangster's scripts for *Taste of Fear*, *Paranoic*, *Nightmare* and *Crescendo*. Sixties starlet Elke Sommer, no stranger to Euro shockers, appears as Frau Lust. Also starring: Allegra Curtis (daughter of Tony, half-sister of Jamie Lee).
Note: This is the English-dubbed version.
High Fliers. July 2003. Cert 18.

Gacy

A biopic of serial killer John Wayne Gacy, who raped, tortured and murdered over 30 young men. On the surface, Gacy seemed the archetypal model citizen, a tireless charity worker and children's clown. Directed by Clive Saunders, *Gacy* largely avoids sensationalism, despite the images of maggots on human flesh. Mark Holton gives a chilling performance as Gacy, who carries out one murder in full clown make-up. That said, the script is sketchy, shedding little light on Gacy's background. Also starring: Adam Baldwin.
DEJ Productions. August 2003. Cert 15.

Gang of Roses

A misfiring hip-hop western that makes *Billy the Kid versus Dracula* look good. Lil' Kim leads an all-female band of outlaws, the Gang of Roses. Mario Van Peebles makes a brief appearance as Jesse Lee, his outlaw character from *Posse* (1993). Feebly scripted, *Gang of Roses* is also filled with

technical errors. The lead performances display more enthusiasm than expertise. Directed by Jean-Claude La Marre, who also plays a supporting role.
Also starring: Bobby Brown.
DEJ Productions. June 2004. Cert 15.

Gang Tapes

A 14 year old gangsta wannabe records his daily routine with a stolen video camera. The end result is a catalogue of drug deals, drive-by shootings, casual violence and rape. Written and directed by Adam Ripp, a reserve police officer with the LAPD, *Gang Tapes* aims for authenticity. Several of the cast are real LA 'gangbangers'. One was in jail for the premiere; four were subsequently arrested for armed robbery. The documentary style creates a feeling of raw realism, making some scenes hard to watch. It's arguable that Ripp, a white film-maker, is too misanthropic, offering little insight into LA's gang culture. Despite good reviews, *Gang Tapes* was abruptly pulled from US cinemas, over fears of inciting violence. The BBFC have cut 3 minutes 37 seconds from this release, removing footage of 'instructive' illegal drug use.
MIA. March 2004. Cert 18.

The Group

Six Hong Kong orphans, raised by a Christian priest, grow up to have successful careers. Once a year, they repay the priest's kindness, performing a good deed for the underprivileged by any means necessary. Made in 1998, *The Group* was produced, co-written and directed by Alfred Cheung, who also co-stars. Best known for his comedies, Cheung's more serious films include the outstanding *On the Run* (1988). *The Group* is an imaginative blend of drama, black comedy and social conscience movie. The early scenes offer some interesting characterisations, emphasising the emotional and sexual tensions within the group. The three men

and three women pool their various skills as film director, private investigator, survival instructor, lawyer, doctor and psychologist. Anthony Wong, a leading Hong Kong actor, plays Chiller, an orphan turned gangster who helps his old friends when they tangle with bent cops. Unfortunately, *The Group* gets hung up on its Robin Hood theme, the group robbing a security van to help 10,000 African orphans. The second half becomes confusing, with too many film references and jolting shifts in tone.
Also starring: Almen Wong, Ken Lo.
Hong Kong Classics. June 2004. Cert 15.

The Job

Splash star Daryl Hannah has enjoyed a comeback as *Kill Bill*'s Elle Driver, a one-eyed assassin with (bad) attitude. If *The Job* is anything to go by, Hannah still has problems carrying a film single-handed. Hannah plays C.J. March, a cold-blooded assassin looking to retire. Undertaking the obligatory One Last Job, she must deal with pregnancy, childhood trauma and a troubled conscience. Compared to Elle Driver, or *Blade Runner*'s Pris, C.J. March seems very tame.
Written and directed by Kenny Golde.
Also starring: Brad Renfro, Dominique Swain, Alex Rocco.
DEJ Productions. March 2004. Cert 15.

Kickboxer 4 – The Aggressor

This middling entry in the *Kickboxer* series is an interesting example of shifting attitudes at the BBFC. Back in 1994, the Board rejected the film outright, on grounds of excessive violence. Ten years later, *Kickboxer 4* has been passed uncut. Sasha Mitchell stars as Sloane, a martial arts master sprung from prison to take out Tong Po (Kamel Krifia), a former rival who kidnapped Sloane's wife. Fans of the original *Kickboxer* (1989), starring Jean-Claude Van Damme, may find something to enjoy here. That said, director Albert Pyun, whose career peaked with *The Sword*

and the Sorcerer (1982), does little new with the material and the tournament format has worn thin. Cast as arch-villain Tong Po, Kamel Krifia gives a performance verging on high camp, presumably not the intention. The supporting cast includes Nicholas Guest, brother of the better known Christopher Guest. Their careers have certainly diverged since *The Long Riders* (1980). Film 2000. March 2004. Cert 18.

The Man From Elysian Fields

Filmed in 2001, *The Man from Elysian Fields* suffered major production setbacks, its schedule cut to a tight 30 days after the money ran out. Despite this handicap, the end result is a witty comedy drama, offbeat and original. Andy Garcia stars as Byron Tiller, an unsuccessful novelist who reluctantly works as a ladies' 'escort' to earn money. Tiller becomes involved with a woman (Olivia Williams), who introduces him to her dying husband (James Coburn), a Pulitzer Prize-winning author struggling to finish his last work. *The Man from Elysian Fields* develops its ideas with confidence and imagination, playing on the themes of compromise and betrayal. The film also features one of James Coburn's last appearances. Julia Margulies gives a sympathetic performance as Garcia's puzzled wife, who wants to know where he goes in the evenings. Occasional actor Mick Jagger is ideally cast as the Mephistophelian head of the Elysian Fields escort agency. Also starring: Angelica Huston.
Note: Director George Hickenlooper is best known for the documentary *Hearts of Darkness: A Filmmaker's Apocalypse* (1991), about the making of *Apocalypse Now*, itself a notoriously troubled production. Entertainment In Video. January 2004. Cert 15.

Masked and Anonymous

Bob Dylan's film 'comeback' goes straight

to video in the UK, following a limited theatrical release in the US. Imaginative and enjoyable, *Masked and Anonymous* is more than a curiosity for Dylan completists. Dylan's erratic feature-film career kicked off with *Pat Garrett and Billy the Kid* (1973), where he played the knife-toting Alias. While Sam Peckinpah's elegiac western now has semi-classic status, neither *Renaldo and Clara* nor *Hearts of Fire* have enjoyed the same reappraisal. For *Masked and Anonymous*, Dylan teamed up with debut director Larry Charles, who worked on the TV hits *Seinfeld* and *Mad About You*. Dylan and Charles also wrote the script, under the pseudonyms 'Sergei Petrov' and 'Rene Fontaine'. Shot in just 20 days, on digital video, *Masked and Anonymous* is set in an alternative USA, where military dictatorship has led to a second civil war. Dylan plays Jack Fate, a veteran protest singer sprung from jail to headline a benefit concert. Dylan and Charles temper the allegory with black humour and offbeat characters. Never the most natural film actor, Dylan is backed by an amazing cast (see below), all of whom worked for token salaries. Hardcore Dylan fans will be pleased to know that a three hour version exists.
Starring: Jeff Bridges, Penelope Cruz, John Goodman, Angela Bassett, Jessica Lange, Bruce Dern, Ed Harris, Luke Wilson, Val Kilmer, Chris Penn, Mickey Rourke, Christian Slater, Fred Ward, Cheech Marin. BBC Worldwide/High Fliers. May 2004. Cert 12.

Naked Weapon

This Hong Kong 'bullets 'n' babes' movie was produced and scripted by Wong Jing, the man behind such schlock classics as *The Seventh Curse* (1987) and *High Risk* (1995). The evil Madam M (Almen Wong) kidnaps teenage girls from around the world, turning them into elite killers. Hawaiian model Maggie Q plays Charlene, one of Madam M's unwilling proteges. On

assignment in Hong Kong, she is reunited with her mother and falls in love with an FBI agent. Can Charlene break from Madam M's grip and reclaim her life? Aimed at the international market, *Naked Weapon* was filmed in English, rather than Cantonese. This proves a bad idea, emphasising the trite script and stilted performances. Even the group showers, catfights and pole-dancing wear thin. Despite the title, nudity is kept to a minimum. Director Ching Siu Tung seems off-form, though the spine-snapping technique wins points for originality. *Naked Weapon* borrows from Wong Jing's *Naked Killer* and John Woo's more upmarket *The Killer*, on which Ching Siu Tung worked as the action choreographer. Wong also steals from *Nikita*, *Iron Monkey*, *Battle Royale*, *Charlie's Angels* and *From Here to Eternity*. Despite the high body count, *Naked Weapon* is slow moving and riddled with plot holes. Even the action sequences become more ludicrous than exciting. The DVD features a commentary from Maggie Q and Hong Kong film expert Bey Logan.
Also starring: Michael Wu, Anya.
Note: Maggie Q's full name is Margaret Quigley.
Hong Kong Legends. September 2003. Cert 18.

A Night at the Golden Eagle

The Golden Eagle is a seedy hotel in downtown Los Angeles, filled with drunks, junkies, whores and general losers. Directed by Adam Rifkin, *A Night at the Golden Eagle* is a compelling, if grim, look at LA's sleazy underbelly. The eclectic cast includes Vinnie Jones, who plays Rodan, a vicious pimp preying on teenage runaways. Jones' accomplished performance won the Best Supporting Actor award at the 2002 New York Film Festival. The film was also a hit at the London Film Festival.
Also starring: Natasha Lyonne, James Caan, Fayard Nicholas, Russ Meyer starlet Kitten

Natividad and porn legend Ron Jeremy. High Fliers. July 2003. Cert 18.

Out for a Kill

Action man Steven Seagal also produced this mediocre thriller, suggesting a lapse of judgement. Seagal plays the improbably-named Robert Burns, an archaeologist who uncovers priceless artefacts in China. Unfortunately, he's duped by the local Triads, framed for murder and thrown into a hellish prison. Can he break out, beat the bad guys and clear his name? Maybe. The title seems derived from the earlier Seagal movies *Out for Justice* and *Hard to Kill*. While these films had their quota of kickass moments, *Out for a Kill* barely flickers into life. Michael Oblowitz's tricksy direction can't disguise his inability to handle action or tell a story. The main rule seems to be: if all else fails, use slow motion. The Chinese setting is unconvincing, and Seagal is probably the world's least likely archaeologist. At least Indiana Jones looks like he's read a book.
Note: Filmed in Bulgaria, which seems to be the location of choice for low budget action movies.
Columbia TriStar. August 2003. Cert 15.

Le Pacte Du Silence

An intriguing mystery starring Gerard Depardieu, France's most prolific movie star. Depardieu plays Dr Joachim Ferrer, a Jesuit priest and physician investigating the case of a young nun, Sarah (Elodie Bouchez), hospitalised with extreme pain and apparent delusion. Ferrer believes that Sarah's suffering is a symptom of her repressing a traumatic memory. He also discovers that Sarah has a twin sister, Gaelle (Bouchez again), living thousands of miles away. Gaelle is serving a prison sentence for the killing of a child, years previously. Is Sarah's illness linked to this tragedy and did Gaelle really commit the murder? Ferrer's curiosity gradually turns to obsession, the

Above: The merry widow: Helen Mirren in Medusa Pictures' *The Roman Spring of Mrs Stone*

priest forced to deal with his attraction to Gaelle, a crisis of faith and dark secrets from his own violent past. While the ending will irritate some viewers, *Le Pacte du Silence* is a worthy companion piece to such 'twin' classics as *The Dark Mirror* and *Dead Ringers*. *Question*: Would Catholic nuns really take part in a voodoo ritual?
Directed by Graham Guit.
Also starring: Carmen Maura.
Columbia TriStar. November 2003.
Cert 18.

The Returner

Directed by Takashi Yamazaki, this Japanese science fiction fantasy borrows freely from scores of earlier movies. Despite the lack of originality, the end result is hugely enjoyable. Starring Takashi Kaneshiro, a big name in Hong Kong, *The Returner* opens in 2084, with the earth threatened by an interplanetary war. To prevent the annihilation of the human race, our heroes must travel back in time and change history. With a nod to galactic brotherhood, the real villain is a corrupt human who kidnapped alien delegates for his own nefarious purposes. The standard time travel plot is complemented by stand-out action sequences, handled with flair and imagination.
Columbia TriStar. January 2004. Cert 15.

The Roman Spring of Mrs Stone

Based on Tennessee Williams' only novel, this florid romantic drama is set in post-war Italy. The recently widowed Karen Stone (Helen Mirren) falls for gigolo Paolo de Lio (Olivier Martinez), knowing their relationship can't last. Produced for US television, *The Roman Spring of Mrs Stone* boasts lavish production

values, authentic Rome locations and a star turn from Helen Mirren. Mrs Stone, a fading Broadway star, is a typical Williams protagonist, looking for romance in a world of sexual opportunism. While Williams' hothouse melodramatics are an acquired taste, the film compares favourably with the 1961 version, starring Vivien Leigh and Warren Beatty.
Directed by Robert Allan Ackerman.
Also starring: Anne Bancroft, Brian Dennehy.
Medusa Pictures. October 2003. Cert 15.

R.S.V.P.

Set in Las Vegas, this murder mystery enlivens the teen-slasher formula with several nods to Alfred Hitchcock. Kevin Smith regular Jason Mewes plays Terry, the stoned anti-hero faced with a mounting pile of corpses. While director Mark Anthony Galluzzo plays down the gore in favour of black humour and suspense, the end result is predictable.
Also starring: Glenn Quinn.
MIA. March 2004. Cert 18.

Sign of the Killer

This harrowing thriller reunites director Kasi Lemmons and star Samuel L. Jackson, who collaborated on the acclaimed drama *Eve's Bayou* (1997). Jackson plays Romulus Ledbetter, a gifted musician afflicted by paranoid schizophrenia. Now a recluse, living rough, Ledbetter is tormented by horrifying visions. When a young man is found dead, the police rule out foul play. Ledbetter is convinced he was murdered, on the orders of a shady businessman. Unable to convince the authorities, Ledbetter becomes the next target.
Produced by Danny De Vito.
Also starring: Colm Feore, Ann Magnuson,

Anthony Michael Hall.
High Fliers. April 2004. Cert 15.

Sin

This mediocre thriller is a criminal waste of a strong cast. Ving Rhames stars as Eddie Burns, a retired homicide cop who goes on the trail of a vice king (Gary Oldman) after his sister disappears. Back in the twilight world of illicit porn and hard drugs, Burns is in danger of losing his way. With a nod to Clint Eastwood's *Tightrope* (1984), among others, the script suggests that cop and criminal are two sides of the same coin, Burns having more in common with his adversary than he cares to admit. Unfortunately, this theme is barely developed. Rhames struggles with a poorly conceived character and Oldman has played the psycho-nutter villain once too often. While the Reno, Nevada setting adds atmosphere, director Michael Stevens does little to enliven the material.
Also starring: Alicia Coppola, Brian Cox.
Columbia TriStar. January 2004. Cert 15.

Skinny Tiger, Fatty Dragon

An entertaining Hong Kong action comedy, starring Sammo Hung and Karl Maka. Hung plays Fatty, a policeman with a Bruce Lee complex. Maka is his partner, the bad-tempered Baldy. Assigned to investigate a drugs ring, Fatty and Baldy are suspended from duty after accidentally wrecking their boss's wedding. Though hardly subtle, *Skinny Tiger, Fatty Dragon* is a rare Hong Kong comedy that won't leave western audiences utterly baffled. Director Liu Chia Liang worked with Hung and Maka on *The Odd Couple* (1979), a more traditional martial arts comedy. Liu's other credits include *Till Death Do We Scare* (1982), an enjoyable ghost comedy. Frequent co-stars Hung and Maka play well together and Hung recreates Bruce Lee's fighting style with uncanny precision. Some argue that the comedy scenes are even more impressive than the fight sequences. The DVD features an audio commentary by Hong Kong film expert Bey Logan.
Note: Sammo Hung fights with Bruce Lee in the opening sequence of *Enter the Dragon*. Sadly, this proved to be the last martial arts scene Lee shot.
Hong Kong Legends. May 2004. Cert 15.

The Sleeping Dictionary

This engaging romantic drama was written and directed by Guy Jenkin, co-creator of the hit sit-com *Drop the Dead Donkey*. Set in 1936 Sarawak, in Malaysia, the film centres on John Truscott (Hugh Dancy), an eager newcomer employed by the British colonial government. When the uptight Truscott falls for a local girl (Jessica Alba), he must choose between social convention and love. While *The Sleeping Dictionary* has little new to say about culture clash and romantic complications, the film is carried by its appealing characters, solid plotting and convincing period atmosphere. Interestingly, Alba's character is herself the product of an Anglo-Malaysian love affair. The strong supporting cast includes Bob Hoskins, Brenda Blethyn, Emily Mortimer and Noah Taylor.
Entertainment in Video. December 2003. Cert 15.

So Close

A high-impact hi-tech thriller from Hong Kong, directed by veteran action specialist Cory Yuen. Qi Shu and Vicky Zhao Wei play sister assassins, hired by a shady businessman to kill his older brother. When cop Karen Mok uncovers the plot, the businessman decides that she and the sisters must die. Hunted down, Qi, Zhao and Mok join forces to take out the big villain. *So Close* has been described as a gender-reversal remake of John Woo's *The Killer* (1989), cop and criminal(s) finding a common bond in the face of greater evil. *So Close*'s English title derives from the Carpenters' hit 'Close to You', which plays over the opening shootout. The standard plot is given imaginative treatment by Cory Yuen, whose credits include the Jet Li classics *Fong Sai Yuk* (1993) and *High Risk* (1995). Like many recent Hong Kong thrillers, *So Close* makes extensive use of CGI effects. While the film avoids CGI overkill, the stylised action set-pieces lack the visceral quality of Yuen's earlier work. *So Close* benefits from a strong dose of wry humour, which balances the sentimental flashbacks and a negligible romantic subplot. The film is also notable for its strong female characters, something lacking in *The Killer*. Karen Mok is especially good as the off-beat cop, who favours plain-speaking and a fine cigar. The mutual attraction between Mok and Zhao is intriguingly understated. A successful singer, Mok also performs the theme song.
Also known as *Virtual Weapon*.
Note: Cory Yuen pays *homage* to his 1985 hit *Yes, Madam!*, starring Michelle Yeoh and Cynthia Rothrock, recreating one of Yeoh's most spectacular stunts.

Columbia TriStar. January 2004. Cert 15.

Sonny

Directed by Nicolas Cage, this uneven melodrama is set in 1981 New Orleans. Sonny (James Franco) returns home from army service and falls in love with local girl Carol (Mena Suvari). Unfortunately, she's the star attraction at his mother's bordello, where Sonny once worked as a gigolo. Hoping to start a new life, Sonny finds himself trapped by the past. Best known for the recent *Spiderman* films, James Franco gives a strong performance as the tormented Sonny. The rest of the film is a mixed blessing, borrowing heavily from the Tennessee Williams school of hothouse dramatics. No stranger to overacting (see *Peggy Sue Got Married*), Nicolas Cage encourages his cast to give it all they've got, with variable results. British actress Brenda Blethyn seems miscast as Jewel, Sonny's manipulative mother. The film has been accused of homophobia, Sonny reduced to gay hustling to survive. Presumably, performing sex acts on women for money isn't degrading. The deliberately ambiguous ending strikes some viewers as a cop-out.
Also starring: Harry Dean Stanton, Nicolas Cage (as Acid Yellow).
Entertainment In Video. February 2004. Cert 18.

13 Dead Men

A formula action thriller, starring Lorenzo Lamas and rapper Mystikal. Jewel thief Caj (Mystikal) is framed for murder and placed on death row. His buddy Santos (Lamas) vows to free him, by any means necessary. Piling on the prison movie cliches, *13 Dead Men* never comes to life. While director Art Camacho can handle fight scenes, the film is undone by a weak script, with glaring plot holes. Opinion is divided over Mystikal's acting skills.
Anchor Bay UK. November 2003. Cert 18.

Three Blind Mice

A taut thriller, set in London and Paris, imaginatively directed by Mathias Ledoux. Thomas Gross (Edward Furlong) is a computer expert who spends too much time on the internet. Gross becomes obsessed with a webcam featuring 'Cathy' (Valerie Decobert), a beautiful young woman. Gross' cyber-voyeurism takes a nasty turn when he witnesses Cathy's murder online. Summoning the police, Gross is unable to give them

Cathy's location or even her real name. Under suspicion, Gross teams up with Clare Bligh (Emilia Fox), an internet crime specialist, to track down the killer. *Three Blind Mice* suggests that the public appetite for 'reality' entertainment may not be a good thing. The final act uses the familiar heroine-as-psycho-bait ploy, Clare setting up her own webcam to lure the murderer.
High Fliers. January 2004. Cert 18.

3 A.M.

Produced for cable network Showtime, this murder mystery promises more than it delivers. When New York's taxi drivers are stalked by a serial killer, veteran cabbie Danny Glover vows to track down the murderer. After a friend of his is killed, it becomes personal. If nothing else, *3 A.M.* shows the flipside to *Taxi Driver*, the vulnerable cab drivers at the mercy of a psychopath. *Lethal Weapon* star Glover lends his character a conviction and depth lacking in the script. Blaxploitation icon Pam Grier provides solid back-up as Glover's waitress girlfriend. Michelle Rodriguez, star of the acclaimed *Girlfight*, plays a rookie taxi driver with a past.
Directed by Lee Davis.
Note: *3 A.M.* was produced by Spike Lee, who plays a cameo role.
Prism Leisure Corporation. September 2003. Cert 15.

Tongan Ninja

A ninja from Tonga, Tongan Ninja (Sam Manu) must battle a succession of bad guys before facing the chief villain. Clearly inspired by the *Austin Powers* series, not to mention *Kung Pow – Way of the Fist* , *Tongan Ninja* is an enjoyable martial arts spoof. Featuring such characters as Gun Man, Knife Man and Asian Sidekick, the films makes no attempt at subtlety.
Directed by Jason Stutter.
High Fliers. August 2003. Cert 12.

Undisputed

Director Walter Hill used to make lean, mean action movies, notably *Hard Times* (1975), *The Warriors* (1979) and *Southern Comfort* (1981). He also co-produced the *Alien* series, making significant script contributions to the 1979 original. After years of mediocre films and box-office flops, notably the interesting *Wild Bill* (1995), *Undisputed* marks a return to form. Ving Rhames stars as boxing champion 'Iceman' Chambers, imprisoned for rape. The warders

decide that Chambers will fight their own champion pugilist, Monroe Hutchens (Wesley Snipes), ten years undefeated. *Undisputed* is an assured piece of film-making, with brutal action, a taut pace and well-defined characters. While Chambers is obviously inspired by Mike Tyson, Ving Rhames brings the character to aggressive life. Snipes is equally impressive as Hutchens, who knows the prison survival rules both inside and outside the ring. Interestingly, Snipes objected to a scene that made Hutchens more sympathetic. Michael Rooker, best known for *Henry: Portrait of a Serial Killer*, plays the sadistic head guard. *Columbo* star Peter Falk provides an entertaining turn as a veteran mobster.
Note: Walter Hill co-scripted *Undisputed* with David Giler, who also worked on *Southern Comfort* and the *Alien* series.
Buena Vista Home Entertainment. August 2003. Cert 15.

Vampire Hunters

In 19th century China, an evil monk unleashes the dreaded Vampire King and his hordes of *kyonsi*, or blood-sucking undead. A Taoist *sifu*, or master, leads his four disciples against the forces of darkness. Produced by Asian movie *maestro* Tsui Hark, *Vampire Hunters* is a rare Hong Kong horror movie to receive international distribution. Tsui's earlier hits include *A Chinese Ghost Story* (1987), a classic of the genre. Wearing his producer's hat, Tsui entrusted *Vampire Hunters* to director Wellson Chin Sing Wai, whose horror credits include the dreadful *Ghostly Vixen* (1990), starring sexploitation favourite Amy Yip. While an improvement on *Ghostly Vixen*, *Vampire Hunters* is only a qualified success. Strong on special effects and action sequences, the film suffers from a disjointed narrative (see note) and minimal characterisation. In line with Chinese folklore, the 'vampires' resemble zombies, with none of the charm or sexual allure of their western counterparts.
Starring: Ken Chang, Michael Chow.
Also known as *Tsui Hark's Vampire Hunters*.
Note: Columbia TriStar cut nearly 20 minutes from the original version of the film, *Era of Vampires*, and changed the ending. According to the Internet Movie Database, the longer cut is only available on DVD in Singapore.
Columbia TriStar. August 2003. Cert 15.

Volcano High

This Korean fantasy could be described as a post-apocalypse high school romance s-f action movie. Life is hard at Volcano High, where supernaturally gifted students battle teachers and eachother. Borrowing freely from *X-Men* and *The Matrix*, *Volcano High* is first rate mindless entertainment. Just remember: uncontrollable telekinesis can lead to expulsion. The DVD features a commentary by Asian film experts Bey Logan and Mike Leeder.
Directed by Kim Tae Gyun.
Starring: Jang Hyuk, Kim Su Ro, Sin Min A.
Premier Asia. February 2004. Cert 15.

The Warrior

This $60 million Korean epic is set in 1375 China, during the turbulent Ming Dynasty. Caught up in the power struggle, a Koryo (Korean) diplomatic expedition must fight their way home. En route, they rescue a Ming princess (Zhang Ziyi) from Mongol soldiers, hoping to appease the emperor with her safe return. Directed by Kim Sung Su, *The Warrior* is a stylish and exciting historical drama. The desert setting, all orange-brown hues, conveys a real sense of heat and dust. The well-staged battles are convincingly brutal, though Kim overdoes the slow motion. The leading Koryo characters include a soldier, diplomat, slave and monk, their internal strife reflecting the universal chaos. Early on, one character suggests that journey's end will bring only humiliation and failure. *The Warrior* borrows from *Seven Samurai*, *The Wild Bunch*, *Conan the Barbarian* and *Once Upon a Time in China*. Zhang Ziyi, star of *Crouching Tiger, Hidden Dragon*, plays another strong-willed character whose recklessness costs many lives.
The best performance comes from Hong Kong actor Yu Rong Guang, cast as a ruthless yet honourable Mongol general. On the downside, the film is overly solemn, with little sense of humour. The bloodbath finale, filled with noble self-sacrifice, will strike some viewers as over the top.
Also known as *Musa – The Warrior*.
The DVD features cast and crew interviews, and a commentary from Asian film experts Bey Logan and Mike Leeder.
Note: This is the 133 minute international version of the film (127 mins at 25 fps), which runs 25 minutes shorter than the full Korean print. The deleted scenes are included on the DVD as an extra. The BBFC have removed an additional 27 seconds, on grounds of animal cruelty.
Premier Asia. October 2003. Cert 18.

Faces of the Year

GAEL GARCÍA BERNAL

Born: 30 November 1978
in Guadalajara, Jalisco, Mexico.
Education: Central School of
Speech and Drama, London.
Past life: A successful child actor, he
starred in a popular TV soap – *El Abuelo
y Yo* – at 12, and appeared in Antonio
Urrutia's Academy-nominated short,
De Tripas, Corazón.
Talents: He speaks English, Italian,
Spanish and French and possesses a rare
boldness that bestows every role he takes
with a stunning and profound sincerity.
His sexy Latin looks don't hurt, either.
Debut: *Amores Perros* (2000) was his
first major feature and an international
critical success.
Other films: *Y tu mamá también* (2001),
El Crimen De Padre Amaro (2002), *Don't
Tempt Me* (2002), *The Motorcycle Diaries*
(2003), *Bad Education* (2004).
Next up: *The King* (2004),
Dot the I and *Alatriste*.
Awards: 2003 MTV Movie Award,
Favourite Actor; 2001 Venice Film
Festival Marcello Mastroianni Award;
2001 Ariel Award for Best Actor.
He said it: 'It's better to take things little
by little. It's better to be the "new big
thing" for 20 years.'
They said it: 'Gael García Bernal exudes
the charm of a young Antonio Banderas.
Poised for international stardom, Gael's
electric screen presence almost guarantees
that he'll be a force in mainstream films
in no time.'

DANIEL CRAIG

Born: 11 November 1968
in Chester, England.
Education: National Youth Theatre,
Guildhall School of Music and Drama.
Past life: An accomplished TV
and stage career.
TV: *Boon* (1986), *Drop the Dead Donkey*,
Between the Lines, *Heartbeat*, *Sharpe's
Eagle*, *Our Friends in the North*, *Kiss and
Tell*, *Moll Flanders*, *Sword of Honour*
Debut: He made his film debut in *The
Power of One*. His first lead in the
U.K. came in 1998 in John Maybury's
Love is the Devil.
Other films: *A Kid in King Arthur's
Court* (1995), *Love & Rage*, *The Trench*,
Some Voices, *Hotel Splendide*, *I Dreamed
of Africa*, *Lara Croft: Tomb Raider*,
Road to Perdition, *Sylvia*, *The Mother*,
Enduring Love, *Layer Cake*.
Next up: *The Jacket*,
Awards: British Independent Film Award
– Best Actor, for Some Voices (2000).

the star comic on *Saturday Night Live*, where his performance won an Emmy nomination.

Talents: An improv maestro and master impersonator (famously of US president George W. Bush), Ferrell excels at delivering over-the-top performances with class. His characters are usually the biggest buffoons imaginable, but he 'overplays' them with an unexpected intelligence.

TV: *Saturday Night Live, Cow and Chicken* (providing various voices).

Debut: *Criminal Hearts*, as a newscaster (uncredited).

Other films: *Austin Powers: International Man of Mystery* (as Mustafa), *A Night at the Roxbury, The Suburbans, Austin Powers: The Spy Who Shagged Me* (as Mustafa), *Dick* (as Bob Woodward), *Superstar, Drowning Mona, The Ladies Man, Jay and Silent Bob Strike Back, Zoolander, Boat Trip* (uncredited), *Old School, Elf , Starsky and Hutch, Anchorman: The Legend of Ron Burgundy*.

Next up: *Winter Passing, Melinda and Melinda, The Wendell Baker Story, Curious George* (voice only), *The Producers, Kicking & Screaming, The Wedding Crashers, Bewitched, Talladega Nights, Joan of Bark: The Dog That Saved France, A Confederacy of Dunces*.

He said it: 'Well, I know Will flew in his acting coach from Kentucky, Jimmy Beam, that night.'

They said: 'Will Ferrell could probably read a circuit board schematic and I'd laugh myself into stomach cramps. Frenziedly charismatic enough to launder unlikeable characters into leading men, the comedian is like a brilliantly free-associating, deadpan-joking cyborg who just can't be shut off.'

He said it: [on becoming an actor] 'I guess I just wanted to show off. A lot of my mother's contemporaries were actors – they were larger than life. Later I found out they were just pissed drunk.'

They said it: 'Remember the name Daniel Craig. His ability to give the slimy Connor Rooney [in *Road to Perdition*] such pathos with a script that gives him little but bile to say is a rare gift.'

WILL FERRELL

Born: 16 July 1967 in Irvine, California, USA.

Education: University High School in Irvine, California.

Past life: After graduating from USC, worked as a sportscaster for a weekly cable series. Will Ferrell started as a member of LA comedy/improve group The Groundlings, went on, via various TV appearances, to become a regular and

JENNIFER GARNER

Born: 17 April 1972
in Houston, Texas, USA.
Education: George Washington High
School in Charleston, West Virginia;
Denison University, Granville Ohio.
Past life: Ballerina-turned-TV actress.
Talents: A trained dancer, she is famous
for her *Buffy*-like action-sequences from
the hit TV spy-show *Alias*. With a face
like an angel and a body made for sin,
she's the uber-girl-next-door with the
chops for comedy and drama, though
the world just wants to see her kick
ass in tight leathers.
TV: *Zoya* (TV Movie), *Felicity*, *Alias*.
Debut: *Harvest of Fire* (1996).
Other films: *Deconstructing Harry*
(1997), *Mr Magoo, Dude, Where's My
Car?, Pearl Harbor, Catch Me If You Can,
Daredevil, 13 Going on 30.*
Next up: *Elektra.*
Awards: 2002 Golden Globe – Best
Performance by an Actress in a Dramatic
Television Series, for *Alias*; 2003 MTV
Movie Award Breakthrough Female
Performance, for *Daredevil.*
She said it: 'When I was first kind of
deciding that I wanted to be an actress,
it was all about words. I just loved
Shakespeare and restoration drama.
The fact that now what I'm known for
is the physical side of it [as an action
star] cracks me up, personally. It's so
much fun and it makes me really happy ;
'I played in the marching band. I didn't
wear cool clothes ever and I wore huge
glasses. I just wanted to grow up and be
able to put one foot in front of the other
and carry on a proper conversation.
Oh, and to wear contact lenses;
I really wanted contacts.'
They said it: 'Jennifer jumps into things
fearlessly. It's amazing to watch someone
who's so game, so hungry to do work.
And what she can't do, she figures out
how to do. She's wildly capable and
smart.' J.J. Abrams.

BRYCE DALLAS HOWARD

Born: 2 March 1981 in Dallas, Texas.
Education: NYU's Tisch School of the
Arts and the Stella Adler Conservatory.
She also attended the Stagedoor Manor
of the Performing Arts, which was the
setting for Todd Graff's 'musical' *Camp*.
Bryce Dallas attended the summer
school with her close friend Natalie
Portman, following in the footsteps
of such other wannabes as Robert
Downey Jr and Jennifer Jason Leigh.
Past life: As the daughter of Richie
Cunningham – er, director Ron Howard
– Bryce Dallas (partially named after
the city in which was conceived) started
early, although she initially toyed with
the idea of becoming a "forensic
anthropologist, a writer, a lawyer, or a
teacher." However, when applying for
drama school she just used the name
Bryce Dallas.
Talents: In a summer of above-average
multiplex fodder, Bryce Dallas outshone
the likes of Tobey Maguire and Daniel
Radcliffe. As the blind and brave Ivy
Walker in M. Night Shyamalan's *The
Village* (which she snared after Kirsten
Dunst dropped out), she brought a
grounded radiance to an otherwise dull
film. *The Village* was not the success that

its supporters had hoped, but B.D.
was seen by enough of the right people
(like, the media) to guarantee her a
smooth road ahead.
Debut: She had bit parts in
Ron Howard's *Parenthood*, Ron Howard's
Apollo 13 and Ron Howard's *The Grinch*,
playing a surprised 'Who' in the last-
named.
Other films: *The Book of Love*, with
Frances O'Connor and Simon Baker.
Next up: Lars von Trier's starry

Manderlay, a story of slavery set in the
American South. B.D. takes the lead role
of Grace (after Nicole Kidman dropped
out) and is supported by Willem Dafoe,
Danny Glover and Lauren Bacall.
She said it: 'The day after I finished
The Village, I had a breakdown. I was
thinking: What did I just destroy? I'm
not worthy of what Night created,
really I'm not.'
They said it: 'I thought she was
breathtaking.' M. Night Shyamalan.

JOHNNY KNOXVILLE

Real name: Phillip John Clapp.
Born: 11 March 1971
in Knoxville, Tennessee.
Education: American Academy of
Dramatic Arts, Pasadena, California.
Past life: While writing an article for a
skateboarding magazine, a story about
self-defence equipment led to a television
show dedicated to sponsoring attempts at
self-inflicted injury produced by MTV
(and co-created by pal Spike Jonze).
It was called *Jackass*.
Talents: Blessed with the ability of a
circus clown to smile through the tears
of severe pain, the streetwise hip 'n cool
stylings of Johnny Knoxville has made
him America's greatest urban street
clown. However, his choice of film roles
defy obvious typecasting and have begun
to demonstrate a proper actor's gift for
taking risks.
TV: *Jackass*.
Debut: *Desert Blues* (1995) (credited as
Phillip John).
Other films: *Big Trouble, The Tree, The
Ranger, Life Without Dick, Men in Black
2, Jackass: The Movie, Grand Theft
Parsons, Walking Tall.*
Next up: *A Dirty Shame, Jackass: Volume
Two, The Ringer, Lords of Dogtown.*
He said it: 'The moral majority led by
some whack in Washington came down
really hard on MTV, who in turn came
down hard on us. But they can kiss my
ass. They care less about the issues and
more about how they are perceived by
the public and how they can further
their own political careers. I didn't
want to do a half-assed, watered-down
version, so I quit. I loved it too much
not to do it properly.'
They said it: 'First of all, let's get one
thing straight: The very idea that we're
reviewing *Jackass: The Movie* shows that
infidels have stormed the castle of
Western civilization – and won.'

DIANE KRUGER

Real name: Diane Heidkrueger.
Born: 15 July 1976 in Algermissen,
near Hildesheim, Germany.
Education: Studied ballet with the
Royal Ballet in London, then joined
the Ecole Florent.
Past life: A dancer until an injury ended
her career, Diane Heidkrueger became a
top fashion model, launching herself at
15 by reaching the finals of Elite's 1992
Look Of The Year competition, until

heeding advice from Luc Besson to
go to Paris and become an actress.
Talents: A stunner, no question,
Diane Kruger has an undeniably regal
grace and handled well the hyped-up
pressures of playing the most beautiful
woman of ancient legend, Helen of Troy.
The fact she studied Latin and Greek
may have helped.
Debut: *The Piano Player*
(aka *The Target*).
Other films: *Mon idole* (2002), *Ni pour,*

ni contre (bien au contraire),
Michel Vaillant, *Troy*, *Wicker Park*.
Next up: *National Treasure*.
She said it: 'After the first two takes,
you know you can pretty much let
yourself go and try anything.'
They said it: 'Diane is not only a
stunning beauty but a gifted actress
with tremendous emotional depth and
presence,' said Petersen. 'The role of
Helen is charged with the grandeur of
history and legend. I am confident that
Diane has the charisma and artistry that
this compelling character demands.'

LINDSAY LOHAN

Born: 2 July 1986
in New York, New York.
Full name: Lindsay Morgan Lohan.
Education: Laurel Springs School.
Past life: Lindsay Lohan started
modelling for the Ford Agency at age 3,
later starring in over 60 commercials and
made her dramatic debut on the
American TV soap Another World
at age 10.
Talents: On screen, a natural ability to
portray every teenage emotion tempered
by a studio-friendly 'deep-down' decency.
Off screen, a tenacious business sense
that has made her one of the highest
paid teen actresses in history (earning a
$7.5 million payday for *Lady Luck*), also
boasting a budding pop music career.
In other words, pure Hollywood candy.
Debut: *The Parent Trap* (1998).
Other films: *Freaky Friday* (2003),
Confessions of a Teenage Drama Queen,
Mean Girls (both 2004).
Next up: *Herbie: Fully Loaded*,
Lady Luck, *Fashionistas*, *Dramarama*
and *Gossip Girl* (all in 2005).
Awards: MTV Movie Award for
Breakthrough Female Performance
She said it: 'It's kind of amazing. It's
really weird. When my agents called me
they were like, 'We have some great news
for you.' I was like, "Oh, what?" They're
like, "You're gonna get $7.5 million for

your next movie!" and I was like, "What? I don't need that – I really don't!"'

They said it: 'Lohan holds her own, registering prim parental disapproval from within the pierced body of a hormonal high-school girl' [on her performance in *Freaky Friday*]

EMMY ROSSUM

Real name: Emmanuelle Grey Rossum.
Born: 12 September 1986 in New York, New York.
Education: Takes classes at Columbia University and tuition from NYU and UCLA, depending on which coast she happens to be on.
Past life: Trained with New York's Metropolitan Opera Children's Chorus, Emmy has performed at the Metropolitan Opera at Lincoln Center and Carnegie Hall with the likes of Placido Domingo, Luciano Pavarotti and Dolly Parton, and has worked under the direction of Franco Zeffirelli.
Talents: The ultimate metropolitan overachiever, Emmy has a wide-eyed beauty that veils a highly ambitious and determined actress, with more cultivation and talent than anyone so young has a right to. Oh, and she can sing a little as well.
TV: *As the World Turns*, *Genius*, *The Audrey Hepburn Story* (as the young Audrey Hepburn, aged 12-16).
Debut: *Songcatcher* (2000).
Other films: *It Had to Be You* (2000), *Passionada*, *Happy Now*, *An American Rhapsody*, *Nola*, *Mystic River* (as the daughter of Sean Penn), *The Day After Tomorrow*.
Next up: *The Phantom of the Opera* (as Christine).
Awards: Sundance Film Festival Special Jury Award for Outstanding Ensemble Performance for *Songcatcher*.
She said it: 'When I was real young, I wanted to be 1,000 different things. In acting, I get to do that every six weeks.'

They said it: 'Emmy was, like, tongue down the throat and the whole thing,' Jake Gyllenhaal marvels. Rossum says: 'I saw my chance, and I was moving right in – even if he was thinking about Kirsten [Dunst]' – on her screen test for *The Day After Tomorrow*.

MICHAEL SHEEN

Born: 5 February 1969 in Newport, Gwent, Wales.
Education: Trained at RADA, where he won the SWET/ Laurence Olivier Bursary.
Past life: Film fans mostly knew Michael Sheen as Kate Beckinsale's ex, though London's theatre-goers knew him best as a bright burning talent with a fearsome stage presence. He has starred at Manchester's Royal Exchange Theatre, the Royal National Theatre and the Royal Shakespeare Company, just to name a few. He is co-founder of the Thin Language Theatre Company and director of The Foundry Production Company.
Talents: Michael Sheen has the kind of acting talent that can ignite a generation. Given ten years to learn his craft on some of the most demanding stages in the world, he has won kudos from critics that read like love notes from theatre groupies. His new focus on a film career should hopefully lead to something special, though his work to date has done more to entice than to edify.
TV: *Lost in France*, *Gallowglass*, *The Deal* (as Tony Blair).
Debut: *Mary Reilly* (1996).
Other films: *Othello* (1995), *Wilde*, *Heartlands*, *The Four Feathers* (as Trench), *Underworld*, *Timeline*, *Bright Young Things*, *Laws of Attraction*.
Next up: *Kingdom of Heaven*, for Ridley Scott.
Awards: 2003 London Critics Circle Theatre Award for Best Actor, and the 2003 London Evening Standard Theatre Award for Best Actor for his performance in *Caligula* at the Donmar Warehouse.
He said it: 'So with Caligula and Jimmy Porter [in *Look Back in Anger*] and *Amadeus*, all those characters who are very extreme, they're very showy parts to play. But never forget that this is *real*. They're not theatrical creations. They should be played as real people. If someone has an ability to impress an audience there's a tendency to be tempted into doing just that.'
They said it: 'Michael Sheen is the most exciting actor of his generation.' 'Sheen, volatile and responsive in an excellent performance, showed us the exhilaration of power and conquest.'
And: Michael Sheen was named best actor for his glittering and scary turn as Caligula in the Donmar's since-closed revival of the Albert Camus play. In his speech, Sheen told the audience it was a critic who made him want to act in the first place: He used to read the writings of the late Kenneth Tynan when he was growing up in Port Talbot, Wales.

Film World Diary
July 2003 – June 2004

JULY 2003

14-year-old Iranian **Hana Makhmalbaf**'s first full-length film, *Joy of Madness*, is up for the £71,000 prize for 'best debut' at the Venice Film Festival • Super-hunk **Brad Pitt** suffer the ignominy of a body double on *Troy* because his legs are too skinny. Parts of the $200 million movie are being re-shot using a muscle-bound stand-in with 'thighs like tree trunks' • James Bond actor **Pierce Brosnan** is to

be awarded an honorary OBE in recognition of his contribution to drama and the British film industry • **Robert Wagner** sues for half the profits from the *Charlie's Angels* movies, because of his involvement in the development of the original TV series. The films, starring **Drew Barrymore**, **Cameron Diaz** and **Lucy Liu**, have so far grossed nearly £120m at the box office • Actor **Jeffrey Jones**, 56, who

appeared in *Beetlejuice*, *Amadeus* and *Sleepy Hollow*, has pleaded no contest to a charge of employing a 14-year-old boy to pose for sexually explicit photos • A season of 23 restored classic Charlie Chan mystery movies, made in the 1930s and 1940s, has been pulled from the Fox Movie Channel on cable TV following complaints that the films are racially insensitive.

AUGUST 2003

Tom Cruise sings Elvis songs with the Japanese Prime Minister Junichiro Koizumi during a visit to Tokyo • **Peter Jackson** is to pick up one of the biggest fees for directing the movie remake of *King Kong*. He will take the lion's share of $20m (against 20 per cent of the gross), the rest to be shared with the film's writers • **George Clooney** has successfully pressured studio bosses to re-release *Confessions of a Dangerous Mind*, which flopped the first time round in spite of decent reviews • **Angelina Jolie** states

that she has disowned her father **Jon Voight**, saying, 'I no longer see us as father and daughter' • **Ashton Kutcher**, 26, splits up with **Brittany Murphy**, 27, only to hook up almost immediately with **Demi Moore**, 41, causing an media furore about his toy-boy status • **Arnold Schwarzenegger** announces his candidacy for the Governorship of California • **Angelina Jolie** is angry that her picture for the poster of her new *Tomb Raider* movie has been airbrushed to remove her nipples • Four acres of beachfront

property near **Katharine Hepburn**'s home in Old Saybrook, Connecticut, will become protected land for public use, according to her will • **Nicole Kidman** has pulled out of the remaining two films in Lars von Trier's American trilogy, which began with *Dogville*, due to incompatible work diaries • **Orson Welles**' Oscar for *Citizen Kane*, expected to fetch up to £250,000 at auction, is withdrawn from sale after the Academy invoked its right to buy it back for 60p.

SEPTEMBER 2003

Emily Mortimer and husband **Alessandro Nivola** are the proud parents of their first child, which weighed in at 7lb 10oz, in London • **Catherine Zeta-Jones** sues the French cosmetics firm Caudalie for £10 million for unauthorised use of her name in

an ad campaign for face creams and their anti-aging spa in Las Vegas • **Sir Anthony Hopkins** gets his star on the Hollywood Walk of Fame • **Russell Crowe** reveals he abstained from sex for months so he could 'perform' to his best on his honeymoon with

Danielle Spencer: 'We spent a lot of time apart – as in not sharing the same bed. I was determined there would be a lot of pent-up energy on the big night' • **Colin Farrell**'s girlfriend Kim Bordenave gives birth to a baby boy in LA.

Farrell wasn't there for the event as he was filming *Alexander* in Morocco • **Jennifer Lopez** and **Ben Affleck** call off their much reported 'hush-hush' wedding • The gritty, digitally-shot thriller *This is Not a Love Song* becomes

the first feature film to premiere on the internet • **Pierce Brosnan** wins control of the internet name www.piercebrosnan.com in a ruling by the World Intellectual Property Organisation.

OCTOBER 2003

Michael Douglas has agreed to host the annual Nobel Peace Prize concert in Norway – on the condition that **Catherine Zeta-Jones** is allowed to join him on stage • After months of on-again-off-again separations, **Jude Law** and **Sadie Frost** are officially granted a divorce by the UK courts • **Halle Berry**'s 007 spin-off *Jinx* has been axed by MGM. The first Bond-based spin-off series in the franchise's 40-year history would have starred Berry as an American super-spy • **Jim Caviezel** and assistant director Michelini were struck by lightning – but were uninjured – on the set of *The Passion of the Christ*. 'I'm about a hundred feet away from them,' producer Steve McEveety said, 'when I glance over and see lightning coming out of Caviezel's ears' • **Robert De Niro**, 60, is diagnosed with prostate cancer • It's announced that 20 Lottery-backed films have notched up £125,790,000 in worldwide ticket sales and more than 31 million cinema visits. From the £13.7 million in grants distributed by the UK Film Council, the average return is £9 million on every £1 million • **Roger Moore**, 75, is knighted. The Bond-actor said, 'I had the worst attack of stage fright in my life. When you realise the gravitas of the situation, it's slightly nerve-racking. It was like a costume drama and I was Sir Ivanhoe – a part I have played, incidentally.' The 75-year-old, who was knighted for his tireless charity work, revealed that the Queen had recognised his dilemma • **Arnold Schwarzenegger** is

elected Governor of California after a campaign that fielded smear attacks accusing him of being a serial sexual harasser and a fan of Hitler • **Mel Gibson** reportedly struggles to find a studio deal for his controversial film about the death of Jesus Christ, *The Passion of the Christ*. Icon Productions has only had interest from small, independent companies that can't be affected by boycotts or protests • A warrant against **Ben Affleck** issued by accuser Tara Ray is dropped after authorities found no evidence to support the woman's claim that Affleck threatened to kill her • Dutch cinema owner **Dirk Holemans** accidentally screened the erotic Michael Haneke film *The Piano*

Teacher instead of Roman Polanski's Oscar-winner *The Pianist* to a group of elderly farmers' wives. Mr Holemans said, 'I noticed too late it was pure porno. But in order not to spoil the ladies' evening, I went on with it' • **Nicole Kidman** walked out of a special screening of *Dogville* because some of her own scenes, specifically a series of violent rapes, were too disturbing to watch. 'It was hard watching it. The screen is huge and the sound and the extremeness of the situation. I was sitting there watching, and I thought, this is too exposing, and so I left' • **Ben Affleck** and **Jennifer Lopez**'s movie *Gigli* is dropped by every cinema in Britain after only a week on screens.

Left: Jinxed? Halle Berry loses her franchise

NOVEMBER 2003

George Lucas finishes shooting *Star Wars: Episode III – Revenge of the Sith*. The movie is scheduled for release in 2005 • Disney studio execs are reportedly outraged by their own *Bad Santa*, a film that features **Billy Bob Thornton** as a sex-crazed, foul-mouthed Father Christmas who tells kids he doesn't exist • **Nisha Ganatra**, confidante to *Bend It Like Beckham*'s writer-director Gurinder Chadha, reveals that the film was initially intended to feature a lesbian relationship between its two stars, **Parminder K Nagra** and **Keira Knightley** • **Katie Holmes**' fiancé **Chris**

Klein buys the sexy nurse's outfit she wears in *The Singing Detective*, paying £100 to beat all other comers • **Ewan McGregor** is disappointed that American audiences will be denied his full frontal nude shot in *Young Adam* as Sony Classics has cut the scene. 'If you want to see my penis, you'll have to fly to Britain,' the retiring lily says • *Love Actually* sets a new opening box-office record for a British rom-com with £6.6 million, beating previous record holders *Bridget Jones's Diary* and *Notting Hill* • 10,000 *Lord of the Rings* fans have signed an online petition

demanding that **Christopher Lee**'s battle with **Sir Ian McKellen** be reinstated in *LOTR: Return of the King*. • Former Glasgow gangster **Jimmy Boyle**, 60, sells the rights to his unpublished book to Disney for £2.1 million. *A Stolen Smile* tells the story of how the *Mona Lisa* is stolen, ending up on a grim housing estate • *The Matrix Revolutions* is released concurrently in 107 countries across the world and makes £25 million at the box office on its first day. This widest-ever release of a feature is a move to deter potential pirates.

DECEMBER 2003

LOTR: The Return of the King sets a new British box office record, taking £3,029,176 on its opening day. It also breaks records for a five-day opening, making £71m at the US box office, beating the £59m record set by *Stars Wars: Episode I – The Phantom Menace* • **Ben Stiller** admits he needed a rabies shot after being bitten by a ferret on the set of *Along Came Polly*. 'Their teeth are sharp, like razors. I mean, they're rat-like creatures. It was a horrible experience' • A *Star Wars* stormtrooper's helmet sells at auction for £20,000 – about five times more than expected • **Peter Jackson** announces that he is relocating Bag End – Bilbo and Frodo Baggins' home in the *LOTR* films – to the back garden of his New Zealand mansion • **Dame Judi Dench** is reportedly desperate to block the nude scenes she filmed 25 years ago with **Jeremy Irons** in *Langrishe, Go Down* from being released on video. Director **David Jones** says, 'I think *Langrishe, Go Down* was Judi's best film performance ever – beautiful, sensual, passionate and very physical, as well as being wickedly funny. She and Irons

Right: Bill Nighy tackles the charts with his rendition of The Troggs' 'Love is all Around'

were just amazing' • Keiko, the 35ft-long, six-ton killer whale – and star of *Free Willy* – dies at 27 years of age after the sudden onset of pneumonia in the Taknes fjord in Norway • **Billy Bob Thornton** is refusing to release his *All the Pretty Horses* movie on DVD until studio bosses agree to show his marathon-length director's cut on the big screen. 'I guess I have enough satisfaction when Matt Damon calls me up and says,

"You know what? Thanks for the best experience I ever had making a movie. That movie we cut, originally, was the best thing I've ever been in."' • **Geena Davis**, 47, and her husband **Reza Jarrahy**, 33, announce that she is pregnant, with twins! • **Steve Coogan** becomes the first person granted permission to be filmed walking the Great Wall Of China for a movie. Significantly, the production, *Around the World in*

80 Days, stars Asia's biggest film star, **Jackie Chan** • From *Love Actually*, Bill Nighy's spoof rendition of The Troggs' 'Love is all Around', titled 'Christmas is all Around', is released as a single in the British market. Colin Firth comments, 'Past the first listen I don't think I'd spend a lot of time with it. It's designed to hurt the eardrums.'

JANUARY 2004

Revealed: More than £1 billion was spent on British filmmaking last year, setting a new record for the UK film industry • Pixar Animation Studios, whose four movies with Disney since *Toy Story* in 1995 generated more than £1.4 billion in total at the box office, has announced a split with its parent company. 'After ten months of trying to strike a deal with Disney, we're moving on,' said Pixar chief executive Steve Jobs. Their last animated

hit, *Finding Nemo*, has made more than £280 million in global ticket sales, making it the most successful animated film ever • **Jennifer Lopez** splits from fiancé **Ben Affleck**, reportedly over his reluctance to make a commitment and his love of gambling. They part ways after an aborted wedding and 18 months together • A Paris court is hearing a case brought by a French author who says his ideas were used in *Finding Nemo*. French children's

author **Franck le Calvez** claims that Disney and Pixar ripped off the fish characters from his illustrated children's book, claiming similarities between his *Pierrot the Clown Fish* and the fishy star of *Finding Nemo* • Four female jazz musicians are suing **Julia Roberts**' production company for discrimination, claiming they were paid less for appearing in her movie, *Mona Lisa Smile*, than their male counterparts • **Mike Newell**,

Left: Tom Cruise works the crowd in Leicester Square

director of *Harry Potter and the Goblet of Fire*, says the fourth film, at around £168 million, will be the most expensive movie ever, even pricier than all three of the *Lord of the Rings* films • TV star **Shane Richie**'s self-funded gangster flick, *Shoreditch*, takes just £2,272 at the box-office, equivalent to just 300 people seeing it • Nearly 241 British

Academy Awards voters are given an extended voting deadline after their nomination forms – originally sent from the United States to Britain – mysteriously go missing • **Tom Cruise** wows 5,000 fans in Leicester Square by treating them to a marathon two-hour autograph-signing session at the premier of *The Last Samurai*, keeping a prior promise to give

an autograph to every fan who wanted one • **Nicole Kidman** is paid £2m for a four-minute Chanel No. 5 commercial directed by Baz Luhrmann, which is possibly the highest 'fee-per-minute' ever paid to an actor for an ad.

FEBRUARY 2004

Catholic bishops worried by **Mel Gibson**'s portrayal of ancient Jews in his *The Passion of the Christ*, publish a 128-page booklet, *The Bible, the Jews and the Death of Jesus: A Collection of Catholic Documents*, warning against assigning Jewish guilt over the Crucifixion • The stunningly awful urban dance film *You Got Served* enters the US box office

chart at number one • **Drew Barrymore** earns her star on Hollywood's Walk of Fame • One-man controversy machine **Mel Gibson** defends his father, Hutton Gibson, over claims that comments he made mark him as a Holocaust denier: 'I love him back. So I'll slug it out, until my heart is black and blue, if anyone ever tries to hurt him.' In an

interview with the *New York Times*, Gibson Sr. responded to a question on the scale of the Holocaust as follows: 'Go and ask an undertaker or the guy who operates the crematorium what it takes to get rid of a dead body. It takes one litre of petrol and 20 minutes. Now, six million?'

MARCH 2004

The Passion of the Christ tops the UK box office, taking more than £2 million on its opening weekend – the highest ever for a subtitled film in the UK. Costing just £14m to make, it has already taken £147 million in the US alone since its release on Ash Wednesday, topping the box office for three weeks • A film fan pays more than £14,000 for a grey riding dress supposedly worn by Liv Tyler in *The Lord of the Rings*, only to be told it is a fake and part of a movie memorabilia scam • Irony rules, as the **George A. Romero** zombie remake *Dawn of the Dead* knocks *The Passion of the Christ* off the top of the US box office • **Julie Andrews** sings again, seven years after her singing voice disappeared following the removal of a cyst in her throat. During filming for *The Princess Diaries 2*, 'She nailed the song on the first take,' observed one

onlooker. 'I saw crew members with tears in their eyes' • According to new reports, **Jim Caviezel** asked **Jennifer Lopez** to put some clothes on before filming a raunchy sex scene in *Angel Eyes*. He didn't want to offend his new wife Kerri: 'I want to respect her,' he said. 'The only bare breasts I want next to me in my life belong to my wife' • Filming of *Mr and Mrs Smith* is halted, reportedly because **Brad Pitt** and **Angelina Jolie** keep passing each other 'a nasty flu-like bug' while kissing each other during steamy love scenes • The ever-surprising **Angelina Jolie** admits to having a string of hotel sex romps with various male friends: 'I went for two years with absolutely no man around me. Then I decided to get closer to men who were already very close friends of mine. It's kind of an adult way of having adult

relationships. As crazy as that sounds, meeting a man in a hotel room for a few hours and not seeing that man again for a few months is about what I can handle' • **Mel Gibson**'s *The Passion of the Christ* breaks US box office records, taking £60m in its first five days, debuting at No.1 • *The Lord of the Rings: Return of the King* wins all eleven Oscar categories for which it was nominated. The second highest-grossing movie of all time, with more than $1b at the global box office, equals the record number of Oscars scooped by *Ben Hur* in 1960 and *Titanic* in 1998 • **Charlie Sheen** and **Denise Richards** are blessed with a daughter, Sam Sheen.

APRIL 2004

Ewan McGregor and **Charlie Boorman** start a 20,000 mile round-the-world motorcycle adventure from London. Their journey is being filmed for a television documentary • Screenwriter **Charlie Kaufman** lambastes **George Clooney** for changing his script for *Confessions of a Dangerous Mind*. He said, 'I was upset by the fact that he took the movie from me and then cut me out after that. I'm unhappy with the end result. And I'm unhappy with George Clooney. I had a movie that I wrote and this isn't it' • **Adam Sandler**'s *50 First Dates* sets a new record for a rom-com – beating *Runaway Bride* – opening in the US with takings of £21.7 million.

Left: Kate Beckinsale is directed to the altar by new hubby Len Wiseman

MAY 2004

Harry Potter and the Prisoner of Azkaban is the first film to make more than £5m on its first day of release in the UK. That is more than twice the first day takings of the first *Harry Potter* film, and nearly three times as much as the second • **Scarlett Johansson** lands a £3m modelling contract as the face of the design house Louis Vuitton. The 19-year old actress is already the star of a Calvin Klein fragrance campaign • Speculation flies over a photograph taken of **Julia Roberts** in Italy with her husband of four years, Danny Moder, about whether she is now pregnant. It is later confirmed that she is – with twins • **Jennifer Lopez**'s new boyfriend **Marc Anthony** has filed for a quickie divorce in the Dominican Republic from ex-Miss Universe Dayanara Torres • *Harry Potter*

star **Rupert Grint** admits to having dressed up as his female drama teacher and doing a rap in order to stand out from the competition in his audition tape: 'I know Ron [Weasley] isn't a girl, but I wanted to get noticed and show I was versatile' • Tempting another kind of curse, it is announced that **Johnny Depp** is to team up with pop star-actress wife **Vanessa Paradis** for the new adaptation of *The Gypsy's Curse* • *Shrek 2* makes an estimated $104.3 million (£58.5m) over its opening weekend, and $125.3 million (£70.2m) since, setting a mid-week opening record of $11.8 million (£6.7m). The 'toon also set a single-day record on Saturday, with takings of $44.8 million, beating the $43.8m set by *Spider-Man* in 2002. Its record-setting American

debut on 4,163 screens may have helped • **Michael Moore**'s *Fahrenheit 9/11* wins the Palme d'Or at the Cannes Film Festival • **Michael Winterbottom**'s *Nine Songs* ('the most sexually explicit film in the history of British cinema') stuns audiences at Cannes with its candid scenes featuring cunnilingus, fellatio and ejaculation. Quote: 'Most films with explicit sex only feature a tiny amount. In *Nine Songs* I didn't want people just to be titillated by a brief glimpse' • **Kate Beckinsale** marries her *Underworld* director **Len Wiseman** in Las Vegas at the weekend. Her five-year-old daughter, Lily – by actor ex **Michael Sheen** – is a bridesmaid • **George Lucas** is to release a director's cut of his 1971 sci-fi drama *THX-1138*.

JUNE 2004

Russian director **Timur Bekmambetov** is sued by Aeroflot over the scenes in his *Night Watch*, on grounds that the film implies that their planes are unsafe • **Nicole Kidman**'s new movie, *Birth,* comes under critical fire for a 'naked bath scene' she shares with ten-year old **Cameron Bright**. New Line Cinema studio boss **Mark Odesky** defends the movie, saying, 'It is meant to be a provocative film, but not in a horrible or salacious way.' The $50m feature – about a woman who believes the boy is a reincarnation of her late husband – has PR companies calling it a 'publicity nightmare' • *Fahrenheit 9/11* becomes the first documentary to top the US box office in its opening weekend, taking $21.8m (£11.9m) in its first three days • **Tom Hanks** won't direct another film because it's too much like hard work. Hanks says, 'I just don't have the

inner drive to direct. It means working under enormous pressure for 24 months without a break. I enjoyed that on a small scale, but I wouldn't want to repeat it. I consider myself an actor first, and a producer second' • **Frank Oz** admits to having filmed a new ending to his remake of *The Stepford Wives.* 'It wasn't that [test audiences] didn't like it. It wasn't satisfying' • After being loudly dropped by Disney, *Fahrenheit 9/11* finally gets a US distributor though a partnership between Lions Gate Films, IFC Films and the Fellowship Adventure Group, the latter formed by **Harvey** and **Bob Weinstein** specifically to market **Michael Moore**'s film. Disney chiefs reportedly banned their subsidiary Miramax from distributing it in North America, on grounds that distributing it was against company interests because it would alienate people of certain political beliefs.

Movie Quotations of the Year

Richard, leafing through his newspaper over breakfast: 'You're nude in *The Telegraph*, dear. Can you pass the bacon?' Graham Crowden to Annette Crosbie in *Calendar Girls*

Sheldon (a seahorse): 'I'm H2O intolerant.' Erik Per Sullivan on the soundtrack of *Finding Nemo*

Miranda Grey: 'I'm not deluded … I'm possessed.' Halle Berry in *Gothika*

An alarmed Jerry Peyser, surveying his exotic dinner: 'My food is still eating!' Albert Brooks in *The In-Laws*

Captain Nathan Algren to Colonel Bagley: 'I'll kill anyone you want for 500 dollars a month. But keep one thing in mind: I'll kill you for free.' Tom Cruise to Tony Goldwyn in *The Last Samurai*

Karen, to Cady: 'If you're from Africa, why are you white?' Gretchen: 'Oh my God, Karen, you can't ask people why they're white!' Amanda Seyfried and Lacey Chabert in *Mean Girls*

Cady, befuddled while in the presence of the hunky Aaron Samuels: 'Grool! I mean, well, I was gonna say cool but then I said great.' Lindsay Lohan in *Mean Girls*

Cady, to Karen: 'Well, there must be something you're good at.' Karen: 'Well, there is this one thing, it's like I have a fifth sense. It's like I have ESPN or something? My breasts can always tell when it's raining.' Amanda

Above: Lindsay Lohan cuts a mean figure in the piquant *Mean Girls*

Seyfried and Lindsay Lohan in *Mean Girls*

Precocious art student Betty Warren: 'Art isn't art until someone says it is.' Kirsten Dunst in *Mona Lisa Smile*

A young Fitz, in snowy Tullybridge, Scotland: 'At Christmas, if you didn't wake up with an erection, chances are you wouldn't have anything to play with.' Jamie Sives on the soundtrack of *One Last Chance*

Womaniser Roger Swanson, expounding on the joys of peeking at the fairer sex: 'Free yourself from the tyranny of eye-level.' Campbell Scott in *Roger Dodger*

Above: Rock star Jack Black teaches the fundamentals

Rock enthusiast Dewey Finn, appalled by the idea that he should sell anything to pay his rent: 'Would Picasso sell one of his guitars?' Jack Black in *School of Rock*

Dewey Finn (raising his first three fingers): 'Read between the lines.' Jack Black in *School of Rock*

Dewey Finn: 'Those that can't do, teach. And those that can't teach, teach ... gym.' Jack Black in *School of Rock* [stealing directly from *Annie Hall*]

Harry Sanborn, in bed with Erica Barry: 'What about birth control?' Erica (who's in her mid-to-late fifties): 'Menopause.' Harry: 'So, who's a lucky boy?!' Jack Nicholson and Diane Keaton in *Something's Gotta Give*

Walt, doing crossword: 'What is a four-letter word for 'snatch'?' Bob: 'Grab.' Walt, furiously crossing out his previous answer: 'Whoops.' Greg Kinnear and Matt Damon in *Stuck On You*

April: 'Can I ask you a personal question?' Walt: 'Nine inches.' Eva Mendes and Greg Kinnear in *Stuck On You*

Cher, apologising for her behaviour: 'I was a total bitch with

a capital C.' Cher in *Stuck On You*
Sylvia Plath, looking to her
mother for approval of her new
husband: 'I love him.' Aurelia
Plath: 'Then I like him.' Gwyneth
Paltrow and Blythe Danner
in *Sylvia*

An apologetic Ted Hughes,
sensing his wife's disapproving
mood: 'I'm sorry.' Sylvia: 'What
for?' Ted: 'I don't know yet.'
Daniel Craig and Gwyneth
Paltrow in *Sylvia*

Sylvia, apologising to her new
neighbour for disturbing him
in the middle of the night:
'You must think I'm some
stupid American bitch.' Professor
Thomas, conciliatorily: 'Oh, not
at all. I assumed you were
Canadian.' Gwyneth Paltrow
and Michael Gambon in *Sylvia*

Terminator-850, to male
stripper: 'Take off your clothes.'
Male Stripper: 'Patience, honey!'
Arnold Schwarzenegger and
Jimmy Snyder in *Terminator 3:
Rise of the Machines*

Terminator-850: 'Anger is more
useful than despair.' Arnold
Schwarzenegger in *Terminator 3:
The Rise of the Machines*

SWAT team leader to a coffin-
carrying Terminator-850: 'Put
down your weapons … and the
coffin.' Matt Gerald to Arnold
Schwarzenegger in *Terminator 3:
Rise of the Machines*

Terminator-850: 'I'm back!'
Arnold Schwarzenegger in

Terminator 3: Rise of the Machines
Jenna Rink, 13: 'I don't want to
be original, Matt. I want to be
cool.' Christa B. Allen in *13
Going on 30*

Jenna's mother, glancing through
the pages of *Poise* magazine: 'Oh,
those aren't people, Honey,
they're models.' Kathy Baker in
13 Going on 30

Jenna Rink, closing her eyes and
wishing: 'I want to be thirty, flirty
and thriving!' Jennifer Garner
in *13 Going on 30*

Jenna Rink, tapping into her
teenage soul: 'We need to
remember what used to be
good.' Jennifer Garner in *13
Going on 30*

Agamemnon on Achilles:
'Of all the war lords loved by
the gods, I hate him the most.'
Brian Cox in *Troy*

Nestor on Achilles:
'That man was born to end
lives.' John Shrapnel in *Troy*

Achilles: 'Everything's more
beautiful *because* we're doomed.'
Brad Pitt in *Troy*

Marcello (applying his best
English), to Frances: 'I am
going to make love all over
your body.' Raoul Bova to
Diane Lane in *Under the
Tuscan Sun*

Professor G.H. Dorr to
Mrs Munson: 'You, madam, are
addressing a man, who is in fact
quiet… and yet, not quiet, if I may
offer to you a riddle.' Tom
Hanks in *The Ladykillers*

Mrs Munson: 'There are two
kinds of folks. Them that have
got the piles and them who are
going to get them.' Irma P. Hall
in *The Ladykillers*

Below:
Tom Hanks
massages the
English language
with Irma P.
Hall in *The
Ladykillers*

Soundtracks

by James Cameron-Wilson

Let's face it, this was not a good year for film music. While the likes of *Spider-Man 2* and *Shrek 2* crowded the soundtrack charts, there was a genuine lack of resonant, original scores. The best film albums seemed to be compilations of earlier times – notably provided by the Primetime label – which merely confirmed the creative drought. One only had to see a film like the IMAX release *Young Black Stallion* – composed by William Ross – to see how indebted contemporary composers are to past glories (in this case, Ross's homage to Maurice Jarre's music for *Lawrence of Arabia*).

This musical deficit was reflected in the Oscars, when the prize for best score went to *The Lord of the Rings: Return of the King* by Howard Shore, who had already won the damn thing for *The Lord of the Rings: The Fellowship of the Ring*. The only extraordinary detail was that John Williams wasn't nominated this year, having secured his 42nd nomination for *Catch Me If You Can* in 2003.

While the re-birth of the musical readied itself in the wings (watch this space), the charts were packed with reissues, such as *The Good, The Bad and The Ugly*, *Saturday Night Fever* and *Top Gun*. There was one musical, *Camp*, which was glorious (see below), albeit largely composed of familiar show tunes, and ditto the soundtrack of *De-Lovely*, which brought the immortal songs of Cole Porter to the screen via the larynges of Kevin Kline, Robbie Williams, Alanis Morissette, Elvis Costello, Sheryl Crow, Diana Krall, et al.

The real saviour of the 2003-

A scene from *Young Black Stallion*, whose music pays homage to Maurice Jarre's *Lawrence of Arabia*

2004 period was not a composer *per se*, but the record producer T-Bone Burnett who, following the success of *O Brother, Where Art Thou?* (still selling well in the summer of 2004), gave us a wonderful flavour of

traditional blues and gospel in, respectively, *Cold Mountain* and *The Ladykillers*. These were soundtracks to cherish and yet another reminder of how thin on the ground exceptional contemporary film music is.

Barbra Streisand's Movie Album
Barbra Streisand can bring magic to a ring tone and the eclectic bunch of movie themes here (running the gamut from *Road to Rio* to *Bagdad Café*) are given a pedestal they may not even deserve. Even so, this is a sumptuous self indulgence, consummately produced and nectar to the ear.

Camp
With more charm and humanity in its little toe than all of *Chicago*, this little musical has a soundtrack to be proud of. A combination of show-stopping Broadway tunes, inspirational gospel, soft rock and two brand-new numbers from Michael Gore and Lynn Ahrens, the album is distinguished by some astonishing singing from its little-known cast. A treasure.

Cold Mountain
Haunting collection of blues excavated from the very fabric of the Deep South, with The White Stripes' Jack White singing five of the fourteen vocal tracks. There's also Alison Krauss contributing her evocative voice to the Gaelic-seasoned 'You Will Be My Ain True Love' (penned by Sting and T-Bone Burnett) and Elvis Costello's sweet and melancholy 'The Scarlet Tide'. The best stuff,

though, are the traditional songs, along with a sparse, poignant score by Gabriel Yared. The legendary T-Bone Burnett produced.

Deep Blue
An impressive symphony of watery torrents, this lacks the magical touch John Barry might have brought it, but is nonetheless an impressive work. George Fenton supplies the chords to what is 90 minutes of pure imagery, a task to which he doesn't entirely rise to. This was a magnificent opportunity for Fenton to produce a work of genuine stature, but much of it just sounds like film music. B-plus.

Eternal Sunshine of the Spotless Mind
A magical mystery tour of beguiling melodies and uplifting songs, this is a joyous indulgence. With the anarchic sound of the garage punk trio The Willowz (on 'Something') pitted against the poetic musings of Beck (on 'Everybody's Gotta Learn Something') – via the sanguine exultation of The Polyphonic Spree – this all fits a great, idiosyncratic movie like a glove. Terrific score by Jon Brion, too.

Freaky Friday
As these compilations go, Mark Waters' slick production well rocks, with wit, vigour and an appealing *joie de vivre*. Lindsay Lohan herself blasts off the proceedings and is followed onto the stage by American Hi-Fi, Bowling for Soup, The Donnas, Ashlee Simpson and a fresh, dynamic crowd. Great covers include Simple Plan's 'Happy Together' and Joey Ramone's 'What a Wonderful World'.

Harry Potter and the Prisoner of Azkaban
This ain't up there with *Jaws* or *Schindler's List*, but this is the best thing John Williams, now 72, has written in a while. At times he reverts to old formulas, but *Azkaban* is for the most part a pleasantly breezy and diverse concoction that touches a number of bases with some skill.

The Haunted Mansion
Terrible film, terrific album – although the latter has little to do with the former. This is a collection of upbeat, spooky rhythms posing as the soundtrack to the Eddie Murphy hit. It's more of a *homage*, though, and is top-loaded with covers unheard in the movie, from Morris Day's sprightly version of Rockwell's

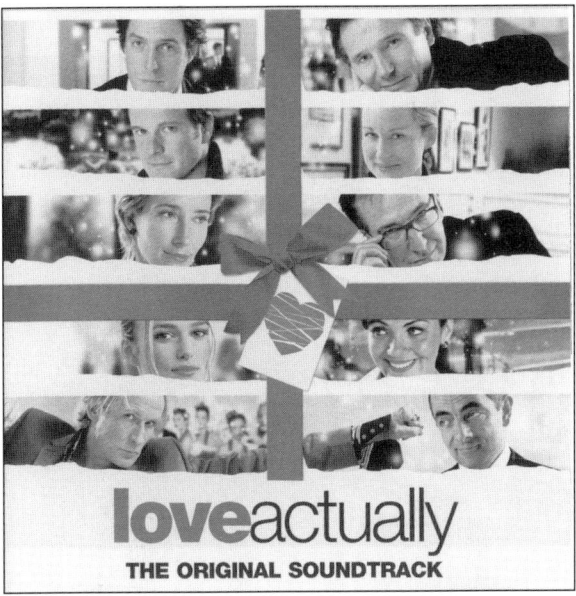

'Somebody's Watching Me' to Brian O'Neal & the Bus Boys' loopy take on The Crypt-Kickers' 'Monster Mash.' Shame there's no 'Ghost Town' or 'Thriller', though.

Hero
The credentials of Tan Dun's follow-up to *Crouching Tiger, Hidden Dragon* are impressive indeed. The Oscar-winning Chinaman has secured the Japanese drumming outfit KODO, the China Philharmonic Orchestra and Chorus and Itzhak Perlman on violin. There is some wonderful stuff here, but the whole fails to capture the sweeping mood and variety of *Crouching Tiger*, its reliance on TD and Perlman's mournful fiddling getting a tad irritating after a while.

Holes
A surprisingly engaging compilation running the gamut from folk and reggae to blues, honky-tonk and funk, this scored higher in the soundtrack charts than the movie did at the box-office. There's plenty of great stuff here, including Shaggy's upbeat hymn to optimism, 'Keep'n It Real', and first-rate tracks from Moby, Keb' Mo', Eagle-Eye Cherry, Eels and the incomparable Dr John.

Kill Bill Vol. 1
As eclectic and episodic as the movie, this is an addictive mix tape of old favourites and wacky numbers you can't stop playing. Sitting cheek-by-jowl is Luis Bacalov's moody theme to *The Grand Duel* and the 5.6.7.8's anarchic 'Woo Hoo'. Quentin Tarantino obviously had fun compiling this and his passion for musical goulash is infectious.

King Arthur
Hans Zimmer is not a composer to disappoint and he certainly supplies some musical muscle for this MTV take of the Camelot tale. There is still a hovering note of familiarity, though, as the army of drums and bellowing brass are brought into the fray, while Clannad's Moya Brennan supplies a traditional note of Celtic class with her vocal. Still, as all the musical cues are blended into six solid suites, the soundtrack is to be praised for its symphonic integrity.

The Ladykillers
This is possibly the year's most divine album, another triumph from producer T-Bone Burnett. An uplifting collection of glorious, pure gospel, this may not exactly reflect the film (other than the music favoured by the

devout Marva Munson), but is as Southern as a dish of corn and black-eyed peas. It's a shame, then, that the 'hippity-hop' anthems of Nappy Roots (preferred by Marlon Wayans' Gawain) clashes so rudely with the celestial voices of Bill Landford and the Landfordaires, The Soul Stirrers and Donnie McClurkin.

The Last Samurai
Another elegiac and epic soundtrack from Hans Zimmer. While not quite in the same league as the gut-flipping sound of *Gladiator* or *Black Hawk Down*, *The Last Samurai* has a sweeping cadence that builds and enraptures in waves of symphonic finesse.

Love Actually
The usual Richard Curtis affair, this (minus the welcome dialogue), with a string of popular classics from a wide range of Woolworth's-friendly personae. Here, we have Dido, Nora Jones, Eva Cassidy, The Calling, Texas, Joni Mitchell, The Beach Boys, Gabrielle, and others. Now That's What I Call a Compilation.

Master and Commander: The Far Side of the World
Like the sublime score for Billy

Bob Thornton's *All the Pretty Horses*, this stirring composition is the collaborative effort of three musicians, namely Iva Davies, Christopher Gordon and Richard Tognetti. Of course, the advantage of hiring three composers is that you get a much more diverse sound, with the artistic input drawn from a wider creative base. Mixed in with some choice snatches of Mozart, Bach and Vaughan Williams, the score is a sweeping, distinctive swell of harmonies, nourished by a wide range of instrumentation, in particular some effective percussion and flute work. Masterful.

The Missing

James Horner's music here is to be applauded on two counts. One, it really does enhance the action of the film and two, it brings a textural edge and cultural resonance to the milieu. It doesn't entirely work as a piece in its own right, but it certainly conjures up the flavour of the film – complete with Apache chants – racing through your loud speakers.

Pieces of April

Regardless of whether or not you have seen this charming, witty film, you should own its blithe, utterly beguiling soundtrack. While the songs are primarily credited to The Magnetic Fields, with two tracks performed by The 6ths, the whole thing is the creation of Stephen Merritt. Such is Merritt's prodigious productivity, he has to write, produce and perform under the umbrella of four different bands (the other two being Future Bible Heroes and The Gothic Archies). Exuding heart-catching melodies, choux pastry arrangements and idiosyncratic lyrics ('The day is beautiful and so are you/My car is ugly but then I'm ugly too') this collection is an addictive delectation.

Reel Chill

This double CD is by no means a must for dedicated cineastes but is a good starter for budding film buffs. Crammed with all the old chestnuts familiar from countless film theme compilations (*Chariots of Fire*, *Bilitis*, *The Mission*, *The Deer Hunter*, *The Piano*) it presents a few surprises, too. Patrick Cassidy's demulcent 'Vide Cor Meum' (sung by Charlotte Kinder and Wills Morgan) from *Hannibal* is an unlikely candidate for aural solace, as are tracks from *Somewhere in Time* (by John Barry), *A.I. Artificial Intelligence* and *Gladiator*. It's also exceptionally well produced, primarily performed by the dependable City of Prague Philharmonic Orchestra. Above all, though, *Reel Chill* achieves its aim: to chill out the listener at the end of a stressful day at the office.

School of Rock

This is one ass-kicking homage to rock 'n' roll, a roll call of the great and noisy (The Who, The Ramones, The Doors, Cream, T.Rex, Stevie Nicks), as well as a showcase for such new boys as The Darkness and The Black Keys. Jack Black himself (of Tenacious D) bookends the album and supplies some choice snatches of dialogue. The actor even sent a videoed plea to Led Zeppelin to convince the legends to contribute their classic 'Immigrant Song'. Way excellent.

Seabiscuit

A vibrant, colourful and varied score, *Seabiscuit* captures the mood of the first decade of the twentieth century with consummate skill. Drawing on his adept knowledge of traditional instruments (the fiddle and use of the guitar, earlier exemplified on the soundtracks of *The Natural* and *Ragtime*), Randy Newman provides an emotive tapestry of melodies of varying hues. A rich, accomplished work.

Veronica Guerin

This is as evocative and accomplished an album as any soundtrack this year, neatly juxtaposing its romantic and dramatic elements with a seductive vigour. Harry Gregson-Williams captures the Irish flavour of the film with a swell of traditional Celtic instruments balanced against the more conventional sounds of piano and violin. There's also a haunting song called 'Fields of Athenry' sung a cappella by Brian O'Donnell, a ten-year-old busker discovered by the composer on his first visit to Dublin.

Wonderland

A stellar, muscular collection of old standards clad this atmospheric if familiar trawl through the underbelly of LA life. The surprise is that well-known tracks – performed by the likes of Bad Company, The Cars, Duran Duran, Roxy Music, Bob Dylan, Billy Joel, Ted Nugent and Patti Smith – actually sound fresh and even salacious in a new context. There's also a tremendously bitter cover of Neil Diamond's 'Love On the Rocks' from Jonathan Davis. Great stuff.

Awards and Festivals

Director Peter Jackson inspects his gold

The 76th American Academy of Motion Picture Arts and Sciences Awards ('The Oscars') and Nominations for 2003, Kodak Theatre, Hollywood & Highland, Los Angeles, 29 February 2004

• **Best Film**: *The Lord of the Rings: The Return of the King*. Nominations: *Lost in Translation, Master and Commander: The Far Side of the World, Mystic River, Seabiscuit*.

• **Best Director**: Peter Jackson, for *The Lord of the Rings: The Return of the King* Nominations: Fernando Meirelles, for *City of God*, Sofia Coppola, for *Lost in Translation*, Peter Weir, for *Master and Commander: The Far Side of the World*, Clint Eastwood, for *Mystic River*.

• **Best Actor**: Sean Penn, for *Mystic River*. Nominations: Jude Law, for *Cold Mountain*, Ben Kingsley, for *House of Sand and Fog*, Bill Murray, for *Lost in Translation*, Johnny Depp, for *Pirates of the Caribbean: The Curse of the Black Pearl*.

• **Best Actress**: Charlize Theron, for

Monster. Nominations: Naomi Watts, for *21 Grams*, Samantha Morton, for *In America*, Diane Keaton, for *Something's Gotta Give*, Keisha Castle-Hughes, for *Whale Rider*.

• **Best Supporting Actor**: Tim Robbins for *Mystic River*. Nominations: Benicio Del Toro, for *21 Grams*, Alec Baldwin, for *The Cooler*, Djimon Hounsou, for *In America*, Ken Watanabe, for *The Last Samurai*.

• **Best Supporting Actress**: Renée Zellweger, for *Cold Mountain*. Nominations: Shohreh Aghdashloo, for *House of Sand and Fog*, Marcia Gay Harden, for *Mystic River*, Patricia Clarkson, for *Pieces of April*, Holly Hunter for *Thirteen*.

• **Best Animated Feature**: *Finding Nemo*. Nominations: *Brother Bear, Belleville Rendezvous (The Triplets of Belleville)*.

• **Best Original Screenplay**: Sofia Coppola, for *Lost in Translation*. Nominations: Denys Arcand, for *The Barbarian Invasions*, Steven Knight, for *Dirty Pretty Things*, Andrew Stanton, Bob Peterson, David Reynolds and Andrew Stanton, for *Finding Nemo*,

Jim Sheridan, Naomi Sheridan and Kirsten Sheridan for *In America*.

• **Best Adapted Screenplay**: Fran Walsh, Philippa Boyens and Peter Jackson for *The Lord of the Rings: The Return of the King*. Nominations: Robert Pulcini and Shari Springer Berman for *American Splendor*, Braulio Mantovani for *City of God*, Brian Helgeland for *Mystic River*, Gary Ross for *Seabiscuit*.

• **Best Cinematography**: Russell Boyd, for *Master and Commander: The Far Side of the World*. Nominations: Cesar Charlone for *City of God*, John Seale for *Cold Mountain*, Eduardo Serra for *Girl with a Pearl Earring*, John Schwartzman for *Seabiscuit*.

• **Best Editing**: Jamie Selkirk, for *The Lord of the Rings: The Return of the King*. Nominations: Daniel Rezende, for *City of God*, Walter Murch, for *Cold Mountain*, Lee Smith, for *Master and Commander: The Far Side of the World*, William Goldenberg, for *Seabiscuit*.

• **Best Original Score**: Howard Shore, for *The Lord of the Rings: The Return of the King*. Nominations: Danny Elfman, for *Big*

Left: Tom Cruise models his garb in *The Last Samurai,* nominated for an Oscar for Best Costume Design

Right: Paul Bettany and Russell Crowe toast their Oscar-winning *Master and Commander* (which won for Best Cinematography and Sound Editing)

Fish, Gabriel Yared, for *Cold Mountain*, Thomas Newman, for *Finding Nemo*, James Horner, for *House of Sand and Fog*.
• **Best Original Song**: 'Into the West' by Fran Walsh (music and lyrics), Howard Shore (music and lyrics) and Annie Lennox (music and lyrics), from *The Lord of the Rings: The Return of the King*. Nominations: 'You Will Be My Ain True Love' by Sting, from *Cold Mountain;* 'Scarlet Tide' by T-Bone Burnett and Elvis Costello, from *Cold Mountain*; 'A Kiss at the End of the Rainbow' by Michael McKean and Annette O'Toole, from *A Mighty Wind*; 'Belleville Rendezvous' by Benoit Charest and Sylvain Chomet, from *Belleville Rendezvous*.
• **Best Art Direction**: Grant Major, Dan Hennah and *Alan Lee for The Lord of the Rings: The Return of the King*. Nominations: Ben Van Os and Cecile Heideman, for *Girl with a Pearl Earring*, Lilly Kilvert and Gretchen Rau, for *The Last Samurai*, William Sandell and Robert Gould, for *Master and Commander: The Far Side of the World*, Jeannine Oppewall and Leslie Pope for *Seabiscuit*.
• **Best Costume Design**: Ngila Dickson and Richard Taylor for *The Lord of the*

Rings: The Return of the King. Nominations: Dien van Straalen, for *Girl with a Pearl Earring*, Ngila Dickson, for *The Last Samurai*, Wendy Stites, for *Master and Commander: The Far Side of the World*, Judianna Makovsky for *Seabiscuit*.
• **Best Sound**: Christopher Boyes, Michael Semanick, Michael Hedges and Hammond Peek for *The Lord of the Rings: The Return of the King*. Nominations: Andy Nelson, Anna Behlmer and Jeff Wexler, for *The Last Samurai*, Paul Massey, D.M. Hemphill and Arthur Rochester for *Master and Commander: The Far Side of the World,* Christopher Boyes, David Parker, David Campbell and Lee Orloff, for *Pirates of the Caribbean: The Curse of the Black Pearl*, Andy Nelson, Anna Behlmer and Tod A. Maitland for *Seabiscuit*.
• **Best Sound Effects Editing**: Richard King, for *Master and Commander: The Far Side of the World*. Nominations: Gary Rydstrom and Michael Silvers, for *Finding Nemo*, Christopher Boyes and George Watters II, for *Pirates of the Caribbean: The Curse of the Black Pearl*.
• **Best Makeup**: Richard Taylor and Peter King, for *The Lord of the Rings: The Return*

of the King. Nominations: Edouard Henriques III and Yolanda Toussieng, for *Master and Commander: The Far Side of the World*, Ve Neill and Martin Samuel, for *Pirates of the Caribbean: The Curse of the Black Pearl*.
• **Best Visual Effects**: Jim Rygiel, Joe Letteri, Randall William Cook and Alex Funke, for *The Lord of the Rings: The Return of the King*. Nominations: Dan Sudick, Stefan Fangmeier, Nathan McGuinness and Robert Stromberg, for *Master and Commander: The Far Side of the World*, John Knoll, Hal Hickel, Charles Gibson and Terry Frazee, for *Pirates of the Caribbean: The Curse of the Black Pearl*.
• **Best Animated Short Film**: *Harvie Krumpet*, by Adam Elliot. Nominations: *Boundin'*, by Bud Luckey; *Destino*, by Dominique Monfery and Roy Edward Disney; *Gone Nutty*, by Carlos Saldanha and John C. Donkin; *Nibbles*, by Chris Hinton.
• **Best Live Action Short Film**: *Two Soldiers*, by Aaron Schneider and Andrew J. Sacks. Nominations: *Torzija [Torsion]*, by Stefan Arsenijevic; *Die Rote Jacket [The Red Jacket]*, by Florian Baxmeyer; *Most [The Bridge]*, by Bobby Garabedian and William Zabka; *Squash,* by Lionel Bailliu.
• **Best Documentary Feature**: *The Fog of War,* by Errol Morris and Michael Williams. Nominations: *Balseros,* by Carlos Bosch and Josep Maria Domenech; *Capturing the Friedmans,* by Andrew Jarecki and Marc Smerling; *My Architect,* by Nathaniel Kahn and Susan R. Behr; *The Weather Underground,* by Sam Green and Bill Siegel.
• **Best Documentary Short**: *Chernobyl Heart,* by Maryann DeLeo. Nominations: *Asylum,* by Sandy McLeod and Gini Reticker; *Ferry Tales*, by Katja Esson.
• **Best Foreign Language Film**: *The Barbarian Invasions* (Canada*).* Nominations: *Evil* (Sweden), *The Twilight Samurai* (Japan), *Twin Sisters* (Netherlands/Luxembourg), *Zelary* (Czech Republic/Slovakia/Austria).
• **Honorary Award**: Blake Edwards

The 45th Australian Film Institute Awards: 21 November 2003

• **Best Film:** *Japanese Story*
• **Best Actor:**
David Wenham, for *Gettin' Square*
• **Best Actress:**
Toni Collette, for *Japanese Story*
• **Best Supporting Actor:**
David Ngoombujarra, for *Black and White*
• **Best Supporting Actress:**
Sacha Horler, for *Travelling Light*
• **Best Director:**
Sue Brooks, for *Japanese Story*
• **Best Original Screenplay:**
Alison Tilson, for *Japanese Story*
• **Best Screenplay Adaptation:**
Tony McNamara, for *The Rage In Placid Lake*
• **Best Cinematography:**
Ian Baker, for *Japanese Story*
• **Best Editing:**
Jill Bilcock, for *Japanese Story*
• **Best Music:**
Elizabeth Drake, for *Japanese Story*
• **Best Costumes:**
Anna Borghesi, for *Ned Kelly*
• **Best Foreign Film:** *The Lord of the Rings: The Return of the King*

• **Best Documentary:**
Michael McMahon, for *Wildness*
• **Best Direction in a Documentary:** Sascha Ettinger-Epstein, for *Painting with Light in a Dark World*
• **Best Short Fiction Film:**
Glendyn Ivin, for *Cracker Bag*
• **Best Screenplay in a Short Fiction Film:**
Glendyn Ivin, for *Cracker Bag*
• **Best Cinematography in a Non-Feature Film:** Anthony Jennings, for *The Projectionist*
• **Best Editing in a Non-Feature Film:**
Roland Gallois and Andrew Arestides, for *Painting with Light in a Dark World*
• **Best Short Animation:** Adam Elliot, for *Harvie Krumpet*
• **Global Achievement Award:**
Geoffrey Rush

The 54th Berlin International Film Festival: 14 February 2004

• **Golden Bear for Best Film:**
Gegen die Wand
• **Silver Bear, Grand Jury Prize:**
El Abrazo partido
• **Silver Bear, Best Director:**
Ki-duk Kim, for *Samaria*

• **Silver Bear, Best Actor:**
Daniel Hendler, for *El Abrazo partido*
• **Silver Bear, Best Actress:** Catalina Sandino Moreno, for *María, llena eres de gracia*; Charlize Theron for *Monster*
• **Silver Bear for Individual Artistic Contribution:** To the ensemble cast of *Om jag vänder mig om*
• **Silver Berlin Bear (Honorable Mention):** Christoph Behl for *Public/Private*
• **Honorary Golden Berlin Bear:**
Fernando E. Solanas
• **Blue Angel Prize:** Björn Runge for *Om jag vänder mig om*
• **Alfred Bauer Prize:** Joshua Marston for *María, llena eres de gracia*
• **Wolfgang Staudt Award:**
Rakesh Sharma for *Final Solution*
• **Golden Bear for Best Short Film:**
Un cartus de kent si un pachet de cafea
• **Silver Bear for Best Short Film:** *Vet!*
• **Silver Bear for Best Film Music:**
Banda Osiris for *Primo amore*
• **Ecumenical Jury Prize:**
Ken Loach, for *Ae Fond Kiss...*
• **Panorama:** Francesca Comencini, for *Mi piace lavorare - Mobbing*
• **Forum:** Dominique Cabrera, for *Folle embellie*

- **Special Prize**: Vinko Bresan, for *Svjedoci*
- **FIPRESCI Prizes**:
- **Best Film**:
Fatih Akin, for *Gegen die Wand*
- **Panorama**: Robert Lepage,
for *La Face cachée de la lune*
- **International Forum**:
Jennifer Todd Reeves, for *The Time We Killed*
- **CICAE** (international confederation of
art cinemas):
- **Panorama**:
Marcos Bernstein for *O Outro Lado da Rua*
- **Forum**: Gonzalo Justiniano for *B-Happy*
- **UIP Berlin Award (European Short
Film)**: Cristi Puiu, for *Un cartus de kent
si un pachet de cafea*
- **German Arthouse Cinemas Guild**:
Ken Loach for *Ae Fond Kiss...*
- **Gay Teddy Bear Award, Best Feature**:
Sébastien Lifshitz, for *Wild Side*
- **Gay Teddy Bear Award, Best Documentary**:
Andrew Horn for *The Nomi Song*
- **Peace Film Prize**:
Vinko Bresan, for *Svjedoci*
- **Panorama Audience Award**:
Andres Veiel, for *Die Spielwütigen*
- **Panorama Audience Award for Short Film**:
Johan Brisinger for *En del av mitt hjärta*
- **Piper Heidsieck New Talent Awards**:
- **Glass Bear for Best Feature Film**:
Maryo J. De los Reyes, for *Magnifico*
- **Glass Bear for Best Short Film**:
Michèle Lemieux, for *Nuit d'orage*
- **Glass Bear, Special Mention Short Film**:
Circuit marine; Marée
- **Glass Bear, Special Mention Feature Film**:
Bernd Sahling for *Die Blindgänger;* Jacques-
Remy Girerd for *La Prophétie des grenouilles*

*Jury: Frances McDormand (president),
Maji-da Abdi, Valeria Bruni Tedeschi,
Samira Makhmalbaf, Peter Rommel,
Gabriele Salvatores, Dan Talbot,
Christine Dollhofer, Sophie Maintigneux,
Vinca Wiedemann*

The 2003 British Academy of Film and Television Arts Awards ('BAFTAs'), Odeon, Leicester Square, 15 February 2004

- **Best Film**: *The Lord of the Rings:
The Return of the King*
- **David Lean Award for Direction**:
Peter Weir, for *Master and Commander:
The Far Side of the World*
- **Best Original Screenplay**:
Thomas McCarthy for *The Station Agent*
- **Best Adapted Screenplay**: Frances Walsh,
Philippa Boyens and Peter Jackson, for *The
Lord of the Rings: The Return of the King*
- **Best Actor**:
Bill Murray, for *Lost in Translation*
- **Best Actress**: Scarlett Johansson,
for *Lost in Translation*
- **Best Supporting Actor**:
Bill Nighy, for *Love Actually*
- **Best Supporting Actress**:
Renée Zellweger, for *Cold Mountain*
- **Best Cinematography**:
Andrew Lesnie, for *The Lord of the Rings:
The Return of the King*
- **Best Production Design**: William
Sandell, for *Master and Commander:
The Far Side of the World*
- **Best Editing**:
Sarah Flack, for *Lost in Translation*
- **Anthony Asquith Award for Film Music**:
Gabriel Yared and T-Bone Burnett,
for *Cold Mountain*
- **Best Costumes**: Wendy Stites, for *Master
and Commander: The Far Side of the World*
- **Best Sound**: Richard King, Doug
Hemphill, Paul Massey and Art Rochester,
for *Master and Commander: The Far Side
of the World*
- **Best Special Visual Effects**: Joe Letteri,
Jim Rygiel, Randall William Cook and
Alex Funke, for *The Lord of the Rings:
The Return of the King*
- **Best Make Up/Hair**: Ve Neill and Martin
Samuel, for *Pirates of the Caribbean: The
Curse of the Black Pearl*
- **Alexander Korda Award for Best British
Film**: *Touching the Void*, by John Smithson
and Kevin Macdonald
- **Best Foreign Language Film**:
In This World
- **Best Short Film**: *Brown Paper Bag*
- **Best Animated Short**: *Jojo in the Stars*
- **Carl Foreman Award for the Most**

Promising Newcomer: Emily Young
(writer-director), for *Kiss of Life*
- **Audience Award**:
The Lord of the Rings: The Return of the King
- **Michael Balcon Award**:
Working Title Films
- **BAFTA Fellowships**:
John Boorman; Roger Graef

The 24th Canadian Film Awards ('Genies'), Toronto, 1 May 2004

- **Best Film**: *Les Invasions Barbares
(The Barbarian Invasions)*
- **Best Director**: Denys Arcand, for *Les
Invasions Barbares (The Barbarian Invasions)*
- **Best Actor**: Rémy Girard, for *Les
Invasions Barbares (The Barbarian Invasions)*
- **Best Actress**:
Sarah Polley, for *My Life Without Me*
- **Best Supporting Actor**:
Stéphane Rousseau, for *Les Invasions
Barbares (The Barbarian Invasions)*
- **Best Supporting Actress**:
Marie-Josée Croze, for *Les Invasions
Barbares (The Barbarian Invasions)*
- **Best Original Screenplay**:
Denys Arcand, for *Les Invasions Barbares
(The Barbarian Invasions)*
- **Best Adapted Screenplay**:
Robert Lepage, for *La Face Cachée
De La Lune (The Far Side of the Moon)*
- **Best Cinematography**: Allen Smith,
for *La Grande Séduction (Seducing Doctor
Lewis)*
- **Best Editing**: David Wharnsby,
for *The Saddest Music In The World*
- **Best Art Direction**: Rob Gray and
Christina Kuhnigk, for *Falling Angels*
- **Best Music (Original Score)**:
Christopher Dedrick,
for *The Saddest Music In The World*
- **Best Music (Original Song)**:
Ken Whiteley , for 'Tell Me' from *Falling Angels*
- **Best Costumes**: Meg Mcmillan, for
The Saddest Music In The World
- **Best Sound Editing**: Michael O'Farrell,
Mark Gingras, Paul Intson, Goro Koyama,
John Laing, Andy Malcolm, Jill Purdy and
John Douglas Smith, for *The Statement*

Below: James Urbaniak as Robert Crumb in *American Splendor*, winner of the International Critics' Award at the Deauville Festival

• **Best Overall Sound:** D. Bruce Carwardine, Todd Beckett, Michael O' Farrell and Don White, for *The Statement*
• **Best Documentary:**
Fix: The Story of an Addicted City, by Betsy Carson and Nettie Wild
• **Best Live-Action Short:** *Noël Blank*, by Christiane Ciupka and Jean-François Rivard
• **Best Animated Short:** *Falling In Love Again*, by Marcy Page and Munro Ferguson

The 57th Cannes Film Festival Awards, 23 May 2004

• **Palme d'Or for Best Film:** *Fahrenheit 911 (Fahrenheit 9/11)*, by Michael Moore
• **Grand Prix du Jury:**
Old Boy, by Park Chan-Wook
• **Best Actor:** Yuuya Yagira, for *Daremo Shiranai (Nobody Knows)*
• **Best Actress:** Maggie Cheung, for *Clean*
• **Best Director:** Tony Gatlif for *Exiles*
• **Best Screenplay:** Agnès Jaoui and Jean-Pierre Bacri for *Comme Une Image (Look At Me)*
• **Palme d'Or for Best Short:**
Trafic, by Catalin Mitulescu
• **Technical Prize:**
Eric Gautier (Cinematography) for *The Motorcycle Diaries* and *Clean*
• **Prix du Jury:** Irma P. Hall, for *The Ladykillers*; Apichatpong Weerasethakul, for *Sud Pralad*
• **Camera d'Or** (for first feature): *Or*, by Keren Yedaya
• **Caméra d'Or** (special mention): *Lu Cheng*, by Yang Chao; *Bitter Dream (Khab É Talkh)*, by Mohsen Amiryoussefi
• **Awards Cinéfondation:**
• **First Prize:** *Happy Now* by Frederikke Aspöck
• **Second Prize:** *99 Vuotta Elämästäni* by Marja Mikkonen; *Calatorie La Oras* by Corneliu Porumboiu
• **Third Prize:**
Fajnie, Ze Jestes, by Jan Komasa
• **FIPRESCI International Critics' Award:** *Fahrenheit 911 (Fahrenheit 9/11)*, by Michael Moore
• **Une Certain Regard:**
Whisky by Juan Pablo Rebella; Pablo Stoll

• **Ecumenical Prize:**
• **Best Film:**
The Motorcycle Diaries by Walter Salles
• **30th Anniversary Prize:**
Ken Loach, for his body of work.
• **Critics' Week:** *Atash* by Tawfik Abu Wael
• **Critics' Week Awards:**
• **Grand Prix:** *Brodeuses*, by Éléonore Faucher ; *Mon Trésor*, by Keren Yedaya

Jury: Quentin Tarantino (president); Emmanuelle Béart, Edwidge Danticat, Tilda Swinton, Kathleen Turner, Benoît Poelvoorde, Jerry Schatzberg, Hark Tsui, Peter von Bagh, Nikita Mikhalkov, Nicole Garcia, Marisa Paredes, Nuri Bilge Ceylan, Pablo Trapero

The 30th Deauville Festival of American Cinema, 14 September 2003

• **Grand Prix for Best Film:**
What Alice Found, by A. Dean Bell
• **Jury Prize:** *Thirteen*, by Catherine Hardwicke

• **International Critics Award:** *American Splendor*, by Shari Springer Berman and Robert Pulcini
• **Short Movie Grand Prix:**
What Are You Having?, by Benjamin Meyer
• **Premiere Award:** *Milwaukee, Minnesota*, by Allan Mindel
• *Journal du Dimanche* **Audience Award:**
Dot the I, by Matthew Parkhill

Jury: Roman Polanski (head of jury); Claudia Cardinale; Nastassja Kinski; Ludivine Sagnier; Ben Kingsley; Fernando Trueba; Tom Tykwer; Zbigniew Preisner; Pawel Edelman; Jacques Fieschi

The 17th European Film Awards ('the Felixes'), Arena, Berlin, 6 December 2003

• **Best Film:** *Good Bye, Lenin!*
• **Best Director:** Lars von Trier, for *Dogville*
• **Best Actor:** Daniel Brühl for *Good Bye, Lenin!*, Germany

• **Best Actress:**
Charlotte Rampling for *Swimming Pool*
• **Best Screenplay:**
Bernd Lichtenberg, for *Good Bye, Lenin!*
• **Best Cinematographer:** Anthony Dod
Mantle, for *28 Days Later*, and *Dogville*
• **Lifetime Achievement Award:**
Claude Chabrol
• **Best Achievement in World Cinema:**
Carlo di Palma
• **Discovery of the Year** (Fassbinder
Award): *Vozvraschenie* (*The Return*)
by Andrei Zvyagintsev
• **Special Mention for:**
Gori Vatra (Fuse) by Pjer Zalica
• **Critics Award, Prix Fipresci:**
Buongiorno, Notte (Goodmorning, Night)
by Marco Bellocchio
• **Documentary, Prix Arte:**
S21, *La Machine De Mort Khmere Rouge*
(*S21: The Khmer Rouge Killing Machine*)
by Rithy Panh
• **Short Film, Prix UIP:**
Torzija by Stefan Arsenijevic
• **Non-European Film, Prix Screen
International:** *Les Invasions Barbares* (*The
Barbarian Invasions*), by Denys Arcand
• **The Jameson People's Choice Awards:**
• **Best European Director:**
Wolfgang Becker for *Good Bye, Lenin!*
• **Best European Actor:**
Daniel Brühl in *Good Bye, Lenin!*
• **Best European Actress:**
Katrin Sass in *Good Bye, Lenin!*

**The Golden Raspberries ('The
Razzies'): Penthouse Suite of the
Four-Points, Sheraton Hotel,
Santa Monica, 28 February 2004**

• **Worst Picture:** *Gigli*
• **Worst Actor:** Ben Affleck, for *Daredevil*
• **Worst Actress:** Jennifer Lopez, for *Gigli*
• **Worst Supporting Actor:** Sylvester
Stallone, for *Spy Kids 3-D: Game Over*
• **Worst Supporting Actress:** Demi Moore,
for *Charlie's Angels: Full Throttle*
• **Worst Director:** Martin Brest, for *Gigli*
• **Worst Screenplay:** Martin Brest, for *Gigli*
• **Worst Remake or Sequel:**

Charlie's Angels: Full Throttle
• **Worst Screen Couple:**
Ben Affleck; Jennifer Lopez in *Gigli*
• **Worst Excuse for an Actual Movie
(All Concept/No Content!):**
The Cat in the Hat
• **Governor's Award:** Travis Payne,
for *From Justin to Kelly*, for distinguished
under-achievement in choreography.

**The 61st Hollywood Foreign Press
Association ('Golden Globes')
Awards, 25 January, 2004**

• **Best Motion Picture – Drama:**
The Lord of the Rings: The Return of the King
• **Best Motion Picture – Musical
or Comedy:** *Lost in Translation*
• **Best Director:** Peter Jackson, for *The Lord
of the Rings: The Return of the King*
• **Best Performance by an Actor in a
Motion Picture – Drama:** Sean Penn
for *Mystic River*
• **Best Performance by an Actress in a
Motion Picture – Drama:** Charlize Theron
for *Monster*
• **Best Performance by an Actor in a
Motion Picture – Comedy/Musical:**
Bill Murray for *Lost in Translation*
• **Best Performance by an Actress in a**

Motion Picture – Comedy/Musical:
Diane Keaton for *Something's Gotta Give*
• **Best Performance by an Actor in a
Supporting Role – Motion Picture:**
Tim Robbins for *Mystic River*
• **Best Performance by an Actress in a
Supporting Role – Motion Picture:**
Renée Zellweger for *Cold Mountain*
• **Best Foreign Language Film:** *Osama*
• **Best Screenplay:** Sofia Coppola for
Lost in Translation
• **Best Original Score:** Howard Shore
for *The Lord of the Rings: The Return
of the King*
• **Best Original Song:** 'Into the West',
by Howard Shore, Fran Walsh and Annie
Lennox, from *The Lord of the Rings:
The Return of the King*
• **Best Television Series – Drama:** *24*
• **Best Television Series – Musical or
Comedy:** *The Office*
• **Best Mini-Series or Motion Picture
made for Television:** *Angels in America*

**The 24th London Film Critics'
Circle Awards, The Dorchester,
London, 11 February 2004**

• **Best Film:** *Master and Commander:
The Far Side of the World*

Sofia Coppola with Bill Murray
on location for *Lost in Translation*

- **Best Actor**: Sean Penn, for *Mystic River*
- **Best Actress**: Julianne Moore, for *Far from Heaven*
- **Best Director**: Clint Eastwood, for *Mystic River*
- **Best Screenwriter**: Peter Weir, for *Master and Commander: The Far Side of the World*
- **Best British Film**: *The Magdalene Sisters*
- **Best British Director**: Peter Mullan, for *The Magdalene Sisters*
- **Best British Screenwriter**: David Hare, for *The Hours*
- **Best British Actor**: Paul Bettany, for *Master and Commander: The Far Side of the World*
- **Best British Actress**: Anne Reid, for *The Mother*
- **Best British Supporting Actor**: Bill Nighy, for *Love Actually*
- **Best British Supporting Actress**: Emma Thompson, for *Love Actually*
- **Best British Newcomer**: David Mackenzie, for *Young Adam*
- **Best Foreign Language Film**: *Good Bye, Lenin!* (Germany)
- **Dilys Powell Award**: Tom Courtenay
- **Life Achievement Award**: Ronald Neame

The Los Angeles Film Critics' Association Awards, Jan. 7, 2004

- **Best Picture**: *American Splendor*
- **Best Actor**: Bill Murray, for *Lost in Translation*
- **Best Actress**: Naomi Watts, for *21 Grams*
- **Best Supporting Actor**: Bill Nighy, for *I Capture the Castle, Lawless Heart*, and *Love Actually*
- **Best Supporting Actress**: Shohreh Aghdashloo, for *House of Sand and Fog*
- **Best Director**: Peter Jackson, for *The Lord of the Rings: The Return of the King*
- **Best Screenplay**: Shari Springer Berman and Robert Pulcini, for *American Splendor*
- **Best Foreign Film**: *The Man on the Train* (France)
- **Best Documentary**: *The Fog of War*
- **Best Cinematography**: Eduardo Serra, for *Girl with a Pearl Earring*
- **Best Music**: Benoit Charest and Mathieu

Chedid, for *Belleville Rendezvous*
- **Best Production Design**: Grant Major, for *The Lord of the Rings: The Return of the King*
- **New Generation Award**: Scarlett Johansson
- **Best Animation**: *The Triplets of Belleville*
- **Best Documentary**: *The Fog of War*
- **Career Achievement Award**: Robert Altman
- **Special Citation**: Disney restoration of the Walt Disney/Salvador Dali short *Destino*

12th MTV Movie Awards, 5 June 2004, Sony Pictures Studio, Culver City, California

- **Best Movie**: *The Lord of the Rings: The Return of the King*
- **Best Male Performance**: Johnny Depp, for *Pirates of the Caribbean: The Curse of the Black Pearl*
- **Best Female Performance**: Uma Thurman, for *Kill Bill, Vol. 1*
- **Best Comedic Performance**: Jack Black, for *School of Rock*
- **Best Onscreen Team**: Adam Sandler and Drew Barrymore, for *50 First Dates*
- **Best Breakthrough Male Performance**: Shawn Ashmore, for *X2: X-Men United*
- **Best Breakthrough Female Performance**: Lindsay Lohan, for *Freaky Friday*
- **Best Villain**: Lucy Liu, for *Kill Bill, Vol. 1*
- **Best Action Sequence**: Battle at Gondor, from *The Lord of the Rings: The Return of the King*
- **Best Fight**: Uma Thurman vs. Chiaki Kuriyama, from *Kill Bill, Vol. 1*
- **Best Kiss**: Owen Wilson, Carmen Electra and Amy Smart, from *Starsky & Hutch*
- **Best Dance Sequence**: Seann William Scott, from *American Wedding*

The 95th National Board of Review of Motion Picture Awards, Tavern on the Green, New York, New York, 3 December 2003

- **Best Film**: *Mystic River*

- **Best Actor**: Sean Penn, for *Mystic River* and *21 Grams*
- **Best Actress**: Diane Keaton, for *Something's Gotta Give*
- **Best Supporting Actor**: Alec Baldwin, for *The Cooler*
- **Best Supporting Actress**: Patricia Clarkson for *Pieces of April* and *The Station Agent*
- **Best Director**: Edward Zwick, for *The Last Samurai*
- **Best Screenplay**: *Cold Mountain* (Best Adapted) and *In America* (Best Original)
- **Best Ensemble Cast**: *The Lord of the Rings: The Return of the King*
- **Best Foreign Film**: *The Barbarian Invasions* (Canada)
- **Best Animated Feature**: *Finding Nemo*
- **Best Documentary**: *The Fog of War*
- **Breakthrough Performances**: Paul Giamatti, for *American Splendor* and Charlize Theron, for *Monster*
- **Best Directorial Debut**: Vadim Perelman, for *House of Sand and Fog*
- **Best Made-for-Cable Movie/Miniseries**: *Angels in America*
- **Special Filmmaking Achievement**: Sofia Coppola, for *Lost in Translation*
- **Career Achievement Awards**: Morgan Freeman (acting), Hans Zimmer (music composition), John Toll (cinematography)
- **Billy Wilder Award for Excellence in Directing**: Norman Jewison
- **William K. Everson Award for Film History**: Richard LaGravenese and Ted Demme, for *A Decade Under the Influence*
- **Producers Award**: Gale Anne Hurde, Kathleen Kennedy, Christine Vachon
- **Special Recognition of Films that Reflect the Freedom of Expression**: *Capturing the Friedmans, Dirty Pretty Things, The Magdalene Sisters*, and *September 11*
- **Special Mention for Excellence in Filmmaking**: *American Splendor, Bend It Like Beckham, The Cooler, Dirty Pretty Things, Girl with a Pearl Earring, Pieces of April, The Secret Lives of Dentists, Shattered Glass, The Statement, Thirteen* and *Whale Rider*

The 38th National Society of Film Critics' Awards, New York, 3 January 2004.

• Best Film: *American Splendor*
• Best Actor: Bill Murray, in *Lost in Translation*
• Best Actress: Charlize Theron, in *Monster*
• Best Director: Clint Eastwood, for *Mystic River*
• Best Supporting Actor: Peter Sarsgaard, in *Shattered Glass*
• Best Supporting Actress: Patricia Clarkson, for *Pieces of April* and *The Station Agent*
• Best Screenplay: Shari Springer Berman and Robert Pulcini, for *American Splendor*
• Best Cinematography: Russell Boyd, for *Master and Commander: The Far Side of the World*
• Best Foreign Film: *Mies vailla menneisyyttä* (*The Man Without a Past*), by Ari Kaurismaki (Finland)
• Best Non-Fiction Film: *To Be and To Have*, by Nicolas Philibert

The 69th New York Film Critics' Circle Awards, December 15, 2003

• Best Film: *The Lord of the Rings: The Return of the King*
• Best Actor: Bill Murray, for *Lost in Translation*
• Best Actress: Hope Davis, for *American Splendor* and *The Secret Lives of Dentists*
• Best Supporting Actor: Eugene Levy, for *A Mighty Wind*
• Best Supporting Actress: Shohreh Aghdashloo, for *House of Sand and Fog*
• Best Director: Sofia Coppola, for *Lost in Translation*
• Best Screenplay: Craig Lucas, for *The Secret Lives of Dentists*
• Best Cinematographer: Harris Savides, for *Elephant and Gerry*
• Best Foreign Film: *City of God*
• Best Nonfiction Film: *Capturing the Friedmans*
• Best Animated Film: *Belleville Rendezvous*

• Best First Feature: Shari Springer Berman and Robert Pulcini, for *American Splendor*

The 20th Sundance Film Festival, Park City, Utah, 25 January 2004.

• The Documentary Grand Jury Prize: *Dig!*
• The Dramatic Grand Jury Prize: *Primer*, directed, written, and produced by Shane Carruth.
• The Documentary Audience Award: *Born into Brothels*, by Ross Kauffman and Zana Briski
• The Dramatic Audience Award: *Maria Full of Grace*, by Joshua Marston and Paul Mezey
• The World Cinema Dramatic Audience Award: *Seducing Doctor Lewis*, directed by Jean-François; *Pouliot*, written by Ken Scott and produced by Roger Frappier and Luc Vandal
• The World Cinema Documentary Audience Award: *The Corporation*, directed by Mark Achbar and Jennifer Abbott, written by Harold Crooks, Joel Bakan, and Mark Achbar, and produced by Bart Simpson and Mark Achbar
• Documentary Directing Award: Morgan Spurlock, for *Super Size Me*
• Dramatic Directing Award: Debra Granik for *Down to the Bone*
• The Excellence in Cinematography Award: Ferne Pearlstein for *Imelda* (Documentary Competition); Nancy Schreiber for *November* (Dramatic Competition)
• The Freedom of Expression Award: *Repatriation*, directed by Kim Dong-won.
• Waldo Salt Screenwriting Award: Larry Gross for *We Don't Live Here Anymore*
• Documentary Jury Special Jury Prize: *Farmingville*, directed and produced by Catherine Tambini and Carlos Sandoval
• Dramatic Jury Special Jury Prizes: *Brother to Brother*, directed by Rodney Evans; Vera Farmiga, for her performance in *Down to the Bone*
• Jury Prize in Short Filmmaking:

When the Storm Came, directed by Shilpi Gupta; *Gowanus, Brooklyn*, directed by Ryan Fleck.
• Jury Prize in International Short Filmmaking: *Tomo*, directed by Paul Catling
• Shorts Jury Honorable Mentions: *Curtis*, directed by Jacob Akira Okada; *Harvie Krumpet*, directed by Adam Elliot; *Krumped*, directed by David LaChapelle; *Papillion d'Amour,* directed by Nicholas Provost; *Spokane*, directed by Larry Kennar
• Alfred P. Sloan Prize: *Primer*, directed by Shane Carruth
• Online Film Festival Jury Awards: *Bathtime in Clerkenwell*, directed by Alex Budovsky (Animation); *Wet Dreams False Images*, directed by Jesse Epstein (Short Subject); *The Dawn at my Back: Memoir of a Texas Upbringing*, directed by Carroll Parrott Blue and Kristy H.A. Kang (New Forms Gallery).
• Sundance/NHK International Filmmakers Award: Gyorgy Palfi, for *Taxidermia* (Europe); Andrucha Waddington, for *House of Sand* (Latin America); Miranda July, for *Me You and Everyone We Know* (United States); Kosuke Hosokaim, for *Tepid Love* (Japan)

Jury: Lisa Cholodenko; Frederick Elmes; Danny Glover; Maggie Gyllenhaal; Ted Hope; Rory Kennedy; Mary Ellen Mark; Robb Moss; Robert Shepard; Chris Smith

The 60th Venice International Film Festival Awards, 6 September 2003

• Golden Lion for Best Film: Andrei Zvyagintsev, for *Vozvrashcheniye*
• Special Jury Grand Prix: Randa Chahal Sabag for *Le Cerf-volant*
• Best Actor: Sean Penn for *21 Grams*
• Best Actress: Katja Riemann for *Rosenstrasse*
• Silver Lion for Outstanding Individual Achievement: Marco Bellocchio for screenwriting *Buongiorno, notte*
• Marcello Mastoianni Award for Emerging Actor: Najat Benssallem in *Raja*

- **FIPRESCI International Critics' Award:** *Bu san* by Ming-liang Tsai
- **Parallel Section:** *Matrubhoomi* by Manish Jha
- **Venezia Opera Prima (Luigi De Laurentiis Award for Best First Feature):** Andrei Zvyagintsev, for *Vozvrashcheniye*; Special Mention to *Ballo a tre passi*; *Poslednij poyezd*

- **San Marco Prize:** Hiner Saleem for *Vodka Lemon*
- **San Marco Special Jury Award:** Michael Schorr, for directing *Schultze Gets the Blues*
- **Career Golden Lion:** Dino De Laurentiis; Omar Sharif
- **Upstream Best Actor:** Tadanobu Asano, for *Ruang rak noi nid mahasan*
- **Upstream Best Actress:**

Scarlett Johansson, for *Lost in Translation*
- **Audience Award:** Zatôichi
- **Special Prize for Direction:** Takeshi Kitano for *Zatôichi*

Jury: Mario Monicelli (head of jury); Stefano Accorsi; Michael Ballhaus; Ann Hui; Pierre Jolivet; Monty Montgomery; Assumpta Serna

Tim Robbins in *Mystic River*, a performance that won him an Oscar and a Golden Globe

In Memoriam

SIR ALAN BATES

Born: 17 February 1934
in Derbyshire, England.
Died: 27 December 2003 in London,
of liver and pancreatic cancer.
Stage and film actor, who starred in a
string of successful films in the 1960s,
including *Zorba the Greek* (1964),
Georgy Girl (1966), *Far From the
Madding Crowd* (1967) and *Women
in Love* (1969). A highly accomplished
stage actor, Bates' big break in films was
playing opposite Laurence Olivier in
The Entertainer (1960). Bates' stature
and popularity grew, and he earned an
Oscar nomination for *The Fixer* (1968).
He later became a prolific character actor
for film and TV, earning a Tony the year
before his death. Other films include
The Running Man (1963), *The Rose*
(1979), *Gosford Park* (2001), *The Sum
of All Fears* (2002) and *The Statement*
(2003).

JONATHAN BRANDIS

Born: 13 April 1976
in Connecticut, USA.
Died: 12 November 2003
in Los Angeles, from suicide.
Former teen heartthrob and American
TV star Brandis' first starring film role

was in *The NeverEnding Story II: The
Next Chapter* . His other films include
The Year that Trembled (2002), *Hart's
War* (2002) and *Puerto Vallarta
Squeeze* (2003).

CHARLES BRONSON

Born: 3 November 1921
in Pennsylvania, USA.
Died: 30 August 2003 in Los Angeles,
of pneumonia.
Real name: Charles Dennis Buchinsky.
Known internationally for his vigilante

tough-guy persona in Michael Winner's
Death Wish movies (1974 onwards),
Bronson's first film was in *You're in the
Navy Now* (1951) which was followed by
a series of character parts in the likes of
Pat and Mike (1952), *The Big House,
USA* (1955) and *House of Wax* (1953).
Machine Gun Kelly (1958) gave him his
first starring role, and was followed by
secondary roles in big films like *The
Magnificent Seven* (1960), *The Great
Escape* (1963), *The Sandpiper* (1965),
Battle of the Bulge and *The Dirty Dozen*
(both 1967). A move to Europe
reworked his image into an anti-heroic
star of rough-and-tough action films,
and an unlikely sex symbol. This period
produced hits like *Adieu L'Ami* (1968),
Once Upon a Time in the West (1969)
and *Rider on the Rain* (1969). Upon his
return to the States his fame grew, and
by 1971 he was named most popular
actor in the world by the Hollywood
Foreign Press Assocation.

ART CARNEY

Born: 4 November 1918,
New York, USA.
Died: 9 November 2003 in Connecticut.
Jackie Gleason's partner in the classic TV
comedy series *The Honeymooners* (1954-
57, then 1966-70), Carney's talents as an
actor were ultimately recognised when he
won an Oscar for his performance in
Paul Mazursky's *Harry and Tonto* (1974).
Active on Broadway, as well as on the
silver screen, his other films include *The
Yellow Rolls-Royce* (1964), *The Late Show*
(1977), *Movie Movie* (1978), *House Calls*
(1978), *Going in Style* (1979), *The
Muppets Take Manhattan* (1984)
and *Last Action Hero* (1993).

JOHNNY CASH

Born: 26 February 1932
in Arkansas, USA.
Died: 12 September 2003 in Nashville
of a diabetes-related nerve disease.
The charismatic 'Man in Black'

Deray worked with the cream of French stars, including Delon, Jean-Paul Belmondo, Lino Ventura, Jean-Louis Trintignant and Yves Montand. After assisting the likes of Luis Bunuel, Henri Verneuil and Jules Dassin, Deray made his directing debut in 1960 with *Le Gigolo*. He immediately found his forte in *Ri-fifi a Tokyo* (1961) and *Symphonie pour un massacre* (1963) amd made it big with *La Piscine* (1969). His other films include: *Borsalino* (1970), *Flic Story* (1975); *Un papillon sur l'epaule* (1978), *Trois hommes a abattre* (1980); and *On ne meurt que deux fois* (1984). Deray's final film was *The Teddy Bear* (1994).

composed over 1000 songs and released 130 albums, his haunting growl, profoundly American outlook, and narrative style lent a cinematic quality to much of his work, making his music a perennial favourite for inclusion in film soundtracks. He also pursued a sporadic acting career, becoming so iconic that he eventually made a mini career cameo-ing as himself.

JEANNE CRAIN

Born: 25 May 1925 in California, USA.
Died: 14 December 2003 in Santa Barbara, of a heart attack.
Her swimsuited and uncredited debut in *The Gang's All Here* (1943) made her a World War Two pin-up and she subsequently appeared in 64 films and numerous TV shows. As a leading lady, she starred in *Home in Indiana* (1944), *In the Meantime, Darling* (1944), *Winged Victory* (1944) and the Rodgers & Hammerstein classic *State Fair* (1945) Notable films include *Margie* (1946), *You Were Meant for Me* (1948), *Apartment for Peggie* (1948), *Lady Windermere's Fan* (1949), *Cheaper by the Dozen* (1950) and *Duel in the Jungle* (1954). Her Academy Award-nomination was for her role as a black

girl passing for white in the controversial Elia Kazan film *Pinky* (1949).

FRANCES DEE

Born: 26 November 1909 in Los Angeles, California, USA.
Died: 6 March 2004 in Norwalk, Connecticut, of complications following a stroke.
She starred opposite Maurice Chevalier in one of the first talkie musicals, *The Playboy of Paris* (1930), and in the 1931 pic *An American Tragedy*. Her other films include: *Little Women* (1933); *Of Human Bondage* (1934); *Souls at Sea* (1937); *Wells Fargo* (1937); and *If I Were King* (1938). Along with her husband, actor Joel McCrea, she bought a large ranch northwest of Los Angeles. As the metropolitan area expanded she became one of the richest landowners in California.

JACQUES DERAY

Born: 19 February 1929 in Lyon, France.
Died: 9 August 2003 in Paris.
Deray directed 24 films, nine featuring Alain Delon, many of them successful police thrillers. A craftsman of the genre (some called him the French Hitchcock),

BUDDY EBSEN

Born: 2 April 1908 in Illinois, USA.
Died: July 2003 in California, from complications related to pneumonia.
Real name: Christian Rudolph Ebsen Jr. Ebsen's showbiz career started in vaudeville where his double-act with his sister led to a kind of fame as the poor man's Fred Astaire and Ginger Rogers. They debuted in films together with *Broadway Melody* (1936). A promising career with MGM was halted by an unofficial blackballing for refusing a seven-year contract offered by Louis B Mayer. Ebsen continued to act on

Broadway and in various bread-and-butter war movies and Westerns until the TV series *Davy Crockett* and *The Beverly Hillbillies* made him a household name. Notable films include *Breakfast at Tiffany's (1961), The Interns* (1961) and *Mail Order Bride* (1964),

JACK ELAM

Born: 13 November 1918 in Arizona, USA.
Died: 21 October 2003 in Oregon, of emphysema.
His sinister looks (thanks to a static eye caused by a childhood accident) marked Elam out as a favourite villain in more than 100 films, mostly Westerns. In fact, his debut credit was as 'The Killer' in *Trailin' West* (1944). His films include: *Rawhide* (1951), *High Noon* (1952), *Rancho Notorious* (1952), *Kiss Me Deadly* (1955), *Gunfight at the OK Corral* (1957), *4 for Texas* (1963), *The Rare Breed* (1966), *Once Upon a Time in the West* (1968), *Support Your Local Sherriff* (1969) and *The Cannonball Run* (1981).

SPALDING GRAY

Born: 5 June 1941 in Providence, Rhode Island, USA.
Died: 7 March 2004 in New York, possibly of suicide.
An actor and renowned monologist, whose authored works were adapted for the films *Swimming to Cambodia* (1987), *Monster in a Box* (1992) and *Gray's Anatomy* (1996) in which he also acted. Gray also appeared in *The Killing Fields* (1984), *Beaches* (1988) and *Kate & Leopold* (2001).

UTA HAGEN

Born: 12 June 1919 in Göttingen, Germany.
Died: 14 January 2004 in Manhattan, USA.
Multiple Tony-awardee, and holder of a

National Medal of the Arts, Uta Hagen was a genuine stage legend whose roles include playing Desdemona to Paul Robeson's *Othello* in the 1940s and Blanche De Bois opposite Marlon Brando in the original production of *A Streetcar Named Desire*. Her handful of film appearances could have been greater but for her blackballing in the 1950s. Films include: *The Other* (1972); *The Boys From Brazil* (1978); and *Reversal of Fortune* (1990).

DAVID HEMMINGS

Born: 18 November 1941 in Surrey, England.
Died: 3 December 2003 in Bucharest, Romania, of a heart attack. From a child soprano to an overnight sensation and cultural icon (thanks to Michelangelo Antonioni's *Blowup*), to a producer and director who famously remarked, 'People thought I was dead. But I wasn't. I was just directing *The A-Team*.' Hemmings had turned full circle, becoming a character actor in Hollywood hits like *Gladiator* (2000), *Spy Game* (2001), *Gangs of New York* (2002), *Equilibrium* (2002), and *The League of Extraordinary Gentleman* (2003) before suffering a heart attack

while filming *Samantha's Child* on location in Romania. Other film appearances include: *Night and the City* (1950); *Saint Joan* (1961); *The Charge of the Light Brigade* (1968); *Camelot* (1967); *Barbarella* (1968); *The Best House in London* (1969); *Voices* (1973); *Murder by Decree* (1980); *The Rainbow* (1989); *Last Orders* (2001); and *Blessed* (2004).

GREGORY HINES

Born: 14 February 1946 in New York, USA.
Died: 9 August 2003 in Los Angeles, of cancer.
Considered by many to be the finest tap-dancer of his generation, with a silky style reminiscent of Fred Astaire's. Hines was a legend on Broadway, which honoured his legacy by dimming its lights the week he passed away. An actor and singer, as well as a dancer, Hines' first film appearance was as a late replacement for Richard Pryor in Mel Brook's *History of the World, Part I* (1981). He also starred with his brother Maurice in Francis Coppola's *The Cotton Club* (1984), *White Nights* (1985) and

Running Scared (1986). Other films include: *Eve of Destruction* (1991); *A Rage in Harlem* (1991); *Renaissance Man* (1994); *Waiting to Exhale* (1995); and *The Preacher's Wife* (1996). From 1999 to 2000 Hines played a semi-regular character in the popular American sitcom *Will & Grace*.

TICKY HOLDAGO

Born: 24 June 1944 in Toulouse, France.
Died: 22 January 2004 in Paris, of cancer.
Real name: Joseph Holgado.
One of France's greatest comic character actors, Holgado got his start when Max Pécas cast him in *Belles, Blondes et Bornzees* (1981). Holgado later worked with the crème of French directors, including Claude Berri, Claude Zidi, Patrice Leconte, Claude Lelouch, Gerard Jugnot and Jean-Pierre Jeunet, coming to international notice in the latter's *Delicatessen* (1991), and later also in *La Cité des Enfants Perdus* (1995), *Amelie* (2001) and *A Very Long Engagement* (2004). Holgado died whilst working on Lelouch's *Les Parisiennes*, which the director has dedicated to his memory. His films include: *Les Ripoux* (1984); *Manon of the Spring* (1986); *Le Mari De La Coiffeuse* (1990); *Wonderful Times* (1992); *Les Misérables* (1995), *Funny Bones* (1995); and *And Now ... Ladies and Gentlemen* (2002).

BOB HOPE

Born: 29 May 1903 in London, England.
Died: 27 July 2003 in Toluca Lake, California, of pneumonia.
Real name: Leslie Townes Hope.
Beloved of the people, 'Rapid Fire Robert' was once clocked at seven jokes a minute and patented the persona of the bumbling, wisecracking coward in *Some Like It Hot* (1939), which he then perfected in the seven *Road to...* movies

he starred in with Bing Crosby; and later as the comic-ironic Casanova is a series of classic romantic comedies. Hope started his career in vaudeville and made his name as a radio star in his 1938 Pepsodent-sponsored show. *The Big Broadcast*, releaed the same year, he duetted with Shirley Ross on the Oscar-winning tune 'Thanks for the Memory', a song he adopted as his signature tune. His acting career, while respectable, was but a modest component of his fame. His immensely popular TV specials, and his worldwide show tours for generations of American military personnel, won him millions of loyal fans, as did his record number of 27 Academy Award appearances, where he joked about never winning one: 'Welcome to the Oscars – or, as it's known in my house, Passover.' Nevertheless, the *Guinness Book of Records* lists him the most decorated man in entertainment, with 1,500 kudos, including five special Academy Awards. His philanthropy and generosity of spirit was legendary. Hope was perhaps the most-loved comedian in showbusiness history.
His movies include: *Going Spanish (aka Bob's Busy Day)* (1934); *Thanks for the Memory* (1938); *Never Say Die*

(1939); *The Cat and the Canary* (1939); *The Road to Singapore* (1940); *The Road to Zanzibar* (1941); *Louisiana Purchase* (1941); *My Favorite Blonde* (1942); *The Road to Morocco* (1942); *Let's Face It* (1943); *The Princess and the Pirate* (1944); *Road to Utopia* (1946); *My Favorite Brunette* (1947); *The Road to Rio* (1947); *The Paleface* (1948); *The Great Lover* (1949); *The Lemon Drop Kid* (1951); *My Favorite Spy* (1951); *Son of Paleface* (1952); *The Road to Bali* (1952); *Here Come the Girls* (1953); *Casanova's Big Night* (1954); *The Iron Petticoat* (1956); *The Road to Hong Kong* (1962); *Call Me Bwana* (1963); *I'll Take Sweden* (1965); *Eight on the Lam* (1967); and *The Muppet Movie* (1979).

MICHAEL KAMEN

Born: 15 April 1948 in New York, USA.
Died: 18 November 2003 in London, Englad, of a heart attack following a recent diagnosis of multiple sclerosis.
Juilliard alumnus Kamen had an ebullient disrespect for genre boundaries – he was equally at home tour-directing David Bowie, collaborating with Metallica, or playing oboe with Leonard Bernstein. Such versatility served him well as one of cinema's great big-budget composers. His first film score was for *The Next Man* (1976). He went on to score more than 60 films, including all four *Lethal Weapons* (1987 onwards), three *Die Hards* (1988 onwards) films, *X-Men* (2000), and *Mr Holland's Opus* (1995) for which he was Oscar-nominated. Hi other films include: The *Dead Zone (1983); Brazil* (1985); *Mona Lisa (1986); The Adventures of Baron Munchausen* (1989); *Licence to Kill* (1989); *Robin Hood: Prince of Thieves* (1991); *Last Action Hero* (1993); *Circle of Friends* (1995); and *The Iron Giant* (1999).

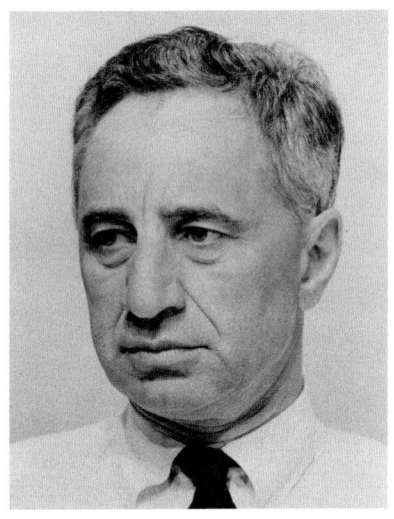

ELIA KAZAN

Born: 7 September 1909
in Constantinople, the old Ottoman Empire.
Died: 28 September 2003
in New York, USA.
Real name: Elia Kazanjoglous.
Elia Kazan was a mesmerising director whose works stand as landmarks of cinematic and stage performance. An advocate of Method acting and co-founder, with Lee Strasberg, of the Actors' Studio, Kazan's first spark on Broadway brought him into the circle of some of the greatest writers of the age, including Tennessee Williams, Arthur Miller, John Steinbeck and William Inge. This led to such great movies as *A Streetcar Named Desire* (1951) and the Oscar-winning *On the Waterfront* (1954), both starring Marlon Brando, and not to mention some of the greatest plays ever written: *Camino Real*, *Cat on a Hot Tin Roof* and *Sweet Bird of Youth* with Williams, and *Death of a Salesman* with Miller. His adaptation of Steinbeck's *East of Eden* (1955) introduced the world to James Dean. He won the Tony for direction three times, the directing Oscar twice (his first for *Gentleman's Agreement*, 1947), and was bestowed a lifetime achievement Oscar in 1999. His films

have garnered a total of 20 Academy Awards. Other notable films include: his debut, *A Tree Grows in Brooklyn* (1945); *Boomerang* (1947); *Pinky* (1949); *Panic in the Streets* (1950); *Viva Zapata* (1952); *Man on a Tightrope* (1953); *A Face in the Crowd* (1957); *Baby Doll* (1956); *Wild River* (1960); *Splendor in the Grass* (1961); and his final movie, *The Last Tycoon* (1976).

ELEM KLIMOV

Born: 9 July 1933
in Stalingrad, the Soviet Union.
Died: 26 October 2003 in Moscow, Russia, of natural causes.
Politically active leader of the Soviet Filmmaker's Union, Klimov was a patriot and a member of the Communist Party whose passionate films often jarred with the establishment. The perestroika movement allowed his most successful film, the apocalyptic *Come and See* (1985) to be watched in its intended form by 29 million ticket-buyers. Other films include: *Welcome, or No Admittance!* (1964); *The Dentist's Apprentice* (1965); *Sport, Sport, Sport* (1970); *Larissa* (1980); *Agony* (1981); and *Farewell to Matyora* (1983).

HOPE LANGE

Born: 28 November 1931
in Redding Ridge, Connecticut, USA.
Died: 19 December 2003
in Santa Monica, Californiaf of ischemic colitis infection.
Hope Lange earned her Oscar nomination playing the incest-abuse victim accused of killing her father in *Peyton Place* (1957). A Broadway veteran since the age of 12, Lange's first big break came playing opposite Marilyn Monroe in *Bus Stop* (1956), which she followed by co-starring with Marlon Brando, Dean Martin and Montgomery Clift in *The Young Lions* (1958) and then opposite Joan Crawford in *The Best of*

Everything (1959). A natural beauty, Lange enjoyed a long and illustrious career on film and in TV, where her work won two Emmys. Marriages to Don Murray and Alan Pakula ended in divorce but she found lasting happiness with third husband Charles Hollerith Jr. Other notable films include: *Wild in the Country* (1961); *Death Wish* (1974); *Blue Velvet* (1986); *Clear and Present Danger* (1994); and *Just Cause* (1995).

MERCEDES McCAMBRIDGE

Born: 17 March 1916
in Joliet, Illinois, USA.
Died: 2 March 2004 in La Jolla, California of natural causes.
Orson Welles called her 'The world's greatest living radio actress', to which she replied: 'How can you be the world's greatest dead radio actress?' An outspoken and talented performer who won an Oscar for her supporting role in *All the King's Men* (1949) and co-starred with James Dean in *Giant* (1956), she nevertheless struggled because of her alcoholism and dreadful family tragedies. Horror buffs will note her as the voice of the demon in *The Exorcist* (1973), which required an appeal by the Screen Actors'

Guild to get William Friedkin to insert her name in the credits. Other films include: *Johnny Guitar* (1954); *A Farewell to Arms* (1957); *Touch of Evil* (1958); *Suddenly Last Summer* (1959); *Cimarron* (1961); *99 Women* (1969); *Thieves* (1977); and *The Concorde – Airport '79* (1979).

ANN MILLER

Born: 12 April 1923
in Houston, Texas, USA.
Died: 22 January 2004 in Los Angeles, California, of lung cancer.
Real name: Johnnie Lucille Collier.
A stunning talent from her teenage years, Ann Miller's legs were once insured for $1 million by RKO. Her 500-taps-a-minute dance routines graced some of the finest musicals in Hollywood history, including *Easter Parade* (1948), *On the Town* (1949) and *Kiss Me Kate* (1953). She debuted in *Stage Door* (1937), which was swiftly followed by *Having a Wonderful Time* (1938), Oscar-winner *You Can't Take It With You* (1938), *Room Service* (1938), and her first starring role, in *Radio City Revels* (1938). Her other films include: *Melody Ranch* (1940); *Hit Parade* (1941); *Carolina Blues* (1944); *The Opposite Sex* (1956); *The Great*

American Pastime (1956); *That's Entertainment!* (1974); and *Mulholland Drive* (2001).

BOB MONKHOUSE

Born: 1 June 1928 in Kent, England.
Died: 29 December 2003 in Bedfordshire, of cancer.
Quick-witted stand-up comic and game show host, tremendously popular with television audiences in his native England for five decades. Bob Monkhouse OBE was a dedicated film enthusiast and collector, and honorary president of the Gothique Film Society. He was also a renowned comedy historian and archivist (the theft of his joke books made headline news). His sporadic film appearances include starring roles in the very first *Carry On*, *Carry On Sergeant* (1958); *Dentist in the Chair* (1960); *Dentist on the Job* (1961); and Hammer Films rarity *A Weekend With Lulu* (1962).

DONALD O'CONNOR

Born: 28 August 1925
in Chicago, Illinois, USA.
Died: 27 September 2003 in Calabasas, California, of heart failure.

O'Connor was a supremely talented song-and-dance man whose career showpiece in *Singin' in the Rain* (1952) had him flipping off walls, a performance that won him a Golden Globe. Born to a performing clan billed as 'The O'Connor Family: The Royal Family of Vaudeville', O'Connor's screen debut was dancing alongside his brother Jack in *Melody for Two* (1937). He made his big break in Bing Crosby's *Sing, You Sinners* (1938), which he followed with child roles in *Tom Sawyer – Detective* and *Beau Geste* (1939). A spell playing teens in forgettable musicals ended with the hit comedy series *Francis the Talking Mule* (1950) which starred O'Connor in four of five sequels, all of which he felt were beneath him. His forte was the acrobatic dance piece in the big-budget musical, of which he had many. Films include: *I Love Melvin* (1953); *Call Me Madam* (1953); *There's No Business Like Show Business* (1954); *Anything Goes* (1956); *The Buster Keaton Story* (1957); *Ragtime* (1981); *Toys* (1992); and *Out to Sea* (1997).

DENIS QUILLEY

Born: 26 December 1927
in London, England.
Died: 5 October 2003
in London, of cancer.
A giant of London's comic and serious theatre who began his career opposite Laurence Olivier and John Gielgud. Quilley had enormous, intelligent presence to go with his rugged handsomeness. His film career pales by comparison to his stage performances and includes: *Life at the Top* (1965); *Anne of the Thousand Days* (1969); *Murder on the Orient Express* (1974); *Evil Under the Sun* (1982); *Privates on Parade* (1982); *Foreign Body* (1986); and *Mr Johnson* (1990).

JOHN RANDOLPH

Born: 1 June 1915 in New York, USA.
Died: 24 February 2004 in Hollywood, California, of natural causes.
Real name: Emanuael Mortimer Cohen. John Randolph studied under Stella Adler and was one of the original members of the Actors' Studio. He debuted on screen in *The Naked City* (1948) but was blacklisted for his leftist views until John Frankenheimer cast him *Seconds* (1966), thereby re-starting a Hollywood career rich in father/authority figure character roles. Notable films include: *Escape from the Planet of the Apes* (1971); *Conquest of the Planet of the Apes* (1972); *Serpico* (1973); *Earthquake* (1974); *All the President's Men* (1976); *King Kong* (1976); *Prizzi's Honor* (1985)*; You've Got M@il* (1998); and *Numb* (2003).

RONALD REAGAN

Born: 6 February 1911
in Tampico, Illinois, USA.
Died: 5 June 2004 in Bel Air, Los Angeles, California, of pneumonia following a long battle with Alzheimer's. Reagan was a studio B-movie player whose film career peaked as a second-lead man in the 1940s and 50s. He subsequently entered politics, winning his greatest role on the world stage as the President of the United States in the 1980s. Known as 'The Great Communicator' because of his powerful charisma and innate instinct for dramatic presentation, Reagan spent a career playing American heroes, first winning fame as secret service agent Brass Bancroft in a studio movie serial. This prompted an historical twist when Jerry Parr, an ex-member of the Junior Brass Bancroft Society, later become the agent who saved President Reagan's life during a 1981 assassination attempt. The two high points of his film career were in *Knute Rockne, All-American* (1940) and *King's Row* (1942). In the former he played George 'the Gipper' Gipp, a persona he later referenced throughout his political career. He launched himself in politics first as the President of the Screen Actors' Guild (1947-52 and 1959-60), then as Governor of California from 1967-75 before winning the US Presidency for two terms from 1980-88. Married twice, first to Jane Wyman in 1940 then to Nancy Wilson in 1952, Reagan was one of the most popular presidents in modern history. His notable films include: *Love is on the Air* (1937); *Dark Victory* (1939); *Desperate Journey* (1942); *The Hasty Heart* (1949); *Bedtime for Bonzo* (1951); *She's Working Her Way Through College* (1952); *Law and Order* (1953); *Cattle Queen of Montana* (1954); *Tennessee's Partner* (1955); *Hellcats of the Navy* (1957); and *The Killers* (1965), in which he played the only vilain of his career.

LENI RIEFENSTAHL

Born: 22 August 1902
in Berlin, Germany.
Died: 8 September 2003
in Poecking, Germany.
Riefenstahl's name will always suffer the shadow of the propagandist Nazi overtones to two of her epic directorial works, *Triumph of the Will* (1934) and *Olympiad* (1938). Ejected from the film industry after World War Two, she turned to photography and, much later, underwater documentary, ever after insisting that she never meant to glorify the Nazi regime with her work. She holds the record for the longest length of time in between film projects, with 48 years separating *Tiefland* (1954) and *Impressionen unter Wasser* (2002), the latter also winning her the oldest-documentary-director record. Her other films include: (as an actress) *Der Heilige Berg* (1926); *The White Hell of Pitz Palu* (1929); *SOS Iceberg* (1933); and, as a director, *The Blue Light* (1932); *Victory of the Faith* (1933); and *The Day of Freedom* (1935).

JOHN RITTER

Born: 17 September 1948
in Burbank, California, USA.
Died: 11 September 2003
in Burbank, of an aortic dissection.
Famous as the star of the 1977-1984 US sitcom *Three's Company*, Ritter's career in film was just at the point of renaissance when he suffered a heart attack on the set of his TV show, *Hooperman*. Ritter's light and easy style belied a capacity for

nuance that indie directors were just coming wise to. His films include: *The Barefoot Executive* (1971); *The Stone Killer* (1973); *Breakfast in Bed* (1978); *Americathon* (1979); *Hero at Large* (1980); *Wholly Moses* (1980); *Skin Deep* (1989); *Problem Child* (1990); *Problem Child 2* (1991); *Noises Off* (1992); *Hacks* (1997); *Nowhere* (1997); *The Joy of Natural Childbirth* (1997); *Bride of Chucky* (1998); *Panic* (2000); *TripFall* (2000); *Lost in the Pershing Point Hotel* (2000); *Nuncrackers* (2001); *Man of the Year* (2002); *Tadpole* (2002); *Bad Santa* (2003); *Manhood* (2003); and *Clifford's Really Big Movie* (2004).

PATRICIA ROC

Born: 7 June 1915 in London, England.
Died: 30 December 2003 in Locarno, Switzerland, of kidney failure.
Real name:
Felicia Miriam Ursula Herold.
This beautiful and talented Rank star was one of the most popular actresses of Britain's post-war years, earning the accolade 'Goddess of the Odeons'. Best-remembered for her co-starring role in the Gainsborough costume drama *The Wicked Lady* (1945), Roc subsequently worked in Eurpoean and American cinema. Her final notable screen appearance was as a guest star in the first episode of the Roger Moore television series *The Saint*. She retired a year later, in 1963. Films include: *Madonna of the Seven Moons* (1944); *Canyon Passage* (1946); *The Brothers* (1947); *When the Bough Breaks* (1947); *The Perfect Woman* (1949); *Return to Life* (1949); *The Man on the Eiffel Tower* (1950); *Circle of Danger* (1951); *Black Jack* (1951); *Something Money Can't Buy* (1952); *The Widow* (1954); *Cartouche* (1954); *The Hypnotist* (1957); *The House in the Woods* (1959); and *Bluebeard's Ten Honeymoons* (1960).

JANICE RULE

Born: 15 August 1931 in Norwood, Ohio, USA.
Died: 17 October 2003 in New York, of a cerebral hemorrhage.
Real name: Mary Janice Rule.
A versatile and accomplished actress with memorable roles in such diverse pictures as *Bell, Book and Candle* (1958), *The Ambushers* (1967) and *3 Women* (1977). Rule's television roles included guest-starring parts in *The Twilight Zone*, *Dr Kildare*, *The Fugitive* and *Murder, She Wrote*. Films include: *Goodbye, My Fancy* (1951); *Starlift* (1951); *Holiday for Sinners* (1952); *The Subterraneans* (1960); *The Swimmer* (1968); *The Chase* (1966); *Welcome to Hard Times* (1967); *Missing* (1982); *American Flyers* (1985); and *LA Bad* (1985)

JOHN SCHLESINGER

Born: 16 February 1926 in London, England.
Died: 25 July 2003 in Palm Springs, California, USA, following a debilitating stroke in December 2000.
A masterful director with meticulous powers of observation and an empathetic feel for character, Schlesinger's career produced enduring works of cinema

including the Oscar Best Pic *Midnght Cowboy* (1969), *Darling* (1965 – and three Oscars) and *Sunday, Bloody Sunday* (1971 – Oscar nominated). After a short stint acting, Schlesinger's directing break came working for the BBC arts series *Monitor*. This led to his documentary about a railway depot, *Terminus* (1961), which won the Golden Lion at the Venice Film Festival as well as a BAFTA. His first feature, *A Kind of Loving* (1962), won the Golden Bear Award at Berlin. *Billy Liar* (1962) and *Darling* (1965) cemented his formidable reputation. Notable films include: *Far From the Madding Crowd* (1967); *Visions of Eight* (1973); *The Day of the Locust* (1975); *Marathon Man* (1976); *Yanks* (1979); *Honky Tonk Freeway* (1981); *An Englishman Abroad* (1983); *The Falcon and the Snowman* (1987); *Madame Sousatzka* (1988); *The Believers* (1989); *A Question of Attribution* (1991); *Pacific Heights* (1990); *The Innocent* (1995); *Eye for an Eye* (1996); and *The Next Best Thing* (2000).

MARY SELWAY

Born: 14 March 1936 in Norwich, England.
Died: 21 April 2004 in London, of cancer.
Mary Selway was widely recognised as Britain's top casting director. She worked on more than 100 films alongside top-flight directors like Steven Spielberg, Roman Polanski, Robert Altman, Ridley Scott, John Boorman, Nic Roeg, James Cameron, Clint Eastwood, John Madden, Michael Apted, Blake Edwards, Fred Schepisi, Sydney Pollack, David Hare, Bertrand Tavernier, Liliana Cavani, Neil LaBute, Fred Zinneman and Bruce Robinson. Her numerous credits include: *Unman, Wittering and Zigo* (1971); *Robin and Marian* (1976); *The Duellists* (1977); *Tess* (1979); *Dracula* (1979); *Raiders of the Lost Ark* (1981); *Excalibur* (1981); *Victor/Victoria* (1982); *Star Wars:*

Episode VI – Return of the Jedi (1983); *Indiana Jones and the Temple of Doom* (1984); *Out of Africa* (1985); *Withnail & I* (1987); *Strapless* (1989); *The Russia House* (1990); *Circle of Friends* (1995); *Emma* (1996); *Notting Hill* (1999); *Gosford Park* (2001); *K-19: The Widowmaker* (2002); *Captain Corelli's Mandolin* (2001); *Master and Commander: The Far Side of the World* (2003); *Love Actually* (2003); *The Mother* (2003); *The Libertine* (2004); *Thunderbirds* (2004); and S*Harry Potter and the Goblet of Fire* (2005)

JACK SMIGHT

Born: 9 March 1925
in Minneapolis, Minnesota, USA
Died: 1 September 2003
in Los Angeles, California, of cancer.
Jack Smight started out as successful TV director before moving onto helming commercial film projects like *Midway* (1976) and *Airport 1975* (1974).
Other films include: *Harper* (1966); *Kaleidoscope* (1966); *The Illustrated Man* (1969); *The Secret War of Harry Figg* (1968); *No Way to Treat a Lady* (1968); *The Traveling Executioner* (1970); *Rabbit, Run* (1970); *Fast Break* (1979); *Number One With a Bullet* (1987); and *The Favorite* (1989).

ELLIOTT SMITH

Born: 6 August 1969 in Omaha, Nebraska, USA.
Died: 21 October 2003 in Los Angeles, California, from self-inflicted stabbing.
Alt-country/folk star Elliott Smith received an Oscar nomination for his songs in *Good Will Hunting* (1997). He also composed music for: *Zero Effect* (1998); *Keeping the Faith* (2000); *Antitrust* (2001); *The Royal Tenenbaums* (2001); and *The Girl Next Door* (2004). He was the subject of Jem Cohen' tribute short *Lucky Three: An Elliott Smith Portrait* (1997).

RAY STARK

Born: 3 October 1914
in Chicago, Illinois, USA.
Died: 17 January 2004 in West Hollywood, California, of heart failure.
Heavyweight film producer Ray Stark was one of the most powerful men in the industry with over 125 films to his credit and more than $1 billion grossed at Columbia studios alone. An incredibly persuasive and a consummate dealmaker, he started his career as an agent in the 1940s and 50s with a roster of clients including John Wayne, Marilyn Monroe, Kirk Douglas, Richard Burton, Ava Gardner, Lana Turner and Ronald Reagan. His first film production was *The World of Suzie Wong* (1960) and his last big hit was *Steel Magnolias* (1989). In between he enjoyed a rich collaboration with Neil Simon. In 1980, the Academy of Motion Picture Arts & Sciences bestowed on Stark the rare honour of an Irving Thalberg Award. Notable films include: *The Night of the Iguana* (1964); *This Property Is Condemned* (1966); *Drop Dead Darling* (1966); *Reflections in a Golden Eye* (1967); *Funny Girl* (1968); *The Owl and the Pussycat* (1970); *Fat City* (1972); *The Way We Were* (1973); *The Black Bird* (1975); *The Sunshine Boys* (1975); *Funny*

Lady (1975); *Murder by Death* (1976); *Robin and Marian* (1976); *The Goodbye Girl* (1977); *California Suite* (1978); *The Cheap Detective* (1978); *Casey's Shadow* (1978); *The Electric Horseman* (1979); *Chapter Two* (1979); *Somewhere in Time* (1980); *Seems Like Old Times* (1980); *The Toy* (1982); *Annie* (1982); *The Slugger's Wife* (1985); *Brighton Beach Memoirs* (1986); *Biloxi Blues* (1988); *Steel Magnolias* (1989); and *Lost in Yonkers* (1993).

INGRID THULIN

Born: 27 January 1926
in Sollefteå, Sweden.
Died: 7 January 2004
in Stockholm, Sweden, of cancer.
A ballerina turned actress, Thulin was a veteran of nine Ingmar Bergman films. She also starred in Luchino Visconti's *The Damned* (1969). Her films include: *Where the Wind Blows* (1948); *Storm Warning* (1949); *Love Will Conquer* (1949); *Foreign Intrigue* (1956); *Wild Strawberries* (1957); *Brink of Life* (1958); *The Face* (1958); *Winter Light* (1962); *The Four Horsemen of the Apocalypse* (1962); *The Silence* (1963); *Return from the Ashes* (1965); *Hour of the Wolf*

(1968); *Cries and Whispers* (1972); *The Cage* (1975); *And Agnes Chose to Die* (1976); *Cassandra Crossing* (1976); *Salon Kitty* (1976); It Rained All Night the Day I Left (1980); *The House of Smiles* (1988); and *The Mother's Heart* (1988).

MARIE TRINTIGNANT

Born: 21 January 1962 in Paris, France.
Died: 1 August 2003 in Hauts-de-Seine, France, murdered by her boyfriend.
Born to one of France's premier showbusiness families, Marie died from head injuries following a dispute with her boyfriend, rocker Bertrand Cantat. Her first film role was at age four in her mother Nadine's film *Mon Amour, Mon Amour* (1967). She subsequently acted in over 40 movies. Notable films include *Serie Noire* (1978); *Story of Women* (1988); *Betty* (1992); In *Nuit d'ete en ville (Summer Night in Town)* (1990); *Les Marmottes (The Groundhogs)* (1993); *Cible emouvante (Wild Target)* (1993); *Les Apprentis* (1995); *Comme elle respire (White Lies)* (1998); *Le Cri de la soie (Scream of Silk)* (1996); *Harrison's Flowers* (2000); *Janis and John* (2003); and *Les Marins perdus (Lost Seamen)* (2003).

SIR PETER USTINOV

Born: 16 April 1921
in London, England.
Died: 28 March 2004 in Genolier, Switzerland, of heart failure.
Possibly the most intellectual, polymathic entertainer of the 20th century, Sir Peter Ustinov was beloved the world over. He was most famous for playing Agatha Christie's Belgian sleuth Hercules Poirot in a series of film adaptations (*Death on the Nile* [1978]; *Evil Under the Sun* [1982]; and *Appointment With Death* [1988]). Ustinov's prodigious talents surfaced early: he started acting at 17, debuting at 21 in Powell and Pressburger's *One of Our Aircraft Is Missing* (1942); sold his first screenplay at 24 (1945's *The True Glory*); and directed his first film, *School for Secrets*, at 25. His acting skills peaked a little later in *Quo Vadis* (1951) where his portrayal of a vain and petulant Emperor Nero won him his first supporting Oscar nomination. He later won Oscars for roles in *Spartacus* (1960) and *Topkapi* (1964). He was also nominated for co-writing *Hot Millions* (1968). His directorial talents bloomed with the startling adaptation of Melville's *Billy Budd* (1960). In a long and varied career, Ustinov seemed to draw effortlessly and gracefully from a bottomless well of talent which served him both in front of, and behind, the lens. In his later years he dvoted himself to tireless charity work on behalf of UNICEF. There will never be another like him. Notable films include: *The Way Ahead* (1944); *Vice Versa* (1948); *Private Angelo* (1949); *The Magic Box* (1951); *The Egyptian* (1954); *We're No Angels* (1955); *The Sundowners* (1956); *Romanoff and Juliet* (1961); *The Comedians* (1967); *Hammersmith Is Out* (1972); *Robin Hood* (1973); *One of Our Dinosaurs Is Missing* (1975); *Logan's Run* (1976); The *Last Remake of Beau Geste* (1977); *The Mouse and His Child* (1977); *Ashanti* (1979); *Grendel, Grendel, Grendel*

(1980); *The Great Muppet Caper; Charlie Chan and the Curse of the Dragon Queen* (both 1981), *Memed My Hawk* (1987); *The French Revolution* (1989); *Lorenzo's Oil* (1992); *The Bachelor* (1999); and *Luther* (2003).

ALEXANDER WALKER

Born: 22 March 1930
in Portadown, Northern Ireland.
Died: 14 July 2003 in London.
Alexander Walker was the erudite and influential film critic for the London *Evening Standard* for 43 years. A graduate in political philosophy from Queens University in Belfast, Walker was hugely respected, profoundly knowledgeable, brutally honest and a tireless campaigner. He was a credit to his profession. His notable books on cinema include acclaimed biographies of Bette Davis, Audrey Hepburn, Stanley Kubrick, Vivien Leigh, Peter Sellers and Elizabeth Taylor. His trilogy of books about the modern British film industry was completed shortly before his death: *Hollywood, England* (1974); *National Heroes* (1985); and *Icons in the Fire* (2004).

Index

Names of films and videos appear in the index in *italics*.
The last separate word of an individual's name is used as the index entry. Thus Jan De Bont appears within Bont, Jan De